Code Reading

Effective SOFTWARE DEVELOPMENT SERIES ♦

Scott Meyers, Consulting Editor

The **Effective Software Development Series** provides expert advice on all aspects of modern software development. Books in the series are well written, technically sound, of lasting value, and tractable length. Each describes the critical things the experts almost always do—or almost always avoid doing—to produce outstanding software.

Scott Meyers (author of the Effective C++ books and CD) conceived of the series and acts as its consulting editor. Authors in the series work with Meyers and with Addison-Wesley Professional's editorial staff to create essential reading for software developers of every stripe.

For more information on books in this series please see www.awprofessional.com/esds

Code Reading

The Open Source Perspective

Diomidis Spinellis

✦Addison-Wesley

Boston · San Francisco · New York · Toronto · Montreal
London · Munich · Paris · Madrid
Capetown · Sydney · Tokyo · Singapore · Mexico City

The publisher offers discounts on this book when ordered in quantity for bulk purchases and special sales. For more information, please contact:

U.S. Corporate and Government Sales
(800) 382-3419
corpsales@pearsontechgroup.com

For sales outside of the U.S., please contact:
International Sales
(317) 581-3793
international@pearsontechgroup.com

Visit Addison-Wesley on the Web: www.awprofessional.com

Library of Congress Cataloging-in-Publication Data

Spinellis, Diomidis.
    Code reading / Diomidis Spinellis.
        p. cm.
    Contents: The open source perspective.
    Includes bibliographical references and Index.
    ISBN 0-201-79940-5 (pbk. : alk. paper)
    1. Computer programming. 2. Coding theory.   I. Title.
    QA76.6 .S675 2003
    005.1–dc21   2002038563

ISBN 0-201-79940-5

Text printed on recycled paper.
1 2 3 4 5 6 7 8 9 10—CRS—0706050403
First printing, May 2003

Contents at a Glance

Contents

Figures

Tables

Foreword

We're programmers. Our job (and in many cases our passion) is to make things happen by writing code. We don't meet our user's requirements with acres of diagrams, with detailed project schedules, with four-foot-high piles of design documentation. These are all wishes—expressions of what we'd like to be true. No, we deliver by writing code: code is reality.

So that's what we're taught. Seems reasonable. Our job is to write code, so we need to learn how to write code. College courses teach us to to write programs. Training courses tell us how to code to new libraries and APIs. And that's one of the biggest tragedies in the industry.

Because the way to learn to write great code is by reading code. Lots of code. High-quality code, low-quality code. Code in assembler, code in Haskell. Code written by strangers ten thousand miles away, and code written by ourselves last week. Because unless we do that, we're continually reinventing what has already been done, repeating both the successes and mistakes of the past.

I wonder how many great novelists have never read someone else's work, how many great painters never studied another's brush strokes, how many skilled surgeons never learned by looking over a colleague's shoulder, how many 767 captains didn't first spend time in the copilot's seat watching how it's really done.

And yet that's what we expect programmers to do. "This week's assignment is to write. . . ." We teach developers the rules of syntax and construction, and then we expect them to be able to write the software equivalent of a great novel.

The irony is that there's never been a better time to read code. Thanks to the huge contributions of the open-source community, we now have gigabytes of source code floating around the 'net just waiting to be read. Choose any language, and you'll be able to find source code. Select a problem domain, and there'll be source code. Pick a level, from microcode up to high-level business functions, and you'll be able to look at a wide body of source code.

Code reading is fun. I love to read others' code. I read it to learn tricks and to study traps. Sometimes I come across small but precious gems. I still remember the pleasure I got when I came across a binary-to-octal conversion routine in PDP-11 assembler that managed to output the six octal digits in a tight loop with no loop counter.

I sometimes read code for the narrative, like a book you'd pick up at an airport before a long flight. I expect to be entertained by clever plotting and unexpected symmetries. Jame Clark's *gpic* program (part of his GNU *groff* package) is a wonderful example of this kind of code. It implements something that's apparently very complex (a declarative, device-independent picture-drawing language) in a compact and elegant structure. I came away feeling inspired to try to structure my own code as tidily.

Sometimes I read code more critically. This is slower going. While I'm reading, I'm asking myself questions such as "Why is this written this way?" or "What in the author's background would lead her to this choice?" Often I'm in this mode because I'm reviewing code for problems. I'm looking for patterns and clues that might give me pointers. If I see that the author failed to take a lock on a shared data structure in one part of the code, I might suspect that the same might hold elsewhere and then wonder if that mistake could account for the problem I'm seeing. I also use the incongruities I find as a double check on my understanding; often I find what I think is a problem, but it on closer examination it turns out to be perfectly good code. Thus I learn something.

In fact, code reading is one of the most effective ways to eliminate problems in programs. Robert Glass, one of this book's reviewers, says, "by using (code) inspections properly, more than 90 percent of the errors can be removed from a software product before its first test.[1] In the same article he cites research that shows "Code-focused inspectors were finding 90 percent more errors than process-focused inspectors." Interestingly, while reading the code snippets quoted in this book I came across a couple of bugs and a couple of dubious coding practices. These are problems in code that's running at tens of thousands of sites worldwide. None were critical in nature, but the exercise shows that there's always room to improve the code we write. Code-reading skills clearly have a great practical benefit, something you already know if you've ever been in a code review with folks who clearly don't know how to read code.

And then there's maintenance, the ugly cousin of software development. There are no accurate statistics, but most researchers agree that more than half of the time we spend on software is used looking at existing code: adding new functionality, fixing bugs, integrating it into new environments, and so on. Code-reading skills are crucial. There's a bug in a 100,000-line program, and you've got an hour to find it. How do

---

[1]http://www.stickyminds.com/se/S2587.asp

you start? How do you know what you're looking at? And how can you assess the impact of a change you're thinking of making?

For all these reasons, and many more, I like this book. At its heart it is pragmatic. Rather than taking an abstract, academic approach, it instead focuses on the code itself. It analyzes hundreds of code fragments, pointing out tricks, traps and (as importantly) idioms. It talks about code in its environment and discusses how that environment affects the code. It highlights the important tools of the code reader's trade, from common tools such as *grep* and *find* to the more exotic. And it stresses the importance of tool building: write code to help you read code. And, being pragmatic, it comes with all the code it discusses, conveniently cross-referenced on a CD-ROM.

This book should be included in every programming course and should be on every developer's bookshelf. If as a community we pay more attention to the art of code reading we'll save ourselves both time and pain. We'll save our industry money. And we'll have more fun while we're doing it.

Dave Thomas
The Pragmatic Programmers, LLC
http://www.pragmaticprogrammer.com

Preface

What do we ever get nowadays from reading to equal the excitement and the revelation in those first fourteen years?

—*Graham Greene*

The reading of code is likely to be one of the most common activities of a computing professional, yet it is seldom taught as a subject or formally used as a method for learning how to design and program.

One reason for this sad situation originally may have been the lack of real-world or high-quality code to read. Companies often protect source code as a trade secret and rarely allow others to read, comment on, experiment with, and learn from it. In the few cases where important proprietary code was allowed out of a company's closet, it spurred enormous interest and creative advancements. As an example, a generation of programmers benefited from John Lions's *Commentary on the Unix Operating System* that listed and annotated the complete source code of the sixth-edition Unix kernel. Although Lions's book was originally written under a grant from AT&T for use in an operating system course and was not available to the general public, copies of it circulated for years as bootleg nth-generation photocopies.

In the last few years, however, the popularity of open-source software has provided us with a large body of code we can all freely read. Some of the most popular software systems used today, such as the *Apache* Web server, the Perl language, the GNU/Linux operating system, the BIND domain name server, and the *sendmail* mail-transfer agent are in fact available in open-source form. I was thus fortunate to be able to use open-source software such as the above to write this book as a primer and reader for software code. My goal was to provide background knowledge and techniques for reading code written by others. By using real-life examples taken out of working, open-source projects, I tried to cover most concepts related to code that are likely to appear before a software developer's eyes, including programming constructs, data types, data structures, control flow, project organization, coding standards, documentation, and architectures. A companion title to this book will cover interfacing and application-oriented code, including the issues of internationalization and portability, the elements of commonly used libraries and operating systems, low-level code, domain-specific and declarative languages, scripting languages, and mixed language systems.

This book is—as far as I know—the first one to exclusively deal with code reading as a distinct activity, one worthy on its own. As such I am sure that there will be inevitable shortcomings, better ways some of its contents could have been treated, and important material I have missed. I firmly believe that the reading of code should be both properly taught and used as a method for improving one's programming abilities. I therefore hope this book will spur interest to include code-reading courses, activities, and exercises into the computing education curriculum so that in a few years our students will learn from existing open-source systems, just as their peers studying a language learn from the great literature.

Supplementary Material

Many of the source code examples provided come from the source distribution of NetBSD. NetBSD is a free, highly portable Unix-like operating system available for many platforms, from 64-bit AlphaServers to handheld devices. Its clean design and advanced features make it an excellent choice for both production and research environments. I selected NetBSD over other similarly admirable and very popular free Unix-like systems (such as GNU/Linux, FreeBSD, and OpenBSD) because the primary goal of the NetBSD project is to emphasize correct design and well-written code, thus making it a superb choice for providing example source code. According to its developers, some systems seem to have the philosophy of "if it works, it's right," whereas NetBSD could be described as "it doesn't work unless it's right." In addition, some other NetBSD goals fit particularly well with the objectives of this book. Specifically, the NetBSD project avoids encumbering licenses, provides a portable system running on many hardware platforms, interoperates well with other systems, and conforms to open systems standards as much as is practical. The code used in this book is a (now historic) export-19980407 snapshot. A few examples refer to errors I found in the code; as the NetBSD code continuously evolves, presenting examples from a more recent version would mean risking that those realistic gems would have been corrected.

I chose the rest of the systems I used in the book's examples for similar reasons: code quality, structure, design, utility, popularity, and a license that would not make my publisher nervous. I strived to balance the selection of languages, actively looking for suitable Java and C++ code. However, where similar concepts could be demonstrated using different languages I chose to use C as the least common denominator.

I sometimes used real code examples to illustrate unsafe, nonportable, unreadable, or otherwise condemnable coding practices. I appreciate that I can be accused of disparaging code that was contributed by its authors in good faith to further the open-source movement and to be improved upon rather than merely criticized. I sincerely apologize in advance if my comments cause any offense to a source code author. In defense I argue that in most cases the comments do not target the particular code excerpt, but rather use it to illustrate a practice that should be avoided. Often the code I am using as a counterexample is a lame duck, as it was written at a time when technological and other restrictions justified the particular coding practice, or the particular practice is criticized out of the context. In any case, I hope that the comments will be received with good humor, and I openly admit that my own code contains similar, and probably worse, misdeeds.

Acknowledgments

A number of people generously contributed advice, comments, and their time help-ing to make this book a reality. Addison-Wesley assembled what I consider a dream team of reviewers: Paul C. Clements, Robert L. Glass, Scott D. Meyers, Guy Steele, Dave Thomas, and John Vlissides graciously read the manuscript in a form much rougher than the one you hold in your hands and shared their experience and wisdom through thoughtful, perceptive, and often eye-opening reviews. In addition, Eliza Fragaki, Georgios Chrisoloras, Kleanthis Georgaris, Isidor Kouvelas, and Lorenzo Vicisano read parts of the manuscript in an informal capacity and contributed many useful comments and suggestions. I was also lucky to get advice on the mechanics of the production process from Bill Cheswick, Christine Hogan, Tom Limoncelli, and Antonis Tsolomitis. Furthermore, George Gousios suggested the use of Tom-cat as Java open-source software material and explained to me details of its oper-ation, pointed me toward the *ant* build tool, and clarified issues concerning the use of the *DocBook* documentation format. Stephen Ma solved the mystery of how vnode pointers end up at the operating system device driver level (see Section 9.1.4). Spyros Oikonomopoulos provided me with an overview of the reverse engineering capabilities of UML-based modeling tools. Panagiotis Petropoulos updated the book references. Konstantina Vassilopoulou advised me on readability aspects of the an-notated code listings. Ioanna Grinia, Vasilis Karakoidas, Nikos Korfiatis, Vasiliki

Tangalaki, and George M. Zouganelis contributed their views on the book's layout. Athan Tolis located the epigram for Chapter 5 in the London Science Museum library.

Elizabeth Ryan and the folks at ITC patiently designed and redesigned the book until we could all agree it had the right look.

My editors, Ross Venables and Mike Hendrickson at Addison-Wesley, handled the book's production with remarkable effectiveness. In the summer of 2001, a week after we first established contact, Ross was already sending the manuscript proposal for review; working with a seven-hour time zone difference, I would typically find any issues I raised near the end of my working day solved when I opened my email in the morning. Their incredible efficiency in securing reviewers, answering my often naive questions, dealing with the book's contractual aspects, and coordinating the complex production process was paramount in bringing this project to fruition. Later on, Elizabeth Ryan expertly synchronized the Addision-Wesley production team; Chrysta Meadowbrooke diligently copy-edited my (often rough) manuscript, demonstrating an admirable understanding of its technical content; ITC handled the demanding composition task; and Jennifer Lundberg patiently introduced me to the mysteries of book marketing.

The vast majority of the examples used in this book are parts of existing open-source projects. The use of real-life code allowed me to present the type of code that one is likely to encounter rather than simplified toy programs. I therefore wish to thank all the contributors of the open-source material I have used for sharing their work with the programming community. The contributor names of code that appears in the book, when listed in the corresponding source code file, appear in Appendix B.

1

Introduction

I regret to report that I've just recently looked again at my programs for prime factors and tic-tac-toe, and they are entirely free of any sort of comments or documentation.

—Donald E. Knuth

Software source code is the definitive medium for communicating a program's operation and for storing knowledge in an executable form. You can compile source code into an executable program, you can read it to understand what a program does and how it works, and you can modify it to change the program's function. Most programming courses and textbooks focus on how to write programs from scratch. However, 40% to 70% of the effort that goes into a software system is expended after the system is first written. That effort invariably involves reading, understanding, and modifying the original code. In addition, the unrelenting, inevitable accumulation of legacy code; the increasing emphasis placed on software reuse; the high human turnover rates associated with the software industry; and the rising importance of open-source development efforts and cooperative development processes (including outsourcing, code walkthroughs, and extreme programming) make code reading an essential skill for today's software engineer. Furthermore, reading real-life well-written code can give you insights on how to structure and program nontrivial systems, a skill that cannot be learned by writing toy-sized programs. Programs should be written to be read, and, whether they are or not, they *need* to be read. Although code reading is, in the words of Robert Glass, "an undersung, undertaught activity," [Gla00] this need not be so.

In this book you will learn how to read code that others have written through concrete examples taken from important, real-life, open-source code systems. We adopt a liberal definition of code and take it to encompass all machine-readable elements of a project: source code (and its commentary), documentation, executable programs, source code repositories, design diagrams, and configuration scripts. Having mastered the book's contents, you will

- Be able to read and understand nontrivial software code
- Appreciate many important software development concepts
- Know how to explore large bodies of code
- Have a reading capability of a multitude of important high- and low-level programming languages
- Appreciate the intricacies of real software projects

Although the book starts with a revision of basic programming structures, we assume you are familiar with either C, C++, or Java and able to use simple tools to examine on-line the code of the examples we provide. In addition, exposure to the systems and applications we discuss, although not required, will enhance your understanding of the presented material.

In the remainder of this chapter you will find a discussion of the different reasons that will prompt you to read code together with the appropriate corresponding reading strategies, and a brief "instruction manual" for following the material we present. Happy (code) reading!

1.1 Why and How to Read Code

You may find yourself reading code because you have to, such as when fixing, inspecting, or improving existing code. You may also sometimes read code to learn how something works, in the manner we engineers tend to examine the innards of anything with a cover that can be opened. You may read code to scavenge for material to reuse or (rarely, but more commonly after reading this book, we hope) purely for your own pleasure, as literature. Code reading for each one of these reasons has its own set of techniques, emphasizing different aspects of your skills.[1]

1.1.1 Code as Literature

Dick Gabriel makes the point that ours is one of the few creative professions in which writers are not allowed to read each other's work [GG00].

---

[1] I am indebted to Dave Thomas for suggesting this section.

The effect of ownership imperatives has caused there to be no body of software as literature. It is as if all writers had their own private companies and only people in the Melville company could read *Moby-Dick* and only those in Hemingway's could read *The Sun Also Rises.* Can you imagine developing a rich literature under these circumstances? Under such conditions, there could be neither a curriculum in literature nor a way of teaching writing. And we expect people to learn to program in this exact context?

Open-source software (OSS) has changed that: we now have access to millions of lines of code (of variable quality), which we can read, critique, and improve and from which we can learn. In fact, many of the social processes that have contributed to the success of mathematical theorems as a scientific communication vehicle apply to open-source software as well. Most open-source software programs have been

- Documented, published, and reviewed in source code form
- Discussed, internalized, generalized, and paraphrased
- Used for solving real problems, often in conjunction with other programs

Make it a habit to spend time reading high-quality code that others have written. Just as reading high-quality prose will enrich your vocabulary, trigger your imagination, and expand your mind, examining the innards of a well-designed software system will teach you new architectural patterns, data structures, coding methods, algorithms, style and documentation conventions, application programming interfaces (APIs), or even a new computer language. Reading high-quality code is also likely to raise your standards regarding the code you produce.

In your code-reading adventures you will inevitably encounter code that should best be treated as an example of practices to avoid. Being able to rapidly differentiate good code from bad code is a valuable skill; exposure to some sound coding counterexamples may help you develop the skill. You can easily discern code of low quality by the following signs:

- An inconsistent coding style
- A gratuitously complicated or unreadable structure
- Obvious logical errors or omissions
- Overuse of nonportable constructs
- Lack of maintenance

You should not, however, expect to learn sound programming from poorly written code; if you are reading code as literature, you are wasting your time, especially considering the amount of available high-quality code you can now access.

Ask yourself: Is the code I am reading really the best of breed? One of the advantages of the open-source movement is that successful software projects and ideas inspire competition to improve on their structure and functionality. We often have the luxury to see a second or third iteration over a software design; in most cases (but not always) the latter design is significantly improved over the earlier versions. A search on the Web with keywords based on the functionality you are looking for will easily guide you toward the competing implementations.

Read code selectively and with a goal in your mind. Are you trying to learn new patterns, a coding style, a way to satisfy some requirements? Alternatively, you may find yourself browsing code to pick up random gems. In that case, be ready to study in detail interesting parts you don't know: language features (even if you know a language in depth, modern languages evolve with new features), APIs, algorithms, data structures, architectures, and design patterns.

Notice and appreciate the code's particular nonfunctional requirements that might give rise to a specific implementation style. Requirements for portability, time or space efficiency, readability, or even obfuscation can result in code with very peculiar characteristics.

- We have seen code using six-letter external identifiers to remain portable with old-generation linkers.

- There are efficient algorithms that have (in terms of source code lines) an implementation that is two orders of magnitude more complex than their naive counterparts.

- Code for embedded or restricted-space applications (consider the various GNU/Linux or FreeBSD on-a-floppy distributions) can go to great lengths to save a few bytes of space.

- Code written to demonstrate the functioning of an algorithm may use identifiers that may be impractically long.

- Some application domains, like copy-protection schemes, may *require* code to be unreadable, in an (often vain) attempt to hinder reverse engineering efforts.

When you read code that falls in the above categories, keep in mind the specific nonfunctional requirements to see how your colleague satisfied them.

Sometimes you may find yourself reading code from an environment completely foreign to you (computer language, operating system, or API). Given a basic familiarity with programming and the underlying computer science concepts, you can in many cases use source code as a way to teach yourself the basics of the new environment. However, start your reading with small programs; do not immediately dive into the study of a large system. Build the programs you study and run them. This will provide you with both immediate feedback on the way the code is supposed to work and a sense of achievement. The next step involves actively changing the code to test your understanding. Again, begin with small changes and gradually increase their scope. Your active involvement with real code can quickly teach you the basics of the new environment. Once you think you have mastered them, consider investing some effort (and possibly some cash) to learn the environment in a more structured way. Read related books, documentation, or manual pages, or attend training courses; the two methods of learning complement each other.

One other way in which you can actively read existing code as literature entails improving it. In contrast to other literal works, software code is a live artifact that is constantly improved. If the code is valuable to you or your community, think about how you could improve it. This can involve using a better design or algorithm, documenting some code parts, or adding functionality. Open-source code is often not well documented; consider reinvesting your understanding of the code in improved documentation. When working on existing code, coordinate your efforts with the authors or maintainers to avoid duplication of work or bad feelings. If your changes are likely to be substantial, think about becoming a concurrent versions system (CVS) committer—an individual with the authority to directly commit code to a project's source base. Consider the benefits you receive from open-source software to be a loan; look for ways to repay it by contributing back to the open-source community.

1.1.2 Code as Exemplar

There are cases where you might find yourself wondering how a specific functionality is realized. For some application classes you may be able to find an answer to your questions in standard textbooks or specialized publications and research articles. However, in many cases if you want to know "how'd they do that" there's no better way than reading the code. Code reading is also likely to be the most reliable way to create software compatible with a given implementation.

The key concept when you are using code as exemplar is to *be flexible*. Be prepared to use a number of different strategies and approaches to understand how the code works. Start with any documentation you might find (see Chapter 8). A formal software design document would be ideal, but even user documentation can be helpful. Actually use the system to get a feeling of its external interfaces. Understand what exactly are you actually looking for: a system call, an algorithm, a code sequence, an architecture? Devise a strategy that will uncover your target. Different search strategies are effective for different purposes. You may need to trace through the instruction execution sequence, run the program and place a breakpoint in a strategic location, or textually search through the code to find some specific code or data elements. Tools (see Chapter 10) will help you here, but do not let one of them monopolize your attention. If a strategy does not quickly produce the results you want, drop it and try something different. Remember, the code you are looking for is there; you just have to locate it.

Once you locate the desired code, study it, ignoring irrelevant elements. This is a skill you will have to learn. Many exercises in this book will ask you to perform exactly this task. If you find it difficult to understand the code in its original context, copy it into a temporary file and remove all irrelevant parts. The formal name of this procedure is *slicing* (see Section 9.1.6), but you can get the idea by examining how we have informally applied it in the book's annotated code examples.

1.1.3 Maintenance

In other cases code, rather than being an exemplar, may actually need fixing. If you think you have found a bug in a large system, you need strategies and tactics to let you read the code at increasing levels of detail until you have found the problem. The key concept in this case is to *use tools*. Use the debugger, the compiler's warnings or symbolic code output, a system call tracer, your database's Structured Query Language (SQL) logging facility, packet dump tools, and Windows message spy programs to locate a bug's location. (Read more in Chapter 10 about how tools will help your code reading.) Examine the code from the problem manifestation to the problem source. Do not follow unrelated paths. Compile the program with debugging support and use the debugger's stack trace facility, single stepping, and data and code breakpoints to narrow down your search.

If the debugger is not cooperating (the debugging of programs that run in the background such as daemons and Windows services, C++ template-based code, servlets, and multithreaded code is sometimes notoriously difficult), consider adding print statements in strategic locations of the program's execution path. When examining Java code consider using AspectJ to insert into the program code elements that will execute only under specific circumstances. If the problem has to do with operating system interfaces, a system call tracing facility will often guide you very near the problem.

1.1.4 Evolution

In most situations (more than 80% of your time by some measurements) you will be reading code not to repair a fault but to add new functionality, modify its existing features, adapt it to new environments and requirements, or refactor it to enhance its nonfunctional qualities. The key concept in these cases is to *be selective* in the extent of the code you are examining; in most situations you will actually have to understand a very small percentage of the overall system's implementation. You can in practice modify a million-line system (such as a typical kernel or window system) by selectively understanding and changing one or two files; the exhilarating feeling that follows the success of such an operation is something I urge you to strive to experience. The strategy for selectively dealing with parts of a large system is outlined below.

- Locate the code parts that interest you.
- Understand the specific parts in isolation.
- Infer the code excerpt's relationship with the rest of the code.

When adding new functionality to a system your first task is to find the implementation of a similar feature to use as a template for the one you will be implementing. Similarly, when modifying an existing feature you first need to locate the underlying code. To go from a feature's functional specification to the code implementation, follow the string messages, or search the code using keywords. As an example, to locate the user authentication code of the *ftp* command you would search the code for the Password string:[2]

```
if (pass == NULL)
    pass = getpass("Password:");
n = command("PASS %s", pass);
```

Once you have located the feature, study its implementation (following any code parts you consider relevant), design the new feature or addition, and locate its impact

---

[2]netbsdsrc/usr.bin/ftp/util.c:265–267

area—the other code parts that will interact with your new code. In most cases, these are the only code parts you will need to thoroughly understand.

Adapting code to new environments is a different task calling for another set of strategies. There are cases where the two environments offer similar capabilities: you may be porting code from Sun Solaris to GNU/Linux or from a Unix system to Microsoft Windows. In these situations the compiler can be your most valuable friend. Right from the beginning, assume you have finished the task and attempt to compile the system. Methodically modify the code as directed by compilation and linking errors until you end with a clean build cycle, then verify the system's functionality. You will find that this approach dramatically lessens the amount of code you will need to read. You can follow a similar strategy after you modify the interface of a function, class, template, or data structure. In many cases, instead of manually locating your change's impact, you follow the compiler's error or warning messages to locate the trouble spots. Fixes to those areas will often generate new errors; through this process the compiler will uncover for you the code location influenced by your code.

When the code's new environment is completely different from the old one (for example, as is the case when you are porting a command-line tool to a graphical windowing environment) you will have to follow a different approach. Here your only hope for minimizing your code-reading efforts is to focus at the point where the interfaces between the old code and the new environment will differ. In the example we outlined, this would mean concentrating on the user interaction code and completely ignoring all the system's algorithmic aspects.

A completely different class of code evolution changes concerns *refactoring*. These changes are becoming increasingly important as some types of development efforts adopt extreme programming and agile programming methodologies. Refactoring involves a change to the system that leaves its static external behavior unchanged but enhances some of its nonfunctional qualities, such as its simplicity, flexibility, understandability, or performance. Refactoring has a common attribute with cosmetic surgery. When refactoring you start with a working system and you want to ensure that you will end up with a working one. A suite of pertinent test cases will help you satisfy this obligation, so you should start by writing them. One type of refactoring concerns fixing a known trouble spot. Here you have to understand the old code part (which is what this book is about), design the new implementation, study its impact on the code that interfaces with your code (in many cases the new code will be a drop-in replacement), and realize the change.

A different type of refactoring involves spending some "quality time" with your software system, actively looking for code that can be improved. This is one of the few cases where you will need an overall picture of the system's design and architecture; refactoring in-the-large is likely to deliver more benefits than refactoring in-the-small. Chapter 6 discusses ways to untangle large systems, while Chapter 9 outlines how to move from code to the system's architecture. When reading code to search for refactoring opportunities, you can maximize your return on investment by starting from the system's architecture and moving downward to look at increasing levels of detail.

1.1.5 Reuse

You might also find yourself reading code to look for elements to reuse. The key concept here is to *limit your expectations*. Code reusability is a tempting but elusive concept; limit your expectations and you will not be disappointed. It is very hard to write reusable code. Over the years comparatively little software has survived the test of time and been reused in multiple and different situations. Software parts will typically become reuse candidates after they have been gracefully extended and iteratively adapted to work on two or three different systems; this is seldom the case in ad-hoc developed software. In fact, according to the COCOMO II software cost model [BCH+95], crafting reusable software can add as much as 50% to the development effort.

When looking for code to reuse in a specific problem you are facing, first isolate the code that will solve your problem. A keyword-based search through the system's code will in most cases guide you to the implementation. If the code you want to reuse is intractable, difficult to understand and isolate, look at larger granularity packages or different code. As an example, instead of fighting to understand the intricate relation of a code piece with its surrounding elements, consider using the whole library, component, process, or even system where the code resides.

One other reuse activity involves proactively examining code to mine reusable nuggets. Here your best bet is to look for code that is already reused, probably within the system you are examining. Positive signs indicating reusable code include the use of a suitable packaging method (see Section 9.3) or a configuration mechanism.

1.1.6 Inspections

Finally, in some work settings, the task of code reading may be part of your job description. A number of software development methodologies use technical reviews such as walkthroughs, inspections, round-robin reviews, and other types of technical assessments as an integral part of the development process. Moreover, when practicing pair programming while applying the extreme programming methodology you will often find yourself reading code as your partner writes it. Code reading under these circumstances requires a different level of understanding, appreciation, and alertness. Here you need to *be thorough*. Examine code to uncover errors in function and logic. The various elements we have marked in the margin as dangerous (see the icon at left) are some of the things you should be wary of. In addition, you should be ready to discuss things you fail to see; verify that the code meets all its requirements.

Nonfunctional issues of the code should absorb an equal part of your attention. Does the code fit with your organization's development standards and style guides? Is there an opportunity to refactor? Can a part be coded more readably or more efficiently? Can some elements reuse an existing library or component? While reviewing a software system, keep in mind that it consists of more elements than executable statements. Examine the file and directory structure, the build and configuration process, the user interface, and the system's documentation.

Software inspections and related activities involve a lot of human interaction. Use software reviews as a chance to learn, teach, lend a hand, and receive assistance.

1.2 How to Read This Book

In this book we demonstrate important code-reading techniques and outline common programming concepts in the form they appear in practice, striving to improve your code-reading ability. Although you will find in the following chapters discussions of many important computer science and computing practice concepts such as data and control structures, coding standards, and software architectures, their treatment is by necessity cursory since the purpose of the book is to get you to examine the use of these ideas in the context of production code, rather than to introduce the ideas themselves. We have arranged the material in an order that will let you progress from the basic to the more sophisticated elements. However, the book is a reader, not a detective novel, so feel free to read it in the sequence that suits your interests.

1.2.1 Typographical Conventions

All code listings and text references to program elements (for example, function names, keywords, operators) are set in `typewriter` font. Some of our examples refer to command sequences executed in a Unix or Windows shell. We display the shell command prompt $ to denote Unix shell commands and the DOS command prompt

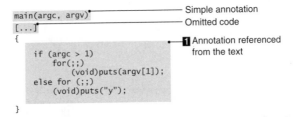

Figure 1.1 Example of an annotated listing.

C:\> to denote the Windows console prompt. Unix shell commands can span more than one line; we use > as the continuation line symbol.

```
$ grep -l malloc *.c |
> wc -l
        8
C:\>grep -l malloc *.c | wc -l
        8
```

The prompts and the continuation line symbol are displayed only to distinguish your input from the system output; you type only the commands after the prompt.

In some places we discuss unsafe coding practices or common pitfalls. These are identified on the margin with a danger symbol. You should be alert for such code when conducting a code walkthrough or just reading code to look for a bug. Text marked on the margin with an i identifies common coding idioms. When we read text we tend to recognize whole words rather than letters; similarly, recognizing these idioms in code will allow you to read code faster and more effectively and to understand programs at a higher level.

The code examples we use in this book come from real-world programs. We identify the programs we use (such as the one appearing in Figure 1.1) in a footnote[3] giving the precise location of the program in the directory tree of the book's companion source code and the line numbers covered by the specific fragment. When a figure includes parts of different source code files (as is the case in Figure 5.17, page 169) the footnote will indicate the directory where these files reside.[4]

Sometimes we omit parts from the code we list; we indicate those with an ellipsis sign [...]. In those cases the line numbers represent the entire range covered by the listed code. Other changes you may notice when referring back to the original code are

---

[3]netbsdsrc/usr.bin/yes/yes.c:53–64
[4]netbsdsrc/distrib/utils/more

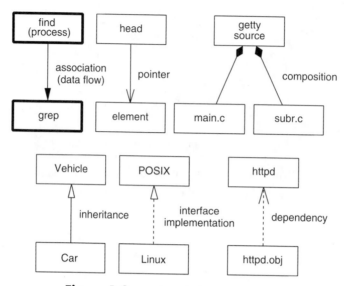

Figure 1.2 UML-based diagram notation.

changes of most C declarations from the old "Kernighan and Ritchie" style to ANSI C and the omission of some comments, white space, and program licensing information. We hope that these changes enhance the readability of the examples we provide without overly affecting the realism of the original examples. Nontrivial code samples are graphically annotated with comments using a custom-built software application. The use of the annotation software ensures that the examples remain correct and can be machine-verified. Sometimes we expand on an annotation in the narrative text. In those cases (Figure 1.1:1) the annotation starts with a number printed in a box; the same number, following a colon, is used to refer to the annotation from the text.

1.2.2 Diagrams

We chose UML for our design diagrams because it is the de facto industry standard. In preparing this book, we found it useful to develop an open-source declarative language for generating UML diagrams,[5] and we also made some small improvements to the code base underlying *GraphViz*[6] tool. We hope you find that the resulting UML diagrams help you better understand the code we analyze.

Figure 1.2 shows examples of the notation we use in our diagrams. Keep in mind the following.

---

[5]http://www.spinellis.gr/sw/umlgraph
[6]http://www.graphviz.org

- We draw processes (for example, filter-style programs) using UML's *active class* notation: a class box with a bold frame (for example, see Figure 6.14, page 213).

- We depict pointers between data elements using an *association navigation* relationship: a solid line with an open arrow. We also split each data structure into horizontal or vertical compartments to better depict its internal organization (for example, see Figure 4.10, page 121).

- We show the direction of associations (for example, to illustrate the flow of data) with a solid arrow located on the association line, rather than on top of it as prescribed by the UML (for example, see Figure 9.3, page 274).

All other relationships use standard UML notation.

- Class inheritance is drawn using a *generalization relationship*: a solid line with an empty arrow (for example, see Figure 9.6, page 277).

- An interface implementation is drawn as a *realization relationship*: a dashed line with an empty arrow (for example, see Figure 9.7, page 278).

- A *dependency* between two elements (for example, between files of a build process) is shown with a dashed line and an open arrow (for example, see Figure 6.8, page 191).

- Compositions (for example, a library consisting of various modules) are depicted through an *aggregation association*: a line ending in a diamond-like shape (for example, see Figure 9.24, page 321).

1.2.3 Exercises

The exercises you will find at the end of most sections aim to provide you with an incentive to apply the techniques we described and to further research particularly interesting issues, or they may be starting points for in-depth discussions. In most instances you can use references to the book's CD-ROM and to "code in your environment" interchangeably. What is important is to read and examine code from real-world, nontrivial systems. If you are currently working on such a system (be it in a proprietary development effort or an open-source project), it will be more productive to target the code-reading exercises toward that system instead of the book's CD-ROM.

Many exercises begin by asking you to locate particular code sequences. This task can be automated. First, express the code you are looking for as a regular expression. (Read more about regular expressions in Chapter 10.) Then, search through the code base using a command such as the following in the Unix environment:

```
find /cdrom -name '*.c' -print | xargs grep 'malloc.*NULL'
```

or using the Perl script codefind.pl[7] in the Windows environment. (Some of the files in the source code base have the same name as old MS-DOS devices, causing some Windows implementations to hang when trying to access them; the Perl script explicitly codes around this problem.)

1.2.4 Supplementary Material

All the examples you will find in this book are based on existing open-source software code. The source code base comprises more than 53,000 files occupying over 540 MB. All references to code examples are unambiguously identified in footnotes so you can examine the referenced code in its context. In addition, you can coordinate your exploration of the source code base with the book's text in three different ways.

1. You can look up the file name (the last component of the complete file path) of each referenced source file in the Index.
2. You can browse Appendix A, which provides an overview of the source code base.
3. You can search Appendix C, which contains a list of referenced source code files sorted according to the code directory structure.

1.2.5 Tools

Some of the examples we provide depend on the availability of programs found under Unix-type operating systems, such as *grep* and *find*. A number of such systems (for example, FreeBSD, GNU/Linux, NetBSD, OpenBSD, and Solaris) are now freely available to download and install on a wide variety of hardware. If you do not have access to such a system, you can still benefit from these tools by using ports that have been made to other operating systems such as Windows. (Section 10.9 contains further details on tool availability.)

---

[7] tools/codefind.pl

1.2.6 Outline

In Chapter 2 we present two complete programs and examine their workings in a step-by-step fashion. In doing so we outline some basic strategies for code reading and identify common C control structures, building blocks, idioms, and pitfalls. We leave some more advanced (and easily abused) elements of the C language to be discussed in Chapters 3 and 5. Chapter 4 examines how to read code embodying common data structures. Chapter 6 deals with code found in really large projects: geographically distributed team efforts comprising thousands of files and millions of lines of code. Large projects typically adopt common coding standards and conventions (discussed in Chapter 7) and may include formal documentation (presented in Chapter 8). Chapter 9 provides background information and advice on viewing the forest rather than the trees: the system's architecture rather than its code details. When reading code you can use a number of tools. These are the subject of Chapter 10. Finally, Chapter 11 contains a complete worked-out example: the code-reading and code-understanding techniques presented in the rest of the book are applied for locating and extracting a phase of the moon algorithm from the NetBSD source code base and adding it as an SQL function in the Java-based HSQL database engine.

In the form of appendices you will find an overview of the code that we used in the examples and that accompanies this book (Appendix A), a list of individuals and organizations whose code appears in the book's text (Appendix B), a list of all referenced source files ordered by the directory in which they occur (Appendix C), the source code licenses (Appendix D), and a list of maxims for reading code with references to the page where each one is introduced (Appendix E).

1.2.7 The Great Language Debate

Most examples in the book are based on C programs running on a POSIX character terminal environment. The reasons behind this choice have to do with the abundance of open-source software portable C code and the conciseness of the examples we found compared to similar ones written in C++ or Java. (The reasons behind this phenomenon are probably mostly related to the code's age or the prevalent coding style rather than particular language characteristics.) It is unfortunate that programs based on graphical user interfaces (GUIs) are poorly represented in our samples, but reading and reasoning about such programs really deserves a separate book volume. In all cases where we mention Microsoft Windows API functions we refer to the Win32 SDK API rather than the .NET platform.

Table 1.1 The Ten Most-Used Languages in
Open-Source Projects

Language	Number of Projects	% of Projects
C	8,393	21.2
C++	7,632	19.2
Java	5,970	15.1
PHP	4,433	11.2
Perl	3,618	9.1
Python	1,765	4.5
Visual Basic	916	2.3
Unix Shell	835	2.1
Assembly	745	1.9
JavaScript	738	1.9

We have been repeatedly asked about the languages used to write open-source
software. Table 1.1 summarizes the number of projects using each of the top ten
most-used languages in the SourceForge.net repository.[8] The C language features
at the top of the list and is probably underrepresented because many very large C
open-source projects such as FreeBSD and GNU/Linux are independently hosted, and
many projects claiming to use C++ are in fact written in C, making very little use
of the C++ features. On the other hand, keep in mind that a similar list compiled for
non-open-source projects would be entirely different, probably featuring COBOL, Ada,
Fortran, and assorted 4GLs at the top of the list. Furthermore, if you are maintaining
code—a very likely if unfashionable reason for reading code—the language you will
be reading would very likely have been adopted (if you are lucky) five or ten years
ago, reflecting the programming language landscape of that era.

The code structures that our examples represent apply in most cases equally well
to Java and C++ programs; many also apply to Perl, Python, and PHP. However, you
can safely skip

- Chapter 3 if you never encounter C (or C++ as a better C) code
- Section 9.3.4 if C++ and Ada are not your cup of tea
- Section 9.1.3 if you have managed to avoid object-oriented approaches, C++,
  Java, Python, Smalltalk, and the object-oriented features of Perl
- Section 5.2 if you are not into Java or C++
- Section 2.8 if you are a structured programming zealot or a devoted Java fan

---

[8]http://sourceforge.net/softwaremap/trove_list.php?form_cat=160

Further Reading

The role of software as a medium for storing executable knowledge is described in Armour [Arm00]. A very readable, all-encompassing introduction to the various coding systems used in computer technology is Petzold's *Code* [Pet99]. Kernighan and Plauger advocate the careful study and imitation of good programs as a way to better writing [KP76]. Code reading and understanding is also an integral part of software maintenance. The costs of software maintenance are analyzed in Chapter 30 of Pressman [Pre00] and in more detail by Boehm [Boe81, Boe83]. Glass presents the social dimension of code reading in an open-source world [Gla00]. Code specifically written to be read is advocated by Knuth's *Literate Programming* methodology. A readable introduction to it is Bentley's "Programming Pearls" column [BK86] while Knuth's opus [Knu92], his two literate programming books [Knu86a, Knu86b], and a series of articles based on the original idea [BKM86, Han87, Jac87, Ham88, WL89] provide additional examples. The act of reading old computer code has recently been described as *software archeology* [HT02].

After more than twenty years the Lions book is now available in an unrestricted edition [Lio96]. Read about the open-source software development processes in Raymond [Ray01]. The ethical dimensions of using open-source software as research (and teaching, we presume) material are discussed in El-Emam [El-01]. The social processes that have contributed to the success of mathematical theorems as a scientific communication vehicle are presented in DeMillo et al. [DLP77]. Aspect-oriented programming may prove to be a valuable addition in the software maintainer's tool chest; read the AspectJ introduction in Kiczales et al. [KHH+01] and the companion articles in the same journal issue. Software maintenance management (and the effort figures we used in Section 1.1.4) is analyzed in Lientz and Swanson [LS80]; read more about refactoring in Fowler [Fow00]. Beck wrote the canonical introduction to extreme programming [Bec00]; you can find the corresponding *Manifesto for Agile Software Development* online.[9] The most important software reuse issues are outlined in two sources [Kru92, MMM95]. Examples of process-level software reuse based on open-source code are described elsewhere [Spi99a, SR00]. The COCOMO II software cost model was first presented in Boehm et al. [BCH+95].

---

[9]http://www.AgileManifesto.org/

2

Basic Programming Elements

What we observe is not nature itself, but nature exposed to our method of questioning.

—Werner Heisenberg

Code reading is in many cases a bottom-up activity. In this chapter we review the basic code elements that comprise programs and outline how to read and reason about them. In Section 2.1 we dissect a simple program to demonstrate the type of reasoning necessary for code reading. We will also have the first opportunity to identify common traps and pitfalls that we should watch for when reading or writing code, as well as idioms that can be useful for understanding its meaning. Sections 2.2 and onward build on our understanding by examining the functions, control structures, and expressions that make up a program. Again, we will reason about a specific program while at the same time examining the (common) control constructs of C, C++, Java, and Perl. Our first two complete examples are C programs mainly because realistic self-standing Java or C++ programs are orders of magnitude larger. However, most of the concepts and structures we introduce here apply to programs written in any of the languages derived from C such as C++, C#, Java, Perl, and PHP. We end this chapter with a section detailing how to reason about a program's flow of control at an abstract level, extracting semantic meaning out of its code elements.

2.1 A Complete Program

A very simple yet useful program available on Unix systems is *echo*, which prints its arguments on the standard output (typically the screen). It is often used to display information to the user as in:

```
echo "Cool! Let's get to it..."
```

in the NetBSD upgrade script.[1] Figure 2.1 contains the complete source code of *echo*.[2]

As you can see, more than half of the program code consists of legal and administrative information such as copyrights, licensing information, and program version identifiers. The provision of such information, together with a summary of the specific program or module functionality, is a common characteristic in large, organized systems. When reusing source code from open-source initiatives, pay attention to the licensing requirements imposed by the copyright notice (Figure 2.1:1).

C and C++ programs need to include header files (Figure 2.1:2) in order to correctly use library functions. The library documentation typically lists the header files needed for each function. The use of library functions without the proper header files often generates only warnings from the C compiler yet can cause programs to fail at runtime. Therefore, a part of your arsenal of code-reading procedures will be to run the code through the compiler looking for warning messages (see Section 10.6).

Standard C, C++, and Java programs begin their execution from the function (method in Java) called `main` (Figure 2.1:3). When examining a program for the first time `main` can be a good starting point. Keep in mind that some operating environments such as Microsoft Windows, Java applet and servlet hosts, palmtop PCs, and embedded systems may use another function as the program's entry point, for example, `WinMain` or `init`.

In C/C++ programs two arguments of the `main` function (customarily named `argc` and `argv`) are used to pass information from the operating system to the program about the specified command-line arguments. The `argc` variable contains the number of program arguments, while `argv` is an array of strings containing all the actual arguments (including the name of the program in position 0). The `argv` array is terminated with a `NULL` element, allowing two different ways to process arguments: either by counting based on `argc` or by going through `argv` and comparing each value against `NULL`. In Java programs you will find the `argv` `String` array and its `length` method used for the same purpose, while in Perl code the equivalent constructs you will see are the `@ARGV` array and the `$#ARGV` scalar.

---

[1] netbsdsrc/distrib/miniroot/upgrade.sh:98
[2] netbsdsrc/bin/echo/echo.c:3–80

```
/*
 * Copyright (c) 1989, 1993
 *      The Regents of the University of California.  All rights reserved.
 *
 * Redistribution and use in source and binary forms, with or without
 * modification, are permitted provided that the following conditions
 * are met:
 * 1. Redistributions of source code must retain the above copyright
 *    notice, this list of conditions and the following disclaimer.
 * 2. Redistributions in binary form must reproduce the above copyright
 *    notice, this list of conditions and the following disclaimer in the
 *    documentation and/or other materials provided with the distribution.
 * 3. All advertising materials mentioning features or use of this software
 *    must display the following acknowledgement:
 *    This product includes software developed by the University of
 *    California, Berkeley and its contributors.
 * 4. Neither the name of the University nor the names of its contributors
 *    may be used to endorse or promote products derived from this software
 *    without specific prior written permission.
 *
 * THIS SOFTWARE IS PROVIDED BY THE REGENTS AND CONTRIBUTORS ``AS IS'' AND
 * ANY EXPRESS OR IMPLIED WARRANTIES, INCLUDING, BUT NOT LIMITED TO, THE
 * IMPLIED WARRANTIES OF MERCHANTABILITY AND FITNESS FOR A PARTICULAR PURPOSE
 * ARE DISCLAIMED.  IN NO EVENT SHALL THE REGENTS OR CONTRIBUTORS BE LIABLE
 * FOR ANY DIRECT, INDIRECT, INCIDENTAL, SPECIAL, EXEMPLARY, OR CONSEQUENTIAL
 * DAMAGES (INCLUDING, BUT NOT LIMITED TO, PROCUREMENT OF SUBSTITUTE GOODS
 * OR SERVICES; LOSS OF USE, DATA, OR PROFITS; OR BUSINESS INTERRUPTION)
 * HOWEVER CAUSED AND ON ANY THEORY OF LIABILITY, WHETHER IN CONTRACT, STRICT
 * LIABILITY, OR TORT (INCLUDING NEGLIGENCE OR OTHERWISE) ARISING IN ANY WAY
 * OUT OF THE USE OF THIS SOFTWARE, EVEN IF ADVISED OF THE POSSIBILITY OF
 * SUCH DAMAGE.
 */

#include <sys/cdefs.h>

#ifndef lint
__COPYRIGHT(
"@(#) Copyright (c) 1989, 1993\n\
        The Regents of the University of California.  All rights reserved.\n");

__RCSID("$NetBSD: echo.c,v 1.7 1997/07/20 06:07:03 thorpej Exp $");
#endif /* not lint */


#include <stdio.h>
#include <stdlib.h>
#include <string.h>


int     main __P((int, char *[]));

int
main(argc, argv)
        int argc;
        char *argv[];
{
        int nflag;

        /* This utility may NOT do getopt(3) option parsing. */
        if (*++argv && !strcmp(*argv, "-n")) {
                ++argv;
                nflag = 1;
        }
        else
                nflag = 0;

        while (*argv) {
                (void)printf("%s", *argv);
                if (*++argv)
                        putchar(' ');
        }
        if (!nflag)
                putchar('\n');
        exit(0);
}
```

1 Comment (copyright and distribution license), ignored by the compiler. This license appears on most programs of this collection. It will not be shown again.

Copyright and program version identifiers that will appear as strings in the executable program

2 Standard library headers for:
    printf
    exit
    strcmp

Function declaration with macro to hide arguments for pre-ANSI compilers

3 The program starts with this function
4 Number of arguments to the program
4 The actual arguments (starting with the program name, terminated with NULL)
5 When true output will not be terminated with a newline

6 The first argument is -n
6 Skip the argument and set nflag

There are arguments to process
7 Print the argument
Is there a next argument? (Advance argv)
Print the separating space

Terminate output with newline unless -n was given
Exit program indicating success

Figure 2.1 The Unix *echo* program.

The declaration of `argc` and `argv` in our example (Figure 2.1:4) is somewhat unusual. The typical C/C++ definition of `main` is[3]

```
int
main(int argc, char **argv)
```

while the corresponding Java class method definition is[4]

```
public static void main(String args[]) {
```

The definition in Figure 2.1:4 is using the old-style (pre-ANSI C) syntax of C, also known as K&R C. You may come across such function definitions in older programs; keep in mind that there are subtle differences in the ways arguments are passed and the checks that a compiler will make depending on the style of the function definition.

When examining command-line programs you will find arguments processed by using either handcrafted code or, in POSIX environments, the `getopt` function. Java programs may be using the GNU `gnu.getopt` package[5] for the same purpose.

The standard definition of the *echo* command is not compatible with the `getopt` behavior; the single `-n` argument specifying that the output is not to be terminated with a newline is therefore processed by handcrafted code (Figure 2.1:6). The comparison starts by advancing `argv` to the first argument of *echo* (remember that position 0 contains the program name) and verifying that such an argument exists. Only then is `strcmp` called to compare the argument against `-n`. The sequence of a check to see if the argument is valid, followed by a use of that argument, combined with using the Boolean AND (`&&`) operator, is a common idiom. It works because the `&&` operator will not evaluate its righthand side operand if its lefthand side evaluates to false. Calling `strcmp` or any other string function and passing it a `NULL` value instead of a pointer to actual character data will cause a program to crash in many operating environments.

Note the nonintuitive return value of `strcmp` when it is used for comparing two strings for equality. When the strings compare equal it returns 0, the C value of false. For this reason you will see that many C programs define a macro `STREQ` to return true when two strings compare equal, often optimizing the comparison by comparing the first two characters on the fly:[6]

```
#define STREQ(a, b) (*(a) == *(b) && strcmp((a), (b)) == 0)
```

---

[3] netbsdsrc/usr.bin/elf2aout/elf2aout.c:72–73
[4] jt4/catalina/src/share/org/apache/catalina/startup/Catalina.java:161
[5] http://www.gnu.org/software/java/packages.html
[6] netbsdsrc/usr.bin/file/ascmagic.c:45

Fortunately the behavior of the Java `equals` method results in a more intuitive reading:[7]

```
if (isConfig) {
    configFile = args[i];
    isConfig = false;
} else if (args[i].equals("-config")) {
    isConfig = true;
} else if (args[i].equals("-debug")) {
    debug = true;
} else if (args[i].equals("-nonaming")) {
```

The above sequence also introduces an alternative way of formatting the indentation of cascading `if` statements to express a selection. Read a cascading `if`-`else if`-`...`-`else` sequence as a selection of mutually exclusive choices.

An important aspect of our `if` statement that checks for the `-n` flag is that `nflag` will always be assigned a value: 0 or 1. `nflag` is not given a value when it is defined (Figure 2.1:5). Therefore, until it gets assigned, its value is undefined: it is the number that happened to be in the memory place it was stored. Using uninitialized variables is a common cause of problems. When inspecting code, always check that all program control paths will correctly initialize variables before these are used. Some compilers may detect some of these errors, but you should not rely on it.

The part of the program that loops over all remaining arguments and prints them separated by a space character is relatively straightforward. A subtle pitfall is avoided by using `printf` with a string-formatting specification to print each argument (Figure 2.1:7). The `printf` function will always print its first argument, the format specification. You might therefore find a sequence that directly prints string variables through the format specification argument:[8]

```
printf(version);
```

Printing arbitrary strings by passing them as the format specification to `printf` will produce incorrect results when these strings contain conversion specifications (for example, an SCCS revision control identifier containing the % character in the case above).

---

[7] jt4/catalina/src/share/org/apache/catalina/startup/CatalinaService.java:136–143
[8] netbsdsrc/sys/arch/mvme68k/mvme68k/machdep.c:347

Even so, the use of printf and putchar is not entirely correct. Note how the return value of printf is cast to void. printf will return the number of characters that were actually printed; the cast to void is intended to inform us that this result is intentionally ignored. Similarly, putchar will return EOF if it fails to write the character. All output functions—in particular when the program's standard output is redirected to a file—can fail for a number of reasons.

- The device where the output is stored can run out of free space.
- The user's quota of space on the device can be exhausted.
- The process may attempt to write a file that exceeds the process's or the system's maximum file size.
- A hardware error can occur on the output device.
- The file descriptor or stream associated with the standard output may not be valid for writing.

Not checking the result of output operations can cause a program to silently fail, losing output without any warning. Checking the result of each and every output operation can be inconvenient. A practical compromise you may encounter is to check for errors on the standard output stream before the program terminates. This can be done in Java programs by using the checkError method (we have yet to see this used in practice on the standard output stream; even some JDK programs will fail without an error when running out of space on their output device); in C++ programs by using a stream's fail, good, or bad methods; and in C code by using the ferror function:[9]

```
if (ferror(stdout))
    err(1, "stdout");
```

After terminating its output with a newline, *echo* calls exit to terminate the program indicating success (0). You will also often find the same result obtained by returning 0 from the function main.

Exercise 2.1 Experiment to find out how your C, C++, and Java compilers deal with uninitialized variables. Outline your results and propose an inspection procedure for locating uninitialized variables.

Exercise 2.2 (Suggested by Dave Thomas.) Why can't the *echo* program use the getopt function?

---

[9] netbsdsrc/bin/cat/cat.c:213–214

Exercise 2.3   Discuss the advantages and disadvantages of defining a macro like STREQ. Consider how the C compiler could optimize strcmp calls.

Exercise 2.4   Look in your environment or on the book's CD-ROM for programs that do not verify the result of library calls. Propose practical fixes.

Exercise 2.5   Sometimes executing a program can be a more expedient way to understand an aspect of its functionality than reading its source code. Devise a testing procedure or framework to examine how programs behave on write errors on their standard output. Try it on a number of character-based Java and C programs (such as the command-line version of your compiler) and report your results.

Exercise 2.6   Identify the header files that are needed for using the library functions sscanf, qsort, strchr, setjmp, adjacent_find, open, FormatMessage, and XtOwn-Selection. The last three functions are operating environment–specific and may not exist in your environment.

2.2 Functions and Global Variables

The program *expand* processes the files named as its arguments (or its standard input if no file arguments are specified) by expanding hard tab characters (\t, ASCII character 9) to a number of spaces. The default behavior is to set tab stops every eight characters; this can be overridden by a comma or space-separated numeric list specified using the -t option. An interesting aspect of the program's implementation, and the reason we are examining it, is that it uses all of the control flow statements available in the C family of languages. Figure 2.2 contains the variable and function declarations of *expand*,[10] Figure 2.3 contains the main code body,[11] and Figure 2.5 (in Section 2.5) contains the two supplementary functions used.[12]

When examining a nontrivial program, it is useful to first identify its major constituent parts. In our case, these are the global variables (Figure 2.2:1) and the functions main (Figure 2.3), getstops (see Figure 2.5:1), and usage (see Figure 2.5:8).

The integer variable nstops and the array of integers tabstops are declared as *global variables*, outside the scope of function blocks. They are therefore visible to all functions in the file we are examining.

The three function declarations that follow (Figure 2.2:2) declare functions that will appear later within the file. Since some of these functions are used before they are defined, in C/C++ programs the declarations allow the compiler to verify the arguments

[i]

---

[10] netbsdsrc/usr.bin/expand/expand.c:36–62
[11] netbsdsrc/usr.bin/expand/expand.c:64–151
[12] netbsdsrc/usr.bin/expand/expand.c:153–185

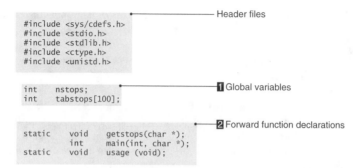

```
#include <sys/cdefs.h>
#include <stdio.h>
#include <stdlib.h>
#include <ctype.h>
#include <unistd.h>
```
— Header files

```
int    nstops;
int    tabstops[100];
```
1 Global variables

2 Forward function declarations

```
static    void    getstops(char *);
          int     main(int, char *);
static    void    usage (void);
```

Figure 2.2 Expanding tab stops (declarations).

passed to the function and their return values and generate correct corresponding code. When no forward declarations are given, the C compiler will make assumptions about the function return type and the arguments when the function is first used; C++ compilers will flag such cases as errors. If the following function definition does not match these assumptions, the compiler will issue a warning or error message. However, if the wrong declaration is supplied for a function defined in another file, the program may compile without a problem and fail at runtime.

Notice how the two functions are declared as `static` while the variables are not. This means that the two functions are visible only within the file, while the variables are potentially visible to all files comprising the program. Since *expand* consists only of a single file, this distinction is not important in our case. Most linkers that combine compiled C files are rather primitive; variables that are visible to all program files (that is, not declared as `static`) can interact in surprising ways with variables with the same name defined in other files. It is therefore a good practice when inspecting code to ensure that all variables needed only in a single file are declared as `static`.

Let us now look at the functions comprising *expand*. To understand what a function (or method) is doing you can employ one of the following strategies.

- Guess, based on the function name.
- Read the comment at the beginning of the function.
- Examine how the function is used.
- Read the code in the function body.
- Consult external program documentation.

In our case we can safely guess that the function `usage` will display program usage information and then exit; many command-line programs have a function with the same name and functionality. When you examine a large body of code, you

```
int
main(int argc, char *argv)
{
    int c, column;                                              ①Variables local to main
    int n;

    while ((c = getopt (argc, argv, "t:")) != -1) {             ②Argument processing using getopt
        switch (c) {
        case 't':                                               ③Process the -t option
            getstops(optarg);
            break;
        case '?': default:                                      Switch labels grouped together
            usage();                                            ④End of switch block
        }
    }
    argc -= optind;
    argv += optind;

    do {                                                        ⑤At least once
                                                                ⑥Process remaining arguments
        if (argc > 0) {
            if (freopen(argv[0], "r", stdin) == NULL) {
                perror(argv[0]);
                exit(1);
            }
            argc--, argv++;
        }
        column = 0;
        while ((c = getchar()) != EOF) {                        ⑦Read characters until EOF
            switch (c) {
            case '\t':                                          Tab character
                if (nstops == 0) {
                    do {
                        putchar(' ');
                        column++;
                    } while (column & 07);
                    continue;                                   ⑧Process next character
                }
                if (nstops == 1) {
                    do {
                        putchar(' ');
                        column++;
                    } while (((column - 1) % tabstops[0]) != (tabstops[0] - 1));
                    continue;                                   ⑧
                }
                for (n = 0; n < nstops; n++)
                    if (tabstops[n] > column)
                        break;
                if (n == nstops) {
                    putchar(' ');
                    column++;
                    continue;                                   ⑧
                }
                while (column < tabstops[n]) {
                    putchar(' ');
                    column++;
                }
                continue;                                       ⑧
            case '\b':                                          Backspace
                if (column)
                    column--;
                putchar('\b');
                continue;                                       ⑧
            default:                                            All other characters
                putchar(c);
                column++;
                continue;                                       ⑧
            case '\n':                                          Newline
                putchar(c);
                column = 0;
                continue;                                       ⑧
            }                                                   End of switch block
        }                                                       End of while block
    } while (argc > 0);                                         End of do block
    exit(0);
}
```

Figure 2.3 Expanding tab stops (main part).

will gradually pick up names and naming conventions for variables and functions. These will help you correctly guess what they do. However, you should always be prepared to revise your initial guesses following new evidence that your code reading will inevitably unravel. In addition, when modifying code based on guesswork, you should plan the process that will verify your initial hypotheses. This process can involve checks by the compiler, the introduction of assertions, or the execution of appropriate test cases.

The role of `getstops` is more difficult to understand. There is no comment, the code in the function body is not trivial, and its name can be interpreted in different ways. Noting that it is used in a single part of the program (Figure 2.3:3) can help us further. The program part where `getstops` is used is the part responsible for processing the program's options (Figure 2.3:2). We can therefore safely (and correctly in our case) assume that `getstops` will process the tab stop specification option. This form of gradual understanding is common when reading code; understanding one part of the code can make others fall into place. Based on this form of gradual understanding you can employ a strategy for understanding difficult code similar to the one often used to combine the pieces of a jigsaw puzzle: start with the easy parts.

Exercise 2.7   Examine the visibility of functions and variables in programs in your environment. Can it be improved (made more conservative)?

Exercise 2.8   Pick some functions or methods from the book's CD-ROM or from your environment and determine their role using the strategies we outlined. Try to minimize the time you spend on each function or method. Order the strategies by their success rate.

2.3 `while` Loops, Conditions, and Blocks

We can now examine how options are processed. Although *expand* accepts only a single option, it uses the Unix library function `getopt` to process options. A summarized version of the Unix on-line documentation for the `getopt` function appears in Figure 2.4. Most development environments provide on-line documentation for library functions, classes, and methods. On Unix systems you can use the *man* command and on Windows the Microsoft Developer Network Library (MSDN),[13] while the Java API is documented in HTML format as part of the Sun JDK. Make it a habit to read the documentation of library elements you encounter; it will enhance both your code-reading and code-writing skills.

---

[13]http://msdn.microsoft.com

GETOPT (3)   UNIX Programmer's Manual   GETOPT (3)

NAME

      getopt – get option character from command line argument list

SYNOPSIS

      `#include <unistd.h>`

      extern char *optarg;
      extern int optind;
      extern int optopt;
      extern int opterr;
      extern int optreset;

      int
      getopt(*int argc, char *const *argv, const char *optstring*)

DESCRIPTION

      The **getopt**( ) function incrementally parses a command line argument list *argv* and returns the next *known* option character. An option character is *known* if it has been specified in the string of accepted option characters, *optstring*.

      The option string *optstring* may contain the following elements: individual characters, and characters followed by a colon to indicate an option argument is to follow. For example, an option string `"x"` recognizes an option "**-x**", and an option string `"x:"` recognizes an option and argument "**-x** *argument*". It does not matter to **getopt**( ) if a following argument has leading white space.

      On return from **getopt**(), *optarg* points to an option argument, if it is anticipated, and the variable *optind* contains the index to the next *argv* argument for a subsequent call to **getopt**(). The variable *optopt* saves the last *known* option character returned by **getopt**().

      The variable *opterr* and *optind* are both initialized to 1. The *optind* variable may be set to another value before a set of calls to **getopt**( ) in order to skip over more or less argv entries.

      The **getopt**( ) function returns –1 when the argument list is exhausted, or a non-recognized option is encountered. The interpretation of options in the argument list may be cancelled by the option '--' (double dash) which causes **getopt**( ) to signal the end of argument processing and returns –1. When all options have been processed (i.e., up to the first non-option argument), **getopt**( ) returns –1.

DIAGNOSTICS

      If the **getopt**( ) function encounters a character not found in the string *optstring* or detects a missing option argument it writes an error message to *stderr* and returns '?'. Setting *opterr* to a zero will disable these error messages. If *optstring* has a leading ':' then a missing option argument causes a ':' to be returned in addition to suppressing any error messages.

      Option arguments are allowed to begin with "–"; this is reasonable but reduces the amount of error checking possible.

HISTORY

      The **getopt**( ) function appeared 4.3BSD.

BUGS

      The **getopt**( ) function was once specified to return EOF instead of –1. This was changed by POSIX 1003.2–92 to decouple **getopt**( ) from `<stdio.h>`.

4.3 Berkeley Distribution   April 19, 1994   1

Figure 2.4 The *getopt* manual page.

Based on our understanding of getopt, we can now examine the relevant code (Figure 2.3:2). The option string passed to getopt allows for a single option -t, which is to be followed by an argument. getopt is used as a condition expression in a while statement. A while statement will repeatedly execute its body as long as the condition specified in the parentheses is true (in C/C++, if it evaluates to a value other than 0). In our case the condition for the while loop calls getopt, assigns its result to c, and compares it with -1, which is the value used to signify that all options have been processed. To perform these operations in a single expression, the code uses the fact that in the C language family assignment is performed by an operator (=), that is, assignment expressions have a value. The value of an assignment expression is the value stored in the left operand (the variable c in our case) after the assignment has taken place. Many programs will call a function, assign its return value to a variable, and compare the result against some special-case value in a single expression. The following typical example assigns the result of readLine to line and compares it against null (which signifies that the end of the stream was reached).[14]

```
if ((line = input.readLine()) == null) [...]
    return errors;
```

It is imperative to enclose the assignment within parentheses, as is the case in the two examples we have examined. As the comparison operators typically used in conjunction with assignments bind more tightly than the assignment, the following expression

```
c = getopt (argc, argv, "t:") != -1
```

will evaluate as

```
c = (getopt (argc, argv, "t:") != -1)
```

thus assigning to c the result of comparing the return value of getopt against -1 rather than the getopt return value. In addition, the variable used for assigning the result of the function call should be able to hold both the normal function return values and any exceptional values indicating an error. Thus, typically, functions that return characters such as getopt and getc and also can return an error value such as -1 or

---

[14]cocoon/src/java/org/apache/cocoon/components/language/programming/java/Javac.java:106–112

EOF have their results stored in an integer variable, *not a character variable*, to hold
the superset of all characters *and* the exceptional value (Figure 2.3:7). The following
is another typical use of the same construct, which copies characters from the file
stream pf to the file stream active until the pf end of file is reached.[15]

```
while ((c = getc(pf)) != EOF)
    putc(c, active);
```

The body of a while statement can be either a single statement or a block: one or
more statements enclosed in braces. The same is true for all statements that control the
program flow, namely, if, do, for, and switch. Programs typically indent lines to
show the statements that form part of the control statement. However, the indentation
is only a visual clue for the human program reader; if no braces are given, the control
will affect only the single statement that follows the respective control statement,
regardless of the indentation. As an example, the following code does not do what is
suggested by its indentation.[16]

```
for (ntp = nettab; ntp != NULL; ntp = ntp->next) {
    if (ntp->status == MASTER)
        rmnetmachs(ntp);
        ntp->status = NOMASTER;
}
```

The line ntp->status = NOMASTER; will be executed for every iteration of the for
loop and not just when the if condition is true.

Exercise 2.9   Discover how the editor you are using can identify matching braces and
parentheses. If it cannot, consider switching to another editor.

Exercise 2.10   The source code of *expand* contains some superfluous braces. Identify
them. Examine all control structures that do not use braces and mark the statements that will
get executed.

Exercise 2.11   Verify that the indentation of *expand* matches the control flow. Do the same
for programs in your environment.

Exercise 2.12   The Perl language mandates the use of braces for all its control structures.
Comment on how this affects the readability of Perl programs.

---

[15]netbsdsrc/usr.bin/m4/eval.c:601–602
[16]netbsdsrc/usr.sbin/timed/timed/timed.c:564–568

2.4 switch **Statements**

The normal return values of getopt are handled by a switch statement. You will find switch statements used when a number of discrete integer or character values are being processed. The code to handle each value is preceded by a case label. When the value of the expression in the switch statement matches the value of one of the case labels, the program will start to execute statements from that point onward. If none of the label values match the expression value and a default label exists, control will transfer to that point; otherwise, no code within the switch block will get executed. Note that additional labels encountered after transferring execution control to a label *will not* terminate the execution of statements within the switch block; to stop processing code within the switch block and continue with statements outside it, a break statement must be executed. You will often see this feature used to group case labels together, merging common code elements. In our case when getopt returns 't', the statements that handle -t are executed, with break causing a transfer of execution control immediately after the closing brace of the switch block (Figure 2.3:4). In addition, we can see that the code for the default switch label and the error return value '?' is common since the two corresponding labels are grouped together.

When the code for a given case or default label does not end with a statement that transfers control out of the switch block (such as break, return, or continue), the program will continue to execute the statements following the next label. When examining code, look out for this error. In rare cases the programmer might actually want this behavior. To alert maintainers to that fact, it is common to mark these places with a comment, such as FALLTHROUGH, as in the following example.[17]

```
case 'a':
    fts_options |= FTS_SEEDOT;
    /* FALLTHROUGH */
case 'A':
    f_listdot = 1;
    break;
```

The code above comes from the option processing of the Unix *ls* command, which lists files in a directory. The option -A will include in the list files starting with a dot (which are, by convention, hidden), while the option -a modifies this behavior by adding to the list the two directory entries. Programs that automatically verify

---

[17] netbsdsrc/bin/ls/ls.c:173–178

source code against common errors, such as the Unix *lint* command, can use the FALLTHROUGH comment to suppress spurious warnings.

A switch statement lacking a default label will silently ignore unexpected values. Even when one knows that only a fixed set of values will be processed by a switch statement, it is good defensive programming practice to include a default label. Such a default label can catch programming errors that yield unexpected values and alert the program maintainer, as in the following example.[18]

```
    switch (program) {
    case ATQ:
[...]
    case BATCH:
        writefile(time(NULL), 'b');
        break;
    default:
        panic("Internal error");
        break;
    }
```

In our case the switch statement can handle two getopt return values.

1. 't' is returned to handle the -t option. Optind will point to the argument of -t. The processing is handled by calling the function getstops with the tab specification as its argument.

2. '?' is returned when an unknown option or another error is found by getopt. In that case the usage function will print program usage information and exit the program.

A switch statement is also used as part of the program's character-processing loop (Figure 2.3:7). Each character is examined and some characters (the tab, the newline, and the backspace) receive special processing.

Exercise 2.13 The code body of switch statements in the source code collection is formatted differently from the other statements. Express the formatting rule used, and explain its rationale.

Exercise 2.14 Examine the handling of unexpected values in switch statements in the programs you read. Propose changes to detect errors. Discuss how these changes will affect the robustness of programs in a production environment.

---

[18]netbsdsrc/usr.bin/at/at.c:535–561

Exercise 2.15   Is there a tool or a compiler option in your environment for detecting missing break statements in switch code? Use it, and examine the results on some sample programs.

2.5 for Loops

To complete our understanding of how *expand* processes its command-line options, we now need to examine the getstops function. Although the role of its single cp argument is not obvious from its name, it becomes apparent when we examine how getstops is used. getstops is passed the argument of the -t option, which is a list of tab stops, for example, 4, 8, 16, 24. The strategies outlined for determining the roles of functions (Section 2.2) can also be employed for their arguments. Thus a pattern for reading code slowly emerges. Code reading involves many alternative strategies: bottom-up and top-down examination, the use of heuristics, and review of comments and external documentation should all be tried as the problem dictates.

After setting nstops to 0, getstops enters a for loop. Typically a for loop is specified by an expression to be evaluated before the loop starts, an expression to be evaluated before each iteration to determine if the loop body will be entered, and an expression to be evaluated after the execution of the loop body. for loops are often used to execute a body of code a specific number of times.[19]

```
for (i = 0; i < len; i++) {
```

[i]   Loops of this type appear very frequently in programs; learn to read them as "execute the body of code len times." On the other hand, any deviation from this style, such as an initial value other than 0 or a comparison operator other than <, should alert you to carefully reason about the loop's behavior. Consider the number of times the loop body is executed in the following examples.

Loop extrknt + 1 times:[20]

```
for ( i = 0; i <= extrknt; i++ )
```

Loop month - 1 times:[21]

```
for (i = 1; i < month; i++)
```

---

[19] cocoon/src/java/org/apache/cocoon/util/StringUtils.java:85
[20] netbsdsrc/usr.bin/fsplit/fsplit.c:173
[21] netbsdsrc/usr.bin/cal/cal.c:332

Loop nargs times:[22]

```
for (i = 1; i <= nargs; i++)
```

Note that the last expression need not be an increment operator. The following line will loop 256 times, decrementing code in the process:[23]

```
for (code = 255; code >= 0; code--) {
```

In addition, you will find for statements used to loop over result sets returned by library functions. The following loop is performed for all files in the directory dir.[24]

```
if ((dd = opendir(dir)) == NULL)
    return (CC_ERROR);
for (dp = readdir(dd); dp != NULL; dp = readdir(dd)) {
```

The call to opendir returns a value that can be passed to readdir to sequentially access each directory entry of dir. When there are no more entries in the directory, readdir will return NULL and the loop will terminate.

The three parts of the for specification are expressions and not statements. Therefore, if more than one operation needs to be performed when the loop begins or at the end of each iteration, the expressions cannot be grouped together using braces. You will, however, often find expressions grouped together using the expression-sequencing comma (,) operator.[25]

```
for (cnt = 1, t = p; cnt <= cnt_orig; ++t, ++cnt) {
```

The value of two expressions joined with the comma operator is just the value of the second expression. In our case the expressions are evaluated only for their side effects: before the loop starts, cnt will be set to 1 and t to p, and after every loop iteration t and cnt will be incremented by one.

Any expression of a for statement can be omitted. When the second expression is missing, it is taken as true. Many programs use a statement of the form for (;;) to perform an "infinite" loop. Very seldom are such loops really infinite. The following

---

[22] netbsdsrc/usr.bin/apply/apply.c:130
[23] netbsdsrc/usr.bin/compress/zopen.c:510
[24] netbsdsrc/usr.bin/ftp/complete.c:193–198
[25] netbsdsrc/usr.bin/vi/vi/vs_smap.c:389

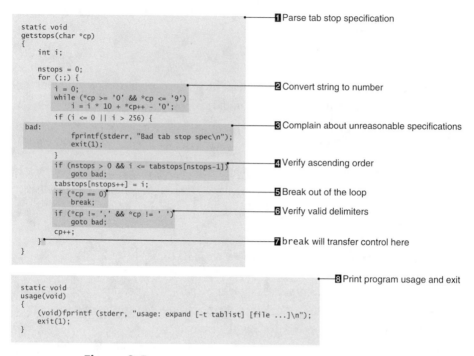

```
static void
getstops(char *cp)                                          ┌─1 Parse tab stop specification
{
    int i;

    nstops = 0;
    for (;;) {
        i = 0;                                              ┌─2 Convert string to number
        while (*cp >= '0' && *cp <= '9')
            i = i * 10 + *cp++ - '0';

        if (i <= 0 || i > 256) {
bad:                                                        ┌─3 Complain about unreasonable specifications
            fprintf(stderr, "Bad tab stop spec\n");
            exit(1);
        }
        if (nstops > 0 && i <= tabstops[nstops-1])          ┌─4 Verify ascending order
            goto bad;
        tabstops[nstops++] = i;
        if (*cp == 0)                                       ┌─5 Break out of the loop
            break;
        if (*cp != ',' && *cp != ' ')                       ┌─6 Verify valid delimiters
            goto bad;
        cp++;
    }                                                       ┌─7 break will transfer control here
}

                                                            ┌─8 Print program usage and exit
static void
usage(void)

{
    (void)fprintf (stderr, "usage: expand [-t tablist] [file ...]\n");
    exit(1);
}
```

Figure 2.5 Expanding tab stops (supplementary functions).

example—taken out of *init*, the program that continuously loops, controlling all Unix processes—is an exception.[26]

```
for (;;) {
    s = (state_t) (*s)();
    quiet = 0;
}
```

In most cases an "infinite" loop is a way to express a loop whose exit condition(s) cannot be specified at its beginning or its end. These loops are typically exited either by a `return` statement that exits the function, a `break` statement that exits the loop body, or a call to `exit` or a similar function that exits the entire program. C++, C#, and Java programs can also exit such loops through an exception (see Section 5.2).

A quick look through the code of the loop in Figure 2.5 provides us with the possible exit routes.

---

[26] netbsdsrc/sbin/init/init.c:540–545

- A bad stop specification will cause the program to terminate with an error message (Figure 2.5:3).
- The end of the tab specification string will break out of the loop.

Exercise 2.16 The for statement in the C language family is very flexible. Examine the source code provided to create a list of ten different uses.

Exercise 2.17 Express the examples in this section using while instead of for. Which of the two forms do you find more readable?

Exercise 2.18 Devise a style guideline specifying when while loops should be used in preference to for loops. Verify the guideline against representative examples from the book's CD-ROM.

2.6 break **and** continue **Statements**

A break statement will transfer the execution to the statement after the innermost loop or switch statement (Figure 2.5:7). In most cases you will find break used to exit early out of a loop. A continue statement will continue the iteration of the innermost loop without executing the statements to the end of the loop. A continue statement will reevaluate the conditional expression of while and do loops. In for loops it will evaluate the third expression and then the conditional expression. You will find continue used where a loop body is split to process different cases; each case typically ends with a continue statement to cause the next loop iteration. In the program we are examining, continue is used after processing each different input character class (Figure 2.3:8).

Note when you are reading Perl code that break and continue are correspondingly named last and next.[27]

```
while (<UD>) {
    chomp;
    if (s/0x[\d\w]+\s+\((.*?)\)// and $wanted eq $1) {
        [...]
        last;
    }
}
```

---

[27]perl/lib/unicode/mktables.PL:415–425

To determine the effect of a break statement, start reading the program upward from break until you encounter the first while, for, do, or switch block that encloses the break statement. Locate the first statement after that loop; this will be the place where control will transfer when break is executed. Similarly, when examining code that contains a continue statement, start reading the program upward from continue until you encounter the first while, for, or do loop that encloses the continue statement. Locate the last statement of that loop; immediately after it (but not outside the loop) will be the place where control will transfer when continue is executed. Note that continue ignores switch statements and that neither break nor continue affect the operation of if statements.

There are situations where a loop is executed only for the side effects of its controlling expressions. In such cases continue is sometimes used as a placeholder instead of the empty statement (expressed by a single semicolon). The following example illustrates such a case.[28]

```
for (; *string && isdigit(*string); string++)
    continue;
```

In Java programs break and continue can be followed by a label identifier. The same identifier, followed by a colon, is also used to label a loop statement. The labeled form of the continue statement is then used to skip an iteration of a nested loop; the label identifies the loop statement that the corresponding continue will skip. Thus, in the following example, the continue skip; statement will skip one iteration of the outermost for statement.[29]

```
skip:
    for ( [...] ) {
        if ( ch == limit.charAt(0) ) {
            for (int i = 1 ; i < limlen ; i++) {
                if ( [...] )
                    continue skip;
            }
            return ret;
        }
    }
```

---

[28] netbsdsrc/usr.bin/error/pi.c:174–175
[29] jt4/jasper/src/share/org/apache/jasper/compiler/JspReader.java:472–482

Similarly, the labeled form of the `break` statement is used to exit from nested loops; the label identifies the statement that the corresponding `break` will terminate. In some cases a labeled `break` or `continue` statements is used, even when there are no nested loops, to clarify the corresponding loop statement.[30]

```
comp : while(prev < length) {
    [...]
    if (pos >= length || pos == -1) {
        [...]
        break comp;
    }
}
```

Exercise 2.19   Locate ten occurrences of `break` and `continue` in the source code provided with the book. For each case indicate the point where execution will transfer after the corresponding statement is executed, and explain why the statement is used. Do not try to understand in full the logic of the code; simply provide an explanation based on the statement's use pattern.

2.7 Character and Boolean Expressions

The body of the `for` loop in the `getstops` function starts with a block of code that can appear cryptic at first sight (Figure 2.5:2). To understand it we need to dissect the expressions that comprise it. The first, the condition in the `while` loop, is comparing `*cp` (the character `cp` points to) against two characters: `'0'` and `'9'`. Both comparisons must be true and both of them involve `*cp` combined with a different inequality operator and another expression. Such a test can often be better understood by rewriting the comparisons to bring the value being compared in the middle of the expression and to arrange the other two values in ascending order. This rewriting in our case would yield

```
while ('0' <= *cp && *cp <= '9')
```

This can then be read as a simple range membership test for a character c.

$$0 \leq c \leq 9$$

---

[30] cocoon/src/scratchpad/src/org/apache/cocoon/treeprocessor/MapStackResolver.java:201–244

Note that this test assumes that the digit characters are arranged sequentially in ascending order in the underlying character set. While this is true for the digits in all character sets we know, comparisons involving alphabetical characters may yield surprising results in a number of character sets and locales. Consider the following typical example.[31]

```
if ('a' <= *s && *s <= 'z')
    *s -= ('a' - 'A');
```

The code attempts to convert lowercase characters to uppercase by subtracting from each character found to be lowercase (as determined by the if test) the character set distance from 'a' to 'A'. This fragment will fail to work when there are lowercase characters in character set positions outside the range a...z, when the character set range a...z contains nonlowercase characters, and when the code of each lowercase character is not a fixed distance away from the corresponding uppercase character. Many non-ASCII character sets exhibit at least one of these problems.

The next line in the block (Figure 2.5:2) can also appear daunting. It modifies the variable i based on the values of i and *cp and two constants: 10 and '0' while at the same time incrementing cp. The variable names are not especially meaningful, and the program author has not used macro or constant definitions to document the constants; we have to make the best of the information available.

We can often understand the meaning of an expression by applying it on sample data. In our case we can work based on the initial value of i (0) and assume that cp points to a string containing a number (for example, 24) based on our knowledge of the formatting specifications that *expand* accepts. We can then create a table containing the values of all variables and expression parts as each expression part is evaluated. We use the notation i' and *cp' to denote the variable value after the expression has been evaluated.

Iteration	i	i*10	*cp	*cp-'0'	i'	*cp'
0	0	0	'2'	2	2	'4'
1	2	20	'4'	4	24	0

The expression *cp - '0' uses a common idiom: by subtracting the ordinal value of '0' from *cp the expression yields the integer value of the character digit pointed to by *cp. Based on the table we can now see a picture emerging: after the

---

[31] netbsdsrc/games/hack/hack.objnam.c:352–253

loop terminates, i will contain the decimal value of the numeric string pointed to by cp at the beginning of the loop.

Armed with the knowledge of what i stands for (the integer value of a tab-stop specification), we can now examine the lines that verify the specification. The expression that verifies i for reasonable values is straightforward. It is a Boolean expression based on the logical OR (| |) of two other expressions. Although this particular expression reads naturally as English text (print an error message if i is either less than or equal to zero, or greater than 255), it is sometimes useful to transform Boolean expressions to a more readable form. If, for example, we wanted to translate the expression into the range membership expression we used above, we would need to substitute the logical OR with a logical AND (&&). This can easily be accomplished by using De Morgan's rules.[32]

```
!(a || b) <=> !a && !b
!(a && b) <=> !a || !b
```

We can thus transform the testing code as follows:

```
i <= 0 || i > 256  <=>
!(!(i <= 0) && !(i > 256)) <=>
!(i > 0 && i <= 256) <=>
!(0 < i && i <= 256) <=>
¬(0 < i ≤ 256)
```

In our example we find both the initial and final expressions equally readable; in other cases you may find that De Morgan's rules provide you a quick and easy way to disentangle a complicated logical expression.

When reading Boolean expressions, keep in mind that in many modern languages Boolean expressions are evaluated only to the extent needed. In a sequence of expressions joined with the && operator (a *conjunction*), the first expression to evaluate to false will terminate the evaluation of the whole expression yielding a false result. Similarly, in a sequence of expressions joined with the | | operator (a *disjunction*), the first expression to evaluate to true will terminate the evaluation of the whole expression yielding a true result. Many expressions are written based on this *short-circuit evaluation* property and should be read in the same way. When reading a conjunction, you can always assume that the expressions on the left of the expression you are examining

---

[32]We use the operator <=> to denote that two expressions are equivalent. This is not a C/C++/C#/Java operator.

are true; when reading a disjunction, you can similarly assume that the expressions on the left of the expression you are examining are false. As an example, the expression in the following if statement will become true only when all its constituent elements are true, and t->type will be evaluated only when t is not NULL.[33]

```
if (t != NULL && t->type != TEOF && interactive && really_exit)
        really_exit = 0;
```

Conversely, in the following example argv[1] will be checked for being NULL only if argv is not NULL.[34]

```
if (argv == NULL || argv[1] == NULL || argv[2] == NULL)
    return -1;
```

[i]   In both cases, the first check guards against the subsequent dereference of a NULL pointer. Our getstops function also uses short-circuit evaluation when checking that a delimiter specified (i) is larger than the previous one (tabstops[nstops-1]) (Figure 2.5:4). This test will be performed only if at least one additional delimiter specification has been processed (nstops > 0). You can depend on the short-circuit evaluation property in most C-derived languages such as C++, Perl, and Java; on the other hand, Fortran, Pascal, and most Basic dialects will always evaluate all elements of a Boolean expression.

Exercise 2.20   Locate expressions containing questionable assumptions about character code values in the book's CD-ROM. Read about the Java Character class test and conversion methods such as isUpper and toLowerCase or the corresponding ctype family of C functions (isupper, tolower, and so on). Propose changes to make the code less dependent on the target architecture character set.

Exercise 2.21   Find, simplify, and reason about five nontrivial Boolean expressions in the source code base. Do not spend time on understanding what the expression elements mean; concentrate on the conditions that will make the expression become true or false. Where possible, identify and use the properties of short-circuit evaluation.

Exercise 2.22   Locate and reason about five nontrivial integer or character expressions in the source code base. Try to minimize the amount of code you need to comprehend in order to reason about each expression.

---

[33] netbsdsrc/bin/ksh/main.c:606–607
[34] netbsdsrc/lib/libedit/term.c:1212–1213

```
static int
gen_init(void)
{
    [...]
    if ((sigaction(SIGXCPU, &n_hand, &o_hand) < 0) &&
        (o_hand.sa_handler == SIG_IGN) &&
        (sigaction(SIGXCPU, &o_hand, &o_hand) < 0))
        goto out;                                     ┤1 Failure; exit with an error

    n_hand.sa_handler = SIG_IGN;
    if ((sigaction(SIGPIPE, &n_hand, &o_hand) < 0) ||
        (sigaction(SIGXFSZ, &n_hand, &o_hand) < 0))
        goto out;                                     ┤2 Failure; exit with an error

    return(0);                                        ┤3 Normal function exit (success)

                                                       ◄─4 Common error handling code
out:
    syswarn(1, errno, "Unable to set up signal handler");
    return(-1);
}
```

Figure 2.6 The goto statement used for a common error handler.

2.8 goto **Statements**

The code segment that complains about unreasonable tab specifications (Figure 2.5:3) begins with a word followed by a colon. This is a label: the target of a goto instruction. Labels and goto statements should immediately raise your defenses when reading code. They can be easily abused to create "spaghetti" code: code with a flow of control that is difficult to follow and figure out. Therefore, the designers of Java decided not to support the goto statement. Fortunately, most modern programs use the goto statement in a small number of specific circumstances that do not adversely affect the program's structure.

  You will find goto often used to exit a program or a function after performing some actions (such as printing an error message or freeing allocated resources). In our example the exit(1) call at the end of the block will terminate the program, returning an error code (1) to the system shell. Therefore all goto statements leading to the bad label are simply a shortcut for terminating the program after printing the error message. In a similar manner, the listing in Figure 2.6[35] illustrates how a common error handler (Figure 2.6:4) is used as a common exit point in all places where an error is found (Figure 2.6:1, Figure 2.6:2). A normal exit route for the function, located before the error handler (Figure 2.6:3), ensures that the handler will not get called when no error occurs.

---

[35] netbsdsrc/bin/pax/pax.c:309–412

```
again:
    if ((p = fgets(line, BUFSIZ, servf)) == NULL)      Read a line; return on EOF
        return (NULL);

    if (*p == '#')                                     Comment? Retry
        goto again;
    cp = strpbrk(p, "#\n");
    if (cp == NULL)                                    Incomplete line? Retry
        goto again;
    *cp = '\0';                                        Complete entry
    [...]
    return (&serv);
```

Figure 2.7 The use of goto to reexecute code.

You will also find the goto statement often used to reexecute a portion of code, presumably after some variables have changed value or some processing has been performed. Although such a construct can often be coded by using a structured loop statement (for example, for (;;)) together with break and continue, in practice the coder's intent is sometimes better communicated by using goto. A single label, almost invariably named again or retry, is used as the goto target. The example in Figure 2.7,[36] which locates the entry of a specific service in the system's database while ignoring comments and overly large lines, is a typical case. (Interestingly, the code example also seems to contain a bug. If a partial line is read, it continues by reading the remainder as if it were a fresh line, so that if the tail of a long line happened to look like a service definition it would be used. Such oversights are common targets for computer security exploits.)

Finally, you will find the goto statement used to change the flow of control in nested loop and switch statements instead of using break and continue, which affect only the control flow in the innermost loop. Sometimes goto is used even if the nesting level would allow the use of a break or continue statement. This is used in large, complex loops to clarify where the flow of control will go and to avoid the possibility of errors should a nested loop be added around a particular break or continue statement. In the example in Figure 2.8[37] the statement goto have_msg is used instead of break to exit the for loop.

Exercise 2.23 Locate five instances of code that use the goto statement in the code base. Categorize its use (try to locate at least one instance for every one of the possible uses we outlined), and argue whether each particular goto could and should be replaced with a loop or other statement.

---

[36] netbsdsrc/lib/libc/net/getservent.c:65–104
[37] netbsdsrc/sys/dev/ic/ncr5380sbc.c:1575–1654

```
for (;;) {                                              ●──── for loop
    [...]
    if ((sc->sc_state & NCR_DROP_MSGIN) == 0) {
        if (n >= NCR_MAX_MSG_LEN) {
            ncr_sched_msgout(sc, SEND_REJECT);
            sc->sc_state |= NCR_DROP_MSGIN;
        } else {
            [...]
            if (n == 1 && IS1BYTEMSG(sc->sc_imess[0]))
                goto have_msg;●────────────────────── Exit the for loop
            [...]
        }
    }
    [...]
}                                                        ──── goto target
have_msg:●──────────────────────────────────────────
```

Figure 2.8 Exiting a loop using the goto statement.

Exercise 2.24 The function getstops produces the same error message for a number of different errors. Describe how you could make its error reporting more user-friendly while at the same time eliminating the use of the goto statement. Discuss when such source code changes are appropriate and when they should be avoided.

2.9 Refactoring in the Small

The rest of the getstops code is relatively straightforward. After checking that each tab stop is greater than the previous one (Figure 2.5:4), the tab stop offset is stored in the tabstops array. After a single tab stop number has been converted into an integer (Figure 2.5:2), cp will point to the first nondigit character in the string (that is, the loop will process all digits and terminate at the first nondigit). At that point, a series of checks specified by if statements control the program's operation. If cp points to the end of the tab stop specification string (the character with the value 0, which signifies the end of a C string), then the loop will terminate (Figure 2.5:5). The last if (Figure 2.5:6) will check for invalid delimiters and terminate the program operation (using the goto bad statement) if one is found.

The body of each one of the if statements will transfer control somewhere else via a goto or break statement. Therefore, we can also read the sequence as:

```
if (*cp == 0)
    break;
else if (*cp != ',' && *cp != ' ')
    goto bad;
else
    cp++;
```

i   This change highlights the fact that only one of the three statements will ever get executed and makes the code easier to read and reason about. If you have control over a body of code (that is, it is not supplied or maintained by an outside vendor or an open-source group), you can profit by reorganizing code sections to make them more readable. This improvement of the code's design after it has been written is termed *refactoring*. Start with small changes such as the one we outlined—you can find more than 70 types of refactoring changes described in the relevant literature. Modest changes add up and often expose larger possible improvements.

As a further example, consider the following one-line gem.[38]

```
op = &(!x ? (!y ? upleft : (y == bottom ? lowleft : left)) :
(x == last ? (!y ? upright : (y == bottom ? lowright : right)) :
(!y ? upper : (y == bottom ? lower : normal))))[w->orientation];
```

i   The code makes excessive use of the conditional operator ?:. Read expressions using the conditional operator like if code. As an example, read the expression[39]

```
sign ? -n : n
```

as follows:

> "If sign is true, then the value of the expression is -n; otherwise, the value of the expression is n".

Since we read an expression like an if statement, we can also format it like an if statement; one that uses x ? instead of if (x), parentheses instead of curly braces, and : instead of else. To reformat the expression, we used the indenting features of our editor in conjunction with its ability to show matching parentheses. You can see the result in Figure 2.9 (*left*).

Reading the conditional expression in its expanded form is certainly easier, but there is still room for improvement. At this point we can discern that the x and y variables that control the expression evaluation are tested for three different values:

1. 0 (expressed as !x or !y)

2. bottom or last

3. All other values

---

[38] netbsdsrc/games/worms/worms.c:419
[39] netbsdsrc/bin/csh/set.c:852

```
op = &(                          op = &(
!x ? (                           !x ? (
    !y ?                             !y ?
        upleft                          upleft
    : (                             : ( y == bottom ?
        y == bottom ?                   lowleft
            lowleft                 :
        :                               left
            left                    )
    )                            ) : ( x == last ? (
) : (                               !y ?
    x == last ? (                       upright
        !y ?                        : ( y == bottom ?
            upright                     lowright
        : (                         :
            y == bottom ?               right
                lowright            )
            :                    ) : (
                right               !y ?
        )                               upper
    ) : (                           : ( y == bottom ?
        !y ?                            lower
            upper                   :
        : (                             normal
            y == bottom ?           )
                lower           )
            :                ))[w->orientation];
                normal
        )
    )
))[w->orientation];
```

Figure 2.9 A conditional expression formatted like an if statement (*left*) and like
cascading if–else statements (*right*).

We can therefore rewrite the expression formatted as a series of cascading if–else
statements (expressed using the ?: operator) to demonstrate this fact. You can see the
result in Figure 2.9 (*right*).

The expression's intent now becomes clear: the programmer is selecting one
of nine different location values based on the combined values of x and y. Both
alternative formulations, however, visually emphasize the punctuation at the expense

```
struct options *locations[3][3] = {                    Location map
    {upleft,  upper,  upright},
    {left,    normal, right},
    {lowleft, lower,  lowright},
};
int xlocation, ylocation;                              To store the x, y map offsets

                                                       Determine x offset
if (x == 0)
    xlocation = 0;
else if (x == last)
    xlocation = 2;
else
    xlocation = 1;

                                                       Determine y offset
if (y == 0)
    ylocation = 0;
else if (y == bottom)
    ylocation = 2;
else
    ylocation = 1;

op = &(locations[ylocation][xlocation])[w->orientation];
```

Figure 2.10 Location detection code replacing the conditional expression.

of the semantic content and use an inordinate amount of vertical space. Nevertheless, based on our newly acquired insight, we can create a two-dimensional array containing these location values and index it using offsets we derive from the x and y values. You can see the new result in Figure 2.10. Notice how in the initialization of the array named `locations`, we use a two-dimensional textual structure to illustrate the two-dimensional nature of the computation being performed. The initializers are laid out two-dimensionally in the program text, the array is indexed in the normally unconventional order [y][x], and the mapping is to integers "0, 2, 1" rather than the more obvious "0, 1, 2", so as to make the two-dimensional presentation coincide with the semantic meanings of the words `upleft`, `upper`, and so on.

The code, at 20 lines, is longer than the original one-liner but still shorter by 7 lines from the one-liner's readable cascading-else representation. In our eyes it appears more readable, self-documenting, and easier to verify. One could argue that the original version would execute faster than the new one. This is based on the fallacy that code readability and efficiency are somehow incompatible. There is no need to sacrifice code readability for efficiency. While it is true that efficient algorithms and certain optimizations can make the code more complicated and therefore more difficult to follow, this does not mean that making the code compact and unreadable will make it more efficient. On our system and compiler the initial and final versions of the code execute at exactly the same speed: 0.6 μs. Even if there were speed differences, the economics behind software maintenance costs, programmer salaries, and CPU performance most of the time favor code readability over efficiency.

However, even the code in Figure 2.10 can be considered a mixed blessing: it achieves its advantages at the expense of two distinct disadvantages. First, it separates the code into two chunks that, while shown together in Figure 2.10, would necessarily be separated in real code. Second, it introduces an extra encoding (0, 1, 2), so that understanding what the code is doing requires two mental steps rather than one (map "0, last, other" to "0, 2, 1" and then map a pair of "0, 2, 1" values to one of nine items). Could we somehow directly introduce the two-dimensional structure of our computation into the conditional code? The following code fragment[40] reverts to conditional expressions but has them carefully laid out to express the computation's intent.

```
op =
   &(         !y ? (!x ?  upleft : x!=last ?  upper :  upright ) :
      y!=bottom ? (!x ?    left : x!=last ? normal :    right ) :
                  (!x ? lowleft : x!=last ?  lower : lowright )
   )[w->orientation];
```

The above formulation is a prime example on how sometimes creative code layout can be used to improve code readability. Note that the nine values are right-justified within their three columns, to make them stand out visually and to exploit the repetition of "left" and "right" in their names. Note also that the usual practice of putting spaces around operators is eschewed for the case of != in order to reduce the test expressions to single visual tokens, making the nine data values stand out more. Finally, the fact that the whole expression fits in five lines makes the vertical alignment of the first and last parentheses more effective, making it much easier to see that the basic structure of the entire statement is of the form

```
op = &(  <conditional-mess>  )[w->orientation];
```

The choice between the two new alternative representations is largely a matter of taste; however, we probably would not have come up with the second formulation without expressing the code in the initial, more verbose and explicit form.

The expression we rewrote was extremely large and obviously unreadable. Less extreme cases can also benefit from some rewriting. Often you can make an expression more readable by adding whitespace, by breaking it up into smaller parts by means of temporary variables, or by using parentheses to amplify the precedence of certain operators.

---

[40]Suggested by Guy Steele.

You do not always need to change the program structure to make it more readable. Often items that do not affect the program's operation (such as comments, the use of whitespace, and the choice of variable, function, and class names) can affect the program's readability. Consider the work we did to understand the code for the getstops function. A concise comment before the function definition would enhance the program's future readability.

```
/*
 * Parse and verify the tab stop specification pointed to by cp
 * setting the global variables nstops and tabstops[].
 * Exit the program with an error message on bad specifications.
 */
```

When reading code under your control, make it a habit to add comments as needed.

In Sections 2.2 and 2.3 we explained how names and indentation can provide hints for understanding code functionality. Unfortunately, sometimes programmers choose unhelpful names and indent their programs inconsistently. You can improve the readability of poorly written code with better indentation and wise choice of variable names. These measures are extreme: apply them only when you have full responsibility and control over the source code, you are sure that your changes are a lot better than the original code, and you can revert to the original code if something goes wrong. Using a version management system such as the Revision Control System (RCS), the Source Code Control System (SCCS), the Concurrent Versions System (CVS), or Microsoft's Visual SourceSafe can help you control the code modifications. The adoption of a specific style for variable names and indentation can appear a tedious task. When modifying code that is part of a larger body to make it more readable, try to understand and follow the conventions of the rest of the code (see Chapter 7). Many organizations have a specific coding style; learn it and try to follow it. Otherwise, adopt one standard style (such as one of those used by the GNU[41] or BSD[42] groups) and use it consistently. When the code indentation is truly inconsistent and cannot be manually salvaged, a number of tools (such as *indent*) can help you automatically reindent it to make it more readable (see Section 10.7). Use such tools with care: the judicious use of whitespace allows programmers to provide visual clues that are beyond the abilities of automated formatting tools. Applying *indent* to the code example in Figure 2.10 would definitely make it less readable.

Keep in mind that although reindenting code may help readability, it also messes up the program's change history in the revision control system. For this reason it

---

[41] http://www.gnu.org/prep/standards_toc.html
[42] netbsdsrc/share/misc/style:1–315

is probably best not to combine the reformatting with any actual changes to the program's logic. Do the reformat, check it in, and then make the other changes. In this way future code readers will be able to selectively retrieve and review your changes to the program's logic without getting overwhelmed by the global formatting changes. On the flip side of the coin, when you are examining a program revision history that spans a global reindentation exercise using the *diff* program, you can often avoid the noise introduced by the changed indentation levels by specifying the –w option to have *diff* ignore whitespace differences.

Exercise 2.25   Provide five examples from your environment or the book's CD-ROM where the code structure can be improved to make it more readable.

Exercise 2.26   You can find tens of intentionally unreadable C programs at the International Obfuscated C Code Contest Web site.[43] Most of them use several layers of obfuscation to hide their algorithms. See how gradual code changes can help you untangle their code. If you are not familiar with the C preprocessor, try to avoid programs with a large number of #define lines.

Exercise 2.27   Modify the position location code we examined to work on the mirror image of a board (interchange the right and left sides). Time yourself in modifying the original code and the final version listed in Figure 2.10. Do not look at the readable representations; if you find them useful, create them from scratch. Calculate the cost difference assuming current programmer salary rates (do not forget to add overheads). If the readable code runs at half the speed of the original code (it does not), calculate the cost of this slowdown by making reasonable assumptions concerning the number of times the code will get executed over the lifetime of a computer bought at a given price.

Exercise 2.28   If you are not familiar with a specific coding standard, locate one and adopt it. Verify local code against the coding standard.

2.10 do **Loops and Integer Expressions**

We can complete our understanding of the *expand* program by turning our attention to the body that does its processing (Figure 2.3, page 27). It starts with a do loop. The body of a do loop is executed at least once. In our case the do loop body is executed for every one of the remaining arguments. These can specify names of files that are to be tab-expanded. The code processing the file name arguments (Figure 2.3:6) reopens the stdin file stream to access each successive file name argument. If no file name arguments are specified, the body of the if statement (Figure 2.3:6) will not get

i

---

[43]http://www.ioccc.org

executed and *expand* will process its standard input. The actual processing involves reading characters and keeping track of the current column position. The `switch` statement, a workhorse for character processing, handles all different characters that affect the column position in a special way. We will not examine the logic behind the tab positioning in detail. It is easy to see that the first three and the last two blocks can again be written as a cascading `if–else` sequence. We will focus our attention on some expressions in the code.

Sometimes equality tests such as the ones used for `nstops` (for example, `nstops == 0`) are mistakenly written using the assignment operator `=` instead of the equality operator `==`. In C, C++, and Perl a statement like the following:[44]

```
if ((p = q))
    q[-1] = '\n';
```

uses a valid test expression for the `if` statement, assigning q to p and testing the result against zero. If the programmer intended to test p against q, most compilers would generate no error. In the statement we examined, the parentheses around (p = q) are probably there to signify that the programmer's intent was indeed an assignment and a subsequent test against zero. One other way to make such an intention clear is to explicitly test against NULL.[45]

```
if ((p = strchr(name, '=')) != NULL) {
    p++;
```

In this case the test could also have been written as `if (p = strchr(name, '='))`, but we would not know whether this was an intentional assignment or a mistake.

Finally, another approach you may come across is to adopt a style where all comparisons with constants are written with the constant on the lefthand side of the comparison.[46]

```
if (0 == serconsole)
    serconsinit = 0;
```

When such a style is used, mistaken assignments to constants are flagged by the compiler as errors.

---

[44] netbsdsrc/bin/ksh/history.c:313–314
[45] netbsdsrc/bin/sh/var.c:507–508
[46] netbsdsrc/sys/arch/amiga/dev/ser.c:227–228

When reading Java or C# programs, there are fewer chances of encountering such errors since these languages accept only Boolean values as control expressions in the corresponding flow statements. We were in fact unable to locate a single suspicious statement in the Java code found in the book's CD-ROM.

The expression `column & 7` used to control the first do loop of the loop-processing code is also interesting. The & operator performs a *bitwise-and* between its two operands. In our case, we are not dealing with bits, but by masking off the most significant bits of the `column` variable it returns the remainder of `column` divided by 8. When performing arithmetic, read `a & b` as `a % (b + 1)` when $b = 2^n - 1$. The intent of writing an expression in this way is to substitute a division with a— sometimes more efficiently calculated—bitwise-and instruction. In practice, modern optimizing compilers can recognize such cases and do the substitution on their own, while the speed difference between a division and a bitwise-and instruction on modern processors is not as large as it used to be. You should therefore learn to read code that uses these tricks, but avoid writing it.

There are two other common cases where bit instructions are used as substitutes for arithmetic instructions. These involve the *shift* operators << and >>, which shift an integer's bits to the left or right. Since every bit position of an integer has a value equal to a power of 2, shifting an integer has the effect of multiplying or dividing it by a power of 2 equal to the number of shifted bits. You can therefore think of shift operators in an arithmetic context as follows.

- Read `a << n` as `a * k`, where $k = 2^n$. The following example uses the shift operator to multiply by 4.[47]

```
n = ((dp - cp) << 2) + 1; /* 4 times + NULL */
```

- Read `a >> n` as `a / k`, where $k = 2^n$. The following example from a binary search routine uses the right shift operator to divide by 2.[48]

```
bp = bp1 + ((bp2 - bp1) >> 1);
```

Keep in mind that Java's logical shift right operator >>> should not be used to perform division arithmetic on signed quantities since it will produce erroneous results when applied on negative numbers.

---

[47] netbsdsrc/bin/csh/str.c:460
[48] netbsdsrc/bin/csh/func.c:106

Exercise 2.29   Most compilers provide a facility to view the compiled code in assembly language. Find out how to generate assembly code when compiling a C program in your environment and examine the code generated by your compiler for some instances of arithmetic expressions and the corresponding expressions using bit instructions. Try various compiler optimization levels. Comment on the readability and the code efficiency of the two alternatives.

Exercise 2.30   What type of argument could cause *expand* to fail? Under what circumstances could such an argument be given? Propose a simple fix.

2.11 Control Structures Revisited

Having examined the syntactic details of the control flow statements we can now focus our attention on the way we can reason about them at an abstract level.

The first thing you should remember is to examine one control structure at a time, treating its contents as a black box. The beauty of structured programming is that the control structures employed allow you to abstract and selectively reason about parts of a program, without getting overwhelmed by the program's overall complexity.

Consider the following code sequence.[49]

```
while (enum.hasMoreElements()) {
    [...]
    if (object instanceof Resource) {
        [...]
        if (!copy(is, os))
            [...]
    } else if (object instanceof InputStream) {
        [...]
        if (!copy((InputStream) object, os))
            [...]
    } else if (object instanceof DirContext) {
        [...]
    }
}
```

Although we have removed a large part of the 20 lines of code, the loop still appears quite complex. However, the way you should read the above loop is

```
while (enum.hasMoreElements()) {
    // Do something
}
```

---

[49] jt4/catalina/src/share/org/apache/catalina/loader/StandardLoader.java:886–905

At that level of abstraction you can then focus on the loop body and examine its functioning without worrying about the control structure in which it is enclosed. This idea suggests a second rule we should follow when examining a program's flow of control: treat the controlling expression of each control structure as an assertion for the code it encloses. Although the above statement may appear obtuse or trivial, its significance to the understanding of code can be profound. Consider again the while statement we examined. The typical reading of the control structure would be that while enum.hasMoreElements() is true the code inside the loop will get executed. When, however, you examine the loop's body (in isolation as we suggested above), you can always assume that enum.hasMoreElements() will be true and that, therefore, the enclosed statement

```
NameClassPair ncPair = (NameClassPair) enum.nextElement();
```

will execute without a problem. The same reasoning also applies to if statements. In the code below you can be sure that when links.add is executed the links collection will not contain a next element.[50]

```
if (!links.contains(next)) {
    links.add(next);
}
```

Unfortunately, some control statements taint the rosy picture we painted above. The return, goto, break, and continue statements as well as exceptions interfere with the structured flow of execution. Reason about their behavior separately since they all typically either terminate or restart the loop being processed. This assumes that for goto statements their target is the beginning or the end of a loop body, that is, that they are used as a multilevel break or continue. When this is not the case, all bets are off.

When going over loop code, you may want to ensure that the code will perform according to its specification under all circumstances. Informal arguments are sufficient for many cases, but sometimes a more rigorous approach is needed.

Consider the binary search algorithm. Getting the algorithm right is notoriously difficult. Knuth [Knu98] details how its use was first discussed in 1946, but nobody published a correct algorithm working for arrays with a size different from $2^n - 1$ until 1962. Bentley [Ben86] adds that when he asked groups of professional programmers to implement it as an exercise, only 10% got it right.

---

[50] cocoon/src/java/org/apache/cocoon/Main.java:574–576

```
void *
bsearch(key, base0, nmemb, size, compar)
    register const void *key;                                   ──── Item to search for
    const void *base0;                                          ──── Start of element array
    size_t nmemb;                                               ──── Number of elements
    register size_t size;                                       ──── Size of each element
    register int (*compar) __P((const void *, const void *));   ──── Function to compare two elements
{
    register const char *base = base0;
    register int lim, cmp;
    register const void *p;

    for (lim = nmemb; lim != 0; lim >>= 1) {
        p = base + (lim >> 1) * size;                           ──── Locate a point in the middle
        cmp = (*compar)(key, p);                                ──── Compare element against key
        if (cmp == 0)                                           ──── Found; return its position
            return ((void *)p);
        if (cmp > 0) {      /* key > p: move right */
            base = (char *)p + size;                            ──── Adjust base upwards
            lim--;                                              ──── Not sure why this is needed
        } /* else move left */
    }
    return (NULL);                                              ──── Not found
}
```

Figure 2.11 Binary search implementation.

Consider the standard C library implementation of the binary search algorithm listed in Figure 2.11.[51]. We can see that it works by gradually reducing the search interval stored in the lim variable and adjusting the start of the search range stored in base, but it is not self-evident whether the arithmetic calculations performed are correct under all circumstances. If you find it difficult to reason about the code, the comment that precedes it might help you.

> The code below is a bit sneaky. After a comparison fails, we divide the work in half by moving either left or right. If lim is odd, moving left simply involves halving lim: e.g., when lim is 5 we look at item 2, so we change lim to 2 so that we will look at items 0 & 1. If lim is even, the same applies. If lim is odd, moving right again involves halving lim, this time moving the base up one item past p: e.g., when lim is 5 we change base to item 3 and make lim 2 so that we will look at items 3 and 4. If lim is even, however, we have to shrink it by one before halving: e.g., when lim is 4, we still looked at item 2, so we have to make lim 3, then halve, obtaining 1, so that we will only look at item 3.

If you—like myself—did not regard the above comment as particularly enlightening or reassuring, you might consider employing more sophisticated methods.

A useful abstraction for reasoning about properties of loops is based around the notions of *variants* and *invariants*. A loop invariant is an assertion about the program

---

[51] netbsdsrc/lib/libc/stdlib/bsearch.c

state that is valid both at the beginning and at the end of a loop. By demonstrating that a particular loop maintains the invariant, and by choosing an invariant so that when the loop terminates it can be used to indicate that the desired result has been obtained, we can ensure that an algorithm's loop will work within the envelope of the correct algorithm results. Establishing this fact, however, is not enough. We also need to ensure that the loop will terminate. For this we use a *variant*, a measure indicating our distance from our final goal, which should be decreasing at every loop iteration. If we can demonstrate that a loop's operation decreases the variant while maintaining the invariant, we determine that the loop will terminate with the correct result.

Let us start with a simple example. The following code finds the maximum value in the depths array.[52]

```
max = depths[n];
while (n--) {
  if (depths[n] > max)
    max = depths[n];
}
```

If we define n_0 as the number of elements in the depths array (initially held in variable n), we can formally express the result we want at the end of the loop as

$$max = maximum\{depths[0 : n_0)\}$$

We use the symbolism $[a : b)$ to indicate a range than includes a but ends one element before b, that is, $[a : b - 1]$. A suitable invariant can then be

$$max = maximum\{depths[n : n_0)\}$$

The invariant is established after the first assignment to max, so it holds at the beginning of the loop. Once n is decremented, it does not necessarily hold, since the range $[n : n_0)$ contains the element at index n, which might be larger than the maximum value held in max. The invariant is reestablished after the execution of the if statement, which will adjust max if the value of the new member of the now extended range is indeed larger than the maximum we had to this point. We have thus shown that the invariant will also be true at the end of every loop iteration and that therefore it will be true when the loop terminates. Since the loop will terminate when n (which we can consider as our loop's variant) reaches 0, our invariant can at that point be rewritten in the form

---

[52] XFree86-3.3/xc/lib/Xt/GCManager.c:252–256

```
register const char *base = base0;          1 R in [base, base + nmemb)
for (lim = nmemb; lim != 0;) {              2 R in [base, base + lim)
    p = base + lim  / 2;
    cmp = (*compar)(key, p);
    if (cmp == 0)
        return ((void *)p);
    if (cmp > 0) {
        /*Key > p: move right*/             3 R in (p, base + lim)
                                               R in [p + 1, base + lim)
        base = p + 1;                        4 base = base_old + lim / 2 + 1
                                               base_old = base - lim / 2 - 1
                                               R in [base, base_old + lim)
                                               R in [base, base - lim / 2 - 1 + lim)
        lim--;                               5 R in [base, base - (lim + 1) / 2 - 1 + lim + 1)
                                               R in [base, base + lim - (lim + 1) / 2)
                                               R in [base, base + lim / 2)
    } /* else move left */                  6 R in [base, p)
                                               R in [base, base + lim / 2)
    lim /= 2;                                7 R in [base, base + lim)
}
return (NULL);
}
```

Figure 2.12 Maintaining the binary search invariant.

of the original specification we wanted to satisfy, demonstrating that the loop does indeed arrive at the result we want.

We can apply this reasoning to our binary search example. Figure 2.12 illustrates the same algorithm slightly rearranged so as to simplify reasoning with the invariant.

- We substituted the right shift operations >> with division.
- We factored out the size variable since it is used only to simulate pointer arithmetic without having to know the pointer's type.
- We moved the last expression of the for statement to the end of the loop to clarify the order of operations within the loop.

A suitable invariant can be the fact that the value we are looking for lies within a particular range. We will use the notation $R \in [a : b)$ to indicate that the result of the search lies between the array elements a (including a) and b (excluding b). Since base and lim are used within the loop to delimit the search range, our invariant will be $R \in [\text{base} : \text{base} + \text{lim})$. We will show that the bsearch function will indeed find the value in the array, if such a value exists, by demonstrating that the invariant is maintained after each loop iteration. Since the comparison function compar is always called with an argument from within the invariant's range (base + lim/2), and since lim (our variant) is halved after every loop iteration, we can be sure that compar will eventually locate the value if that value exists.

At the beginning of the bsearch function we can only assert the function's specification: $R \in [\text{base0} : \text{base0} + \text{nmemb})$. However, after Figure 2.12:1 this can be expressed as $R \in [\text{base} : \text{base} + \text{nmemb})$, and after the for assignment (Figure 2.12:2) as $R \in [\text{base} : \text{base} + \text{lim})$—our invariant. We have thus established that our invariant holds at the beginning of the loop.

The result of the compar function is positive if the value we are looking for is greater than the value at point p. Therefore, at Figure 2.12:3 we can say that

$$R \in (\text{p} : \text{base} + \text{lim}) \equiv$$
$$R \in [\text{p} + 1 : \text{base} + \text{lim}).$$

If we express the original base value as base_{old} our original invariant, after the assignment at Figure 2.12:4, is now

$$R \in [\text{base} : \text{base}_{old} + \text{lim}).$$

Given that p was given the value of $\text{base} + \text{lim}/2$, we have

$$\text{base} = \text{base}_{old} + \frac{\text{lim}}{2} + 1 \Leftrightarrow$$
$$\text{base}_{old} = \text{base} - \frac{\text{lim}}{2} - 1.$$

By substituting the above result in the invariant we obtain

$$R \in \left[\text{base} : \text{base} - \frac{\text{lim}}{2} - 1 + \text{lim}\right).$$

When lim is decremented by one at Figure 2.12:5 we substitute $\text{lim} + 1$ in our invariant to obtain

$$R \in \left[\text{base} : \text{base} - \frac{\text{lim}+1}{2} - 1 + \text{lim} + 1\right) \equiv$$
$$R \in \left[\text{base} : \text{base} + \text{lim} - \frac{\text{lim}+1}{2}\right) \equiv$$
$$R \in \left[\text{base} : \text{base} + \frac{\text{lim}}{2}\right).$$

By a similar process, in the case where the result of the compar function is negative, indicating that the value we are looking for is less than the value at point p, we obtain

$$R \in [\text{base} : \text{p}) \equiv$$
$$R \in \left[\text{base} : \text{base} + \frac{\text{lim}}{2}\right).$$

Note that the invariant is now the same for both comparison results. Furthermore, when lim is halved at Figure 2.12:7 we can substitute its new value in the invariant to obtain $R \in [\text{base} : \text{base} + \text{lim})$, that is, the invariant we had at the top of the loop. We have thus shown that the loop maintains the invariant and therefore will correctly locate the value within the array. Finally, when lim becomes zero, the range where the value can lie is empty, and it is therefore correct to return NULL, indicating that the value could not be located.

Exercise 2.31   Locate five control structures spanning more than 50 lines in the book's CD-ROM and document their body with a single-line comment indicating its function.

Exercise 2.32   Reason about the body of one of the above control structures, indicating the place(s) where you use the controlling expression as an assertion.

Exercise 2.33   Provide a proof about the correct functioning of the insertion sort function[53] found as part of the radix sort implementation in the book's CD-ROM. *Hint:* The innermost for loop just compares two elements; the swap function is executed only when these are not correctly ordered.

Further Reading

Kernighan and Plauger [KP78] and, more recently, Kernighan and Pike [KP99, Chapter 1] provide a number of suggestions to improve code style; these can be used to disentangle badly written code while reading it. Apart from the specific style sheets mentioned in Section 2.9, a well-written style guide is the *Indian Hill C Style and Coding Standard*; you can easily find it on-line by entering its title in a Web search engine. For a comprehensive bibliography on programming style, see Thomas and Oman [TO90]. The now classic article presenting the problems associated with the goto statement was written by Dijkstra [Dij68]. The effects of program indentation on comprehensibility are studied in the work by Miara et al. [MMNS83], while the effects of formatting and commenting are studied by Oman and Cook [OC90]. For an experiment of how comments and procedures affect program readability, see Tenny [Ten88]. Refactoring as an activity for improving the code's design (and readability) is presented in Fowler [Fow00, pp. 56–57]. If you want to see how a language is introduced by its designers, read Kernighan and Ritchie [KR88] (covering C), Stroustrup [Str97] (C++), Microsoft Corporation [Mic01] (C#), and Wall et al. [WCSP00] (Perl). In addition, Ritchie [Rit79] provides an in-depth treatment of C and its libraries, while Linden [Lin94] lucidly explains many of the C language's finer points.

Invariants were introduced by C. A. R. Hoare [Hoa71]. You can find them also described in references [Ben86, pp. 36–37; Mey88, pp. 140–143; Knu97, p. 17; HT00, p. 116.] A complete analysis of the binary search algorithm is given in Knuth [Knu98].

---

[53] netbsdsrc/lib/libc/stdlib/radixsort.c:310–330

3

Advanced C Data Types

A common mistake that people make when trying to design something completely foolproof is to underestimate the ingenuity of complete fools.

—Douglas Adams

Pointers, structures, unions, dynamic memory, and type name declarations are the basic building elements for more sophisticated C data types and algorithms. Although we have encountered them a number of times up to now, their uses are sufficiently diverse, specialized, and idiomatic to merit in-depth treatment. In this chapter we examine how pointers, structures, and unions are typically used in programs and provide examples for each usage pattern. By recognizing the function served by a particular language construct, you can better understand the code that uses it.

The ability to establish new data storage locations as the program executes by dynamically allocating and disposing of memory areas is one other powerful concept often used in conjunction with pointers and structures to create and manipulate new data types. Understand the few common idioms used for managing dynamic memory and a lot of the mystique will disappear.

3.1 Pointers

Most people learning C initially view pointers with a mixture of awe and fear. It is true that pointer-based code is sometimes inscrutable and often a source of subtle errors and unsightly crashes. The main reason for this is that a pointer is a low-level, powerful, yet blunt tool. Learn to distinguish its uses and common coding patterns will emerge; view the remaining few code instances you cannot classify with suspicion.

$\boxed{\text{i}}$ You will find pointers used in C programs in the following ways:

- To construct linked data structures
- To reference dynamically allocated data structures
- To implement call by reference
- To access data elements and iterate through them
- When passing arrays as arguments
- For referring to functions
- As an alias for another value
- To represent character strings
- For direct access to system memory

We will examine some representative cases for each use in turn. Where appropriate we will point toward sections that discuss a particular use in detail. The purpose of the following paragraphs is to provide a summary, taxonomy, and road map for reading pointer-based code.

3.1.1 Linked Data Structures

At the lowest level, a pointer is just a memory address. It is therefore uniquely suited for representing links between data structure elements. At the conceptual level, data structures such as linked lists, trees, and graphs consist of elements (*nodes*) joined together by *vertices* or *edges*. A pointer can represent a directed vertex between two nodes by storing in one node the address of another. In addition, pointers are used when processing such data structures for accessing their elements and performing house-keeping operations. We examine linked data structures in Section 4.7 and onward.

3.1.2 Dynamic Allocation of Data Structures

Vector-type data structures are often allocated dynamically to have their sizes correspond to runtime information about the number of elements required. We examine this in detail in Section 3.4. Pointers are used to store the starting addresses of such data structures. In addition, programs often dynamically construct C structures to pass them between functions or use them as building elements for linked data structures. In this case pointers are used to store the memory location of the allocated struct, as is the case in the following example.[1]

---

[1] netbsdsrc/sbin/fsck/preen.c:250–280

```
static struct diskentry *
finddisk(const char *name)
{
    struct diskentry *d;
    [...]
    d = emalloc(sizeof(*d));
    d->d_name = estrdup(name);
    d->d_name[len] = '\0';
    [...]
    return d;
}
```

The code for allocating memory equal to the size of a struct and casting the result to an appropriate pointer is often delegated to a macro with a name such as new after the equivalent C++ operator.[2,3]

```
#define new(type)    (type *) calloc(sizeof(type), 1)
    [...]
    node = new(struct codeword_entry);
```

3.1.3 Call by Reference

Pointers are also used in functions that receive arguments passed *by reference*. Function arguments passed by reference are used for returning function results or for avoiding the overhead of copying the function's argument. When pointer-type arguments are used for returning function results, you will see these arguments assigned a value within the function body, as is the case with the following function that sets gid to the group identifier of the given group's name.[4]

```
int
gid_name(char *name, gid_t *gid)
{
    [...]
    *gid = ptr->gid = gr->gr_gid;
    return(0);
}
```

---

[2]XFree86-3.3/xc/doc/specs/PEX5/PEX5.1/SI/xref.h:113
[3]XFree86-3.3/xc/doc/specs/PEX5/PEX5.1/SI/xref.c:268
[4]netbsdsrc/bin/pax/cache.c:430–490

The function's return value is used only to indicate an error condition. Many functions of the Windows API use such a convention. On the caller side you will typically see the respective argument passed to the function by applying the address-of operator (&) to a variable.

[i]   Pointer-type arguments are also used to avoid the overhead of copying large elements on each function call. Such arguments are typically structures; seldom, they are double-precision floating-point numbers. Arrays are always passed by reference, and in most architectures other primitive C types are more efficiently copied on a function call than passed by reference. The following function uses the two structure arguments (now and then) passed by reference only to calculate the results without modifying the structure contents. It was presumably coded in that way to avoid the timeval structure copy overhead on each call.[5]

```
static double
diffsec(struct timeval *now,
    struct timeval *then)
{
    return ((now->tv_sec - then->tv_sec)*1.0
        + (now->tv_usec - then->tv_usec)/1000000.0);
}
```

[i]   In modern C and C++ programs you can often identify arguments passed by reference for efficiency purposes because they are identified by a const declarator.[6]

```
static char *ccval (const struct cchar *, int);
```

The role of each argument is also sometimes identified using a comment marked IN or OUT, as is the case in the following (pre-ANSI C) function definition.[7]

```
int
atmresolve(rt, m, dst, desten)
    register struct rtentry *rt;
    struct mbuf *m;
    register struct sockaddr *dst;
    register struct atm_pseudohdr *desten;    /* OUT */
{
```

---

[5]netbsdsrc/sbin/ping/ping.c:1028–1034
[6]netbsdsrc/bin/stty/print.c:56
[7]netbsdsrc/sys/netinet/if_atm.c:223–231

Table 3.1 Index and Pointer Code for Accessing an
Array a with Elements of Type T

Array Index Code	Pointer Code
int i;	T *p;
i = 0	p = a or p = &a[0]
a[i]	*p
a[i].f	p->f
i++	p++
i += K	p += K
i == N	p == &a[N] or p == a + N

```
stackp = de_stack;                     ── Initialize stack
[...]
*stackp++ = finchar;                   ── Push finchar into stack
[...]
do {
    if (count-- == 0)
        return (num);
    *bp++ = *--stackp;                 ── Pop from stack into *bp
} while (stackp > de_stack);           ── Check if stack is empty
```

Figure 3.1 Pointer access for an array-based stack.

3.1.4 Data Element Access

In Section 4.2 we present how to use a pointer as a database cursor to access table elements. The key ideas for reading pointer-based array access code are that a pointer to an array element address can be used to access the element at the specific position index and that arithmetic on array element pointers has the same semantics as arithmetic on the respective array indices. Table 3.1 shows examples for most common operations used when accessing an array a with elements of type T. Figure 3.1[8] provides an example of pointer-based code for accessing a stack.

3.1.5 Arrays as Arguments and Results

In C and C++ programs, pointers crop up when arrays are passed to functions and returned as results. In C code when the name of an array is used as a function argument, all that is passed to the function is the address of the array's first element. As a result, any modifications made to the array data while the function is executing will affect the

---

[8]netbsdsrc/usr.bin/compress/zopen.c:523–555

elements of the array passed by the function's caller. This implicit *call by reference* behavior for arrays is different from the way all other C types are passed to functions and can therefore be a source of confusion.

Similarly, C functions can return only a pointer to an array element, not a complete array. Thus, when a function builds a result within an array and then returns an appropriate pointer, it is important to ensure that the array is not a local variable allocated on that function's stack. In such a case the array's space may be overwritten once the function exits, and consequently the function's result will be invalidated. One way to avoid this problem is to declare such arrays as static, as is the case in the following function that converts an Internet address into its dotted decimal representation.[9]

```c
char *inet_ntoa(struct in_addr ad)
{
    unsigned long int s_ad;
    int a, b, c, d;
    static char addr[20];

    s_ad = ad.s_addr;
    d = s_ad % 256;
    s_ad /= 256;
    c = s_ad % 256;
    s_ad /= 256;
    b = s_ad % 256;
    a = s_ad / 256;
    sprintf(addr, "%d.%d.%d.%d", a, b, c, d);
    return addr;
}
```

The function builds the result in the addr buffer. If that buffer were not declared as static, its contents (the readable representation of the Internet address) would be invalidated once the function returned. Even the above construct is not completely safe. Functions using global or static local variables are in most cases not reentrant. This means that the function cannot be called from another program execution thread while another instance of that function is executing. Even worse, in our case, the function's result has to be saved into another place (using, for example, a call to strdup) before the function is called again; otherwise it will be overwritten by the

---

[9]netbsdsrc/libexec/identd/identd.c:120–137

new result. As an example, the implementation of the inet_ntoa function we listed could not have been used in place of naddr_ntoa in the following context.[10]

```
(void)fprintf(ftrace, "%s Router Ad"
        " from %s to %s via %s life=%d\n",
        act, naddr_ntoa(from), naddr_ntoa(to),
        ifp ? ifp->int_name : "?",
        ntohs(p->ad.icmp_ad_life));
```

In this case, to circumvent the problem we described, the function naddr_ntoa is used as a wrapper for inet_ntoa, storing its result into a circular list of four different temporary buffers.[11]

```
char *
naddr_ntoa(naddr a)
{
#define NUM_BUFS 4
    static int bufno;
    static struct {
        char    str[16];            /* xxx.xxx.xxx.xxx\0 */
    } bufs[NUM_BUFS];
    char *s;
    struct in_addr addr;

    addr.s_addr = a;
    s = strcpy(bufs[bufno].str, inet_ntoa(addr));
    bufno = (bufno+1) % NUM_BUFS;
    return s;
}
```

3.1.6 Function Pointers

It is often useful to parameterize a function by passing to it another function as an argument. The C language, however, does not allow functions to be passed to others as arguments. It does, however, allow passing as an argument a *pointer* to a function. In Figure 3.2[12] the function getfile, which is used to process files during a backup recovery process, receives as parameters fill and skip; these are used to indicate

---

[10] netbsdsrc/sbin/routed/rdisc.c:121–125
[11] netbsdsrc/sbin/routed/trace.c:123–139
[12] netbsdsrc/sbin/restore/tape.c:177–837

```
/*
 * Verify that the tape drive can be accessed and
 * that it actually is a dump tape.
 */
void
setup()
{
    [...]
    getfile(xtrmap, xtrmapskip);                    ■1 Call with function arguments
    [...]
}

/* Prompt user to load a new dump volume. */
void
getvol(int nextvol)
{
    [...]
    getfile(xtrlnkfile, xtrlnkskip);                ■1
    [...]
    getfile(xtrfile, xtrskip);                      ■1
    [...]
}

/*
 * skip over a file on the tape
 */
void
skipfile()
{
    curfile.action = SKIP;
    getfile(xtrnull, xtrnull);                      ■1
}

/* Extract a file from the tape. */
void
getfile(void (*fill)(char *, long), (*skip)(char *, long))
{
    [...]
    (*fill)((char *)buf, (long)(size > TP_BSIZE ?   ■2 Call function argument
        fssize : (curblk - 1) * TP_BSIZE + size));
    [...]
    (*skip)(clearedbuf, (long)(size > TP_BSIZE ?    ■2
        TP_BSIZE : size));
    [...]
    (*fill)((char *)buf, (long)((curblk * TP_BSIZE) + size)); ■2
    [...]
}
```

■3 Functions to be passed as argument parameters

```
/* Write out the next block of a file. */
static void
xtrfile(char *buf, long size)
{ [...] }
/* Skip over a hole in a file. */
static void
xtrskip(char *buf, long size)
{ [...] }
/* Collect the next block of a symbolic link. */
static void
xtrlnkfile(char *buf, long size)
{ [...] }
/* Skip over a hole in a symbolic link */
static void
xtrlnkskip(char *buf, long size)
{ [...] }
/* Collect the next block of a bit map. */
static void
xtrmap(char *buf, long size)
{ [...] }
/* Skip over a hole in a bit map */
static void
xtrmapskip(char *buf, long size)
{ [...] }
/* Noop, when an extraction function is not needed. */
void
xtrnull(char *buf, long size)
{ return; }
```

Figure 3.2 Parameterization using function arguments.

how to read or skip over data. The function is called (Figure 3.2:1) with different arguments (Figure 3.2:3) to perform an initial scan over the data or to recover or skip over data files.

A number of C library files, such as qsort and bsearch, receive function arguments that specify how they operate.[13]

```
getnfile()
{
    [...]
    qsort(nl, nname, sizeof(nltype), valcmp);
    [...]
}

valcmp(nltype *p1, nltype *p2)
{
    if ( p1 -> value < p2 -> value ) {
        return LESSTHAN;
    }
    if ( p1 -> value > p2 -> value ) {
        return GREATERTHAN;
    }
    return EQUALTO;
}
```

In the above example the way qsort will compare the elements of the array it sorts is specified by the valcmp function.

Finally, function pointers can be used to parameterize control within a body of code. In the example that follows, closefunc is used to store the function that will be called to close the fin stream, depending on how it was opened.[14]

```
void
retrieve(char *cmd, char *name)
{
    int (*closefunc)(FILE *) = NULL;
    [...]
    if (cmd == 0) {
        fin = fopen(name, "r"), closefunc = fclose;
```

---

[13] netbsdsrc/usr.bin/gprof/gprof.c:216–536
[14] netbsdsrc/libexec/ftpd/ftpd.c:792–860

```
[...]
if (cmd) {
    [...]
    fin = ftpd_popen(line, "r", 1), closefunc = ftpd_pclose;
    [...]
    (*closefunc)(fin);
}
```

3.1.7 Pointers as Aliases

Pointers are often used to create an *alias* for a particular value.[15]

```
struct output output = {NULL, 0, NULL, OUTBUFSIZ, 1, 0};
[...]
struct output *out1 = &output;
```

In the example code above, the dereferenced pointer out1 can be used in the place of the original value of the variable output. You will find aliasing used for a number of different reasons.

Efficiency Concerns

Assigning a pointer is more efficient than assigning a larger object. In the following example curt could have been a structure variable instead of a pointer to such a structure. However, the corresponding assignment statement would have been less efficient since it would have to copy the contents of the entire structure.[16]

```
static struct termios cbreakt, rawt, *curt;
    [...]
    curt = useraw ? &rawt : &cbreakt;
```

Reference to Statically Initialized Data

A variable is used to point to different values of static data. The most common example in this case involves character pointers set to point to different strings.[17]

```
char *s;
[...]
s = *(opt->bval) ? "True" : "False";
```

---

[15] netbsdsrc/bin/sh/output.c:81–84
[16] netbsdsrc/lib/libcurses/tty.c:66–171
[17] netbsdsrc/games/rogue/room.c:629–635

Implementation of Variable Reference Semantics in a Global Context

The daunting title merely refers to the equivalent of the call-by-reference pointer usage, but using a global variable instead of a function argument. Thus, a global pointer variable is used to refer to data that is to be accessed and modified in another place. In the following random-number generator, fptr is initialized to point to an entry in a table of random-number seeds; it is also set in a similar fashion in srrandom(). Finally, in rrandom() the variable fptr is used to modify the value it points to.[18]

```
static long rntb[32] = {
    3, 0x9a319039, 0x32d9c024, 0x9b663182, 0x5da1f342,
    [...]
};

static long *fptr = &rntb[4];
[...]

void
srrandom(int x)
{
    [...]
    fptr = &state[rand_sep];
    [...]
}

long
rrandom()
{
    [...]
    *fptr += *rptr;
    i = (*fptr >> 1) & 0x7fffffff;
```

The equivalent result could have been obtained by passing fptr as an argument to srrandom() and rrandom().

A similar approach is also often used to access a modifiable copy of global data.[19]

```
WINDOW scr_buf;
WINDOW *curscr = &scr_buf;
```

---

[18] netbsdsrc/games/rogue/random.c:62–109
[19] netbsdsrc/games/rogue/curses.c:121–157

```
[...]
move(short row, short col)
{
    curscr->_cury = row;
    curscr->_curx = col;
    screen_dirty = 1;
}
```

3.1.8 Pointers and Strings

In the C language string literals are represented by a character array terminated with the null character '\0'. As a consequence, character strings are represented by a pointer to the first character of a null-terminated sequence. In the following code excerpt you can see how the code of the strlen C library function advances a pointer through the string passed as the function's parameter until it reaches the string's end. It then subtracts the pointer to the string's start from the pointer to its terminating null character to calculate and return the string's length.[20]

```
size_t
strlen(const char *str)
{
    register const char *s;

    for (s = str; *s; ++s)
        ;
    return(s - str);
}
```

When reading string-based code, be careful to distinguish between character pointers and character arrays. Although you will find both often used to represent strings (since a character array is automatically converted into a pointer to the first character of the array when passed to a function), the underlying types and operations you can perform on them are different. As an example, the following code fragment defines pw_file as a character pointer pointing to a string constant that contains the sequence "/etc/passwd".[21]

```
static char *pw_file = "/etc/passwd";
```

---

[20] netbsdsrc/lib/libc/string/strlen.c:51–59
[21] netbsdsrc/distrib/utils/libhack/getpwent.c:45

The size of the pw_file variable on our machine is 4, and it can be modified to point elsewhere, but trying to change the contents of the memory it points to will result in undefined behavior.

On the other hand, the following line defines line as an array of characters initialized to contain the sequence "/dev/XtyXX" followed by a null.[22]

```
static char line[] = "/dev/XtyXX";
```

Applying the sizeof operator on line returns 11; line will always refer to the same storage area, and the elements it contains can be freely modified.[23]

```
line[5] = 'p';
```

Keeping the distinction between character arrays and pointers in mind while reading code is important since they are both used, often interchangeably, for similar purposes. Crucially, all C compilers we are aware of will not warn you when the two are accidentally mixed up across different files. Consider the following two (unrelated) definitions and the associated declaration.[24,25,26]

```
char version[] = "332";
char *version = "2.1.2";
extern char *version;
```

Both definitions are used to define a version string that is probably subsequently printed by passing it to a printf function. However, the extern char *version declaration can be used only to access the variable defined as char *version. Although linking the source file with the file containing the char version[] definition will typically not produce an error, the resulting program will fail at runtime. The version variable, instead of pointing to a memory area that contains the version string, will probably point to the memory area whose address is represented by the bit pattern of the character string "332" (0x33333200 on some processor architectures).

⚠

---

[22] netbsdsrc/lib/libutil/pty.c:71
[23] netbsdsrc/lib/libutil/pty.c:81
[24] netbsdsrc/usr.bin/less/less/version.c:575
[25] netbsdsrc/libexec/identd/version.c:3
[26] netbsdsrc/libexec/identd/identd.c:77

3.1.9 Direct Memory Access

☐ Since a pointer is internally represented as a memory address, you will find low-level code using pointers to access hardware-specific memory areas. Many peripherals, such as graphics and network adapters, use a commonly accessible memory area to interchange data with the system's main processor. A variable initialized to point to that area can be conveniently used to communicate with the given device. In the following example, the video variable is set to point to a memory area occupied by the screen adapter (0xe08b8000). Writing to that area at an offset determined by the specified row and column (vid_ypos and vid_xpos) will make the corresponding character (c) appear on the screen.[27]

```
static void
vid_wrchar(char c)
{
    volatile unsigned short *video;

    video = (unsigned short *)(0xe08b8000) +
            vid_ypos * 80 + vid_xpos;
    *video = (*video & 0xff00) | 0x0f00 | (unsigned short)c;
}
```

Keep in mind that modern operating systems prevent user programs from direct hardware access without prior arrangements. You are likely to encounter such code only when examining embedded system code or kernel and device-driver internals.

Exercise 3.1 Reimplement the pointer-based stack in the *compress* library[28] by using an array index. Measure the speed difference and comment on the readability of the two implementations.

Exercise 3.2 Locate in the book's CD-ROM three instances of code using pointers for each one of the reasons we outlined.

Exercise 3.3 If you are familiar with C++ or Java, explain how it is possible to minimize (in C++) or avoid (in Java) the use of pointers.

---

[27] netbsdsrc/sys/arch/pica/pica/machdep.c:951–958
[28] netbsdsrc/usr.bin/compress/zopen.c

Exercise 3.4   How does a C pointer differ from a memory address? How does that affect your understanding of code? Which tools take advantage of the difference?

Exercise 3.5   Should program version strings be represented as character arrays or as pointers to a string? Justify your answer.

3.2 Structures

A C struct is a grouping of data elements that makes it possible to use them as a whole. You will find structures used in C programs in the fo llowing ways:

- To group together data elements typically used as a whole
- To return multiple data elements from a function
- To construct linked data structures (see Section 4.7)
- To map the organization of data on hardware devices, network links, and storage media
- To implement abstract data types (Section 9.3.5)
- To program in an object-oriented fashion

The following paragraphs expand on uses of structures we do not cover in other sections.

3.2.1 Grouping Together Data Elements

Structures are often used to form a group out of related elements typically used as a whole. The prototypical example is the representation of the coordinates of a location on the screen.[29]

```
struct point {
    int col, line;
};
```

Other cases you will encounter include complex numbers and fields forming table rows.

---

[29] netbsdsrc/games/snake/snake/snake.c:75–77

3.2.2 Returning Multiple Data Elements from a Function

When the result of a function is expressed using more than a single basic data type, the multiple result elements can be returned either through function arguments passed to the function by reference (see Section 3.1.3) or by grouping them together into a structure and returning that structure. In the following example `difftv` returns the difference between the two times passed in seconds (`tv_sec`) and microseconds (`tv_usec`) in the form of the `timeval` structure.[30]

```
static struct timeval
difftv(struct timeval a, struct timeval b)
{
    static struct timeval diff;

    diff.tv_sec = b.tv_sec - a.tv_sec;
    if ((diff.tv_usec = b.tv_usec - a.tv_usec) < 0) {
        diff.tv_sec--;
        diff.tv_usec += 1000000;
    }
    return(diff);
}
```

3.2.3 Mapping the Organization of Data

When data is moved over a network or transferred to or from secondary storage, or when programs interface directly with hardware, structures are often used to represent how data is organized on that other medium. The following structure represents an Intel EtherExpress network interface card command block.[31]

```
struct fxp_cb_nop {
    void *fill[2];
    volatile u_int16_t cb_status;
    volatile u_int16_t cb_command;
    volatile u_int32_t link_addr;
};
```

---

[30] netbsdsrc/usr.sbin/named/dig/dig.c:1221–1233
[31] netbsdsrc/sys/dev/pci/if_fxpreg.h:102–107

The volatile qualifier is used to denote that the underlying memory fields are used [i]
by entities outside the control of the program (in this case, the network interface card).
The compiler is thus prohibited from performing optimizations on these fields such
as removing redundant references.

In certain cases a *bit field* may be declared to specify a precise range of bits used [i]
to hold a particular value on the given device.[32]

```
struct fxp_cb_config {
    [...]
    volatile u_int8_t    byte_count:6,
                :2;
    volatile u_int8_t    rx_fifo_limit:4,
            tx_fifo_limit:3,
            :1;
```

In the above example the byte_count to be transferred is specified to occupy 6
bits, while the receiver and the transmitter FIFO queue limits occupy 4 and 3 bits,
respectively, on the hardware device.

Network data packets are also often encoded using a C structure to delineate
their elements, as demonstrated by the following classic definition of the TCP packet
header.[33]

```
struct tcphdr {
    u_int16_t th_sport;      /* source port */
    u_int16_t th_dport;      /* destination port */
    tcp_seq   th_seq;        /* sequence number */
    tcp_seq   th_ack;        /* acknowledgement number */
    [...]
```

Finally, structures are also used to map how data is stored on peripheral media such
as disks and tapes. As an example, the disk characteristics of MS-DOS disk partitions
are determined by the so-called BIOS parameter block. Its fields are specified using
the following structure.[34]

```
struct bpb33 {
    u_int16_t bpbBytesPerSec; /* bytes per sector */
```

---

[32] netbsdsrc/sys/dev/pci/if_fxpreg.h:116–125
[33] netbsdsrc/sys/netinet/tcp.h:43–47
[34] netbsdsrc/sys/msdosfs/bpb.h:22–34

```
    u_int8_t  bpbSecPerClust; /* sectors per cluster */
    u_int16_t bpbResSectors;  /* number of reserved sectors */
    u_int8_t  bpbFATs;        /* number of FATs */
    u_int16_t bpbRootDirEnts; /* number of root directory entries */
    u_int16_t bpbSectors;     /* total number of sectors */
    u_int8_t  bpbMedia;       /* media descriptor */
    u_int16_t bpbFATsecs;     /* number of sectors per FAT */
    u_int16_t bpbSecPerTrack; /* sectors per track */
    u_int16_t bpbHeads;       /* number of heads */
    u_int16_t bpbHiddenSecs;  /* number of hidden sectors */
};
```

▲   The way fields are ordered within a structure is architecture- and compiler-dependent. In addition, the representation of various elements within the structure is architecture- and operating system–dependent (the operating system may force a particular processor to adopt a specific byte ordering). Even simple data types such as integers can have their bytes stored in different ways. Therefore, the use of structures to map external data is inherently nonportable.

3.2.4 Programming in an Object-Oriented Fashion

[i]   In C programs structures are sometimes used to create object-like entities by grouping together data elements and function pointers to simulate a class's fields and methods. In the following example, the domain structure, representing different domains of network protocols (for example, Internet, SNA, IPX), groups together data about the particular domain, such as its family dom_family, and methods for operating on it, such as the routing table initialization method dom_rtattach.[35]

```
struct   domain {
  int      dom_family;        /* AF_xxx */
  char     *dom_name;
  void     (*dom_init)(void); /* initialize domain data structures */
  [...]
  int      (*dom_rtattach)(void **, int);
                              /* initialize routing table */
  int      dom_rtoffset;      /* an arg to rtattach, in bits */
  int      dom_maxrtkey;      /* for routing layer */
}
```

---

[35] netbsdsrc/sys/sys/domain.h:50–65

Following such a declaration, variables of the specific structure type or, more often, pointers to the structure type can be treated—after being suitably initialized—in ways resembling the use of C++ or Java objects.[36]

```
for (dom = domains; dom; dom = dom->dom_next)
    if (dom->dom_family == i && dom->dom_rtattach) {
        dom->dom_rtattach((void **)&nep->ne_rtable[i],
            dom->dom_rtoffset);
        break;
```

Since "objects" can be initialized with different "methods" (function pointers) and yet be used through the same interface (calls through the same structure member names), the technique we outlined implements the *virtual methods* available in object-oriented languages and *polymorphic programming*. In fact, because objects of the same class share their methods (but not their fields), the method pointers are often shared between different objects by storing in the "objects" structure only a pointer to another structure containing pointers to the actual methods.[37]

```
struct file {
    [...]
    short   f_type;          /* descriptor type */
    short   f_count;         /* reference count */
    short   f_msgcount;      /* references from message queue */
    struct  ucred *f_cred;   /* credentials associated with descriptor */
    struct  fileops {
        int     (*fo_read)(struct file *fp, struct uio *uio,
                                struct ucred *cred);
        int     (*fo_write)(struct file *fp, struct uio *uio,
                                struct ucred *cred);
        int     (*fo_ioctl)(struct file *fp, u_long com,
                                caddr_t data, struct proc *p);
        int     (*fo_poll)(struct file *fp, int events,
                                struct proc *p);
        int     (*fo_close)(struct file *fp, struct proc *p);
    } *f_ops;
    off_t   f_offset;
    caddr_t f_data;              /* vnode or socket */
};
```

---

[36] netbsdsrc/sys/kern/vfs_subr.c:1436–1440
[37] netbsdsrc/sys/sys/file.h:51–73

In the above example, each object representing an open file or socket shares its read, write, ioctl, poll, and close methods through the structure member f_ops pointing to the shared fileops structure.

Exercise 3.6 An alternative way for passing array-type data to functions by value and returning it as a real value is to embed the array within a structure. Locate such examples in the book's CD-ROM. Suggest reasons explaining why this approach is not used more often.

Exercise 3.7 Locate 20 separate instances of structures in the book's CD-ROM and classify the reasons behind their use. Familiarize yourself with a general-purpose data structure library such as the C++ STL or java.util and indicate which instances could have been coded using library functionality. Minimize the time you spend on each instance.

Exercise 3.8 A number of technologies, libraries, and tools support the portable encoding of data for transfer between applications. Outline the technologies applicable in your environment, and compare them against using ad hoc approaches based on C structures.

3.3 Unions

A C union groups together items that share the same storage area. Only one of the items sharing the area can be accessed at the time. You will find unions used in C programs in the following ways:

- To use storage efficiently
- To implement polymorphism
- To access data using different internal representations

3.3.1 Using Storage Efficiently

A common justification for unions you will encounter concerns sharing the same area of storage for two different purposes; the intent is to save a few precious memory bytes. There are cases where unions are used exactly for this purpose. However, in an industry where even embedded devices sport several megabytes of memory, this use is becoming increasingly rare. Apart from legacy code, you will also encounter cases where a very large number of objects based on a union justifies the extra effort needed to write the appropriate code. The following example from the standard C library memory allocation function malloc is a typical case.[38]

---

[38] netbsdsrc/lib/libc/stdlib/malloc.c:78–92

```
union   overhead {
    union   overhead *ov_next;   /* when free */
    struct {
        u_char  ovu_magic;       /* magic number */
        u_char  ovu_index;       /* bucket # */
#ifdef RCHECK
        u_short ovu_rmagic;      /* range magic number */
        u_long  ovu_size;        /* actual block size */
#endif
    } ovu;
#define ov_magic    ovu.ovu_magic
#define ov_index    ovu.ovu_index
#define ov_rmagic   ovu.ovu_rmagic
#define ov_size     ovu.ovu_size
};
```

Memory blocks can be either free or occupied. Different values need to be stored in each case, and since a block cannot be at the same time both free and occupied these can share the same memory space. The extra programming cost for maintaining this arrangement is amortized over the trillions of items that will be allocated by calls to the C library over its lifetime.

Note the macro definitions following the definition of the ovu structure; such definitions are often used as shortcuts for referring directly to structure members within a union without prepending the union member name in front. Thus, in the code you see[39]

```
op->ov_index = bucket;
```

instead of more verbose references to op->ovu.ovu_index.

3.3.2 Implementing Polymorphism

By far the most common use of unions you will encounter concerns the implementation of polymorphism. Here the same object (typically represented by a C structure) is used to represent different types. The data for those different types is stored into separate union members. Polymorphic data stored in a union also saves space over alternative memory arrangements; however, the union is used in this case to express our intent of

---

[39] netbsdsrc/lib/libc/stdlib/malloc.c:213

[i] having an object store different data types rather than show off our frugality. Unions used in this way are typically embedded within a C structure containing a type field that denotes what kind of data is stored in the union. This field is often represented by using an enumerated type, and its name is often, predictably enough, type. The following example, part of the Sun RPC (Remote Procedure Call) library, contains the structure used for representing an RPC message. Two different message types are supported: a call and a reply. The msg_type enum distinguishes between the two types, while a union contains a structure with the data elements for each type.[40]

```
enum msg_type {
    CALL=0,
    REPLY=1
};
[...]
struct rpc_msg {
    u_int32_t        rm_xid;
    enum msg_type        rm_direction;
    union {
        struct call_body RM_cmb;
        struct reply_body RM_rmb;
    } ru;
};
```

3.3.3 Accessing Different Internal Representations

The final use of unions we will examine involves storing data into one union field and accessing another in order to transfer data between different internal representations. Although this use is inherently nonportable, there are some conversions that are safe to perform and others that are useful in specific machine-dependent ways. The following structure definition is used by the *tar* file archive program to represent the information about each file in the archive.[41]

```
union record {
    char         charptr[RECORDSIZE];
    struct header {
        char     name[NAMSIZ];
        char     mode[8];
```

---

[40] netbsdsrc/include/rpc/rpc_msg.h:54–158
[41] netbsdsrc/usr.bin/file/tar.h:36–54

```
        char    uid[8];
        char    gid[8];
        char    size[12];
        char    mtime[12];
        char    chksum[8];
        char    linkflag;
        char    linkname[NAMSIZ];
        char    magic[8];
        char    uname[TUNMLEN];
        char    gname[TGNMLEN];
        char    devmajor[8];
        char    devminor[8];
    } header;
};
```

To detect data corruption, a checksum field `chksum` contains the sum of all record bytes comprising a file (including the header record). Programs use the `charptr` union member to iterate over the header data byte-by-byte to calculate the checksum and the `header` member to access specific header fields. Since integral types in C (including characters) are valid over all possible bit patterns they can represent, accessing the internal representation of other C types (pointers, floating-point numbers, other integral types) as an integral type is guaranteed to be a legal operation. However, the converse operation—the generation of another type through its integral representation—will not always yield proper values. Under most architectures one safe operation you may encounter involves generating nonintegral types from data that was an older copy of their value.

The second, inherently nonportable use of structures is to access architecture-specific data elements in some other format. This can be useful for interpreting a data type based on its representation or for creating a data type from its representation. In the example in Figure 3.3[42] the union u is used to access the internal representation of the floating-point number v as a mantissa, an exponent, and a sign. The conversion is used to break floating-point numbers into a normalized fraction and an integral power of 2.

Exercise 3.9 Locate 20 separate instances of unions in the book's CD-ROM and classify the reasons behind their use. Minimize the time you spend on each instance. Create a graph depicting the frequency with which constructs are used for a particular reason.

---

[42] netbsdsrc/lib/libc/arch/i386/gen/frexp.c:48–72

```
double
frexp(double value, int *eptr)          ──────── Exponent to return
{
    union {
        double v;                        ──────── Store value in this field
                                         ──────── Access internal representation from this field
        struct {
            u_int u_mant2 : 32;          ──────── Mantissa
            u_int u_mant1 : 20;
            u_int   u_exp : 11;          ──────── Exponent
            u_int  u_sign :  1;
        } s;
    } u;
    if (value) {
        u.v = value;                     ──────── Store value
        *eptr = u.s.u_exp - 1022;        ──────── Retrieve and set signed exponent
        u.s.u_exp = 1022;                ──────── Zero exponent
        return(u.v);                     ──────── Return normalized mantissa
    } else {
        *eptr = 0;
        return((double)0);
    }
}
```

Figure 3.3 Accessing internal type representation by using a union.

Exercise 3.10 Propose portable alternatives for implementing the nonportable constructs used with structures and unions. Discuss your proposal in terms of implementation cost, maintainability, and efficiency.

3.4 Dynamic Memory Allocation

A data structure whose size is not known when the program is written, or one that grows while the program is running, is stored in memory allocated *dynamically* while the program is running. Programs refer to dynamically allocated memory through the use of pointers. In this section we examine how memory can be dynamically allocated for vector structures; however, the code sequences we list are very similar or identical to those used for storing other data structures.

Figure 3.4[43] is a typical example of how data space is dynamically allocated and used. In this case the code allocates space to store a sequence of integers as an array, so RRlen is first defined as a pointer to these integers (Figure 3.4:1). Pointer-type variables have to be initialized by making them point to a valid memory area. In this case the program uses the C library malloc function to obtain from the system the address of a memory area large enough to store c integers. The argument of malloc is the number of bytes to allocate. Its calculation here is typical: it consists of the product of the number of elements to allocate (c) multiplied by the size of each

---

[43] netbsdsrc/usr.sbin/named/named/ns_validate.c:871–1231

```
int
update_msg(uchar *msg, int *msglen, int Vlist[], int c)
{
    [...]
    int *RRlen;                                       ①Pointer to an integer
    [...]                                                ──── Number of elements
    RRlen = (int *)malloc((unsigned)c*sizeof(int));      ── Size of each element
                                                         ②Handle memory exhaustion
    if (!RRlen)
        panic(errno, "malloc(RRlen)");
    [...]
    for (i = 0;  i < c;  i++) {                        ──── Iterate over all elements
        [...]
                                                       ──── Use RRlen as an array
        RRlen[i] = dn_skipname(cp, msg + *msglen);
        [...]
    }
    [...]
    free((char *)RRlen);       ──── Free allocated memory
    return (n);
}
```

Figure 3.4 Dynamic storage allocation.

element (`sizeof(int)`). If a system's memory is exhausted the `malloc` function indicates this by returning `NULL`; robustly written programs should always check for such a case (Figure 3.4:2). From that point onward the program can dereference RRlen (using the [] or the * operator) as if it were an array consisting of c elements. Keep in mind, however, that the two are not equivalent: most notably `sizeof` applied to an array variable will return the size of the array (for example, 40 for an array of 10 four-byte integers), whereas the same operator when applied on a pointer will return only the storage required to store that pointer in memory (for example, 4 in many modern architectures). Finally, when the storage allocated is no longer needed, it must be freed by calling the `free` function. From that point onward trying to dereference the pointer will lead to undefined results. Failing to free the memory is also a mistake that can lead to programs exhibiting *memory leaks* that gradually appropriate and waste a system's memory resources.

When memory is exhausted there is not a lot a program can do; in most cases printing an error message and exiting is the only viable strategy. For this reason, and to avoid the burden of checking the return value of `malloc` after every call, `malloc` is wrapped inside a function (typically named `xmalloc`) that performs this check and is always called instead of `malloc`, as in the following example.[44]

---

[44] netbsdsrc/usr.bin/sed/misc.c:63–107

```
void
remember_rup_data(char *host, struct statstime *st)  ———————————— Index larger than allocated size?
{
        if (rup_data_idx >= rup_data_max) {
                rup_data_max += 16;  ———————————————————————————— New size
                rup_data = realloc (rup_data,  ——————————————————— Adjust allocation
                rup_data_max * sizeof(struct rup_data));
                if (rup_data == NULL) {
                        err (1, "realloc");
                }
        }
        rup_data[rup_data_idx].host = strdup(host);  ————————————— Store data
        rup_data[rup_data_idx].statstime = *st;
        rup_data_idx++;  ———————————————————————————————————————— New index
}
```

Figure 3.5 Memory allocation readjustment.

```
void *
xmalloc(u_int size)
{
    void *p;

    if ((p = malloc(size)) == NULL)
        err(FATAL, "%s", strerror(errno));
    return (p);
}
    [...]
    oe = xmalloc(s);
    (void)regerror(errcode, preg, oe, s);
```

In some cases the size of an array is determined while elements are actually being stored in it. This is typically the case when processing input data: the data is stored in an array, but the number of elements that need to be stored may not be known until all elements have been read. Figure 3.5[45] demonstrates such a case. Before an element is stored, the current array index is checked against the size of the elements in the allocated memory block. If more space is needed, the `realloc` C library function is called to adjust the space pointed to by its first argument to the new amount specified by the function's second argument. The function returns a pointer to the adjusted memory block because its address may not be the same as that of the original block. In that case, the contents of the original block are copied to the new location. Keep in mind that any pointer variables pointing to locations in the original block will now point to undefined data. The example in Figure 3.5 linearly increments the size

---

[45] netbsdsrc/usr.bin/rup/rup.c:146–164

of the memory block by 16 bytes each time the allocated memory is exhausted. An exponential increase of the allocated memory space is also very common.[46]

```
if (cur_pwtab_num + 1 > max_pwtab_num) {
  /* need more space in table */
  max_pwtab_num *= 2;
  pwtab = (uid2home_t *) xrealloc(pwtab,
                      sizeof(uid2home_t) * max_pwtab_num);
```

3.4.1 Managing Free Memory

Earlier we mentioned that failing to free a memory block leads to programs exhibiting memory leaks. However, you will often encounter programs that allocate memory and never free it.[47] Such programs get away with it when they are short-lived; when a program terminates, all memory it has allocated is automatically reclaimed by the operating system. Such is the case in the implementation of the *skeyinit* program.[48]

```
int
main(int argc, char *argv[])
{
    [...]
    skey.val = (char *)malloc(16 + 1);
    [... no call to free(skey.val) ]
    exit(1);
}
```

The *skeyinit* program is used to change a password or add a user in Bellcore's S/Key authentication system. It performs its work and then immediately exits, thus relinquishing the memory it allocates. This careless coding practice, however, may create problems when the same code is reused in a program with a larger lifespan (for example, as part of a router software system). In such a case the program will appear to leak memory, a fact that can often be ascertained by using a process view command such as *ps* or *top* under Unix or the task manager under Windows. Note that in the example above *skeyinit* could have simply set `skey.val` to point to a fixed size array, allocated as a local variable on the stack.

---

[46]netbsdsrc/usr.sbin/amd/hlfsd/homedir.c:521–525
[47]netbsdsrc/bin/mv/mv.c:260
[48]netbsdsrc/usr.bin/skeyinit/skeyinit.c:34–233

```
main(int argc, char *argv[])
{
    char valspace[16 + 1];
    [...]
    skey.val = valspace;
```

⚠   It is a common misconception of novice C/C++ programmers that all pointers must be initialized to `malloc`-allocated memory blocks. Although code written in this style is not wrong, the resulting programs are often more difficult to read and maintain.

In a few cases you may encounter programs that contain a *garbage collector* to automatically reclaim unused storage. Such a technique is often used when the memory blocks allocated are difficult to follow throughout their lifetime because, for example, they are shared between different variables. In such cases you will see a *reference count* associated with each block. This can be maintained by incrementing it every time a new reference for the block is created[49]

```
req.ctx = ctx;
req.event.time = time;
ctx->ref_count++;
```

and decrementing it every time a reference is destroyed.[50]

```
XtFree((char*)req);
ctx->req = NULL;
ctx->ref_count--;
```

When the reference count reaches 0, the block is no longer used and can be freed.[51]

```
if (--ctx->ref_count == 0 && ctx->free_when_done)
    XtFree((char*)ctx);
```

Another, less frequently used approach involves using a *conservative garbage collector* that scans all the memory of a process looking for addresses that match existing allocated memory blocks. Any blocks not encountered in the scan are then freed.

---

[49] XFree86-3.3/xc/lib/Xt/Selection.c:1540–1542
[50] XFree86-3.3/xc/lib/Xt/Selection.c:744–746
[51] XFree86-3.3/xc/lib/Xt/Selection.c:563–564

Finally, some versions of the C library implement a nonstandard function called alloca. This function allocates a memory block using the same interface as malloc, but instead of allocating the block in the program's *heap* (the general-purpose memory area belonging to the program), it allocates it on the program's *stack* (the area used for storing function return addresses and local variables).[52]

```
int
ofisa_intr_get(int phandle, struct ofisa_intr_desc *descp,
               int ndescs)
{
    char *buf, *bp;
    [...]
    buf = alloca(i);
```

The block returned by alloca is automatically reclaimed when the function it was allocated in returns; there is no need to call free to dispose the allocated block. Naturally, the address of alloca-allocated memory should never be passed to the callers of the function it was allocated in, as it will be invalid when the function returns. The use of alloca is discouraged in some programming environments like FreeBSD because it is considered nonportable and machine-dependent; in other cultures like GNU its use is encouraged because it reduces accidental memory leaks.

3.4.2 Structures with Dynamically Allocated Arrays

Sometimes a single dynamically allocated structure is used to store some fields and an array containing structure-specific, variable-length data. This construct is used to avoid the pointer indirection and memory overhead associated with having a structure element contain a pointer to the variable-length data. Thus instead of a definition like:[53]

```
typedef struct {
    XID            id_base;
    [...]
    unsigned char    *data;
    unsigned long    data_len;    /* in 4-byte units */
} XRecordInterceptData;
```

---

[52] netbsdsrc/sys/dev/ofisa/ofisa.c:563–564
[53] XFree86-3.3/xc/include/extensions/record.h:99–108

you will see a definition like:[54]

```
typedef struct {
    char *user;
    char *group;
    char *flags;
    char data[1];
} NAMES;
```

The `data` array structure element is used as a placeholder for the actual data. When memory for holding the structure is allocated, its size is adjusted upward based on the number of elements in the `data` array. From that point onward the array element is used as if it contained space for those elements.[55]

```
if ((np = malloc(sizeof(NAMES) +
    ulen + glen + flen + 3)) == NULL)
        err(1, "%s", "");
np->user = &np->data[0];
(void)strcpy(np->user, user);
```

Notice how the example above apparently allocates one byte more than what is actually needed. The size of the memory block is calculated as the sum of the structure size and the associated data elements: the size of the three strings (`ulen`, `glen`, `flen`) and their corresponding null terminating characters (3). However, the structure size already includes one placeholder byte for the associated data that is not taken into account when calculating the memory block size. The micromanagement of memory storage structures is a perilous and error-fraught activity.

Exercise 3.11   Locate in the book's CD-ROM a medium-sized C program that depends on dynamic memory allocation. Measure the percentage of the program's code that is used for managing the dynamically allocated memory structures. Estimate the percentage again, assuming that memory disposal was automatically managed by a garbage collector, as is the case in Java programs.

Exercise 3.12   Most modern programming environments offer specialized libraries, compilation options, or other tools for detecting memory leaks. Identify the facility available in your environment, and use it on three different programs. Comment on the results you obtain.

---

[54] netbsdsrc/bin/ls/ls.h:69–74
[55] netbsdsrc/bin/ls/ls.c:470–475

3.5 typedef **Declarations**

The examples in the previous section used a typedef declaration to create new data type names. A typedef declaration adds a new name, a synonym, for an already existing type. Thus after the following declaration[56]

```
typedef unsigned char cc_t;
```

you should read unsigned char whenever you see the identifier cc_t. C programs use typedef declarations to promote abstraction and enhance the code's readability, to guard against portability problems, and to emulate the class declaration behavior of C++ and Java.

The combined use of prefix and postfix types in C declarations sometimes conspires to make some typedef declarations difficult to read.[57]

```
typedef char ut_line_t[UT_LINESIZE];
```

However, decrypting such declarations is not too difficult. Consider typedef to be a storage class specifier like extern or static, and read the declaration as a variable definition.

```
static char ut_line_t[UT_LINESIZE];
```

The name of the variable being defined (ut_line_t in the case above) is the type's name; the variable's type is the type corresponding to that name.

When a typedef declaration is used as an abstraction mechanism, an abstract name is defined as a synonym for its concrete implementation. As a result, code that uses the declared name is better documented since it is written in terms of the appropriately named abstract concept, instead of the incidental implementation details. In the example below, DBT defines a database *thang*, a structure containing a key or a data element.[58]

```
typedef struct {
    void    *data;        /* data */
    size_t  size;         /* data length */
} DBT;
```

---

[56] netbsdsrc/libexec/telnetd/defs.h:124
[57] netbsdsrc/libexec/rpc.rusersd/rusers_proc.c:86
[58] netbsdsrc/include/db.h:72–75

Following the above declaration, all database access routines are specified to operate on DBT (and other `typedef`ed) entities.[59]

```
int   __rec_get (const DB *, const DBT *, DBT *, u_int);
int   __rec_iput(BTREE *, recno_t, const DBT *, u_int);
int   __rec_put (const DB *dbp, DBT *, const DBT *, u_int);
int   __rec_ret (BTREE *, EPG *, recno_t, DBT *, DBT *);
```

Since in C and C++ the hardware details of the language's data types depend on the underlying architecture, compiler, and operating system, `typedef` declarations are often used to enhance a program's portability by either creating portable names for known hardware quantities by a series of implementation-dependent declarations[60]

```
typedef __signed char    int8_t;
typedef unsigned char    u_int8_t;
typedef short            int16_t;
typedef unsigned short   u_int16_t;
typedef int              int32_t;
typedef unsigned int     u_int32_t;
typedef long             int64_t;
typedef unsigned long    u_int64_t;
```

or by creating abstract names for quantities with a known hardware representation using one of the previously declared names.[61]

```
typedef u_int32_t in_addr_t;
typedef u_int16_t in_port_t;
```

Finally, `typedef` declarations are also commonly used to emulate the C++ and Java behavior where a class declaration introduces a new type. In C programs you will often find a `typedef` used to introduce a type name for a `struct` (the nearest concept C has for a class) identified by the same name. Thus, the following example declares `path` to be a synonym for `struct path`.[62]

```
typedef struct path path;
struct path {
    [...]
```

---

[59] netbsdsrc/lib/libc/db/recno/extern.h:47–50
[60] netbsdsrc/sys/arch/alpha/include/types.h:61–68
[61] netbsdsrc/sys/arch/arm32/include/endian.h:61–62
[62] netbsdsrc/sbin/mount_portal/conf.c:62–63

Exercise 3.13   Locate in the book's CD-ROM five different instances for each use of the typedef functionality we discussed.

Exercise 3.14   How can the use of typedef declarations negatively affect code readability?

Further Reading

If the concepts we discussed in this chapter are not familiar to you, consider refreshing your knowledge of C [KR88]. Theoretical arguments regarding the implementation of recursive data structures without the explicit use of pointers are advanced in Hoare [Hoa73]. The use of pointers in C is concisely presented in Sethi and Stone [SS96], while a number of pitfalls regarding the use of pointers are discussed in Koenig [Koe88, pp. 27–46]. One reference [CWZ90] contains an analysis of pointers and structures. There are a number of interesting articles regarding the manipulation of pointer-based data structures and exploitation of pointer properties [FH82, Suz82, LH86]. A description of how virtual functions are typically realized in C++ implementations (and, as we described, also in C programs) can be found in Ellis and Stroustrup [ES90, pp. 217–237]. Algorithms behind dynamic storage allocation are discussed in Knuth [Knu97, pp. 435–452] and their practical implications in two other sources [Bru82, DDZ94]. The concept of reference-counted garbage collection is discussed in Christopher [Chr84], while the implementation of a conservative garbage collector is outlined in Boehm [Boe88].

C Data Structures

The ignoring of data is, in fact, the easiest and most popular mode of obtaining unity in one's thought.

—William James

Programs work by applying algorithms on data. The internal organization of data plays an important role in how algorithms operate.

You will find elements with the same type organized as a collection using a number of different mechanisms, each having different affordances regarding data storage and access. A *vector*, implemented as an array, offers random access to all elements, but it can be inefficient to change in size at runtime. A vector can also be used to organize groups of elements in the form of a *table* or stacked into two dimensions to create a *matrix*. Operations on a vector are sometimes restricted to occur at one end, in which case we talk about a *stack*, or in a first-in first-out order, treating the vector as a *queue*. When the order of the elements is not important, *maps* are used to create lookup tables and *sets* employed to form element collections.

The ability to link data elements together using pointers gives rise to a number of other structures you will often encounter. A *linked list* easily grows dynamically but offers only serial access (including stack and queue operations), whereas a suitably organized *tree* can be used to access data elements based on a key and can also easily grow dynamically while allowing traversal in an orderly fashion. We finish our discussion of C data structures with an examination of some applications and code patterns relating to *graphs*—the most flexible representation of linked data structures you will encounter.

Languages such as Java, C++, and C# offer abstractions for implementing these data structures as part of the language's library. In C these data structures are typically explicitly coded within the code body that uses them, however, their properties and the operations performed on them are common. The objective of this chapter is to learn how to read explicit data structure operations in terms of the underlying abstract data class.

4.1 Vectors

By far the most common data structures we encounter in C programs are *vectors* (when used for temporary storage, often referred to as *buffers*). These are used to store elements of the same type in a block and process them in a linear or random-access fashion. Vectors are typically realized in C using the built-in array type without attempting to abstract the properties of the vector from the underlying implementation. As an example, the vector's first element is always accessed at the array's position 0.[1]

```
ProgramName = argv[0];
```

To avoid confusion, from this point onward, we use the term *array* to refer to the array-based vector implementation that is prevalent in C programs. The application domain of vectors is extremely broad and seems to tempt us programmers to demonstrate all our resourcefulness and creativity. There are few distinguishable coding patterns (other than having the sequence buf appear in the array's name—we counted more than 50,000 occurrences in the BSD source base), numerous ways to err, and only a small number of methods to disentangle difficult sequences of code.

The typical way to process all elements of an array is with a for loop.[2]

```
char pbuf0[ED_PAGE_SIZE];

for (i = 0; i < ED_PAGE_SIZE; i++)
  pbuf0[i] = 0;
```

[i]   An array of *N* elements is completely processed by the sequence for (i = 0; i < *N*; i++); all other variations should raise your defenses. It is safe to terminate the loop's processing early with a continue statement or to break out of the loop with ▲   a break statement. However, if you see the loop index being incremented within the loop, you must reason very carefully about the way the code works.

---

[1] XFree86-3.3/contrib/programs/viewres/viewres.c:884
[2] netbsdsrc/sys/arch/bebox/isa/if_ed.c:1184–1187

You will find that the C library `memset` and `memcpy` functions are often used to initialize arrays and copy their contents. The initialization code sequence we listed above appears in other programs more concisely expressed as follows.[3]

```
static char buf[128];

memset(buf, 0, sizeof(buf));
```

`memset` will set a memory area to the value of its second argument. It is convenient for initializing single-byte character sequences to a predetermined value (for example, a space) or integers to 0. All other uses, such as the initialization of wide (for example, Unicode) characters or floating-point numbers are risky and nonportable. There is absolutely no guarantee that the repetition of a given byte value will yield a certain floating-point number or arbitrary Unicode character.

The expression `sizeof(x)` always yields the correct number of bytes for processing an array x (not a pointer) with `memset` or `memcpy`. It has the advantage (over explicitly passing the array size) that changes in the array's number of elements or their individual size will be reflected automatically by the value of the `sizeof` expression. Note, however, that applying `sizeof` on a pointer to a dynamically allocated memory block will yield only the size of the actual pointer, *not* the size of the block.

Correspondingly, `memcpy` is often used to copy data between two arrays.[4]

```
int     forcemap[MAPSZ];   /* map for blocking <1,x> combos */
int     tmpmap[MAPSZ];     /* map for blocking <1,x> combos */
[...]
    memcpy(forcemap, tmpmap, sizeof(tmpmap));
```

(Note that in the example above it would have been safer to apply the `sizeof` operator to the output buffer, the `forcemap` array, since having `memcpy` copy more bytes than the size of the destination will have unpredictable results.) `memcpy` and `memset` short-circuit the language's type system; you need to verify manually that the source and destination arguments refer to elements of the same type. In addition, the behavior of `memcpy` is undefined if the source and destination regions overlap; the function `memmove` should have been used in such a case.

---

[3]netbsdsrc/bin/chio/chio.c:659–662
[4]netbsdsrc/games/gomoku/pickmove.c:68–324

[i]   The elements of an array are often saved to a file using the `fwrite` C library function.[5]

```
if (fwrite(buf, sizeof(char), n, fp) != n) {
  message("write() failed, don't know why", 0);
```

The corresponding `fread` function is then used to read the elements from the file into the main memory.[6]

```
if (fread(buf, sizeof(char), n, fp) != n) {
  clean_up("read() failed, don't know why");
```

These functions store in the file a copy of the internal representation of the data. This data is inherently nonportable between different system architectures (for example, an Intel machine and a Power PC Macintosh). Both functions return the number of complete elements read or written. Programs should verify that the function behaved as expected by testing the function's return value.

The most common problem you may encounter when inspecting programs involving array processing is code that might access an element outside the range covered by the array. Some languages such as Java, C#, and Ada treat such an error by raising an exception. Others like C and C++ return an undefined value or store a value in a random memory address (probably one used to store another variable), while others like Perl and Tcl/Tk extend the array range. In all cases you want to ensure that such errors do not occur. In simple loops you can often construct an informal argument that demonstrates that only legal array values are accessed. In more complicated situations you can use the notion of a *loop invariant* based on the array index to construct a more rigorous argument proving your case. We presented an example of this approach in Section 2.11.

This problem can also occur when we call functions that take an array as an argument. The size of the array is often communicated to the function by using an out-of-band mechanism, typically an additional argument, for example, as is the case for the C library functions `qsort` and `memcpy`. In some infamous cases involving functions such as `gets` and `sprintf` the called function has no way of knowing the size of the array. In this case the called function may easily write outside the array

---

[5]netbsdsrc/games/rogue/save.c:382–383
[6]netbsdsrc/games/rogue/save.c:370–371

limits, and there is almost nothing a programmer can do to prevent it. Consider the following code.[7]

```
main()
{
    char    p[80];
    [...]
    if (gets(p) == NULL || p[0] == '\0')
        break;
```

If the program receives at its input more than 80 characters, these will overwrite other variables or even control information stored in the stack. This type of problem, called a *buffer overflow*, is constantly being exploited by worm and virus writers to subtly manipulate programs and thereby gain privileged system access. For this reason C library functions that may overwrite their buffer argument such as `strcat`, `strcpy`, `sprintf`, `vsprintf`, `gets`, and `scanf` should be used—if at all—only in circumstances where the amount of data to be written is controlled and verified by the code that calls them. For most functions, the standard C library or operating system–specific extensions provide safe alternatives such as `strncat`, `strncpy`, `snprintf`, `vsnprintf`, and `fgets`. For the `gets` function, controlling the data copied is very difficult since its data is the program's input. The following code excerpt correctly represents the guilt one should feel when using functions that write to a buffer without checking its size.[8]

```
/* Yes, we use gets not fgets.  Sue me. */
extern char *gets();
```

   Note that, although it is illegal to access elements outside those prescribed by an array's limits, ANSI C and C++ allow the calculation of the address of the element immediately after the array's end. Calculating the address of any other element outside the array limits is illegal and can lead to undefined behavior in some architectures even if no actual access takes place. The address of the element beyond the end is used as an indicator for marking the end of the range and iterating through it.[9]

---

[7]XFree86-3.3/xc/config/util/mkshadow/wildmat.c:138–157
[8]XFree86-3.3/xc/config/util/mkshadow/wildmat.c:134–135
[9]netbsdsrc/sbin/routed/rdisc.c:84–120

```
#define MAX_ADS 5
struct dr {                 /* accumulated advertisements */
    [...]
    n_long  dr_pref;    /* preference adjusted by metric */
} *cur_drp, drs[MAX_ADS];
[...]
    struct dr *drp;
    [...]
    for (drp = drs; drp < &drs[MAX_ADS]; drp++) {
        drp->dr_recv_pref = 0;
        drp->dr_life = 0;
    }
```

In the above example, although it is illegal to access drs[MAX_ADS], its address is legally used to represent the first element outside the array range. Ranges are typically represented using the first element of the range and the first beyond it. An equivalent mathematical formulation for this convention is that ranges are represented *inclusive*—closed—of their lower-bound element and *exclusive*—open—of their upper-bound element. This idiom for representing ranges helps programmers avoid off-by-one errors. When reading code that employs such *asymmetric bounds*, you can easily reason about the range they represent.

- The number of elements in an asymmetric range equals the difference between the upper bound and the lower bound.

- When the upper bound of an asymmetric range equals the lower bound, the range is empty.

- The lower bound in an asymmetric range represents the first occupied element; the upper bound, the first free one.

Exercise 4.1   Select a large software system, locate where arrays are used, and categorize their uses. Describe three instances where alternative, more disciplined data structures [such as the C++ standard template library (STL) vector class] would have been appropriate. Discuss the advantages and disadvantages of using the vector abstract data type over explicitly using the built-in array type. Try to locate code sequences that could not be coded using the vector interface.

Exercise 4.2   Fixed-length arrays notoriously impose arbitrary limits to a program's operation. Locate 10 instances of such limits in existing code and check whether these are documented in the respective system's documentation.

Exercise 4.3   Devise an expression that is true when the arguments passed to memcpy represent nonoverlapping memory areas. (Assume that memory addresses are coded in a linear fashion, but keep in mind that this assumption is not true on a number of processor architectures.) Explain how such an expression could result in more robust systems if coded as an assertion.

Exercise 4.4   Locate instances where functions susceptible to a buffer overflow problem are called, and either construct an argument to show that such a problem cannot occur or provide an example of the circumstances that can result in a buffer overflow.

4.2 Matrices and Tables

You will typically find a two-dimensional data structure referred to as a *table* in data-processing contexts and as a *matrix* in mathematical contexts. The two structures are also differentiated by the fact that matrix elements are all of the same type, whereas table elements are in most cases of different types. This distinction dictates how C elements are used to store each structure.

You will find tables stored and processed as arrays of C structs. Tables are intimately related to relational databases. Each table row (array element) is used to represent a *record*, while each table column (structure member) is used to represent a *field*. Memory-based tables can be allocated statically as is the case for the lookup tables we examined in Section 4.5 or in the following example that converts Internet control message protocol (ICMP) numerical codes into a string representation.[10]

```
static struct tok icmp2str[] = {
    { ICMP_ECHOREPLY,        "echo reply" },
    { ICMP_SOURCEQUENCH,     "source quench" },
    { ICMP_ECHO,             "echo request" },
    [...]
    { 0,               NULL }
};
```

Tables can also be dynamically allocated by using malloc, passing to it as an argument the product of the table size and the size of the C structure it contains (Figure 4.1:1).[11]

---

[10]netbsdsrc/usr.sbin/tcpdump/print-icmp.c:109–120
[11]netbsdsrc/usr.sbin/quot/quot.c:423–445

```
struct user *usr, *usrs;
[...]
if (!(usrs = (struct user *)malloc(nusers * sizeof(struct user))))     ❶ Allocate table memory
    errx(1, "allocate users");
[...]

for (usr = usrs, n = nusers; --n >= 0 && usr->count; usr++) {          ❸ Traverse table
    printf("%5ld", (long)SIZE(usr->space));                            ❷ Field access
    if (count)
        printf("\t%5ld", (long)usr->count);                            ❷
    printf("\t%-8s", usr->name);                                       ❷
    [...]
}
```

Figure 4.1 A structure pointer as a table cursor.

When tables are processed, we often need to refer to a particular table row and access its elements. One alternative is to use an integer index variable (tvc in the example that follows) to represent a table row.[12]

```
struct vcol *vc;
int tvc;
[...]
cnt = vc[tvc].cnt;
```

However, in these cases, information about the particular table we are accessing is lost; all that remains is an integer, which can mean many different (incompatible) things. It is better to use a pointer to a particular structure element to represent both the table and the location within the table. This pointer can be incremented and decremented to move within the table and dereferenced using the -> operator to access structure fields (Figure 4.1:2). Database systems refer to such an abstraction as a *cursor*.

Matrices are allocated and processed using a different set of techniques. Since all matrix elements are of the same type, you will encounter many alternative ways used to store and process them. The most obvious way is to use a two-dimensional array to allocate storage and access its elements.[13]

```
typedef double Transform3D[4][4];
[...]
IdentMat(Transform3D m)
{
    register int i;
    register int j;

    for (i = 3; i >= 0; --i)
```

---

[12] netbsdsrc/usr.bin/pr/pr.c:314–530
[13] XFree86-3.3/contrib/programs/ico/ico.c:110–1151

```
    {
        for (j = 3; j >= 0; --j)
            m[i][j] = 0.0;
        m[i][i] = 1.0;
    }
}
```

This method, however, cannot be used to deal with dynamically allocated matrices. When matrices are of fixed size, or when the number of columns is known, you will find code that declares variables that point to an array column and allocates memory based on the number of rows and the size of each column. The example below[14] declares rknots as a matrix with MAXORD columns and dynamically allocates the memory required to store all the numKnots rows.[15]

```
ddFLOAT  (*rknots)[MAXORD]=0;    /* reciprocal of knot diff */
[...]
if ( !( rknots = (ddFLOAT (*)[MAXORD])
    xalloc( MAXORD * numKnots * sizeof(float))) )
```

These variables can then be passed to functions and used as two-dimensional arrays (kr in the following example) because one can omit the first dimension of an array in C.[16]

```
    mi_nu_compute_nurb_basis_function( order, i, knots, rknots, C );
    [...]
void
mi_nu_compute_nurb_basis_function( order, span, knots, kr, C )
    [...]
    ddFLOAT kr[][MAXORD]; /* reciprocal of knots diff */
    [...]
{
    [...]
    for ( k = 1; k < order; k++ ) {
        t0 = t1 * kr[span-k+1][k];
```

---

[14]XFree86-3.3/xc/programs/Xserver/PEX5/ddpex/mi/level2/miNCurve.c:364–511

[15]Dave Thomas commented when reviewing the manuscript: The rknots code is an accident waiting to happen, as the type of the elements in the matrix is not related in the code to the xalloc used to allocate the space: the declaration uses ddFLOAT and the xalloc uses float. This is a good example of code that I personally like to see written as rknots = xalloc(MAXORD * numKnots * sizeof(rknots[0][0]));.

[16]XFree86-3.3/xc/programs/Xserver/PEX5/ddpex/mi/level2/minurbs.c:154–179

```
PclFontMapRec ** index;                          Matrix declaration
[...]
index = (PclFontMapRec **)xalloc(sizeof(PclFontMapRec *)*nindex_row);     Allocate row pointers
[...]
for (i=0; i<nindex_row; i++) {                        Allocate row contents
    index[i] = (PclFontMapRec *)xalloc(sizeof(PclFontMapRec)*nindex_col);
    [...]
    for (j=0; j<=nindex_col; j++)
        index[i][j].fid = 0x0;           Array-like access
}
```

Figure 4.2 A pointer-based matrix.

An alternative, used when the size of each row is different (as is the case in diagonal or symmetric matrices), is to store the matrix by separately allocating memory for each row. An array of pointers to pointers to elements is then used to store the address of each row. Thus, given a pointer to this structure p, the location of the fifth row can be found at `*(p + 5)`, while the third element in that row will be represented as `*(*(p + 5) + 3)`. Thankfully, because array indexing can be used in C as a shorthand for dereferencing a pointer with an offset, the above can be written as `p[5][3]`. It is important to note that p is not a two-dimensional array; it occupies additional space for storing the row pointers, and element access involves a pointer lookup rather than the calculation of the element location using multiplication. As you can see in Figure 4.2,[17] elements for this structure are allocated in two phases: first an array of pointers to each row, then each row's individual elements. From that point onward operations that resemble two-dimensional array access can be used.

Finally, it is also possible to emulate the way C accesses two-dimensional array elements by using an explicit code or a macro. Figure 4.3 shows such an example.[18] In this case the matrix is allocated as a flat array of elements, and a multiplication based on the matrix's row size (n) determines the offset of a particular row; the element in the row is then located by adding the column number to that offset.

Exercise 4.5   For the relational database management system of your choice, locate documentation regarding cursors. Compare the functionality offered by cursors to the functionality offered by pointers to structures.

Exercise 4.6   Tables are also sometimes stored as vectors, using one different array for each field. Locate one such instance in the book's CD-ROM and explain how this could be rewritten by using an array of structures.

---

[17]XFree86-3.3/xc/programs/Xserver/Xprint/pcl/PclText.c:638–655
[18]XFree86-3.3/xc/programs/xieperf/convolve.c:91–434

```
#define    DATA( n, i, j ) ( float * ) ( *data + ( i * n ) ) + j        Array access macro
[...]
int    Boxcar3( float **data )
{
    int    i, j;

    if ( ( *data = ( float * ) malloc( sizeof( float ) * 9 ) ) ==       Allocate flat memory
        ( float * ) NULL )
        return( -1 );
    for ( i = 0; i < 3; i++ )
        for ( j = 0; j < 3; j++ )
            *(DATA( 3, i, j )) = 0.11111111;                            Array element access
    return( 3 );
}
```

Figure 4.3 Explicit matrix element access.

Exercise 4.7 A number of linear algebra and matrix libraries are available on the Web in open-source form. Download two such packages and identify how matrices are stored.

4.3 Stacks

The ways we can access a *stack* data structure are much more restricted than those offered by a vector. A stack only allows elements to be added (*pushed*) or removed (*popped*) from its end in a *last-in-first-out* (LIFO) order. In addition, we can query the stack to find out if it is empty. The LIFO access order afforded by a stack matches particularly well recursively defined data structures and algorithms. Consider the simple example of processing parenthesized arithmetic expressions: the last parenthesis opened is the first one that will be closed. Expressions are in fact often recursively defined as operators applied on plain operands or parenthesized expressions. A stack of intermediate results is an ideal structure for processing such expressions. Apart from arithmetic expressions, you will find recursive definitions and stacks used for block-structured programming and markup languages; data types; hierarchical data structures; execution, traversal, and search strategies; graphics algorithms; processing interrupts; and the implementation of the *undo* command in user applications.

When examining code you will often find stacks implemented in C using an array. In structured programs the basic stack operations will probably be abstracted as

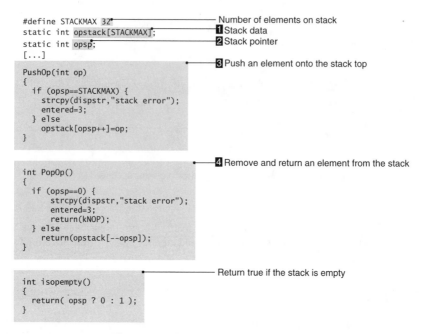

```
#define STACKMAX 32                        — Number of elements on stack
static int opstack[STACKMAX];              1 Stack data
static int opsp;                           2 Stack pointer
[...]
                                           3 Push an element onto the stack top
PushOp(int op)
{
  if (opsp==STACKMAX) {
    strcpy(dispstr,"stack error");
    entered=3;
  } else
    opstack[opsp++]=op;
}

                                           4 Remove and return an element from the stack
int PopOp()
{
  if (opsp==0) {
    strcpy(dispstr,"stack error");
    entered=3;
    return(kNOP);
  } else
    return(opstack[--opsp]);
}

                                           — Return true if the stack is empty
int isopempty()
{
  return( opsp ? 0 : 1 );
}
```

Figure 4.4 A stack abstract data type.

separate functions in the form of an *abstract data type* (ADT) as shown in Figure 4.4.[19] For the program's original author and its maintainers, an ADT isolates the implementation of the data type from its use by providing an interface that does not depend on the underlying implementation. For you as a reader, an ADT provides a measure of confidence regarding the way the underlying implementation elements will be used (or abused). Some languages and implementation methods can completely isolate the interface from the implementation, making it very difficult to manipulate the data without using the interfaces provided by the ADT. An array-based stack will typically consist of an array where the stack elements are stored (Figure 4.4:1) and the *stack pointer*, an integer array index indicating the position where the next element will be stored or, alternatively, retrieved from (Figure 4.4:2). Both conventions are followed; in our case the stack pointer sp indexes the array position where new stack elements are to be copied. Notice how the stack pointer is postincremented when elements are added (Figure 4.4:3) but predecremented when elements are removed (Figure 4.4:4). This (or the opposite) symmetry must always exist in push and pop operations. Look for this symmetry when reading code with explicitly coded stack access sequences,

---

[19]XFree86-3.3/contrib/programs/xcalc/math.c:827–860

as in the following example; note that the two operations are in different functions, separated by 84 lines of code.[20]

```
if (regretp >= 0) {
    strcpy(lexstring, string_stack[regretp]);
    lexnumber = numberstack[regretp];
    return(regretstack[regretp--]);
}
[...]
if (++regretp >= REGDEP)
    errx(1, "Too many regrets");
regretstack[regretp] = token;
```

A particular problem with stack operations randomly interspersed in a program's code concerns the checking of overflow and underflow. Notice how the stack ADT we examined contains checks for both conditions. When the stack operations are performed in-line, these checks are often omitted out of laziness or a misplaced interest in brevity or efficiency. In such cases it is very difficult to argue about the program's correctness since we cannot determine whether the original author correctly reasoned that the stack would not overflow or underflow in that particular case or whether the author simply forgot to check.[21]

```
de_stack[--stack_top] = '0' + c % 8;
de_stack[--stack_top] = '0' + (c / 8) % 8;
de_stack[--stack_top] = '0' + c / 64;
```

Exercise 4.8 Locate instances of a stack data structure in the book's CD-ROM. Compare the number of implementations using an ADT versus the number using explicit code. Count implementations where the stack pointer points to the first empty array element and implementations where the stack pointer points to the last occupied element. Discuss the results you obtained.

Exercise 4.9 Examine the stack operations performed on implementations based on explicit code. Identify those operations that do not fit into the model we described. Propose function names and code for implementing them.

Exercise 4.10 Reason whether overflow could indeed occur in the unchecked stack push example provided in this section.

4.4 Queues

A *queue* is a collection of elements that allows items to be added at the end (the *tail*) and removed from the beginning (the *head*) in a *first-in-first-out* (FIFO) order.

---

[20] netbsdsrc/usr.bin/mail/list.c:518–617
[21] XFree86-3.3/xc/util/compress/compress.c:1325–1327

You will often find queues used in places where two systems are connected. In the real world, queues form where one entity (for example, members of the general public, orders) interfaces with another (for example, a bank teller, a check-in counter, a bus, a manufacturing line). Similarly, in the software world you will find queues used when two software systems are connected together or where a software system interfaces with hardware. In both cases the queue is used to manage the different data generation and processing characteristics of the two systems. Examples of the former case include the connection of window systems with user applications, the operating system processing of incoming network packets, and the way mail messages are forwarded between mail transfer agents. Examples of queues used for hardware interfacing include the processing of requests and data generated by network interface cards, disk drives, serial communication devices, and printers. In all cases data generated from the one system is placed in a queue and processed by the other at appropriate intervals.

When implemented by using an array, you will find a queue often called a *circular* or *ring buffer*. As it is inefficient to shift forward the queue elements every time an item is removed from the head, you will often find array-based queues implemented by using two array indices: one pointing at the array position where elements are added, and one pointing at the position where elements are removed. When these indices reach the end of the array they must wrap around to its beginning. This is typically implemented by using a conditional statement[22]

```
if (++adbInHead >= ADB_QUEUE)
    adbInHead=0;
```

a conditional expression[23]

```
static int     history_head, history_tail;
#define hist_bump(h)    ((++(h) == NUM_HISTORY) ? ((h) = 0) : 0)
[...]
    for (i = history_tail; i != history_head; hist_bump(i))
        DrawPoints (old_pixmaps[i], bit_0_gc, xp, n);
```

or modulo arithmetic.[24]

```
adb_evq[(adb_evq_len + adb_evq_tail) % ADB_MAX_EVENTS] =
    *event;
```

---

[22] netbsdsrc/sys/arch/mac68k/dev/adb_direct.c:1610–1611
[23] XFree86-3.3/xc/programs/beforelight/b4light.c:76–166
[24] netbsdsrc/sys/arch/mac68k/dev/adb.c:133–134

Many queues are implemented by using a head and a tail index.[25]

```
volatile int        rnd_head;
volatile int        rnd_tail;
[...]
volatile rnd_event_t    rnd_events[RND_EVENTQSIZE];
```

Such implementations often have the head indexing the first element to remove and the tail indexing the first empty element. An empty queue is thus denoted by the head and tail containing the same index[26]

```
/*
 * check for empty queue
 */
if (rnd_head == rnd_tail)
    return;
```

and a full queue by the tail indexing one element before the head.[27]

```
/*
 * check for full ring.  If the queue is full and we have not
 * already scheduled a timeout, do so here.
 */
nexthead = (rnd_head + 1) & (RND_EVENTQSIZE - 1);
if (nexthead == rnd_tail) {
```

Note that in the implementation we examined, elements are added in the queue's head and removed from its tail. Also note that this scheme wastes one queue element, always keeping it empty to distinguish a full queue from an empty one. Convince yourself of this fact by considering how you would represent an empty queue and a full queue of a single element. We can avoid this problem and the resultant confusion by explicitly storing the number of elements in the queue, as is the case in Figure 4.5.[28] This storage method can also be optimized to store only the queue's tail and number of elements.[29]

---

[25] netbsdsrc/sys/dev/rnd.c:99–102
[26] netbsdsrc/sys/dev/rnd.c:826–830
[27] netbsdsrc/sys/dev/rnd.c:763–768
[28] netbsdsrc/sys/arch/mac68k/dev/adb_direct.c:239–1611
[29] netbsdsrc/sys/arch/mac68k/dev/adb.c:72–74

```
struct     adbCommand adbInbound[ADB_QUEUE];          ─── Queue array

int    adbInCount=0;                                  ─── Element count
int    adbInHead=0;                                   ─── First element to remove
int    adbInTail=0;                                   ─── First empty element

void
adb_pass_up(struct adbCommand *in)
{
    if (adbInCount>=ADB_QUEUE) {                       ─── Check for queue overflow
        printf_intr("adb: ring buffer overflow\n");
        return;
    }
    [...]
    adbInbound[adbInTail].cmd=cmd;                     ─── Add element

    adbInCount++;                                      ─── Adjust tail and element count
    if (++adbInTail >= ADB_QUEUE)
        adbInTail=0;

    [...]
void
adb_soft_intr(void)
{
    [...]
    while (adbInCount) {                               ─── While there are elements in the queue
        [...]
        cmd=adbInbound[adbInHead].cmd;                 ─── Extract one element
        [...]
        adbInCount--;                                  ─── Adjust head and element count
        if (++adbInHead >= ADB_QUEUE)
                adbInHead=0;
    }
```

Figure 4.5 A queue with an explicit element count.

```
static adb_event_t adb_evq[ADB_MAX_EVENTS]; /* ADB event queue */
static int adb_evq_tail = 0;     /* event queue tail */
static int adb_evq_len = 0;      /* event queue length */
```

Exercise 4.11   Locate ten queue instances in the book's CD-ROM and identify the systems they are used to interface.

Exercise 4.12   In the book's CD-ROM count examples where elements are added in a queue's head and examples where elements are added in a queue's tail. Propose a strategy for avoiding this confusion.

Exercise 4.13   Look for the word "queue" in the source code documentation and try to identify the corresponding data structure. Locate at least two cases where a corresponding queue data structure is not used and justify the discrepancy.

4.5 Maps

When we use an array index variable to access array elements, we perform a very efficient operation, typically implemented with one or two machine instructions. This feature makes arrays ideal for organizing simple *maps* or *lookup tables* keyed by sequential integers starting from zero. In cases where the array elements are known in advance, they can be used to directly initialize the array contents.[30]

```
static const int      year_lengths[2] = {
       DAYSPERNYEAR, DAYSPERLYEAR
};
```

The array defined in this example contains just two elements denoting the number of days in normal and leap years. What is important is not the array's size but the uniform random access made possible through its index.[31]

```
janfirst += year_lengths[isleap(year)] * SECSPERDAY;
[...]
while (days < 0 || days >= (long) year_lengths[yleap = isleap(y)]) {
[...]
yourtm.tm_mday += year_lengths[isleap(i)];
```

The same principle is also often employed for tables of more than one dimension.[32]

```
static const int      mon_lengths[2][MONSPERYEAR] = {
  { 31, 28, 31, 30, 31, 30, 31, 31, 30, 31, 30, 31 },
  { 31, 29, 31, 30, 31, 30, 31, 31, 30, 31, 30, 31 }
};
```

The above example initializes a two-dimensional array to store the number of days for each month in normal and leap years. You may find the information stored in the mon_lengths array trivial and a waste of space. Far from it—as in this case, arrays are often used to efficiently encode control structures, thus simplifying a program's logic.

⊡

---

[30] netbsdsrc/lib/libc/time/localtime.c:453–455
[31] netbsdsrc/lib/libc/time/localtime.c:832–1264
[32] netbsdsrc/lib/libc/time/localtime.c:448–451

```
static struct key {
    char *name;                         ──────── Command name
    void (*f)(struct info *);           ──────── Function to process it
    [...]
} keys[] = {
                                        ●───── Command and function table
    { "all",    f_all,      0 },
    { "cbreak", f_cbreak,   F_OFFOK },
    [...]
    { "tty",    f_tty,      0 },
};
[...]
int
ksearch(char ***argvp, struct info *ip)
{
    char *name;
    struct key *kp, tmp;

    name = **argvp;
    [...]
    tmp.name = name;
    if (!(kp = (struct key *)bsearch(&tmp, keys,         ●── Look for command in table
        sizeof(keys)/sizeof(struct key), sizeof(struct key), c_key)))
        return (0);
    [...]
    kp->f(ip);                          ──────── Execute the respective function
    return (1);
}

                                        ●── Processing function for the "all" command
void
f_all(struct info *ip)
{
    print(&ip->t, &ip->win, ip->ldisc, BSD);
}
```

Figure 4.6 Table-driven program operation.

Consider how the following code excerpts would have to be coded using explicit if statements.[33]

```
value += mon_lengths[leapyear][i] * SECSPERDAY;
[...]
if (d + DAYSPERWEEK >= mon_lengths[leapyear][rulep->r_mon - 1])
[...]
i = mon_lengths[isleap(yourtm.tm_year)][yourtm.tm_mon];
```

The logical conclusion of using an array to encode a program's control elements is the complete table-driven operation of a program. In the most common case arrays are used to associate data with code by storing in each position a data element and a pointer to the element's processing function. The example in Figure 4.6[34] uses an array initialized with command names and pointers to the function used to execute

---

[33] netbsdsrc/lib/libc/time/localtime.c:682–1373
[34] netbsdsrc/bin/stty/key.c:74–148

each respective command. The ksearch function performs a binary search for the command name over the array contents (sorted in ascending order by the command name). If an entry for the command is found, ksearch will call the respective function. Generalizing from the above examples, we note that arrays can control a program's operation by storing data or code used by *abstract* or *virtual machines* implemented within that program. Typical examples of this approach include the implementation of parsers and lexical analyzers using pushdown and stack automata and the realization of interpreters based on the execution of virtual machine instructions.

A minor but frequently encountered idiom used in Figure 4.6 concerns the calculation of the number of elements of the key array. When the key array is defined, its size is not given; the compiler determines it based on the number of elements used to initialize it. Within the program, in places where the number of array elements is needed, it can be obtained as the result of the expression sizeof(keys)/sizeof (struct key). You can always read the expression sizeof(x)/sizeof(x[0]) as the number of elements of the array x. The number of elements is calculated as a compile-time constant by dividing the size needed for the whole array by the size needed for each of its elements. Since the result of this operation is a compile-time constant you will often see it used for specifying the size of or initializing other arrays.[35]

```
struct protosw impsw[] = {
{ SOCK_RAW,      &impdomain, 0, PR_ATOMIC|PR_ADDR,
  [...]
},
};


struct domain impdomain =
  { AF_IMPLINK, "imp", 0, 0, 0,
    impsw, &impsw[sizeof (impsw)/sizeof(impsw[0])] };
```

4.5.1 Hash Tables

Lookup tables are not always initialized from static data and accessed using a zero-based key index. Very often we use the efficient random-access mode that arrays give us to organize a map that changes during a program's operation and to implement element lookup schemes with keys different from a simple array index. You will find such schemes referred to as *hash tables*. The main idea behind such a scheme is to

---

[35] netbsdsrc/sys/netinet/in_proto.c:167–177

⊡   construct an array index out of the lookup key we want to use. When the lookup key is
another (potentially very large) integer, a simple solution involves using the remainder
of the key divided by the number of array elements as the array index.[36]

```
/*
 * hash inode number and look for this file
 */
indx = ((unsigned)arcn->sb.st_ino) % L_TAB_SZ;
if ((pt = ltab[indx]) != NULL) {
```

In the above example a file's unique identifying number st_ino (called the *inode* number) is used as an array index for the ltab array, with L_TAB_SZ elements. The result
of the modulo operation is guaranteed to match exactly the range of allowable array indices and is therefore then directly used to access array elements. Often the cost of the
modulo operation is avoided by having the array contain a number of elements equal
to a power of 2 and using a bitwise-AND operation, as we described in Section 2.10,
instead.

When the index variable we want to use on the map is not an integer, you will
find it converted into an integer by using a *hash function*. The hash function combines
the key data elements so as to convert them into an integer. As an example, the hash
function in Figure 4.7:1[37] converts a string into an integer by using the exclusive-OR of
each string's character element with the accumulated hash value shifted left by three
bit positions; negative results are converted to positive at the end of the conversion.
Before looking up the array, the computed value is again confined to the legal array
index values by using a bitwise-AND operation (Figure 4.7:2). Keep in mind that many
different map index values may hash into the same array position. Therefore, after
locating the array position, we need to check that the element in that position is indeed
the element we were looking for (Figure 4.7:3). A final complication arises from the
fact that more than one element may need to be stored in the same position. A strategy
often used in this case is calculating new candidate array positions by using another
function (Figure 4.7:4). These alternative positions are then used for placing elements
when their primary position is occupied and for searching elements when the primary
position does not contain the element we were looking for (Figure 4.7:5).

---

[36] netbsdsrc/bin/pax/tables.c:163–167
[37] XFree86-3.3/xc/lib/font/util/atom.c:55–173

```
static
Hash(char *string, int len)
{
    int    h;

    h = 0;
    while (len--)
        h = (h << 3) ^ *string++;
    if (h < 0)
        return -h;
    return h;
}
```
1 Hash function

```
[...]
Atom
MakeAtom(char *string, unsigned len, int makeit)
{
    int         hash, h, r;

    hash = Hash (string, len);
    if (hashTable) {
        h = hash & hashMask;
        if (hashTable[h]) {

            if (hashTable[h]->hash == hash &&
            hashTable[h]->len == len &&
                NameEqual (hashTable[h]->name, string, len))
                    return hashTable[h]->atom;


        r = (hash % rehash) | 1;


        for (;;) {
            h += r;
            if (h >= hashSize)
                h -= hashSize;
            if (!hashTable[h])
                break;
            if (hashTable[h]->hash == hash &&
                hashTable[h]->len == len &&
                NameEqual (hashTable[h]->name, string, len))
                    return hashTable[h]->atom;
        }
    }
```

Compute hash value
2 Limit hash value to the array size
3 Verify that the correct element was found
4 Value for calculating alternative positions
5 Search alternative positions

Figure 4.7 Hash function and hash table access.

Exercise 4.14   Locate in the book's CD-ROM an instance where an array is used to encode control information. Rewrite the code using explicit control statements. Measure the difference in lines of code and comment on the relative maintainability, extensibility, and efficiency of the two approaches.

Exercise 4.15   Locate code where explicit control structures can be substituted by an array lookup mechanism. Explain how the code would be implemented.

Exercise 4.16   Locate in the book's CD-ROM at least three different implementations of a string hash function. Select a representative set of input strings and compare the implementations based on the number of elements that collide in the same array position and the execution time of each function.

Exercise 4.17   Do you envisage any difficulties in implementing a hash-based map as an abstract data type? Suggest ways to overcome them.

4.6 Sets

There are cases where we want to efficiently represent and process sets of elements. When these elements can be expressed as relatively small integers, you will find that the typical implementation used involves representing the set as an array of bits, with set membership of each element based on the value of a particular bit. The C language does not have a data type for directly representing and addressing bits as arrays. For this reason you will see that programs use one of the integral data types (char, int) as an underlying storage element and address specific bits using shift and bitwise AND/OR operators. As an example the following line will make the set pbitvec contain j as a member.[38]

```
pbitvec[j/BITS_PER_LONG] |= ((unsigned long)1 << (j % BITS_PER_LONG));
```

The array pbitvec is composed of long integers, each containing BITS_PER_LONG bits. Each array element can therefore store information about BITS_PER_LONG set members. We therefore divide the set element number j by BITS_PER_LONG to find the array position that contains information about the particular element and then use the division's remainder to shift left a 1 bit to bring it at the bit position where information about the particular element is stored. By performing a bitwise-OR between the existing array value and the bit value we created, we set that bit in the array to 1, denoting set membership of j. Similarly, we can test whether an element is a member of a set with a binary-AND between the constructed bit and the appropriate array element.[39]

```
#define FD_ISSET(n, p) \
  ((p)->fds_bits[(n)/NFDBITS] & (1 << ((n) % NFDBITS)))
```

Finally, we can remove an element from the set using a binary-AND between the array element and the one's complement of the constructed bit.[40]

```
#define FD_CLR(n, p) \
  ((p)->fds_bits[(n)/NFDBITS] &= ~(1 << ((n) % NFDBITS)))
```

---

[38] XFree86-3.3/xc/programs/Xserver/record/set.c:269
[39] XFree86-3.3/xc/include/Xpoll.h:99
[40] XFree86-3.3/xc/include/Xpoll.h:96

The one's complement of the bit will have 1s in all bit positions apart from the position containing the element we want to remove, in effect masking the array's value to clear the specific bit. In Section 2.10 we outlined how shift and bitwise-AND operations are often used in place of the division and remainder operators; you will often encounter the set operations we described implemented by using the bit-based operators.[41]

```
resourceQuarks[q >> 3] |= 1 << (q & 0x7);
```

Using the representation we outlined, you will also sometimes see set-union and set-intersection implemented by using the bitwise-OR and bitwise-AND operators to directly combine the array elements.[42]

```
#define XFD_ANDSET(dst,b1,b2) \
 (dst)->fds_bits[0] = ((b1)->fds_bits[0] & (b2)->fds_bits[0]); \
```

Exercise 4.18   In the book's CD-ROM, locate ADT implementations of sets using bit-operators and arithmetic operations. Also, implement the same ADT as an array of characters, Booleans, and integers. Write a small program to compare the five different implementations in terms of efficiency. Justify the results for both medium-sized (1,000 elements) and very large (five times your machine's memory size) sets.

Exercise 4.19   Locate instances in the book's CD-ROM where sets are being used. Suggest other implementation strategies for each particular problem. Comment on whether a set data type is used partly because it is easy to create an efficient implementation for it.

4.7 Linked Lists

The simplest and most common linked data structure you will encounter in C programs is a *linked list*. It is constructed by joining together, through a pointer, structures representing the list elements. Elements are typically added to the front of the list—the list *head*. However, because all list elements are linked together using pointers, elements can be efficiently added or removed from any list position, an operation that may require a significant amount of overhead in large arrays. To locate a particular item in the list, the list must be traversed from its beginning; it is not possible to randomly access elements in it. You will find lists often used to store sequentially accessed data that expands dynamically during the program's operation.

---

[41] XFree86-3.3/xc/lib/X11/Xrm.c:990
[42] XFree86-3.3/xc/include/Xpoll.h:133–134

```
struct host_list {
    struct host_list *next;          ——— 1 Next list element
    struct in_addr addr;             ——— 2 List node data
} *hosts;                            ——— 3 List head
```

                                               •——— Search for an item in the list
```
int
search_host(struct in_addr addr)
{
    struct host_list *hp;

    [...]
    for (hp = hosts; hp != NULL; hp = hp->next) {  •——— 4 Iterate through list elements
        if (hp->addr.s_addr == addr.s_addr)         ——— Item found
            return(1);
    }
    return(0);                                   ——— Item not found
}
```

                                               •——— Add a list item
```
void
remember_host(struct in_addr addr)
{
    struct host_list *hp;

    if (!(hp = (struct host_list *)malloc(sizeof(struct host_list)))) {
        err(1, "malloc");
        /* NOTREACHED */
    }
    hp->addr.s_addr = addr.s_addr;      ——— Store data
    hp->next = hosts;                   ——— 5 Link element into list
    hosts = hp;
}
```

Figure 4.8 Linked list definition and basic operations.

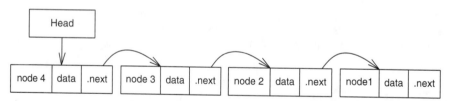

Figure 4.9 A singly linked list.

Linked lists are usually coded using a very specific style; it's therefore easy to identify what a code sequence is used for. A structure with an element titled next pointing to itself typically defines a node of a singly linked list. The list node consists of data (other structure fields; see Figure 4.8:2[43]) and the next pointer that points to the next list element (Figure 4.8:1). A permanent (for example, global, static, or heap allocated) pointer to a list node will often represent the list head (Figure 4.8:3). This arrangement is shown in Figure 4.9. When the list head has the value of NULL the list is empty. Linked lists are traversed by using a list node pointer that starts from the list head and is advanced using each node's next pointer. A for loop is often used to code this sequence, as is the case in Figure 4.8:4. Note that in the list we defined

[43] netbsdsrc/usr.bin/rup/rup.c:60–97

in Figure 4.8 it's only possible to traverse its elements in a *forward* manner. When looking for a particular element, an early exit from the `for` loop is used when the element is found; if the loop ends normally, the particular element wasn't found. New elements are added to a list by using a carefully choreographed yet common sequence: after allocating memory for the new node and storing its data, the new node is set to point to the node where the old list head was pointing, and the list head is set to point to the new list node (Figure 4.8:5). Removing the list's head element is easy: the head is made to point to the list's next element. For this reason you will find linked lists also often used for representing a stack.[44]

```
/* push alias expansion */
[...]
s->next = source;
source = s;
[...]
source = s->next;    /* pop source stack */
```

Removing an arbitrary element from a list is a more complicated affair because we need a variable to point to the particular element's pointer. A pointer to a list pointer is used for this purpose, as in the following example.[45]

```
STATIC int
unalias(char *name)
{
    struct alias *ap, **app;

    app = hashalias(name);
    for (ap = *app; ap; app = &(ap->next), ap = ap->next) {
        if (equal(name, ap->name)) {
            [...]
            *app = ap->next;
            ckfree(ap->name);
            ckfree(ap->val);
            ckfree(ap);
            [...]
            return (0);
        }
    }
    return (1);
}
```

---

[44] netbsdsrc/bin/ksh/lex.c:639–644,845
[45] netbsdsrc/bin/sh/alias.c:120–152

Here app initially points to the linked list head. The variable ap is used to traverse through the linked list, while app always points to the location where the current element's pointer is stored. Thus, when the element to be deleted is found, *app is set to point to its next element, effectively removing the found element from the list chain.

Note that in the previous example, after an element is deleted, ap could not have been used to advance to the next element because its contents (including ap->next) have been freed. Accessing the next member of deleted linked list elements is a common mistake.[46]

```
for (; ihead != NULL; ihead = ihead->nextp) {
    free(ihead);
    if ((opts & IGNLNKS) || ihead->count == 0)
        continue;
    if (lfp)
        log(lfp, "%s: Warning: missing links\n",
                ihead->pathname);
}
```

In the above example, ihead->nextp and ihead->count are accessed after freeing ihead. While this code may work in some architectures and C library implementations, it works only by accident since the contents of a freed memory block are not available for further access. The mistake is particularly common when deleting a complete linked list. The correct way to delete such elements involves either using a temporary variable for storing the address of each next element[47]

```
for (j = job_list; j; j = tmp) {
    tmp = j->next;
    if (j->flags & JF_REMOVE)
        remove_job(j, "notify");
}
```

or storing in a temporary variable the address of the element to be freed before advancing the list pointer.[48]

---

[46] netbsdsrc/usr.bin/rdist/docmd.c:206–213
[47] netbsdsrc/bin/ksh/jobs.c:1050–1054
[48] netbsdsrc/bin/sh/alias.c:164–177

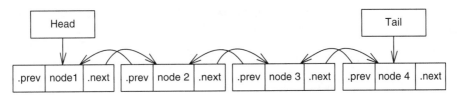

Figure 4.10 A doubly linked list.

```
struct alias *ap, *tmp;
[...]
while (ap) {
    ckfree(ap->name);
    ckfree(ap->val);
    tmp = ap;
    ap = ap->next;
    ckfree(tmp);
}
```

Linked lists come in a number of different flavors; the single linked list we outlined above is by far the most commonly used. One variation involves linking each list element both with its predecessor and its successor. Such a list is called a *doubly linked list* (Figure 4.10). The telltale sign of a doubly linked list is an element pointer titled prev.[49]

```
struct queue {
    struct queue *q_next, *q_prev;
};
```

Two advantages of a doubly linked list are (1) the ability to insert and remove elements at arbitrary list positions without any additional context beyond a pointer to the element where the insertion or removal will take place, and (2) the possibility of traversing the list in a backward direction. Doubly linked lists are often used to implement a *double-ended queue*, also known as a *deque*: a queue in which elements can be added or removed on both ends.

---

[49] netbsdsrc/sys/arch/arm32/arm32/stubs.c:82–84

Traversing a doubly linked list in the backward direction is typically performed using a `for` loop.[50]

```
for (p2 = p2->prev; p2->word[0] != ')'; p2 = p2->prev)
```

The operations for adding and removing elements from a doubly linked list may appear complicated, but you can easily follow them by drawing boxes to represent the elements and arrows to represent the changing pointers. Consider the following code fragment, which adds an `elem` list node after the `head` node.[51]

```
register struct queue *next;

next = head->q_next;
elem->q_next = next;
head->q_next = elem;
elem->q_prev = head;
next->q_prev = elem;
```

The corresponding steps, illustrated in Figure 4.11, clearly demonstrate how the data structure pointers are gradually adjusted to link `elem` into the list. The above example uses the `next` temporary variable to simplify the pointer expressions. In other cases, adjacent list elements are directly expressed by using the `prev` and `next` pointers of the anchor element.[52]

```
ep->prev->next = ep->next;
if (ep->next)
    ep->next->prev = ep->prev;
```

Although such code may initially appear daunting, a bit of reasoning with a pencil and paper will quickly unravel its function (the above example removes element `ep` from the doubly linked list).

Sometimes the last element of a list, instead of containing `NULL`, will point back to the list's first element (Figure 4.12). Such a list is called a *circular list* and is often used for implementing ring buffers or other structures that exhibit wraparound behavior. A circular list cannot be traversed using the `for` sequences we have seen so far since there is no end element to terminate the loop. Instead, you will see that code traversing a circular list, stores in a variable the first element accessed, and loops until that element is reached again.[53]

---

[50] netbsdsrc/bin/csh/parse.c:170
[51] netbsdsrc/sys/arch/arm32/arm32/stubs.c:96–102
[52] netbsdsrc/usr.bin/telnet/commands.c:1735–1747
[53] netbsdsrc/bin/csh/lex.c:187–202

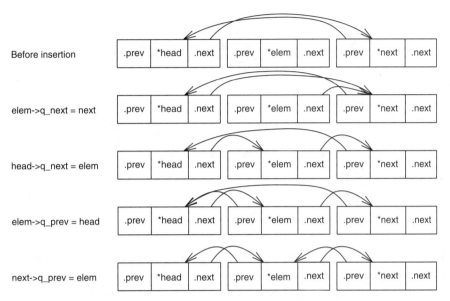

Figure 4.11 Adding an element in a doubly linked list.

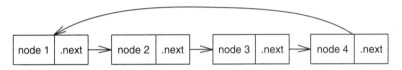

Figure 4.12 A circular linked list.

```
void
prlex(FILE *fp, struct wordent *sp0)
{
    struct wordent *sp = sp0->next;

    for (;;) {
        (void) fprintf(fp, "%s", vis_str(sp->word));
        sp = sp->next;
        if (sp == sp0)
            break;
        if (sp->word[0] != '\n')
            (void) fputc(' ', fp);
    }
}
```

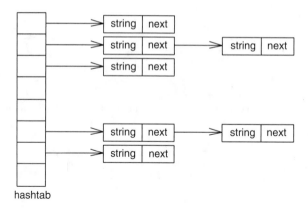

Figure 4.13 A hash table of linked lists.

The above example prints the contents of a circular linked list starting from position sp using sp0 as the loop exit marker.

Linked lists are also used when storing more than one element in a single hash table entry, as illustrated in Figure 4.13. When looking for an element in the map, the hash function efficiently locates which linked list to search for, and a simple list traversal is then used to locate the particular element.[54]

```
struct wlist *
lookup(char *s)
{
    struct wlist *wp;

    for (wp = hashtab[hash(s)]; wp != NULL; wp = wp->next)
        if (*s == *wp->string && strcmp(s, wp->string) == 0)
            return wp;
    return NULL;
}
```

Such a structure offers efficient access to data elements (identifiers) with a modest implementation cost. You will find it often used for constructing symbol tables. (A symbol table is often used in language processors, such as interpreters and compilers, for storing and retrieving the details associated with a particular identifier, for example the type of a given variable name.)

---

[54] netbsdsrc/games/battlestar/parse.c:70–80

Exercise 4.20   Locate five instances of singly and doubly linked lists in the book's CD-ROM and explain the functions they perform.

Exercise 4.21   The following function is called with a pointer to a doubly linked list element.[55]

```
void
_remque(void *v)
{
    register struct queue *elem = v;
    register struct queue *next, *prev;

    next = elem->q_next;
    prev = elem->q_prev;
    next->q_prev = prev;
    prev->q_next = next;
    elem->q_prev = 0;
}
```

By means of a diagram, explain the operation it performs.

4.8 Trees

A number of algorithms and methods of organizing information rely on *trees* as the underlying data structure. The formal definition of a tree states that its nodes are joined by edges in a way that there is exactly one path from each node to the tree's root. The way a tree's nodes expand at each level is often exploited to efficiently organize and process data. Consider that a binary tree 20 levels deep (20 nodes from the lowest level to the root) can hold approximately one million (2^{20}) elements. Many searching,[56] sorting,[57] language processing,[58] graphics,[59] and compression[60] algorithms rely on the tree data structure. In addition, you will find trees used to organize database files,[61] directories,[62] devices,[63] memory hierarchies,[64] properties (consider the Microsoft

---

[55] netbsdsrc/sys/arch/arm32/arm32/stubs.c:109–121
[56] netbsdsrc/games/gomoku/pickmove.c
[57] netbsdsrc/usr.bin/ctags/ctags.c
[58] netbsdsrc/bin/sh/eval.c
[59] XFree86-3.3/xc/programs/Xserver/mi/mivaltree.c
[60] netbsdsrc/lib/libz/infblock.c
[61] netbsdsrc/lib/libc/db/btree
[62] netbsdsrc/usr.bin/find/find.c
[63] netbsdsrc/sys/dev/isapnp/isapnpres.c
[64] XFree86-3.3/xc/programs/Xserver/hw/xfree86/accel/cache/xf86bcache.c

Windows registry and the X Window System default specifications), network routes,[65] document structures,[66] and display elements.[67]

In languages that support pointers (Pascal, C, C++) or object references (Java, C#), trees are typically implemented by linking a parent node with its descendants. This is specified by using a recursive type definition in which a tree is declared to consist of pointers or references to other trees. The following excerpt defines a *binary tree*: each node can have at most two other nodes.[68]

```
typedef struct tree_s {
        tree_t      data;
        struct tree_s   *left, *right;
        short       bal;
    }
    tree;
```

You will find binary tree nodes typically named `left` and `right`, to denote their positions inside the tree. Binary trees are often used to efficiently sort and search through data on which an ordering can be defined. The declaration we examined is used by the Internet name server *named* to organize Internet addresses. The tree is constructed so that nodes with a value greater than the one stored in a given parent node will always be on its right and nodes with lower value on its left. We illustrate an example of such a tree in Figure 4.14.

The recursive definition of the tree data structure lends itself to manipulation by recursive algorithms. As these algorithms are more complicated than the one-liners we saw used for processing linked lists (Section 4.7), they are typically written in the form of a function that takes as a parameter another function specifying the operation to perform on the structure. In languages that support type parameterization, such as Ada, C++, and Eiffel, the same effect is more efficiently achieved by using a template argument. In the case of a binary tree, this external function specifies the ordering to be used by the tree elements. Thus, in our example below, the same tree structure and processing functions are used for binary trees containing IP addresses and trees containing host names. In the former case the comparison function `pfi_compare` compares the integer representation of the IP addresses; in the latter, it compares

---

[65] netbsdsrc/sbin/routed/radix.c
[66] XFree86-3.3/xc/doc/specs/PEX5/PEX5.1/SI/xref.c
[67] XFree86-3.3/xc/programs/Xserver/dix/window.c
[68] netbsdsrc/usr.sbin/named/named/tree.h:34–39

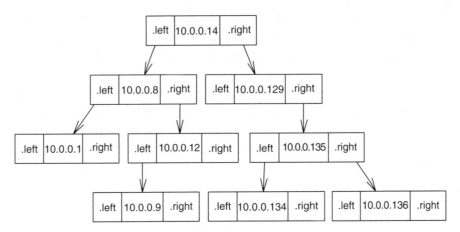

Figure 4.14 A binary tree of name-server Internet addresses.

strings. The function that searches for the element p_user in the tree pointed to by ppr_tree is coded in our case as follows.[69]

```
tree_t
tree_srch(tree **ppr_tree, int (*pfi_compare)(), tree_t p_user)
{
    register int    i_comp;

    ENTER("tree_srch")
    if (*ppr_tree) {
        i_comp = (*pfi_compare)(p_user, (**ppr_tree).data);
        if (i_comp > 0)
            return (tree_srch(&(**ppr_tree).right, pfi_compare, p_user))
        if (i_comp < 0)
            return (tree_srch(&(**ppr_tree).left, pfi_compare, p_user))
        /* not higher, not lower... this must be the one.
         */
        return ((**ppr_tree).data)
    }
    /* grounded. NOT found.
     */
    return (NULL)
}
```

---

[69] netbsdsrc/usr.sbin/named/named/tree.c:98–129

All the function does is compare the element with the current tree element and recursively search the left or right nodes of the tree, or return the node where the element was found. The first if checks for an empty tree, ensuring that the function will terminate.

Another common operation on a tree involves the systematic visiting of all its elements. This *traversal* of the tree is also typically coded in a recursive fashion and often parameterized by using a function, one that specifies the operation to perform on each node. In the following example[70] tree_trav calls the function pfi_uar for every tree node. It works by recursively visiting the left node, calling pfi_uar, and then recursively visiting the right node. As usual, an early check will immediately exit the function when an empty tree is encountered.

```
int
tree_trav(tree **ppr_tree, int (*pfi_uar)())
{
    [...]
    if (!*ppr_tree)
        return (TRUE)
    if (!tree_trav(&(**ppr_tree).left, pfi_uar))
        return (FALSE)
    if (!(*pfi_uar)((**ppr_tree).data))
        return (FALSE)
    if (!tree_trav(&(**ppr_tree).right, pfi_uar))
        return (FALSE)
    return (TRUE)
}
```

We will not provide any code examples for adding and removing elements from a tree because there is simply too much variation in current practice. Implementations range from the nonexistent (many trees are often only grown and never have elements removed from them), to the trivial, to the baroque (involving algorithms that keep trees balanced to preserve algorithm efficiency). Keep in mind that, because trees are in most cases built following specific rules based on the ordering of their elements, modifying an element's data in-place may render a tree invalid. Algorithms operating on such a tree may return incorrect results or further corrupt the tree's order.

A different yet quite common application of trees involves the representation of the syntactic structure of various languages. Many information processing tasks are

---

[70]netbsdsrc/usr.sbin/named/named/tree.c:164–181

formally specified in terms of a *language*. This need not be a full-blown general-purpose programming language. Command-line interfaces, arithmetic expressions, macro languages, configuration files, data interchange standards, and many file formats are often specified and processed using the same standard techniques. A set of elements (*tokens*) is *parsed* to analyze their relationship with each other. This relationship (typically specified by means of a *grammar*) is then represented in the form of a *parse tree*.

To avoid the complication of an example based on an obscure language, we will demonstrate how the *lint* C program verifier stores C expressions in the form of a tree. The tree structure defined for the C expressions is our familiar recursive definition.[71]

```
typedef struct tnode {
    op_t    tn_op;       /* operator */
    [...]
    union {
        struct {
            struct  tnode *_tn_left;    /* (left) operand */
            struct  tnode *_tn_right;   /* right operand */
        } tn_s;
        sym_t   *_tn_sym;   /* symbol if op == NAME */
        val_t   *_tn_val;   /* value if op == CON */
        strg_t  *_tn_strg;  /* string if op == STRING */
    } tn_u;
} tnode_t;
```

Expressions are represented as nodes with the operator stored in `tn_op` and the left and right operands stored in `_tn_left` and `_tn_right`,[72] respectively. Other elements (for example, symbols, constant values, and strings) are pointed to by different tree elements. In contrast to a binary tree, tree nodes are arranged not according to a fixed ordering of the operator values but according to the way expressions appear in the source code parsed by *lint*. Thus the expression[73]

```
kp->flags & F_NEEDARG && !(ip->arg = *++*argvp)
```

will be represented by the parse tree illustrated in Figure 4.15. As you might expect, parse trees are also often processed by using recursive algorithms. They are also often   ⬚

---

[71] netbsdsrc/usr.bin/xlint/lint1/lint1.h:265–280
[72] Note that ANSI C prohibits the use of a leading underscore in user-program identifiers.
[73] netbsdsrc/bin/stty/key.c:135

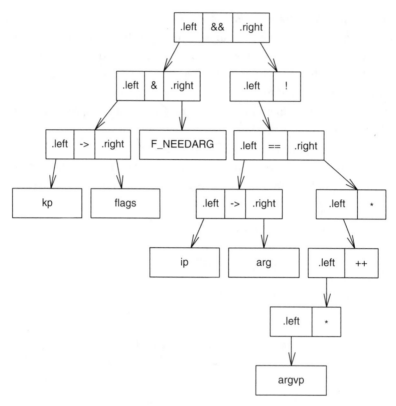

Figure 4.15 Parse tree generated by *lint* for the expression `kp->flags & F_NEEDARG &&`
`!(ip->arg = *++*argvp)`

generated by recursively recognizing parts of the language using a *recursive descent parser*[74] or by means of specialized parser generators[75] like *yacc*.

Exercise 4.22   Draw a binary tree that contains the host names in your e-mail address book. Add the names in a random order, not alphabetically. Systematically walk through the tree to derive a sorted listing of the host names. Construct a new tree, adding the host names in the order they appear in the listing you constructed. Comment on the efficiency of searching data in the two trees.

Exercise 4.23   Read about AVL trees in an algorithm textbook and follow the corresponding operations in one of the implementations found in the book's CD-ROM.

Exercise 4.24   Locate in the book's CD-ROM other cases where parse trees are generated. Draw a representative tree for specific input data.

---

[74] netbsdsrc/bin/expr/expr.c
[75] netbsdsrc/usr.bin/xlint/lint1/cgram.y

4.9 Graphs

A *graph* is defined as a set of *vertices* (or nodes) joined by *edges*. This definition is extremely broad and encompasses data organization structures such as trees (directed graphs with no cycles), sets (graphs with no edges), and linked lists (directed graphs with exactly one edge leading to each vertex). In this section we examine the cases that do not fall in the above categories. Unfortunately, the generality of the graph data structure and the wide variety of requirements of programs that use it conspire to provide us with a bewildering number of options for storing and manipulating graphs. Although it is not possible to discern a small number of "typical" graph data structure patterns, we can analyze any graph data structure by establishing its position on a few design axes. We thus provide answers to the following questions.

- How are nodes stored?
- How are edges represented?
- How are edges stored?
- What are the properties of the graph?
- What separate structures does the "graph" really represent?

We will examine each question in turn.

4.9.1 Node Storage

Algorithms that process a graph need a reliable way to access all nodes. Unlike a linked list or a tree, the nodes of a graph are not necessarily joined together by edges; even when they are, *cycles* within the graph structure may render a systematic traversal that follows the edges difficult to implement. For this reason, an external data structure is often used to store and traverse the graph nodes as a set. The two most common approaches you will encounter involve storing all nodes into an *array* or linking them together as a *linked list*, as is the case in the way nodes are stored in the Unix *tsort* (topological sort) program[76]

```
struc node_str {
    NODE **n_prevp;     /* pointer to previous node's n_next */
    NODE *n_next;       /* next node in graph */
```

---

[76]netbsdsrc/usr.bin/tsort/tsort.c:88–97

```
    NODE **n_arcs;        /* array of arcs to other nodes */
    [...]
    char n_name[1];       /* name of this node */
};
```

In the case above, nodes are linked together in a doubly linked list using the n_prevp and n_next fields. In both the linked list and the array representations, the edge structure is superimposed on the storage structure using one of the methods we will outline in the following subsection. In a few cases you will indeed find the graph node set represented and accessed using the edge connections. In such a case a single node is used as a starting point to traverse all graph nodes. Finally, there are cases where a mixture of the two representation methods or another data structure is used. As an example we will examine the graph structure used in the network packet capture library *libpcap*. This library is used by programs like *tcpdump* to examine the packets flowing on a network. The packets to be captured are specified by using a series of blocks, which are our graph's nodes. To optimize the packet capture specification, the block graph is mapped into a tree-like structure; each level of the tree nodes is represented by a linked list of nodes anchored at a level-dependent position of an array. Each block also contains a linked list of edges arriving into it; edges specify the blocks they link.[77]

```
struct edge {
    int id;
    int code;
    uset edom;
    struct block *succ;
    struct block *pred;
    struct edge *next;  /* link list of incoming edges for a node */
};

struct block {
    int id;
    struct slist *stmts;/* side effect stmts */
    [...]
    struct block *link; /* link field used by optimizer */
    uset dom;
```

---

[77] netbsdsrc/lib/libpcap/gencode.h:96–127

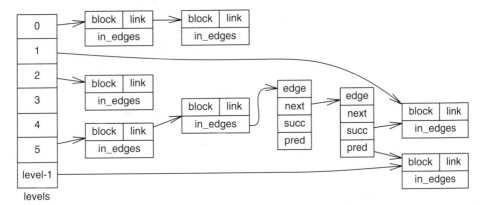

Figure 4.16 Graph nodes accessed through an array of linked lists.

```
    uset closure;
    struct edge *in_edges;
    [...]
};
```

A representative snapshot of the data structure is illustrated in Figure 4.16. In the code example, blocks are linked together in a list using the link field, while the edges for each block are anchored at the in_edges field; these edges are linked in a list through the edge next field, while the blocks they join are specified by the succ and pred fields. Each list of blocks starts from a different element of a levels array. Given this representation, a traversal of all graph nodes is coded as a linked list traversal inside an array loop.[78]

```
struct block **levels;
[...]
    int i;
    struct block *b;
    [...]
    for (i = root->level; i >= 0; --i) {
        for (b = levels[i]; b; b = b->link) {
            SET_INSERT(b->dom, b->id);
```

---

[78] netbsdsrc/lib/libpcap/optimize.c:150,255–273

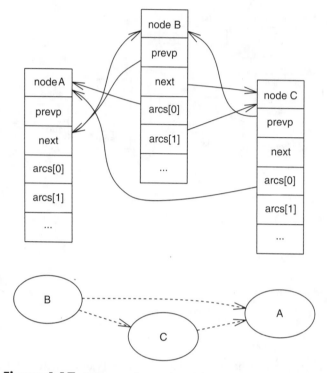

Figure 4.17 A three-node graph and its representation in *tsort*.

4.9.2 Edge Representation

The edges of a graph are typically represented either implicitly through pointers or explicitly as separate structures. In the implicit model, an edge is simply represented as a pointer from one node to another. This is the model used for representing the *tsort* nodes we listed in Section 4.9.1. In each graph node, the array n_arcs contains pointers to the other nodes it connects to. You can see a three-node graph and the way its edges are represented as pointers in Figure 4.17.

In many cases, graph edges are represented explicitly so that additional information can be stored in them. As an example, consider the program *gprof*, used to analyze the runtime behavior of programs. (You can find more details about *gprof*'s operation in Section 10.8.) An important part of this information is a program's *call graph*: the way program functions call each other. This is represented in *gprof* by using a graph; the edges (*arcs* in *gprof* terminology) of the graph are used to store information about other related edges.[79]

---

[79]netbsdsrc/usr.bin/gprof/gprof.h:110–121

```
struct arcstruct {
  struct nl        *arc_parentp;   /* pointer to parent's nl entry */
  struct nl        *arc_childp;    /* pointer to child's nl entry */
  long             arc_count;      /* num calls from parent to child */
  double           arc_time;       /* time inherited along arc */
  double           arc_childtime;  /* childtime inherited along arc */
  struct arcstruct *arc_parentlist;/* parents-of-this-child list */
  struct arcstruct *arc_childlist; /* children-of-this-parent list */
  struct arcstruct *arc_next;      /* list of arcs on cycle */
  unsigned short   arc_cyclecnt;   /* num cycles involved in */
  unsigned short   arc_flags;      /* see below */
};
```

Each arc joins two nodes (represented by a struct nl) to store a *call* relationship from a parent to a child, for example, main calls printf. This relationship is represented by an arc pointing to the respective parent (arc_parentp) and child (arc_childp) nodes. Given an arc, the program needs to find out other arcs that store similar relationships regarding the parent (caller) or the child (callee) of a node. Links to such arcs are stored in the form of a linked list in arc_parentlist and arc_childlist. To illustrate this structure we can examine how a small program fragment will be represented. Consider the following code.[80]

```
int
main(int argc, char **argv)
{
[...]
        usage();
[...]
        fprintf(stderr, "%s\n", asctime(tm));
[...]
    exit(EXIT_SUCCESS);
}

void
usage()
{
    (void) fprintf(stderr, "%s%s%s%s",
        "Usage: at [-q x] [-f file] [-m] time\n", [...]
    exit(EXIT_FAILURE);
}
```

---

[80]netbsdsrc/usr.bin/at

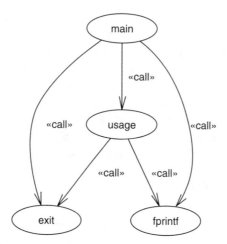

Figure 4.18 A simple call graph.

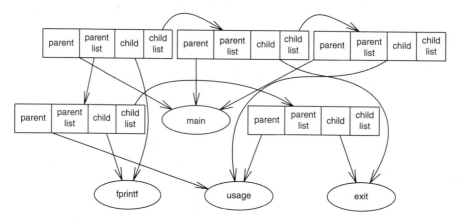

Figure 4.19 A call graph represented as a *gprof* data structure.

The call graph of the above code is illustrated in Figure 4.18; arrows denote a function call. You can see the respective *gprof* data structure in Figure 4.19. Here the arrows are represented using the `parent` and `child` fields of `arcstruct` records; the records are also linked together into lists denoting parents and children of the same children and parents. To simplify our presentation we have not discussed the pointers from the nodes to the edges. If you—justifiably—feel intimidated by this level of complexity, try to follow a couple of caller-callee relationships and one of the arc linked lists on the graph we illustrate. In addition, consider that the data structure we examined stresses, in our opinion, the limits of a complicated structure a human brain can comprehend as a whole. More complex structures should be, and typically are, broken down into separate entities, each of which stands or falls on its own.

4.9.3 Edge Storage

Graph edges are typically stored by using two different methods: as an array inside each node structure (as was the case in the *tsort* example illustrated in Figure 4.17) or as a linked list anchored at each graph node. Since in most cases a graph changes its structure over its lifetime, this array is dynamically allocated and used via a pointer stored at the node. We can study graph edges stored as a linked list anchored at the node by considering the way the *make* program stores element dependencies.

Examine again the full definition of a node used by the *make* program. Each node (typically part of a program build configuration) depends on other nodes (its children) and is used to build other nodes (its parents). Both are stored as linked lists inside the node structure.[81]

```
typedef struct GNode {
    [...]
    Lst        parents;    /* Nodes that depend on this one */
    Lst        children;   /* Nodes on which this one depends */
    [...]
} GNode;
```

Now consider the dependencies represented by the following simple Makefile (*make* program build specification) used for compiling the *patch* program under Windows NT.[82]

```
OBJS = [...] util.obj version.obj
HDRS = EXTERN.h INTERN.h [...]

patch.exe: $(OBJS)
    $(CC) $(OBJS) $(LIBS) -o $@ $(LDFLAGS)

util.obj: $(HDRS)
version.obj: $(HDRS)
```

---

[81] netbsdsrc/usr.bin/make/make.h:112–165
[82] XFree86-3.3/xc/util/patch/Makefile.nt:15–40

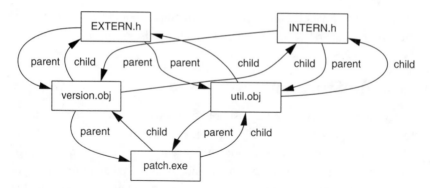

Figure 4.20 Program dependencies represented by a Makefile.

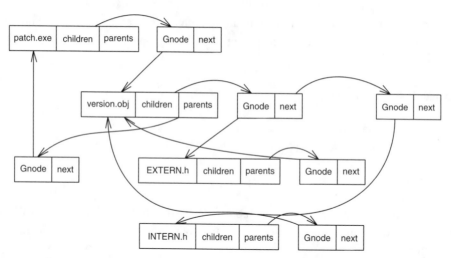

Figure 4.21 Program dependencies represented in a *make* data structure.

The dependencies represented by the Makefile (patch.exe depends on util.obj, util.obj depends on EXTERN.h, and so on) are depicted in Figure 4.20. The respective data structure generated by *make* contains for each node a list of its children (version.obj is a child of patch.exe) and a list of its parents (EXTERN.h and INTERN.h are parents of version.obj). Both relationships are represented in the data structure. As you can see in Figure 4.21, each element of the linked list contains a Gnode pointer, used to denote a node that has a particular relationship (parent or child) with a given node, and a next pointer, used to link to other edges having the same relationship.

4.9.4 Graph Properties

Some graph properties are important for more reasons than passing "Data Structures 101" exams: they guide us on how to read graph-related code. In a *directional* graph, edges (often called *arcs* in this case) are associated with a direction from one edge to another. This property affects the way graph elements are represented, added, and processed. In a nondirectional graph (when the nodes across an edge are not associated with a direction or attribute), the data representation should treat both nodes as equal (perhaps by storing edges for both directions), and processing code should similarly not discriminate edges based on their direction.

In a *connected* graph, there is always a path from one node to another, while in a graph containing a *cycle*, there is more than one path joining two nodes. Both properties affect the way a graph is traversed. On nonconnected graphs, traversal code should be coded so as to bridge isolated subgraphs. When dealing with graphs that contain cycles, traversal code should be coded so as to avoid looping while following a graph cycle. The avoidance of cycles is typically implemented by marking nodes visited and avoiding a subsequent visit.[83]

```
/*
 * avoid infinite loops and ignore portions of the graph known
 * to be acyclic
 */
if (from->n_flags & (NF_NODEST|NF_MARK|NF_ACYCLIC))
    return (0);
from->n_flags |= NF_MARK;
```

4.9.5 Hidden Structures

Many so-called "graph" data structures are sometimes more complicated than their names suggest. Since there is no concrete abstract data type or established practice for representing a graph, often a single data structure is used to represent a number of different entities superimposed on each other. A telltale sign for such a case is the maintenance of multiple edge structures. Consider again the full definition of a node used by the *make* program.[84]

---

[83] netbsdsrc/usr.bin/tsort/tsort.c:397–403
[84] netbsdsrc/usr.bin/make/make.h:112–165

```
typedef struct GNode {
    [...]
    Lst    cohorts;    /* Other nodes for the :: operator */
    Lst    parents;    /* Nodes that depend on this one */
    Lst    children;   /* Nodes on which this one depends */
    Lst    successors; /* Nodes that must be made after this one */
    Lst    preds;      /* Nodes that must be made before this one */
    [...]
} GNode;
```

It is logical to have a node contain `parent` and `children` Gnode linked lists to represent dependence relationships in two directions. However, we see that each node of this graph also contains lists of `successors`, `preds`, and, aptly named, `cohorts`! Clearly, inside this node dependency graph, there is another graph struggling to get our attention.

4.9.6 Other Representations

Graph representations different from the ones we examined surely exist. In the computer science literature, for example, you will find graphs represented using a two-dimensional array. Array element $A(m, n)$ represents an edge from the vertex m to vertex n. You will rarely encounter such a representation in a production program; probably the difficulty of dynamically resizing two-dimensional arrays makes this representation less than ideal.

Exercise 4.25   Locate in the book's CD-ROM or in your environment three code instances using a graph structure. Explain how nodes and edges are stored and represented, outline the graph's important properties, and draw a diagram illustrating how the graph structure is organized.

Further Reading

The canonical reference for the material we have discussed is Knuth's *The Art of Computer Programming* series, and in particular Chapter 2 in Volume 1 [Knu97] dealing with information structures and Chapter 6 in Volume 3 [Knu98] discussing searching techniques such as hashing. The performance of the structures we examined, from a theoretical point of view, is presented in Aho et al. [AHU74], while concrete algorithms in C can be found in Sedgewick [Sed97, Sed01]. Keep in mind that theoretical predictions of data structure efficiency do not always match practice. As an example, it has been found that a hashed data structure or a simple binary tree are in practice often more efficient than more sophisticated self-balancing tree structures [WZH01].

Buffer overflow attacks are a constant theme in system exploitations. An early such attack was the 1988 Internet Worm [ER89, Spa89]. A number of compile-time, runtime, and library-based defense methods have been developed to avoid buffer overflow problems; one recent such approach is described in Baratloo et al. [BTS00]. Asymmetric ranges and how they help avoid off-by-one errors are eloquently described in Koenig [Koe88, pp. 36–46].

You may sometimes encounter a static hash-based map without any collisions or wasted space. The hash function used for generating this map is called a *perfect hash function*. Such functions are sometimes created by hand by dedicated, creative, or bored programmers; they can also be automatically created by using the *gperf* program [Sch90].

Advanced Control Flow

It is necessary for technical reasons that these warheads be stored upside down, that is, with the top at the bottom and the bottom at the top. In order that there may be no doubt as to which is the bottom and which is the top, it will be seen to it that the bottom of each warhead immediately be labeled with the word TOP.

—British Admiralty Regulation

In Chapter 2 we examined a number of statements that influence the control flow of a program's instruction sequence. Although the control statements we described suffice for most common programming tasks and are the ones you will most often encounter, some less common elements are nevertheless important for a number of applications. *Recursive code* often mirrors data structures or algorithms with a similar definition. *Exceptions* are used in C++ and Java to streamline error handling. By using software or hardware *parallelism*, programs can enhance responsiveness, structure work allocation, or effectively use computers with multiple processors. When parallelism facilities are not available, programs may have to resort to the use of *asynchronous signals* (signals that can be delivered at any arbitrary point of time) and *nonlocal jumps* to respond to external events. Finally, in the name of efficiency, programmers sometimes use the *macro substitution* facilities of the C preprocessor in the place of the usual C function call mechanism.

5.1 Recursion

A number of data structures such as trees and the heap, operations such as type inference and unification, mathematical entities such as the Fibonacci numbers and fractal graphs, and algorithms such as quicksort, tree traversals, and recursive descent parsing are defined recursively. A *recursive definition* of an entity or an operation defines its object in terms of itself. Such definitions are not infinitely circular, as they may initially appear, because a *base case definition* typically defines a special case that does not depend on a recursive definition. As an example, although the factorial of an integer n, $n!$, can be defined as $n(n-1)$, we also define a base case as $0! = 1$.

Recursively defined algorithms and data structures are often implemented by using recursive function definitions. Although recursive function calls are just a special case of the function call we examined in Section 2.2, the way they are coded and the way they should be read are sufficiently different to merit special treatment.

Consider the task of parsing shell commands. The command structure supported by the Unix Bourne shell is quite sophisticated. A representative part of the shell command grammar is outlined in Figure 5.1; a command type appearing before a colon is defined by one of the rules following in the indented lines. Notice how many

simple-command:

> *item*
> *simple-command item*

command:

> *simple-command*
> (*command-list*)
> { *command-list* }
> for *name* do *command-list* done
> for *name* in *word* ... do *command-list* done
> while *command-list* do *command-list* done
> until *command-list* do *command-list* done
> case *word* in *case-part* ... esac
> if *command-list* then *command-list* else *else-part* fi

pipeline:

> *command*
> *pipeline* | *command*

andor:

> *pipeline*
> *andor* && *pipeline*
> *andor* || *pipeline*

command-list:

> *andor*
> *command-list* ;
> *command-list* &
> *command-list* ; *andor*
> *command-list* & *andor*

Figure 5.1 Bourne shell command grammar.

commands are in more than one way recursively defined: a *pipeline* can be a *command*, or a *pipeline* followed by the pipe symbol (|), followed by a *command*; or a *command* can be a parentheses-enclosed *command-list*, which can be an *andor*, which can be a *pipeline*, which can again be a *command*. Given such a grammar we typically want to recognize commands, store them in a suitable data structure, and process the data structure. Recursion is a key tool for all these tasks.

Individual shell commands are stored internally as a tree. Since various command types can alternatively consist of different elements, all tree nodes are represented by using a union of all possible elements.[1,2]

```c
union node {
        int type;
        struct nbinary nbinary;
        struct ncmd ncmd;
        struct npipe npipe;
        struct nif nif;
        struct nfor nfor;
        struct ncase ncase;
        struct nclist nclist;
        [...]
};
```

Each element type is recursively defined as a structure containing pointers to command tree nodes appropriate for the given type.

```c
struct nif {
        int type;
        union node *test;
        union node *ifpart;
        union node *elsepart;
};
```

Note that in the above code the union and the corresponding struct share the common int type element. In this way the individual structures can access the union's type field by using the corresponding struct's field with the same name. This is not a particularly good programming practice since the layout correspondence between the fields of the struct and the union is manually maintained by the programmer and never verified by the compiler or the runtime system. Should one of the layouts

---

[1] netbsdsrc/bin/sh/nodetypes; used as an input file to automatically generate node definitions.
[2] Notice how the same name is being used both as a structure tag and as a union member.

```
STATIC void
cmdtxt(union node *n)
{
        union node *np;
        struct nodelist *lp;

        if (n == NULL)                          1 Base case: empty command; return
            return;
        switch (n->type) {
                                                4 command1 ; command2
        case NSEMI:
            cmdtxt(n->nbinary.ch1);             2 Recursively print first command
            cmdputs("; ");
            cmdtxt(n->nbinary.ch2);             3 Recursively print second command
            break;

                                                4 command1 && command2
        case NAND:
            cmdtxt(n->nbinary.ch1);
            cmdputs(" && ");
            cmdtxt(n->nbinary.ch2);
            break;

        /* ... */
                                                4 Command pipeline
        case NPIPE:
            for (lp = n->npipe.cmdlist ; lp ; lp = lp->next) {   5 Recursively print each command
                cmdtxt(lp->n);
                if (lp->next)
                    cmdputs(" | ");
            }
            break;

        /* ... */
        }
}
```

Figure 5.2 Recursively printing the parsed command tree.

change, the program will still compile and run but may fail in unpredictable ways. In addition, according to our interpretation of the C standard, the correlation between the two layouts is guaranteed to hold only for dereferencing via a pointer the first element of a structure.

Figure 5.2[3] is the code used to print the Unix shell command(s) executing in the background as a response to the shell *jobs* built-in command. The cmdtxt function has as its only argument a pointer to the command tree that is to be displayed. The first test inside the cmdtxt function (Figure 5.2:1) is crucial: it ensures that commands represented by a NULL pointer (for example, an empty else part in an if command) are correctly handled. Notice that the handling of empty commands does not involve recursion; the cmdtxt function simply returns. Since commands are represented as a tree and all the trees leaves (terminal nodes) are NULL, recursive descends of tree branches will eventually reach a leaf and terminate. This *base case test* and its nonrecursive definition guarantees that the recursive function will eventually terminate. Informal

---

[3] netbsdsrc/bin/sh/jobs.c:959–1082

arguments such as the above are an important tool for understanding code involving recursion. Once we understand how a function defined in terms of itself can work, the rest of its code falls easily into place. A case for each different nonempty command (tree node) type (Figure 5.2:4) prints the command based on its constituent parts. As an example, a semicolon-separated command list is displayed by printing the first command of the list (Figure 5.2:2), a semicolon, and the second command (Figure 5.2:3).

The recursive grammar definition we saw in Figure 5.1 also lends itself for parsing by using a series of functions that follow the grammar's structure—a *recursive descent parser*. This approach is often used when parsing relatively simple structures such as command- or domain-specific languages, expressions, or text-based data files. Figure 5.3[4] contains representative elements of the code used for parsing shell commands. Notice the symmetry between the parsing code and the grammar; it extends even to the naming of identifiers, although the specific parser was written by Kenneth Almquist at least ten years after Stephen Bourne implemented the original shell and documented its grammar. The structure of the recursive descent parser is remarkably simple. Each function is responsible for parsing a specific grammar element (a command list, an andor command, a pipeline, or a simple command) and for returning a node consisting of that element. All functions work by calling other functions to parse the grammar elements that make up the given command and the `readtoken()` function to read plain tokens such as `if` and `while`.

The functions that print command nodes and parse commands are not strictly recursive since no statement in the function body directly calls the function that contains it. However, the functions call other functions, which call other functions, which may call the original functions. This type of recursion is called *mutual recursion*. Although code based on it may appear more difficult to understand than simple recursive functions, one can easily reason about it by considering the recursive definition of the underlying concept.

When all recursive calls to a function occur exactly before the function's return points, we say that the function is *tail recursive*. Tail recursion is an important concept because the compiler can optimize these calls into simple jumps, thus saving the function call time and memory overhead. Tail-recursive calls are equivalent to a loop going back to the beginning of the function. You will sometimes see tail-recursive calls used instead of conventional loops, a `goto`, or a `continue` statement. The code in Figure 5.4[5] is a representative example. The object is to locate a server (termed

[4]netbsdsrc/bin/sh/jobs.c:157–513
[5]netbsdsrc/games/hunt/hunt/hunt.c:553–619

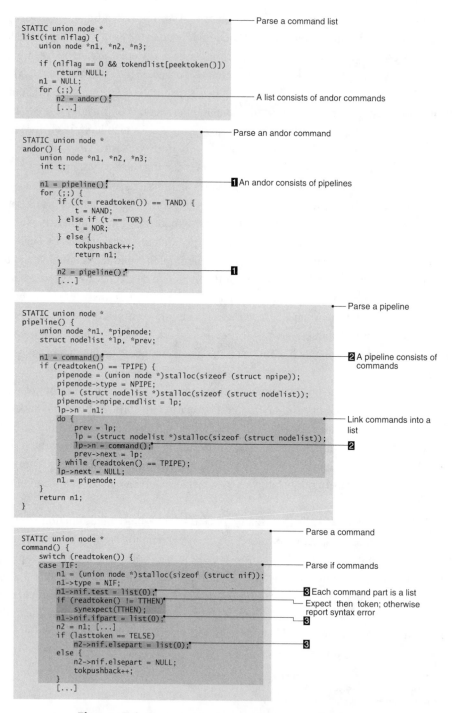

```
                                               ●────── Parse a command list
STATIC union node *
list(int nlflag) {
    union node *n1, *n2, *n3;

    if (nlflag == 0 && tokendlist[peektoken()])
        return NULL;
    n1 = NULL;
    for (;;) {
        n2 = andor();●────────────── A list consists of andor commands
        [...]
```

```
                                               ●────── Parse an andor command
STATIC union node *
andor() {
    union node *n1, *n2, *n3;
    int t;

    n1 = pipeline();●──────────────■ An andor consists of pipelines
    for (;;) {
        if ((t = readtoken()) == TAND) {
            t = NAND;
        } else if (t == TOR) {
            t = NOR;
        } else {
            tokpushback++;
            return n1;
        }
        n2 = pipeline();●────────■
        [...]
```

```
                                                    ●────── Parse a pipeline
STATIC union node *
pipeline() {
    union node *n1, *pipenode;
    struct nodelist *lp, *prev;

    n1 = command();●──────────────────────────────■ A pipeline consists of
    if (readtoken() == TPIPE) {                      commands
        pipenode = (union node *)stalloc(sizeof (struct npipe));
        pipenode->type = NPIPE;
        lp = (struct nodelist *)stalloc(sizeof (struct nodelist));
        pipenode->npipe.cmdlist = lp;
        lp->n = n1;
        do {                                       ●────── Link commands into a
            prev = lp;                                     list
            lp = (struct nodelist *)stalloc(sizeof (struct nodelist));
            lp->n = command();●────────────────────■
            prev->next = lp;
        } while (readtoken() == TPIPE);
        lp->next = NULL;
        n1 = pipenode;
    }
    return n1;
}
```

```
                                                    ●────── Parse a command
STATIC union node *
command() {
    switch (readtoken()) {
    case TIF:                                       ●────── Parse if commands
        n1 = (union node *)stalloc(sizeof (struct nif));
        n1->type = NIF;
        n1->nif.test = list(0);●──────────────■ Each command part is a list
        if (readtoken() != TTHEN)●─────────────── Expect then token; otherwise
            synexpect(TTHEN);                       report syntax error
        n1->nif.ifpart = list(0);●────────────■
        n2 = n1; [...]
        if (lasttoken == TELSE)
            n2->nif.elsepart = list(0);●──────────────■
        else {
            n2->nif.elsepart = NULL;
            tokpushback++;
        }
        [...]
```

Figure 5.3 Recursive descent parser for shell commands.

```
void
find_driver(FLAG do_startup)
{
    SOCKET    *hosts;

    hosts = list_drivers();                     Locate a driver
    if (hosts[0].sin_port != htons(0)) {
        int    i, c;
                                                 Exactly one driver found; use it and return
        if (hosts[1].sin_port == htons(0)) {
            Daemon = hosts[0];
            return;
        }

        /* go thru list and return host that matches daemon */
                                                 More than one driver found; have the
        [...]                                    user select the driver and return
        Daemon = hosts[c];
        clear_the_screen();
        return;

    }
    if (!do_startup)                             Startup already tried; fail
        return;
                                                 Attempt to start-up a new driver and retry
    start_driver();
    sleep(2);
    find_driver(FALSE);

}
```

Figure 5.4 Tail recursion used instead of a loop.

driver in the source code) for the multiuser game *hunt*. If no server is found, the code attempts to launch a new server, waits for the server to register, and performs the server location procedure again using a tail-recursive call.

Exercise 5.1 The informal argument we used to reason about the termination of the cmdtxt function is just that: an informal argument. Provide an example of a data structure that could cause cmdtxt to enter an infinite recursive loop. What additional guarantees are needed to prevent this from happening?

Exercise 5.2 Based on the example provided in Section 10.5, construct a simple tool to locate recursive function definitions. Run it on the provided source code and reason about the workings of three different recursive functions.

Exercise 5.3 Construct the grammar accepted by the *expr* command based on the recursive descent parser it uses to evaluate expressions.[6]

Exercise 5.4 Examine whether your compiler optimizes tail recursion by inspecting the generated symbolic code for a trivial tail-recursive example. Do not forget to specify through a compiler switch the highest level of optimization.

---

[6] netbsdsrc/bin/expr/expr.c:240–525

```
public void remove(String id) throws IOException {          ❶ Exceptions generated by this function
    Connection _conn = getConnection();
    String removeSql = "DELETE FROM "+sessionTable+" WHERE "+
        sessionIdCol+" = ?"; [...]
    try {
                                                             ❷ Catch exceptions for these statements
        if(preparedRemoveSql == null)
            [...]
        preparedRemoveSql.setString(1, id);
        preparedRemoveSql.execute();

    } catch(SQLException e) {                                Type of exception to catch
        log(sm.getString(getStoreName()+".SQLException", e));  ❸ Code to execute when an
    } finally {                                                    exception occurs
        release(_conn);           ❹ Code always executed after the try block
        _conn = null;
    }
    if (debug > 0)           This code is executed unless an IOException is raised
        log([...]);
}
```

Figure 5.5 Exception handling in Java.

5.2 Exceptions

An *exception* mechanism allows programmers to isolate the handling of errors from the code's normal flow of control. You will encounter similar constructs in both C++ and Java programs; some of the errors handled in these languages via exceptions are reported to C programs by signals (examined in Section 5.4). Error handling that uses exceptions differs from C signal-based code in that exceptions, being part of the language (rather than a library facility), propagate along the program's lexical and function or method call stack, allowing the programmer to process them in a structured manner.

Java exception-handling code can consist of:

- A series of statements for which exceptions are to be caught inside a `try` block (Figure 5.5:2)[7]

- Zero or more `catch` clauses, to be matched when an exception occurs (Figure 5.5:3)

- An optional `finally` clause block, which is always executed after the `try` block (Figure 5.5:4)

Java exceptions are objects generated by subclasses of the `java.lang.Throwable` class, which has two standard subclasses: `java.lang.Error` (mostly used to indicate nonrecoverable errors) and `java.lang.Exception` (used to indicate conditions that

---

[7]jt4/catalina/src/share/org/apache/catalina/session/JDBCStore.java:572–595

can be caught and recovered from). You will find many cases where new exception classes are defined by subclassing the above.[8]

```
public final class LifecycleException extends Exception {
```

Exceptions are generated either explicitly in response to an error condition[9]

```
public void addChild(Container child) { [...]
    if (children.get(child.getName()) != null)
        throw new IllegalArgumentException(
"addChild:  Child name '" + child.getName() + "' is not unique");
```

or implicitly as a result of calling a method that triggers an exception. In both cases, if the expression generated is not a subclass of (the ubiquitously generated) `Error` or `RuntimeException` exceptions, the method must declare the exception via a `throws` clause (Figure 5.5:1). An example of an exception that is implicitly generated is the `IOException` in Figure 5.5. You can easily locate the methods that might throw an implicitly generated exception by running the Java compiler on the class source after removing the `throws` clause from the method definition.

If an exception is not caught inside the method in which it is thrown, it will propagate upward the method call stack to its caller, to its caller's caller, and so on, until it is caught. In the code in Figure 5.6, the `LifecycleException` thrown inside the `validatePackages` method[10] is not caught when called by the `start` method[11] but is finally caught when `start` is called by the `ContainerBase setLoader` method.[12] Uncaught exceptions terminate the program with a diagnostic message and a stack trace. This behavior will confound the unwary user with an obscure error report, so you should verify that programs check and gracefully handle all generated exceptions.

Sometimes you will see empty `catch` clauses.[13]

```
try {
    [...]
} catch (MalformedURLException e) {
} catch (IOException e) {
}
```

---

[8] jt4/catalina/src/share/org/apache/catalina/LifecycleException.java:77
[9] jt4/catalina/src/share/org/apache/catalina/core/ContainerBase.java:775–781
[10] jt4/catalina/src/share/org/apache/catalina/loader/StandardLoader.java:1273–1268
[11] jt4/catalina/src/share/org/apache/catalina/loader/StandardLoader.java:583–666
[12] jt4/catalina/src/share/org/apache/catalina/core/ContainerBase.java:345–378
[13] jt4/catalina/src/share/org/apache/catalina/loader/StandardLoader.java:1028–1044

```
public final class StandardLoader [...] { [...]
    private void validatePackages() throws LifecycleException {
    [...]

        if (!found)
            throw new LifecycleException                    ●———— Throw exception
                ("Missing optional package " + required[i]);

        [...]
    } [...]
}

    public void start() throws LifecycleException {
        [...]
        validatePackages();●———— Exception can be generated, but is not caught
        [...]
    } [...]
}

public abstract class ContainerBase [...] { [...]
    public synchronized void setLoader(Loader loader) { [...]
        if (started && (loader != null) &&
            (loader instanceof Lifecycle)) {
                                                        ●——— Exception is caught here
            try {
                ((Lifecycle) loader).start();
            } catch (LifecycleException e) {
                log("ContainerBase.setLoader: start: ", e);
            }

        }
    } [...]
}
```

Figure 5.6 Exception propagation across method calls.

Empty `catch` clauses are used to ignore exceptions, presumably because they are unimportant for the code being executed, as illustrated by the following comment.[14]

```
} catch (NamingException e) {
    // Silent catch: it's valid that no /WEB-INF/lib directory
    //exists
}
```

You may also encounter `finally` clauses used without any corresponding `catch` clauses. These are in most cases used to specify some processing that will occur once the `try` clause has exited, either by the code reaching its end or through a `return` or a (labeled) `break` or `continue` statement. As an example, in the following code

---

[14]jt4/catalina/src/share/org/apache/catalina/startup/ContextConfig.java:1065–1068

the reset(mark) call will always be executed—even in the case where the flow of
control reaches the return values statement.[15]

```
try {
    if ( nextChar() == '>' )
      return values;
} finally {
    reset(mark);
}
```

Thus the code can be read as:

```
if ( nextChar() == '>' ) {
  reset(mark);
  return values;
}
reset(mark);
```

You will often also see a finally clause used to clean up acquired resources
such as file descriptors, connections, locks, and temporary objects. In the following
code excerpt the Connection conn will be closed no matter what happens inside the
28 lines of the try block.[16]

```
conn = getConnection();
try {
    [...]
} catch ( SQLException e ) {
    transformer.getTheLogger().error("Caught a SQLException", e);
    throw e;
} finally {
    conn.close();
    conn = null;
}
```

The handling of exceptions in C++ is very similar to that of Java, with the following
differences.

---

[15]jt4/jasper/src/share/org/apache/jasper/compiler/JspReader.java:606–611
[16]cocoon/src/java/org/apache/cocoon/transformation/SQLTransformer.java:978–1015

- Exception objects can be of any type.
- There is no provision for a `finally` clause.
- Local object destructors get called as the stack unwinds.
- Functions declare thrown exceptions by using the declarator `throw` instead of the Java `throws` clause.

Exercise 5.5 Locate a C++ or Java function calling sequence that signals errors through exceptions, and rewrite it so that it does not rely on them by modifying the function return values. Compare the readability of the two approaches.

Exercise 5.6 Compile a Java method after removing its `throws` clause to find the methods generating the thrown exception. Repeat this procedure for the exception-throwing methods, drawing in the process an expression propagation tree.

Exercise 5.7 The tape-handling code of the BSD backup restore program[17] has numerous cases where system calls are explicitly checked against the `-1` return value that indicates failure. Sketch how parts of the code could be rewritten in C++ using exceptions.

5.3 Parallelism

Some programs execute part of their code in parallel to enhance responsiveness to their environment, to structure work allocation, or to effectively use multiple computers or computers with multiple processors. The design and implementation of such programs is an ongoing research area; you are therefore likely to come across many different abstractions and programming models. In this section we examine some representative examples of commonly encountered work distribution models, eschewing more exotic implementations such as those involving fine-grained parallel or vector computation operations. The ability to execute operations in parallel can be exposed at the hardware or the software layer.

5.3.1 Hardware and Software Parallelism

At the hardware layer some types of parallelism you are likely to encounter include the following.

The Operation of Multiple Execution Units within a Processor Unless you are working on a compiler or an assembler, you will deal with these only when

---

[17] netbsdsrc/sbin/restore/tape.c

reading or writing symbolic code for processor architectures that place the burden of instruction synchronization on the programmer.

Intelligent Integrated or External Peripherals Modern peripherals such as disk and tape drives, graphics and network adapters, modems, and printers have their own processors and execute high-level commands (for example, write a disk track, render a polygon) in parallel with the computer's main processor. Code for these devices is isolated and abstracted by the operating system and device drivers.

Hardware Support for Multitasking Most modern processors include a number of features such as interrupts and memory management hardware that allow operating systems to schedule multiple tasks in a way that provides the illusion that they are executing in parallel. The code implementing this functionality is part of the operating system, while two common software abstractions we will examine, the *process* and the *thread*, are used to encapsulate the tasks executing in parallel.

Machines with Multiple Processors These are becoming commonplace, and therefore software implementations are pressured to use the available computing power. Here again, processes and threads are typically used to help the underlying operating system distribute work among the processors. By using the same abstractions for single processor multitasking and multiprocessor environments, we achieve code portability across the two different classes of hardware architectures.

Coarse-Grained Distributed Models Networked computers are increasingly used in parallel to solve problems requiring substantial computing resources or to provide increased performance or reliability. Typical applications include scientific computations (such as the factoring of large numbers or the search for extraterrestrial intelligence) and the operation of centralized e-business infrastructure based on multiple servers. Code for such systems either relies on existing clustering operating systems, middleware, or application programs or is custom-written based on networking primitives.

At the software level the models used for representing code that executes, or appears to execute, in parallel are the following.

The Process A process is an operating system abstraction representing a single instance of an executing program. Operating systems use the underlying hardware to switch between processes offering more efficient hardware utilization, a structuring mechanism for complicated systems, and a flexible and responsive execution environment. The creation, termination, and switching between processes are relatively expensive events; therefore processes tend to be allocated large chunks of work. Communication and synchronization between processes is handled by various mechanisms provided by the operating system such as shared memory objects, semaphores, and pipes.

The Thread   A single process can consist of many threads: flows of control operating in parallel. Threads can be implemented at the user level or be natively supported by the operating system. All threads in a process share a number of resources, most importantly the global memory; therefore thread creation, termination, and switching are lightweight events and threads are often allocated many small chunks of work. Communication between threads often occurs by using the process's global memory, with synchronization primitives, such as mutual exclusion functions, used to maintain consistency.

Ad Hoc Models   For various real or imaginary reasons having to do with the availability of the two abstractions we described above, maintainability, efficiency, or plain ignorance, some programs implement their own support for real or virtual parallel execution. Such programs rely on underlying primitives such as interrupts, asynchronous signals, polling, nonlocal jumps, and architecture-dependent stack manipulations. We will examine some of these primitives in Sections 5.4 and 5.5. A typical example of such code is the operating system kernel, which often provides the underlying support for processes and threads.

Many operating systems will distribute processes or threads across multiple processors. For this reason code using multiprocessor machines is often structured around processes or threads.

5.3.2 Control Models

You will find that code using parallelism is typically structured around three different models:

1. The *work crew model*, where a set of similar tasks operate in parallel
2. The *boss/worker model*, where a boss task distributes work among workers

```
main(int argc, char **argv)
{
    [...]
    /* start all but one here */
    for (i=1; i<nthreads; i++) {
        closure = (struct closure *) xalloc(sizeof(struct closure));
        xthread_fork(do_ico_window, closure);              └─ Start a thread for each window
    }
    [...]
                                       •─────────────────────────── Function executed for each thread
void * do_ico_window(closure)
    struct closure *closure;
{
```

Figure 5.7 Work crew multithreaded code.

3. The *pipeline model*, where a series of tasks operate on the data and pass it to
   the next task

We will examine each model in detail in the following paragraphs.

The *work crew model* is used for performing similar operations in parallel by
allocating them to a number of tasks. Each task executes the same code as the others,
often differing only in the work allocated to it. The work crew parallelism model is
employed to distribute work among processors or to create a pool of tasks to be used for
allocating standardized chunks of incoming work. As an example, many Web server
implementations allocate a work crew of processes or threads to deal with incoming
HTTP requests. Figure 5.7 shows a typical instance of work crew code.[18] The program
draws bouncing shapes in multiple windows. Each window is handled by a different
thread that executes the do_ico_window function. Since all threads share the same
global memory pool, the thread creation code allocates the closure memory area
for storing private thread information. Although you are likely to encounter a large
number of interfaces for managing threads, most of them start threads in a way similar
to the one in the example: the thread start-up function specifies the function to execute
and a parameter that will be passed to the function instance of the specific thread. The
parameter typically points to a memory area used for storing thread-specific data or
for passing information unique to the specific thread created.

The *boss/worker* model—more imaginatively known as the *master/slave* model—
has one task, the boss, allocating different chunks of work to worker tasks it creates
when needed. This technique is typically used when a boss thread receives commands
from the user and, to maintain responsiveness, fires off a worker thread to deal with
each new task. Application programs often delegate operations that can block or take
long to complete, such as saving or printing, to separate threads to continue processing

---

[18]XFree86-3.3/contrib/programs/ico/ico.c:227–369

```
param = (XAmChanDesc **) xalloc(sizeof(XAmChanDesc *));        ──────── Allocate and set private
*param = chandesc;                                                       reader thread memory
result = thread_newthread(XAmReaderThread, THREAD_STACK_SIZE,  ──────── Start TCP/IP reader thread
                    (char *)param, sizeof(XAmChanDesc *));
[...]
if (thread_newthread(TcpIpReaderThread, MAXBUFSIZE + CONNECTOR_STACK,   ──────── Start TCP/IP connection
                 (char *)param, sizeof(XAmChanDesc *)) == 0) {                   threads
   Error(("TCPconn refused: Cannot start reader thread\n"));
[...]
if (thread_newthread(AmConnectorThread,                        ──────── Start native Amoeba service
                 CONNECTOR_STACK, 0, 0) <= 0) {                         threads
   Fatal(("Cannot start Amoeba connector thread\n"));
}
[...]
if (thread_newthread(AmTCPConnectorThread,                     ──────── Start TCP/IP service threads
                 CONNECTOR_STACK, 0, 0) <= 0)
   Fatal(("Cannot start TCP connector thread\n"));
```

Figure 5.8 Boss/worker multithreaded code.

```
                                         ──────── Shared global resource
static XrmQuark nextUniq = -1;     /* next quark from XrmUniqueQuark */
[...]
XrmQuark XrmUniqueQuark()
{
    XrmQuark q;

    _XLockMutex(_Xglobal_lock);          ──────── Lock access
                                         ──────── Access shared resources
    if (nextUniq == nextQuark)
    q = NULLQUARK;
    else
    q = nextUniq--;                             ■
    _XUnlockMutex(_Xglobal_lock);        ──────── Unlock access
    return q;
}
```

Figure 5.9 A code block protected by mutual exclusion locks.

user commands. The code in Figure 5.8[19] creates no less than four different threads for managing the connections between an X Window System server and its clients under the *Amoeba* distributed operating system environment.

An important issue when working with multiple threads or processes concerns the handling of shared resources. The issue is most prevalent in multithreaded programs because these share all their global memory. The function XrmUniqueQuark in Figure 5.9[20] returns a unique integer by decrementing the global counter nextUniq. However, if one thread assigns to q the current nextUniq value (Figure 5.9:1), and

---

[19]XFree86-3.3/xc/lib/xtrans/Xtransam.c:495–1397
[20]XFree86-3.3/xc/lib/X11/quarks.c:401–433

before nextUniq is decremented another thread gains execution control and requests a unique integer, then the same nonunique integer will be returned for both requests. This problem is avoided by defining a *mutual exclusion* (also known as *mutex*) abstraction that is used for assigning exclusive access to the resource. At most one thread or process can have access to a mutex at a time. A mutex-locking operation tries to gain mutex access; if that mutex is already locked by another task, then the current task is blocked until the mutex is unlocked. After a task accesses the shared resource it unlocks the mutex to free it for other tasks. Code accessing a shared global resource is therefore enclosed in mutex lock/unlock pairs as in Figure 5.9.

On single-processor machines, task concurrency is often implemented by the processor switching the execution context in response to external events called *interrupts*. These are used to inform the machine that a slow peripheral needs servicing (for example, a disk block has been read or a new network packet has arrived) or that a certain time interval has elapsed and therefore the currently executing task can be switched for another. When mutual exclusion operations are not available, code accessing shared resources can control concurrency at a lower level. The following fragment[21] ensures that no other operations will get executed concurrently with ofw_client_services_handle by disabling interrupts until the function returns.

```
saved_irq_state = disable_interrupts(I32_bit);
ofw_result = ofw_client_services_handle(args);
(void)restore_interrupts(saved_irq_state);
```

Notice the similarity between the code above and the mutex-based code. Both enclose the code accessing shared resources within a block defined by statements limiting the access to those resources. You can verify a large percentage of shared resource access code by looking for this symmetric structure. Although the lack of this structure is not necessarily an error, an entry or exit point (a goto label or a return statement) in such a block lacking the appropriate locking statements should raise your defenses.

The boss/worker model of parallelism is also used as a way to separate concerns between different parts of a system. Separate well-defined tasks of the system are handled by different processes, reaping the benefits of reuse and isolating the tasks from unwanted interactions between them. This model is typically used when two processes communicate with a simple interface and the work delegated is nontrivial. Examples include the delivery of mail (handled in Unix systems by invoking the

---

[21] netbsdsrc/sys/arch/arm32/ofw/ofw.c:325–327

```
/* Fork off a child for sending mail */
pid = fork();                                          ─── Split process into parent and child
if (pid < 0)
    perr("Fork failed");
                                                    ● ─── Child process
else if (pid == 0) {
    if (open(filename, O_RDONLY) != STDIN_FILENO)    ─── Redirect input to filename
        perr("Cannot reopen output file");
    execl(_PATH_SENDMAIL, _PATH_SENDMAIL, mailname,  ─── Replace process with the sendmail program
        (char *) NULL);
    perr("Exec failed");
}

waitpid(pid, (int *) NULL, 0);                         ─── Parent process waits for child to terminate
```

Figure 5.10 Spawning off a separate process to send mail.

sendmail process) and the printing of documents. In addition, operations requiring special security privileges are often delegated to a process responsible only for that operation to avoid exposing a large body of code to the security implications of possessing those privileges. One other case where the boss/worker model is used concerns the delegation of a background-running operation (such as committing disk writes to fixed storage or periodically indexing an archive) to a low-priority worker process, allowing the boss to efficiently handle high-priority requests.

A representative example is the code fragment from the *at* program in Figure 5.10.[22] When the program needs to send a mail message to a user, it uses the fork Unix system call to spawn a separate running copy of itself. That child copy redirects its standard input to the file that needs to be sent and replaces its instance with the *sendmail* program and suitable arguments. *sendmail* will deliver the mail as specified. The parent process then waits for the *sendmail* process to terminate.

The procedure we outlined uses a widely available program with a standard interface (*sendmail*) to handle the task of delivering mail. The use of *sendmail* is so widespread that other alternative mail transfer agents that run under Unix such as *smail* or MMDF provide a *sendmail*-compatible program to handle mail delivery. An alternative approach favored in the Microsoft Windows world uses a specific API for delivering mail. This dichotomy exists for other services as well: printing and shutting down the system are normally handled by calling separate programs in the Unix world (*lpr* and *shutdown*) but have a separate API under Windows.

When examining code that spawns off separate processes, always verify that the arguments passed to each process cannot be manipulated by malicious users to trick the process into performing an unintended operation. Consider the code fragments

---

[22] netbsdsrc/libexec/atrun/atrun.c:228–239

```
                        ┌────────── The shell command argument is constructed here
(void)snprintf(bp, len, "exec %s %s -n %s %s '%s%s%s:%s'",
    _PATH_RSH, argv[i], cmd, src, tuser ? tuser : "", tuser ? "@" : "",
    thost, targ);       └── A user argument becomes part of the shell command
(void)susystem(bp);     └── The shell command is passed to the shell
[...]
int
susystem(char *s)
{
    pid_t pid;

    pid = vfork();
    switch (pid) {                       ┌─ The command can contain arbitrary shell metacharacters
    [...]
    case 0:
        execl(_PATH_BSHELL, "sh", "-c", s, NULL);
```

Figure 5.11 Potential security hole created by passing unverified arguments to the shell.

```
egrep '\.[0].(gz|Z)$' $LIST |        ────── Locate all compressed formatted manual pages
                                     ◄── For each matching page
while read file
do
                                     ────── Decompress
    gzip -fdc $file |                ────── Extract summary information
    sed -n -f /usr/share/man/makewhatis.sed;
done >> $TMP
```

Figure 5.12 Pipeline to summarize a list of compressed manual page files.

in Figure 5.11.[23,24] The argument passed to the shell for execution with the -c option can contain shell metacharacters that will be interpreted before the shell executes the command constructed by the snprintf statement. For example, if the user passes as the first argument to the program the command rm /etc/passwd enclosed in backquotes, the shell will interpret the backquotes by executing the command and replacing the backquotes with its output. If the command were executed with superuser privileges, the system's password file would be deleted.

Finally, the *pipeline model* is often used when tasks process data in a serial manner. Each task receives some input, performs some processing on it, and passes the resulting output to the next task for some different processing. Unix *filter*-based programs are typical examples of this technique. The code in Figure 5.12[25] is a representative instance. The object of the code is to create a file containing summary information for every manual page file. Given a file containing the names of all files located in the manual page directory, *egrep* matches from the list only the compressed

---

[23] netbsdsrc/bin/rcp/rcp.c:292–297
[24] netbsdsrc/bin/rcp/util.c:113–127
[25] netbsdsrc/libexec/makewhatis/makewhatis.sh:31–34

formatted pages. The next stage of the pipeline consists of a loop that reads file names and processes each file using another, separate, pipeline. That pipeline decompresses each file (*gzip*) and then extracts the summary information from the result by using a *sed* script.

5.3.3 Thread Implementations

In the thread examples we have examined so far you have probably noticed the multitude of different functions used to achieve similar results. The reason behind this phenomenon is that the C and C++ languages do not offer a standard thread and synchronization library. As a result, multiple slightly incompatible libraries were created to satisfy the need. Some software implementations (such as the X Window System,[26] Perl,[27-30] and the *apache* Web server[31-33]) have custom code that implements a higher-level interface to provide thread and mutual exclusion functionality in a portable way.

Table 5.1 shows how a number of common thread and synchronization primitives are named in three different APIs. One other common thread API, the Unix System V, is very similar to the POSIX API but substitutes the thr prefix in place of pthread for the thread functions, removes the pthread_ prefix for the mutex and cond functions, and uses mutex_clear instead of pthread_mutex_destroy.

The pthread_create and CreateThread functions start a new thread and begin its execution at the function passed as an argument. The Java thread implementation differs: a Thread class is used either as a base class for thread classes derived from it or as a constructor taking as an argument classes that implement the runnable interface. In both cases, the class must supply a run method, which is the thread's entry point. Java threads begin their execution by calling the class's start method.[34]

```
class LogDaemon extends Thread { [...]
    public void run() {
        while (true)
```

[26] XFree86-3.3/xc/include/Xthreads.h

[27] perl/thread.h

[28] perl/os2/os2thread.h

[29] perl/win32/win32thread.h

[30] perl/win32/win32thread.c

[31] apache/src/os/netware/multithread.c

[32] apache/src/os/win32/multithread.c

[33] apache/src/include/multithread.h

[34] jt4/jasper/src/share/org/apache/jasper/logging/JasperLogger.java:77–260

Table 5.1 Common POSIX, Win32, and Java Thread and Synchronization Primitives

POSIX	Win32	Java
pthread_create	CreateThread	Thread
pthread_exit	ExitThread	stop
pthread_yield	Sleep(0)	yield
sleep	Sleep	sleep
pthread_self	GetCurrentThreadId	currentThread
pthread_mutex_init	CreateMutex	—
pthread_mutex_lock	WaitForSingleObject	synchronized[a]
pthread_mutex_unlock	ReleaseMutex	synchronized[b]
pthread_mutex_destroy	CloseHandle	—
pthread_cond_init	CreateEvent	—
pthread_cond_wait	WaitForSingleObject	wait
pthread_cond_signal	PulseEvent	notify
pthread_cond_destroy	CloseHandle	—

[a]Enter method or code block.
[b]Exit method or code block.

```
            flusher.run();
    } [...]
}
public class JasperLogger extends Logger { [...]
    private void init() { [...]
        LogDaemon logDaemon = new LogDaemon([...]);
        logDaemon.start();
    } [...]
}
```

Threads terminate their execution by calling the pthread_exit and ExitThread functions or the object's stop method. Since threads execute concurrently, in some situations a thread might need to relinquish control to other threads; this is accomplished by the pthread_yield and Sleep(0) functions and the yield method. The various calls to sleep allow a thread to pause its execution for the given interval.

Mutual exclusion is handled very differently under the three APIs. Whereas the POSIX and Win32 APIs provide functions for creating, locking (waiting), unlocking (releasing), and destroying (closing) mutexes (Win32 also provides a separate family of critical region and semaphore functions), the Java language provides the same functionality through the synchronized keyword. Object methods declared as synchronized will never execute concurrently for the same underlying object. Similarly, class

```
public synchronized void put(Object object) {
    vector.addElement(object);         ── Change the isEmpty condition
    notify();                          ── Notify waiting threads
} [...]

public synchronized Object pull() {    ── Loop waiting for condition
    while (isEmpty())
    try {
        wait();
    } catch (InterruptedException ex) {
    }
    return get();
}
```

Figure 5.13 Thread synchronization in Java.

methods declared as `synchronized` will lock the entire class during their execution, while a `synchronized` statement will acquire an exclusive lock on its argument before executing the statement that follows it.[35]

```
synchronized (this) {
    mThread = mCurrentThread++;
}
```

Synchronized methods are also used in Java to arrange for one thread to wait for another. The same task is accomplished under POSIX threads by using `pthread_cond_wait` and `pthread_cond_signal`, and under Win32 by means of events. In Java two threads achieve the same effect by using synchronized methods of the same thread object, with calls to the `wait` and `notify` methods, while testing and changing a condition, respectively. You can see an illustration of this code idiom in Figure 5.13,[36] where a queue `pull` method will `wait` in a loop until notified by the queue `put` method that an element is available.

Exercise 5.8 Outline the types of software and hardware parallelism most prevalent in your environment.

Exercise 5.9 The sharing of resources in processes and threads often depends on the operating system and the software libraries. For your environment research and tabulate the software abstractions (file descriptors, signals, memory, mutexes) shared between processes and threads that have the same ancestor.

---

[35] hsqldb/src/org/hsqldb/ServerConnection.java:70–72
[36] jt4/catalina/src/share/org/apache/catalina/util/Queue.java:77–93

```
int
main(int argc, char **argv)
{
    [...]
    (void)signal(SIGINT, intr);          ──────── Install signal handler

                                         ──────── The default operation is an infinite loop
    /* Now ask the questions. */
    for (;;) {
        for (cnt = NQUESTS; cnt--;)
            if (problem() == EOF)
                exit(0);
        showstats();
    }
}
[...]
void                                     ──────── Signal handler
intr(int dummy)
{
    showstats();                         ──────── Print score and exit
    exit(0);
}
```

Figure 5.14 A signal handler and its installation.

Exercise 5.10   Locate calls to the `tsleep` function within the kernel source code.[37] Explain how these are used to support concurrency.

Exercise 5.11   Look for code that invokes a subprocess and discuss the security implications of the operation.

Exercise 5.12   Define a rule specifying when Java methods should be declared `synchronized`. Locate code that uses the keyword and test your rule against it.

5.4 Signals

Application-level C programs receive external asynchronous events in the form of *signals*. Examples of signals include a user interrupting a process (SIGINT), the execution of an illegal instruction or an invalid memory reference (SIGILL, SIGSEGV), a floating-point exception (SIGFPE), or the resumption of a stopped process (SIGCONT). Code responding to signals consists of a *signal handler*: a function specified to be executed when a given signal is received by the application. In Figure 5.14[38] the program will enter into an infinite loop quizzing the user with arithmetic problems. However, when the user interrupts the application by typing ˆC, the signal handler `intr` gets called. The handler prints the quiz statistics and exits the program.

---

[37] netbsdsrc/sys
[38] netbsdsrc/games/arithmetic/arithmetic.c:115–168

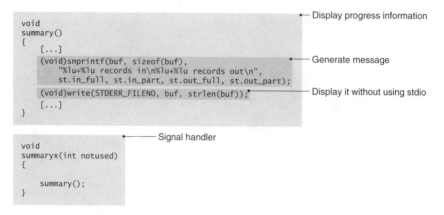

Figure 5.15 Avoiding nonreentrant code in a signal handler.

Signal handlers are not exclusively used for gracefully terminating applications; they often provide more sophisticated functionality. However, because a signal handler can get executed at any time during the program's operation, the code it contains has to be very careful about the assumptions it makes. Many parts of the C library are *nonreentrant*, meaning that calling such functions concurrently with other code may yield unexpected results. The code in Figure 5.15[39] is a signal handler that responds when a user asks the program to display informational output (using the ^T key on the BSD-derived versions of Unix). To avoid using file-based *stdio* file routines, which can be nonreentrant, the handler writes the messages in a memory buffer and copies that to the program's terminal by using the `write` system call.

When two concurrently executing parts of a program alter common data structures so that the end result depends on the order of their execution, this creates a *race condition*. Race conditions are subtle and often have the code leading to them spread over multiple functions or modules; the resultant problems are therefore difficult to isolate. Consider the C++ code in Figure 5.16.[40] The `ForkProcess` constructor function is used to create a new process by means of the `fork` system call. Unix processes that terminate must rendezvous with their parent again (get *reaped*) by means of the `wait` system call; otherwise they remain in a *zombie* state: terminated and waiting for their parent to collect their exit status and resource usage statistics. Our constructor function arranges for this by installing a signal handler for the SIGCHLD

---

[39] netbsdsrc/bin/dd/misc.c:61–98
[40] socket/Fork.C:43–159

```
Fork::ForkProcess::ForkProcess (bool kill, bool give_reason)
 : kill_child (kill), reason (give_reason), next (0)
{
   if (list == 0) {            ── No handler installed?
                                               ── Set up SIGCHLD signal handler
      struct sigaction sa;
      sa.sa_handler = sighnd (&Fork::ForkProcess::reaper_nohang);
      sigemptyset (&sa.sa_mask);
      sa.sa_flags = SA_RESTART;
      sigaction (SIGCHLD, &sa, 0);

   }
   pid = fork ();
   if (pid > 0) {
      next = list;             ──█1 Might point to an element that will be removed

      list = this;
   } [...]
}

void Fork::ForkProcess::reaper_nohang (int signo)  ── Signal handler
{ [...]
   ForkProcess* prev = 0;
   ForkProcess* cur  = list;
   while (cur) {
      if (cur->pid == wpid) {  ── Is this the terminated process?

        cur->pid = -1;
        if (prev)
          prev->next = cur->next;
        else
          list = list->next;   ──█2 Might remove the element pointed by a newly inserted item

        [...]
        delete cur;            ──█3 Might conflict with other memory pool operations

        break;
      }
      prev = cur;
      cur  = cur->next;
   } [...]
}
```

Figure 5.16 Race conditions introduced by a signal handler.

signal, which is delivered to a process when one of its children terminates (dies). The signal handler is installed using the `sigaction` system call; it functions like the `signal` system call but offers more options for specifying exactly how signals are to be handled. All created processes are inserted into a linked list, used by the signal handler to locate the details of the terminated process.

And this is where the trouble begins. The signal handler traverses the list to locate the terminated process by means of its process id `wpid`. Once the process is found, it is removed from the linked list, and the memory that was dynamically allocated for it is freed by means of a `delete` operation. However, because the signal handler is invoked asynchronously, it can run just after the statement in Figure 5.16:1 is executed. If the terminated process is the first in the list, the statement in Figure 5.16:2 will attempt to remove the process from the list, but because the terminated process is already pointed to by the newly inserted element, we will end up with a list containing the details of a process that was already reaped, stored in memory space that will be disposed. A second race condition can be triggered by the delete operation (Figure 5.16:3). If the signal handler, and consequently the delete operation, is run during the time another part of the program executes a new or another delete operation, the two can get intermixed, corrupting the program's dynamic memory pool. A *multithreaded* version of the C++ library might contain safeguards against the second race condition, but in an application we know, it was not used since the program was not explicitly using threads. As a result, the application worked reliably to create many thousands of processes but would crash unexpectedly once the system load increased over a certain threshold. Since the crash was triggered by a corrupted memory pool, the crash position was totally unrelated to the race condition that caused it. The moral of this example is that you should view with extreme suspicion data structure manipulation code and library calls that appear within a signal handler. In particular note that the ANSI C standard specifies that implicitly invoked signal handlers may call only the functions abort, exit, longjmp, and signal and can assign values only to static objects declared as volatile sig_atomic_t; the result of any other operations is undefined.

One often-used approach for handling signals in a clean way involves setting a flag in response to a signal to be examined in a convenient context. The code in Figure 5.17[41] demonstrates such a setup and some additional signal-handling concepts. The function init_signals, when called to enable signal handling, will install the signal handler winch to respond to SIGWINCH (the signal notifying an application that the dimensions of its display window have changed). The code in the signal handler is very simple: it reenables the handling of the signal (signal handling reverts to the default behavior when a signal is received) and sets the sigs flag to contain the signal received. Each iteration of the program's main loop checks the sigs flag and performs, if needed, the necessary processing (Figure 5.17:3). Also interesting is the code that disables the signal handlers: the handling of the interrupt signal SIGINT is restored to the implementation-defined default behavior (Figure 5.17:1), while window size change signals are simply ignored (Figure 5.17:2).

Exercise 5.13   Locate three nontrivial signal handlers and reason about the ways they work.

Exercise 5.14   Examine how threads interoperate with signal handlers in your environment.

---

[41] netbsdsrc/distrib/utils/more

```
init_signals(int on)                            ●── Setup signal handling
{
    if (on) {
        [...]
        (void)signal(SIGWINCH, winch);          ●── Install signal handler
    } else {
        [...]
        (void)signal(SIGINT, SIG_DFL);          ■1 Default action on signal
        (void)signal(SIGWINCH, SIG_IGN);        ■2 Ignore signal
    }
}

[...]
                                                ●── Signal handler
void
winch()
{
    (void)signal(SIGWINCH, winch);              ●── Restore signal behavior
    sigs |= S_WINCH;                            ●── Set flag to be processed synchronously

    [...]
}

[...]
commands()
{
    [...]
                                                ●── Main command loop
    for (;;) {
        [...]
        if (sigs) {                             ■3 Check for received signals, and respond
            psignals();
            if (quitting)
                quit();
        }
        [...]
```

Figure 5.17 Synchronous handling of signals.

Exercise 5.15   ANSI C does not guarantee library functions to be reentrant. Examine signal handlers in the code base for calls to nonreentrant functions.

5.5 Nonlocal Jumps

The C library `setjmp` and `longjmp` functions allow programs to jump back from a function without having to `return` from each function in the sequence. The functions are typically used to immediately exit from a deeply nested function, often as a response to a signal. The functions are designed to be used together. At the point where nested function calls will return, a `setjmp` is used to store in a buffer variable the environment's context. From then onward until the function that called `setjmp` exits, calls to `longjmp`, with a pointer to the saved environment as an argument, will return execution to the point where `setjmp` was originally called. To distinguish between the original `setjmp` call and subsequent returns to it via `longjmp`, `setjmp` returns 0 in the first case and a nonzero value in the latter one.

```
int
main(int argc, char *argv[])
{
    [...]
    signal(SIGINT, signal_int);                    ──────── Set signal handler
    if ((status = setjmp(env)) != 0) {
        fputs("\n?\n", stderr);                     ──── 1 Control arrives here by calling longjmp
        sprintf(errmsg, "interrupt");
    } else {
        init_buffers();                             ──── 2 Control arrives here after the setjmp call
        [...]
    }
    for (;;) {                                      ──────── Command processing loop
        [...]
        if (prompt) {
            printf("%s", prompt);
            fflush(stdout);
        }
        [...]

void                                               ── Signal handler; calls handle_int
signal_int(int signo)
{
    [...]
    handle_int(signo);
}

void
handle_int(int signo)                              ── Called by the signal handler
{
    [...]
    longjmp(env, -1);                              ── Jump back to the top of the command loop
}
```

Figure 5.18 A nonlocal jump using longjmp.

The example in Figure 5.18[42] is a typical case. Users of the *ed* line-oriented text editor can stop lengthy operations and return to the command-prompt mode by issuing an interrupt (^C). This is accomplished by installing a signal handler for the keyboard interrupt and calling setjmp before the command-processing loop. The original call to setjmp will return 0 and the program will perform the normal start-up processing (Figure 5.18:2). When the user presses ^C (to interrupt, for example, a lengthy listing), the signal handler signal_int will call handle_int, which will longjmp back to the top of the command loop (Figure 5.18:1).

Although at first sight the code appears to be error-free, a number of complications can arise. A signal arriving at the wrong moment in conjunction with a longjmp to the top of the command loop can result in resource leakage (for example, leaving a file open or not freeing a temporarily allocated memory block), or worse, in data structures left in an inconsistent state. The code we examined uses mutual exclusion regions to

---

[42]netbsdsrc/bin/ed/main.c:114–1417

```
int mutex = 0;          /* if set, signals set "sigflags" */
int sigflags = 0;       /* if set, signals received while mutex set */

#define SPL1() mutex++          ———— Enter a critical region; delay signal handling
```
                                                              ———— Exit a critical region
```
#define SPL0() \
if (--mutex == 0) { \
    if (sigflags & (1 << (SIGHUP - 1))) handle_hup(SIGHUP); \     ———— Handle pending signals
    if (sigflags & (1 << (SIGINT - 1))) handle_int(SIGINT); \
}
```
                                                ———— Signal handler
```
void
signal_int(int signo)
{
    if (mutex)
        sigflags |= (1 << (signo - 1));    ———— In a mutex region;
    else                                        just set the flag for delayed handling
        handle_int(signo);                 ———— No mutex set; immediately handle the interrupt
}
```
                                    ———— Immediate or delayed handling of the interrupt signal
```
void
handle_int(int signo)
{
    [...]
    sigflags &= ~(1 << (signo - 1));    ———— Reset the interrupt flag
    longjmp(env, -1);                   ———— Jump back to the command loop
}

void
clear_active_list()
{
    SPL1();          ———— Enter critical region
                                                         ———— Critical region
    active_size = active_last = active_ptr = active_ndx = 0;
    free(active_list);
    active_list = NULL;

    SPL0();          ———— Exit critical region
}
```

Figure 5.19 Setting mutual exclusion regions to protect data structures.

avoid this problem. The fragments in Figure 5.19[43] detail how this is accomplished. Two macros, SPL1 and SPL0, are defined to enter and exit critical regions. (The macro names are derived from the functions used to set interrupt priority levels in early versions of the Unix kernel.) SPL1 sets the mutex variable. The signal handlers examine this variable: if it is set, instead of calling handle_int, they simply store the signal number in the sigflags variable. SPL0—called at the end of a critical region—decrements mutex, examines sigflags for any pending signals received while the critical region was executing, and calls handle_int if needed. Using this scheme, responses to signals are simply delayed until the exit from a critical region.

---

[43] netbsdsrc/bin/ed

Exercise 5.16 Explain how, in Figure 5.19, the definitions of SPL0 and SPL1 allow the nested operation of critical regions.

Exercise 5.17 Locate five calls to longjmp and list the reasons they were used. For extra credit try to locate longjmp calls not associated with signals.

Exercise 5.18 How does the longjmp code you located avoid resource leakage and inconsistent data structures?

Exercise 5.19 Propose a way to verify that longjmp is not called after the function containing setjmp has exited. Is this a compile or a runtime method?

5.6 Macro Substitution

The flexibility of the C preprocessor is often used to define simple functions as macros.[44]

```
#define IS_IDENT(c)      (isalnum(c) || (c) == '_' || (c) == '.' \
            || (c) == '$')
#define    IS_OCTAL(c)      ((c) >= '0' && (c) <= '7')
#define    NUMERIC_VALUE(c)     ((c) - '0')
```

When reading code that contains macros, keep in mind that macros are neither functions nor statements. Careful coding practices need to be employed when macros are defined to avoid some common pitfalls. Consider the way c is parenthesized in the definition of the NUMERIC_VALUE macro above. Using c without parentheses would cause an expression of the type NUMERIC_VALUE(charval = b) to evaluate as charval = (b - '0') instead of the intended (charval = b) - '0'. By parenthesizing all macro arguments the code avoids precedence problems. A more difficult case concerns the number of times macro arguments are evaluated. Writing code of the form

```
while (IS_IDENT(a = getchar()))
    putchar(a);
```

would expand into

```
while ((isalnum(a = getchar()) || (a = getchar()) == '_' ||
        (a = getchar()) == '.' || (a = getchar()) == '$'))
            putchar(a);
```

---

[44]netbsdsrc/usr.bin/yacc/defs.h:131–133

reading as many as four different characters in every loop iteration, which is certainly not what was intended. In general, be very careful when you see macro arguments that have side effects such as assignment, pre/post increment/decrement, input/output, and function calls with these effects.

When you see macros used as statements, different problems may result. Consider the definition[45]

```
#define    ASSERT(p)    if (!(p)) botch(__STRING(p))
```

used in the following context.

```
if (k > n)
    ASSERT(process(n) == 0);
else
    ASSERT(process(k) == 0);
```

Once the macro expands the code will read as

```
if (k > n)
        if (!(process(n) == 0))
            botch(__STRING(process(1) == 0));
        else
            if (!(process(k) == 0))
                botch(__STRING(process(k) == 0));
```

which is not what was intended. To avoid this problem we could try to define macros containing an if statement as a block.[46]

```
#define    NOTE(str)    \
    { if (m->eflags&REG_TRACE) printf("=%s\n", (str)); }
```

However, using the NOTE macro in the context

```
if (k > 1)
    NOTE("k > 1");
else
    process(k);
```

---

[45] netbsdsrc/lib/libc/stdlib/malloc.c:130
[46] netbsdsrc/lib/libc/regex/engine.c:128

⚠ will expand into

```
if (k > 1) {
    if (m->eflags&REG_TRACE) printf("=%s\n", ("k > 1"));
}; else
        process(k);
```

which will not compile since there is an extraneous semicolon before the `else`. For these reasons in macro definitions you will often encounter statement sequences inside a do { ... } while (0) block.[47]

```
#define    getvndxfer(vnx)    do {                                    \
    int s = splbio();                                                 \
    (vnx) = (struct vndxfer *)get_pooled_resource(&vndxfer_head);    \
    splx(s);                                                          \
} while (0)
```

ⅈ   The blocks, apart from creating a scope where local variables can be defined, are enclosed within a do ... while statement to protect `if` statements from unwanted interactions. As an example, the code[48]

```
#define DPRINTF(f, m) do {        \
    if (vmswapdebug & (f))        \
        printf m;                 \
} while(0)
```

can be placed in an `if` branch without any of the problems we described above. The result of the macro expansion is not a statement but a statement fragment that requires a following semicolon in all circumstances. Therefore an invocation of a macro that expands to such a form must be written with a following semicolon; there is no choice in the matter. Thus such a macro invocation will always look exactly like a statement and the user of the macro cannot be misled or confused in the ways we discussed.

An alternative approach involves coding conditional operations as expressions by using the C ?: operator or the short-circuit evaluation property of the Boolean operators.[49]

```
#define   SEETWO(a, b)   (MORE() && MORE2() && PEEK() == (a) && \
                            PEEK2() == (b))
#define    EAT(c)    ((SEE(c)) ? (NEXT(), 1) : 0)
```

---

[47] netbsdsrc/sys/vm/vm_swap.c:293–297
[48] netbsdsrc/sys/vm/vm_swap.c:101–104
[49] netbsdsrc/lib/libc/regex/regcomp.c:153–154

```
#define    PEEK()     (*p->next)
#define    GETNEXT()  (*p->next++)
#define    MORE()     (p->next < p->end)

static void
p_str(register struct parse *p)
{
    REQUIRE(MORE(), REG_EMPTY);
    while (MORE())
        ordinary(p, GETNEXT());
}
[...]
static int             /* the value */
p_count(register struct parse *p)
{
    register int count = 0;
    register int ndigits = 0;

    while (MORE() && isdigit(PEEK()) && count <= DUPMAX) {
        count = count*10 + (GETNEXT() - '0');
        ndigits++;
    }
```

Figure 5.20 Macros using locally defined variables.

Although the macro code above looks almost like a function definition, it is crucial to remember that the sequence is not called, like a function, but is lexically replaced at each point it is invoked. This means that identifiers within the macro body are resolved within the context of the function body they appear in and that any variable values modified within the macro body are propagated to the point the macro was "called." Consider the use of the argument p in the definition of the macros PEEK, GETNEXT, and MORE (Figure 5.20:1).[50] The p refers to the argument of the function p_str (Figure 5.20:2) when used in that function and the argument of the function p_count later (Figure 5.20:3).

In addition, variables passed to macros can be modified inside the macro body, as demonstrated by the following code.[51]

```
#define getnum(t) (t) = 0; while (isdigit(*cp)) (t) = (t) * 10 \
                + (*cp++ - '0');

cp = buf;
if (*cp == 'T') {
    setimes++;
    cp++;
    getnum(mtime.tv_sec);
    if (*cp++ != ' ')
        SCREWUP("mtime.sec not delimited");
    getnum(mtime.tv_usec);
    if (*cp++ != ' ')
        SCREWUP("mtime.usec not delimited");
    getnum(atime.tv_sec);
```

---

[50] netbsdsrc/lib/libc/regex/regcomp.c:150–677
[51] netbsdsrc/bin/rcp/rcp.c:595–606

In the above example each argument to getnum is assigned a value according to the string pointed to by cp. If getnum were defined as a proper C function, a *pointer* to the respective variables would need to have been passed instead.

One final difference between macro substitution and function definitions results from the preprocessor's ability to concatenate macro arguments using the ## operator. The following code[52]

```
#define DOVREG(reg) tf->tf_vm86_##reg = (u_short) \
                         vm86s.regs.vmsc.sc_##reg
#define DOREG(reg) tf->tf_##reg = (u_short) vm86s.regs.vmsc.sc_##reg

    DOVREG(ds);
    DOVREG(es);
    DOVREG(fs);
    DOVREG(gs);
    DOREG(edi);
    DOREG(esi);
    DOREG(ebp);
```

will expand into

```
tf->tf_vm86_ds = (u_short) vm86s.regs.vmsc.sc_ds;
tf->tf_vm86_es = (u_short) vm86s.regs.vmsc.sc_es;
tf->tf_vm86_fs = (u_short) vm86s.regs.vmsc.sc_fs;
tf->tf_vm86_gs = (u_short) vm86s.regs.vmsc.sc_gs;
tf->tf_edi = (u_short) vm86s.regs.vmsc.sc_edi;
tf->tf_esi = (u_short) vm86s.regs.vmsc.sc_esi;
tf->tf_ebp = (u_short) vm86s.regs.vmsc.sc_ebp;
```

thus dynamically creating code to access structure fields with names such as tf_vm86_ds and sc_ds.

[i] Older, pre-ANSI C compilers did not support the ## operator. However, they could be tricked into concatenating two tokens by separating them by an empty comment (/**/); you are likely to encounter this use when reading pre-ANSI C code. In the following code excerpt you can see exactly how the effect of the ## operator was achieved in earlier programs.[53]

---

[52] netbsdsrc/sys/arch/i386/i386/vm86.c:153–154
[53] netbsdsrc/sys/arch/bebox/include/bus.h:97–103

```
#ifdef __STDC__
#define CAT(a,b) a##b
#else
#define CAT(a,b) a/**/b
#endif
```

Exercise 5.20   Locate all definitions of the min and max macros in the source code base, counting the ones that are correctly defined and the ones that can result in erroneous code.

Exercise 5.21   C++ and some C compilers support the inline keyword to define functions that are directly compiled at the point they are called, avoiding the associated function call overhead and providing the compiler with additional optimization opportunities in the context of the caller. Discuss how this facility relates to macro definitions in terms of readability, maintainability, and flexibility of code that uses each method.

Exercise 5.22   Compare the readability of C++ template-based code (Section 9.3.4) with similar functionality implemented by using macros. Create, using both approaches, a simple example and compare the compiler error messages after introducing a syntax and a semantic error in your code.

Further Reading

The complete grammar for the Unix shell mentioned in Section 5.1 appears in Bourne [Bou79]. You can read more about recursive-descent parsing in Aho et al. [ASU85, pp. 44–55]. Works on computer architecture and operating systems provide a lot of material on how parallelism can be provided and exploited at various hardware and software levels [Tan97, HP96, PPI97, BST89]. More specifically, threads are covered in two other references [NBF96, LB97] and the operation of signals and threads in Robbins and Robbins [RR96]. Many examples of pipeline-based programming can be found in Kernighan and Pike [KP84], while the theoretical background behind pipelines is elaborated in Hoare [Hoa85]. The design of operating systems provides numerous opportunities for dealing with concurrency issues; these are discussed in several references [Bac86, Tan97, LMKQ88, MBK96]. Common problems with macro definitions are discussed in Koenig [Koe88], while the benefits and shortcomings of inlined functions are exhaustively treated in Meyers [Mey98].

Tackling Large Projects

A Large System, Produced By Expanding The Dimensions of A Smaller System, Does Not Behave Like The Smaller System.

—John Gall

L arge, multifile projects differ from smaller ones not only in the challenges you will encounter when examining their code but also in the opportunities they provide for understanding them. In this chapter we review some common techniques used in the implementation of large projects and then examine specific elements typically comprising the development process of such projects. We will describe how large projects are organized, their build and configuration process, how different file versions are controlled, the special role of project-specific tools, and typical testing strategies. For these elements we sketch characteristic setups you will encounter and provide some hints on how you can use them to enhance your navigation and comprehension capabilities.

6.1 Design and Implementation Techniques

Large coding efforts, due to their size and scope, often justify the use of techniques whose use might not be worthwhile in other situations. We discuss many of these techniques in separate parts of this book; however, it is useful to outline at this point some of the design and implementation methods you are likely to encounter and to provide you with pointers to the appropriate chapters or sections.

Visible Software Process and Disciplined Practices   In large projects, elements of the software lifecycle that are implicitly handled in smaller undertakings are often part of the software code base. In addition, the inherent complexity and the large number of developers participating in nontrivial projects necessitate the adoption of formal practices. These typically specify how a particular language is to be used, the way the project's elements are to be organized, what is to be documented, and processes for most of the project's lifecycle activities. We present coding standards in Chapter 7, the build process in Section 6.3, testing procedures in Section 6.7, configuration methods in Section 6.4, revision control in Section 6.5, and documentation practices in Chapter 8.

Nontrivial Architecture   Whereas small projects can sometimes get away with piling code blocks together until the required specifications are met, large software endeavors need to structure the system being built by using an appropriate architecture to tame its complexity. This architecture typically dictates the system's structure, the way control is handled, and the modular decomposition of the system's elements. Large systems are also likely to reuse architectural ideas through frameworks, design patterns, and domain-specific architectures. We discuss all these aspects in Chapter 9

Merciless Decomposition   At the implementation level, in large projects, you will find building elements aggressively decomposed by using mechanisms such as functions, objects, abstract data types, and components. We discuss all these aspects in Chapter 9.

Support for Multiple Platforms   Large applications often tend to attract a proportionally wide community of users. As a result, such applications often need to address a number of portability concerns that are sometimes conveniently ignored in less ambitious projects.

Object-Oriented Techniques   The complexity of large systems is often tamed by using object-oriented design and implementation techniques. Objects are typically organized into hierarchies. Inheritance (discussed in Section 9.1.3) is then used to factor out common behavior, and dynamic dispatch techniques (Section 9.3.3) make it possible for a single code block to process collections of different objects.

Operator Overloading   Significant code collections written in languages such as C++ and Haskell use operator overloading to promote project-specific data types into first-class citizens that are then manipulated using the language's built-in operator set. You can find representative examples in Section 9.3.3.

Libraries, Components, and Processes   At a higher level of granularity, the code of large systems is often decomposed into libraries of object modules, reusable components, and even separate processes. We discuss these techniques in Section 9.3.

Domain-Specific and Custom Languages and Tools   Large coding efforts often involve the creation of specialized tools or benefit from existing ones used in similar endeavors. You can read more on how specialized tools are used in the build process in Section 6.6.

Aggressive Use of Preprocessing   Projects implemented in assembly language, C, and C++ often use a preprocessor to extend the language with domain-specific structures. Modern projects are rarely coded in symbolic language; we discuss the use of the C preprocessor in Section 5.6.

Exercise 6.1   Propose ways to quickly determine whether a given project follows one of the design or implementation techniques we described. Test your proposal against one of the major projects available in the book's CD-ROM.

Exercise 6.2   Locate recommended design and implementation practices in a software engineering textbook. Explain how these are reflected in a project's source code.

6.2 Project Organization

You can examine a project's organization by browsing its source code tree—the hierarchical directory structure containing the project's source code. The source tree often reflects the project's architectural and software process structure. Consider the source code tree of the *apache* Web server (Figure 6.1). At the top level it mirrors a typical Web server installation: there are directories for storing server scripts (cgi-bin), configuration files (conf), static content (htdocs), icons, and the server logs. Often the source code tree of an application mirrors the application's deployment structure. The actual program source code is stored in a directory called src, a directory name often employed for this purpose. The other directories contain example files and templates for setting up the deployed application. In addition, in the case of *apache*, its documentation is stored as static Web pages under the htdocs/manual directory. The program source code is also organized using directories with typical names: lib contains library code, main contains the server's base code, include contains common header files, modules contains code for installable optional parts, and os contains operating system–specific code. Some of these directories are further subdivided. The lib directory is divided into separate directories for the XML parser code (expat-lite) and for the hashed database library (sdbm). The os directory is also divided into different subdirectories: one for each operating system or platform type. A common strategy for developing multiplatform applications is to

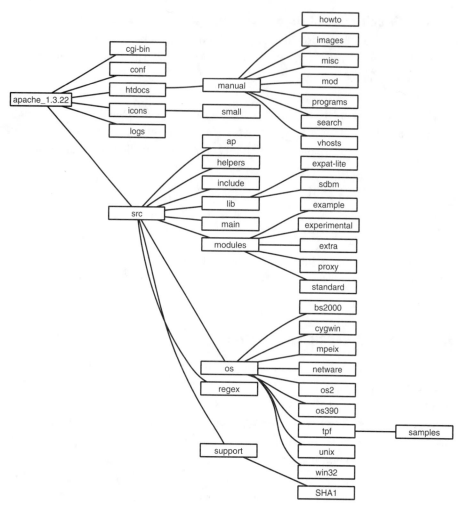

Figure 6.1 The source code tree structure of the *apache* Web server.

isolate the platform-specific code customizing it for each platform. This code can then be put into separate directories; one of these is configured to take part in the build process, depending on the target platform. We summarize directory names commonly found across different projects in Table 6.1. Depending on the system's size, the directories we describe can be common for the whole system, or each part of the system can have its own separate directory structure. The choice between the two organization strategies depends on how the development and maintenance process is organized.

Table 6.1 Common Project Subdirectory Names

Directory	Contents
src	Source code
TLD (e.g., org or edu)	Root of Java source code
main	Source code for the main program; platform-independent, excludes libraries
program-name	Source code for *program-name*
lib	Library source code
lib*name*	Library *name* source code
common	Code elements shared between applications
include	Common C and C++ header files
doc	Documentation
man	Unix manual pages
rc / res	Microsoft Windows (bitmaps, resource files dialogs, icons) in source/compiled form
arch	Code specific to a given processor architecture
os	Operating system–specific code
CVS / RCS / SCCS	Revision control system files
build / compile / classes / obj / Release / Debug	Compilation directory
tools	Tools used during the build process
test	Test scripts and input and output files
conf	Buildtime configuration information
etc	Runtime configuration information
eg	Examples
bin	Depository for executable files and shell scripts
contrib	User-contributed tools and code; typically maintained outside the main project

Centralized processes tend to use common directories, thus exploiting commonality between different applications, while federated development processes duplicate the structure in each different project, thus achieving maintenance independence.

As the size of a project increases, its directory structure becomes tailored to its specific requirements. Often history influences the structure of a project's directories since developers and maintainers are reluctant to restructure a code base they have become accustomed to. Compare the directory structure of the NetBSD kernel (Figure 6.2) with the structure of the Linux kernel (Figure 6.3). The Linux kernel directory structure is more uniformly divided into subdirectories; in the NetBSD kernel a number of directories that could have been grouped under a common directory appear at the top level for historical reasons. A typical example is the organization of the

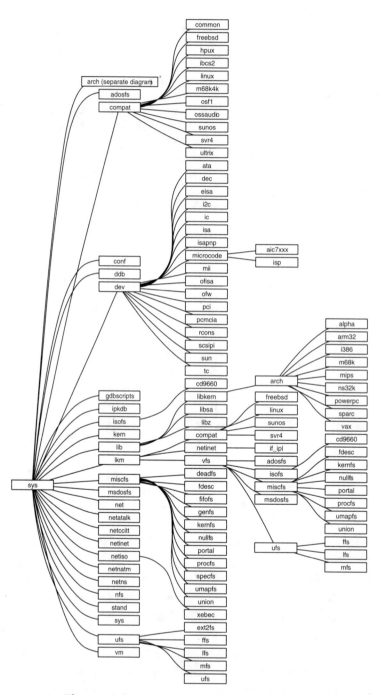

Figure 6.2 The NetBSD kernel main source tree.

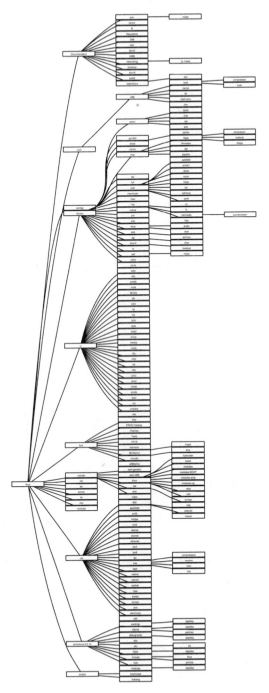

Figure 6.3 The Linux kernel source tree.

networking code. Different networking protocols (TCP/IP,[1] ISO,[2] ATM,[3] AppleTalk[4]) appear as top-level directories under the NetBSD kernel but are organized under a common `net` directory under Linux. Although the developers of the BSD networking code had at the time of its design the forethought to use a networking directory naming scheme that would allow it to be extended to cover additional protocols, they did not take the extravagant step to create a separate directory just to hold what was then support for a single networking protocol.

Sometimes a well-defined process for creating new code yields very orderly directory structures. Consider the architecture-specific part of the NetBSD kernel depicted in Figure 6.4. Over the years NetBSD has been ported to tens of different architectures. The architecture-specific parts are grouped into a separate directory[5] and are appropriately linked to the master source code tree during the configuration and build process.

Do not let huge source code collections daunt you; typically these are better organized than smaller, ad hoc efforts. Figure 6.5 depicts the source code outline of the entire FreeBSD system, including the kernel, libraries, documentation, user, and system tools. Despite its size (it comprises almost 3,000 directories without counting the configuration file repositories), it is trivial to locate the source code for a specific tool: the tool source is located in a directory named after the tool's name appended to a name matching the tool's path. As an example, the source code for the *make* tool (installed as `/usr/bin/make`) can be found under `/usr/src/usr.bin/make`. When you work on a large project for the first time, spend some time acquainting yourself with its directory tree structure. For this task many people prefer to use graphical tools such as the Windows Explorer or the GNU midnight commander.[6] If none of these are available to you, you can explore graphically the directory structure by using a Web browser opened at the local source directory. Under most Unix systems you can also use the *locate* command to find the location of the file you are looking for, while under Windows the Explorer's file search mechanism can do a similar job.

When browsing a large project, keep in mind that a project's "source code" encompasses a lot more than the computer language instructions that are compiled to obtain an executable program; a project's source tree typically also includes specifications, end-user and developer documentation, test scripts, multimedia resources,

---

[1] netbsdsrc/sys/netinet
[2] netbsdsrc/sys/netiso
[3] netbsdsrc/sys/netnatm
[4] netbsdsrc/sys/netatalk
[5] netbsdsrc/sys/arch
[6] http://www.ibiblio.org/mc/

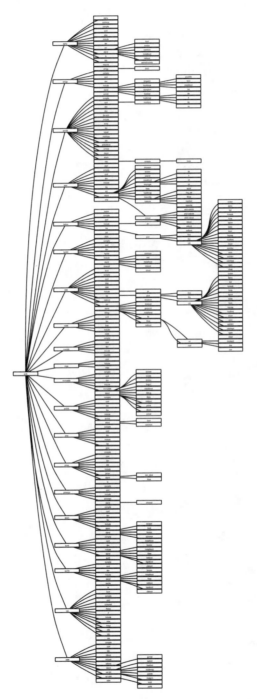

Figure 6.4 The source tree of the architecture-specific part of the NetBSD kernel.

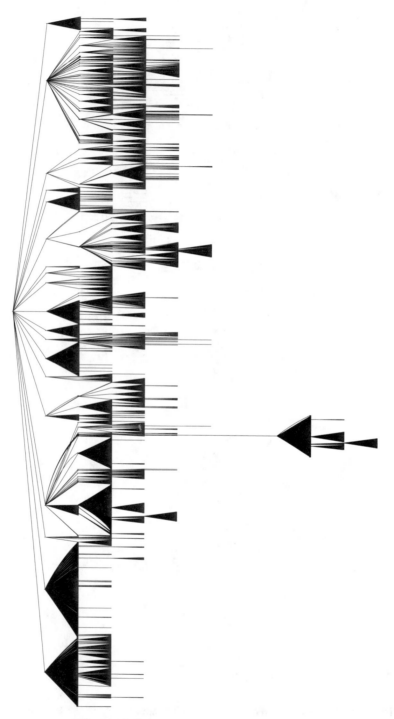

Figure 6.5 The FreeBSD system source tree.

build tools, examples, localization files, revision history, installation procedures, and licensing information.

Exercise 6.3   Describe the directory structure used in the book's CD-ROM or in projects in your organization.

Exercise 6.4   How can a standardized directory structure be used for automating aspects of the software development process?

Exercise 6.5   Examine and describe the directory structure of an installed version of Microsoft Windows.

Exercise 6.6   Outline which elements, apart from source code, are packaged in the Perl distribution that is available in the book's CD-ROM.

6.3 The Build Process and Makefiles

Most large projects use a sophisticated build process. Such a process can typically handle configuration options, multiple types of input and output files, complex inter-dependencies, and several build targets. Since the build process ultimately affects the resultant output, it is important for you to be able to "read" a project's build process as well as a project's code. Unfortunately, there is no standardized way to specify and execute a build process. Each large project and development platform seems to employ its own proprietary way to organize a build. However, some elements are common among most build processes; we outline these in the following paragraphs.

The steps followed in a typical build process are illustrated in Figure 6.6. The first step involves configuring software options and determining what exactly you want to build. (We discuss configuration in Section 6.4.) Based on the project's configuration we can create a *dependency graph*. Large projects typically involve tens to thousands of different components; many of them are based on others. The dependency graph specifies the correct order in which various project components are to be built.

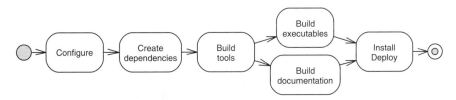

Figure 6.6   The steps of a typical build process.

Often some parts of the build process are not performed by using standard development tools such as the compiler or linker but require tools that have been developed for the specific project. A typical example is the *imake* tool, used to standardize the build process across the X Window System. After the project-specific tools are built they can be used, together with other standard tools, to preprocess, compile, and link the project's executable files. As a parallel step, the project's documentation is often converted from a "source" format into the final distribution format. This can involve the compilation of help files used by Microsoft Windows applications or the typesetting of Unix manual pages. Finally, the resultant executables and documentation are installed on the target system or prepared for larger-scale deployment or distribution. Typical distribution methods include the Red Hat Linux RPM files, the Windows installer format, or the uploading of the appropriate files on a Web site.

By far the most intricate part of a build process concerns the definition and management of the project's dependencies. These specify how different project parts depend on each other and, therefore, the order in which the project's parts are to be built. We illustrate a typical set of project dependencies in Figure 6.7. The project's distribution files depend on the existence of the executable and documentation files;

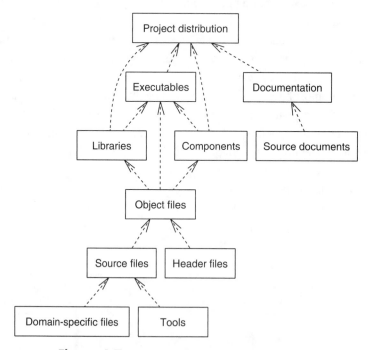

Figure 6.7 A typical set of project dependencies.

sometimes project-specific dynamically loaded libraries and software components are also part of a distribution. The executable files depend on object files, libraries, and components as these are linked together to create the executable files. Libraries and components also depend on object files. Object files in turn depend on the compilation of the corresponding source files and, in the case of languages such as C and C++, on header files that the source files include. Finally, some source files are automatically created from domain-specific files (for example, a *yacc*-specified grammar file is often used to create a parser written in C); therefore the source files depend on the domain-specific code and the corresponding tools. In our description, notice how dependencies and the build process are intimately linked together. We will discuss how this relationship is exploited to guide the process immediately after our description of a specific dependency graph.

You can see a concrete example of project dependencies in Figure 6.8, which depicts a small but representative part of the relationships involved in the build of the *apache* Web server. The installation process depends on the *apache* daemon httpd. The daemon executable httpd depends on a number of object files (among them buildmark.o and modules.o) and libraries such as the XML library libexpat.a and libap.a. The XML parsing library depends on a number of different object files; we illustrate that one of them (xmltok.o) depends on the corresponding C source file xmltok.c.

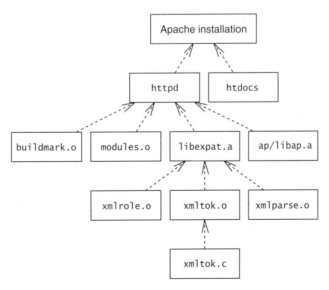

Figure 6.8 Representative dependencies in the *apache* Web server.

In large projects, dependencies involve thousands of source code files and can change according to the specific project configuration. As an example, the Windows build of the *apache* server does not depend on the Unix-specific source code files. Projects written in C and C++ further complicate dependencies because each object file depends not only on the corresponding C or C++ source file but also on all the header files included in the source file. The process of moving from dependencies to a concrete build process is not trivial. It involves performing a topological sort on the dependency graph; the result of this sort is the order on which the build targets are to be constructed (for example, compile the object files used in a library before building the library). Thankfully the process is typically automated by using specialized tools such as *make*, *nmake*, and *ant*.

When using a tool such as *make*, the dependencies and rules for constructing files from their constituents are specified in a special file, typically named *makefile* or *Makefile*. Most parts of the build process are then automated by running *make* with the makefile as an (often implicit) argument. *make* reads and processes the makefile and then issues the appropriate commands for building the specified targets. A makefile mostly consists of elements that specify a target, its dependencies, and rules for generating the target from those dependencies. As an example, the following lines specify that the target `patch.exe` depends on some object files (`$(OBJS)`) and a rule for invoking the C compiler to build it.[7]

```
patch.exe: $(OBJS)
    $(CC) $(OBJS) $(LIBS) -o $@ $(LDFLAGS)
```

A number of mechanisms are used to increase the expressiveness of makefiles; you can see some of them used in the *apache* makefile in Figure 6.9. Keep in mind that in large projects makefiles are often dynamically generated after a configuration step; you will need to perform the project-specific configuration before examining the makefile.

Often *variables* (also called *macros*) are defined—using the syntax VARIABLE = *text*—to abstract widely used file lists and tool options. The definition in Figure 6.9:1 defines the variable OBJS to contain the object files on which the *apache* executable directly depends. Variables are typically written in all-uppercase letters, and, in addition, some standard variable names are often employed for expressing typical concepts. Variables are used within a makefile by employing the syntax $L

---

[7]XFree86-3.3/xc/util/patch/Makefile.nt:23–24

Table 6.2 User Variables
Commonly Defined in Makefiles

Variable	Contents
SRCS	Source files
INCLUDES	Include files
OBJS	Object files
LIBS	Libraries
CC	C compiler
CPP	C preprocessor
CFLAGS	C compiler flags
LFLAGS	Linker flags
INSTALL	Install program
SHELL	Command shell

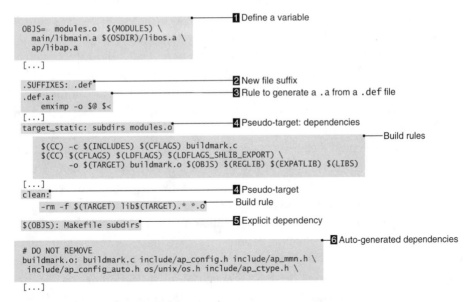

1 Define a variable

```
OBJS=  modules.o  $(MODULES) \
  main/libmain.a $(OSDIR)/libos.a \
  ap/libap.a

[...]
```

2 New file suffix
3 Rule to generate a .a from a .def file

```
.SUFFIXES: .def

.def.a:
     emximp -o $@ $<
[...]
target_static: subdirs modules.o
```

4 Pseudo-target: dependencies
Build rules

```
    $(CC) -c $(INCLUDES) $(CFLAGS) buildmark.c
    $(CC) $(CFLAGS) $(LDFLAGS) $(LDFLAGS_SHLIB_EXPORT) \
        -o $(TARGET) buildmark.o $(OBJS) $(REGLIB) $(EXPATLIB) $(LIBS)

[...]
clean:
```

4 Pseudo-target
Build rule

```
    -rm -f $(TARGET) lib$(TARGET).* *.o

$(OBJS): Makefile subdirs
```

5 Explicit dependency
6 Auto-generated dependencies

```
# DO NOT REMOVE
buildmark.o: buildmark.c include/ap_config.h include/ap_mmn.h \
  include/ap_config_auto.h os/unix/os.h include/ap_ctype.h \

[...]
```

Figure 6.9 Makefile from the *apache* Web server.

(for single-letter variable names) or $(NAME) for multiple-letter names. In Table 6.2 we summarize some user-defined variables you will often encounter.

To avoid the repetition of common rules, *make* provides the possibility of defining a rule for creating a target file based on the suffixes of the files participating in the transformation process. In Figure 6.9:3 a rule specifies how to generate an OS/2

Table 6.3 Variables Maintained by *make*

Variable	Contents
$$	The $ sign
$@	Name of the file to be made
$?	Names of files younger than the target
$>	The list of all sources for the target
$<	Name of the file from which the target is to be transformed
$*	The file prefix of the target without preceding directory components or a suffix

import library (.a) from its definition (.def) by invoking the *emximp* command. Most implementations of *make* maintain a large internal set of transformation rules and available file suffixes. These typically specify how to compile files written in C, C++, assembly, or Fortran, how to convert *yacc* and *lex* files into C, and how to extract source files stored under revision control. When a suffix is not one of the *make*-known suffixes, it needs to be defined by using a special .SUFFIXES command (Figure 6.9:2). To allow users to specify abstract file names in rules, *make* maintains a number of variables automatically, changing their contents based on the targets and dependencies of the rule being processed. We summarize the most important *make*-maintained variables in Table 6.3.

The targets in a makefile need not necessarily be files generated during the build process. *Pseudo-targets* are often defined by using arbitrary names to specify build sequences that are to be executed when the specific target is given as an argument to *make* or as a dependency for another target (Figure 6.9:4). Some common pseudo-target names include all or build for building all the project's targets, doc for building the project's documentation, depend for generating dependency information, test for running postbuild regression tests, install for performing the installation steps, and clean for removing the files generated during the build process.

Not all dependencies need to be followed by a build rule (Figure 6.9:5). Dependencies without a rule are used to specify that if one of the sources is more recent than the target, then the target needs to be rebuilt (using another rule for that target). The dependency in Figure 6.9:5 is used to express that the object files need to be rebuilt if the makefile is changed, presumably because a change in the makefile might involve a change in a compile-time configuration flag. Dependencies without rules are also often used to specify how object files depend on some header files: when a header file included in C code is modified, the corresponding C file needs to be recompiled.

In a large project each C or C++ file typically includes tens of header files, and some of the header files may recursively include other files. Generating correct dependencies to reflect this situation by hand is very difficult. Fortunately, there are a number of ways to generate this information automatically. The GNU C compiler provides a –M option to generate such dependencies, while in BSD systems the *mkdep* tool provides similar functionality. Automatically generated dependencies are typically appended at the end of a makefile following a suitable marker (Figure 6.9:6). A makefile rule (typically called depend) is then used to maintain and refresh those dependencies after changes in the source code or a project's configuration.

[i]

The success of the original *make* program spawned a number of descendants. Newer-generation versions of *make* typically support conditional processing, include files and system-wide specifications, and maintain large collections of internal implicit rules. Some versions of *make* can run the build process in parallel across a number of machines to improve its speed. Large projects typically use these features to centralize the configuration of a build process spanning multiple subprojects and directories. As an example, the X Window System uses *imake* to preprocess makefiles so that system-wide definitions and tools will be consistently used across different subprojects. Similarly, the *make* tool used in the FreeBSD system reads common definitions and default rules maintained in /usr/share/mk before processing a local file; as a result the per-project makefiles are functional and terse to the extreme.

Dependencies are not always specified declaratively as parts of a makefile; they are sometimes described in a procedural fashion as parts of an explicit description of the build process. An example of an imperative specification can be found in the build process of the *apache* Web server: it involves the explicit execution of a build step in all subdirectories prior to building and linking the main program executable.[8]

```
target_static: subdirs modules.o
    [...]
subdirs:
    @for i in $(SUBDIRS); do \
        [...]
        cd $$i && $(MAKE) [...]
    done
```

In the above example the subdirs pseudo-target will always be executed when building target_static. The subdirs target causes *make* to be executed in each

---

[8]apache/src/Makefile.tmpl:33–71

directory appearing in the SUBDIRS variable. A procedural specification of parts of the build process is often used to decouple a long dependency chain, providing a more modular description. Information between the one *make* process and its descendents is automatically passed by using environment variables: all variable definitions are exported to the descendents as environment variables, and all environment variables appear within a *make* process as variable definitions. Procedural specifications are also used on platforms that do not support makefiles or particular features needed for a declarative description. Consider the makefile used for compiling *apache* under Windows. Two targets have as their rule large sequences of commands that are to be run for building and installing *apache*.[9]

As makefiles grow, they become difficult to read and reason about. Fortunately, there is a convenient shortcut for disentangling a complicated build process. You can dry-run *make* by using the -n switch to inspect the steps of a large build process. When executing a dry run, *make* will display the commands it would execute without actually executing them. You can then redirect the output of *make* into a file and inspect it carefully with your favorite editor. You will probably find that the ability to search for strings—representing tools, command-line arguments, input and output files—within the build listing is particularly useful.

Makefiles are seldom portable between different operating systems since they often contain platform-dependent build commands. Newer build-management tools like *jam*[10] and *ant*[11] are explicitly designed with operating system portability in mind. *jam* achieves *jamfile* (the *jam* equivalent of a makefile) portability through installation-time configuration and by internally handling operating system–specific differences like directory path separators, and complicated tasks like C header dependency scanning. *ant* follows a different approach, using XML to express the build tasks and Java classes to extend its functionality (see Figure 6.10[12]). However, the basic concepts behind the way to read the corresponding files remain the same.

Exercise 6.7   Download and build a relatively large open-source project (such as *apache*, Perl, the X Window System, or a Unix-like kernel). Document the steps of the build process.

Exercise 6.8   Compare the use of a declarative versus the use of a procedural specification for a build process.

---

[9]apache/src/makefile.win:61–242

[10]http://www.perforce.com/jam/jam.html

[11]http://jakarta.apache.org/ant/index.html

[12]jt4/webapps/manager/build.xml

```
<project name="manager" default="build-main" basedir=".">     •————————  Project specification
  [...]
  <!-- See "build.properties.sample" in the top level directory for all    -->  •————  Comments
  <!-- property values you must customize for successful building!!!         -->

  <property file="build.properties"/>         •————————————  Inherit project-wide properties
  <property file="../build.properties"/>
  [...]
                                              •————  Specify project properties
  <property name="build.compiler"   value="classic"/>
  <property name="webapps.build"    value="../build"/>
  <property name="webapps.dist"     value="../dist"/>
  <property name="webapp.name"      value="manager"/>


                                              •————  Rule
  <target name="build-prepare">
    <mkdir dir="${webapps.build}"/>           •————  Commands
    <mkdir dir="${webapps.build}/${webapp.name}"/>
  </target>

  [...]
  <target
    name="build-static"•————————————————————  Rule name
                                              Rule dependency
    depends="build-prepare">

                                              •————  Command
    <copy todir="${webapps.build}/${webapp.name}">
      <fileset dir=".">                       •————  Command parameters
        <exclude name="build.*"/>
      </fileset>
    </copy>

  </target>
  [...]
</project>
```

Figure 6.10 An *ant* build file written in XML.

Exercise 6.9   If you are using an integrated development environment, describe how the build process is specified. Comment on the specification's readability, maintainability, and portability.

Exercise 6.10   Select four variants of the *make* program and compare the additional features they offer.

Exercise 6.11   Read the documentation of a *make* program to find out how you can create a listing of its implicitly defined rules. Select five of these rules and explain their operation.

6.4 Configuration

A software system whose configuration can be controlled allows its developers to build, maintain, and evolve a single official version of the source code. Having a single copy of the source code simplifies change and evolution management. By using the appropriate configuration, the same source code body:

- Creates products with different features
- Builds the project on different architectures or operating systems
- Is maintained under different development environments
- Links with different libraries
- Executes using runtime specified configuration options

A system's configuration can occur either at buildtime, in which case it affects both the build process and its results, or dynamically at runtime, in which case it affects only the program's operation. In common with other large system features, you should be able to recognize and reason about the configuration process elements. Typical configuration options addressed at buildtime include the product's supported features, the compilation and target architecture and operating system, the compiler and its options, the need for header files and libraries, installation and administration policies, and default values. The last two elements are also often addressed through runtime configuration.

Following the principle of dependency isolation, the configuration elements are typically isolated in a few files. Configuration information that relates to the way the system is built (for example, installation directories, tool names and paths, whether debugging symbols will be included in the executable, the level of optimization to apply, libraries and object files used) is often expressed in the form of variable definitions inside the project's makefile.[13]

```
ARCHDIR     = ..\lib\$(ARCHNAME)
COREDIR     = ..\lib\CORE
AUTODIR     = ..\lib\auto
[...]
LIBC        = msvcrt.lib
[...]
OPTIMIZE    = -O1 -MD -DNDEBUG
```

When the system is built using an integrated development environment (IDE) or another build management tool, the corresponding information is stored in the corresponding project configuration file, as can be seen in the following excerpt from an *ant* configuration file.[14]

---

[13] perl/win32/Makefile:333–388
[14] jt4/build.properties.sample:13–26

```
# ----- Compile Control Flags -----
compile.debug=on
compile.deprecation=off
compile.optimize=on
# ----- Default Base Path for Dependent Packages -----
base.path=/usr/local
# ----- Jakarta Regular Expressions Library, version 1.2 -----
regexp.home=${base.path}/jakarta-regexp-1.2
regexp.lib=${regexp.home}
regexp.jar=${regexp.home}/jakarta-regexp-1.2.jar
```

Similarly, configuration data that affects how the actual program will compile (runtime file directories, macros affecting conditional compilation of features, portability-related options) is often stored as compiler macro definitions in a file named config.h.[15]

```
/* Define if your OS maps references to /dev/fd/n to file descriptor n */
#define HAVE_DEV_FD 1
/* Default PATH (see comments in configure.in for more details) */
#define DEFAULT_PATH "/bin:/usr/bin:/usr/ucb"
/* Include ksh features? (see comments in configure.in for more details) */
#define KSH 1
```

Since many of the configuration options (especially those that affect operating system and processor architecture portability) are common among different systems, a number of methods and tools have been devised to automate their generation. As a concrete example, the numerous configuration systems generated using the GNU *autoconf* tools follow at buildtime the process illustrated in Figure 6.11. The first part of the configuration process has a shell script, called configure, run to determine a number of the system characteristics. A precise ordering of the detection functions ensures that more complicated functions can be built on earlier determined results. Specifically, elements are checked in the following order: available programs, libraries, header files, typedefs, structures, compiler characteristics, library functions, and system services. The results from this system probing are stored in a humanly readable form in a file called config.log, in a form from which they can be reread to avoid the time-consuming probe sequence in the file config.cache, and in a form that is used for the final configuration in the file config.status. In the second step

---

[15] netbsdsrc/bin/ksh/config.h:192–199

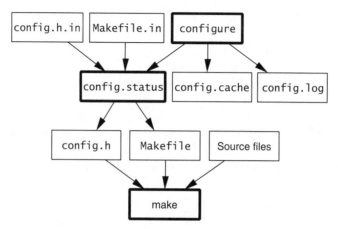

Figure 6.11 The configuration process of GNU *autoconf*.

of the configuration process, the `config.status` file reads the two parameterized
template files, `config.h.in` and `Makefile.in`, to generate the actual `Makefile` and
`config.h` files.

At runtime portable programs read configuration data either from an ad hoc
configuration file[16, 17]

```
/*
 * set_profile reads $HOME/.indent.pro and ./.indent.pro
 * and handles arguments given in these files.
 */
void
set_profile()
{
    FILE    *f;
    char    fname[BUFSIZ];
    static char prof[] = ".indent.pro";

    sprintf(fname, "%s/%s", getenv("HOME"), prof);
    if ((f = fopen(option_source = fname, "r")) != NULL) {
        scan_profile(f);
        (void) fclose(f);
    }
    if ((f = fopen(option_source = prof, "r")) != NULL {
```

---

[16]netbsdsrc/usr.bin/indent/args.c:284–303
[17]Can you spot in the code fragment the buffer overflow possibility?

```
        scan_profile(f);
        (void) fclose(f);
    }
```

or from process configuration commands written in a general-purpose interpreted language like Tcl/Tk or Perl.

In addition, programs running on a POSIX-like platform often obtain configuration data from environment variables by using the getenv function.[18]

```
arcname = getenv("TAPE");
```

Java programs use the System.getProperty method.[19]

```
String useNamingProperty = System.getProperty("catalina.useNaming");
```

Windows programs query the Windows registry by using the SDK RegOpenKey, RegQueryValueEx, and RegCloseKey functions.[20]

```
bSuccess = RegOpenKey(HKEY_LOCAL_MACHINE,newkey,&hk);
[...]
bSuccess = RegQueryValueEx(hk, /* subkey handle */
    "Bind",                    /* value name */
    NULL,                      /* must be zero */
    NULL,                      /* value type not required */
    (LPBYTE) &bindservicenames, /* address of value data */
    &sizeofbindnames);         /* length of value data */
[...]
RegCloseKey(hk);
```

Programs in the X Window System use functions like XtGetApplicationResources.[21]

```
static struct resources {
    Boolean     rpn;    /* reverse polish notation (HP mode) */
    Boolean     stipple; /* background stipple */
    Cursor      cursor;
} appResources;
```

---

[18] netbsdsrc/bin/pax/options.c:800
[19] jt4/catalina/src/share/org/apache/catalina/core/StandardContext.java:800
[20] netbsdsrc/usr.sbin/xntp/xntpd/ntp_io.c:2355–2377
[21] XFree86-3.3/contrib/programs/xcalc/xcalc.c:95–131

```
#define offset(field) XtOffsetOf(struct resources, field)
static XtResource Resources[] = {
{"rpn",          "Rpn",        XtRBoolean, sizeof(Boolean),
    offset(rpn),         XtRImmediate, (XtPointer) False},
{"stipple",      "Stipple",    XtRBoolean, sizeof(Boolean),
    offset(stipple),    XtRImmediate, (XtPointer) False},
{"cursor",       "Cursor",     XtRCursor,  sizeof(Cursor),
    offset(cursor),     XtRCursor,     (XtPointer)NULL}
};
[...]
XtGetApplicationResources(toplevel, (XtPointer)&appResources,
    Resources, XtNumber(Resources), (ArgList) NULL, ZERO);
```

⚠   Configuration data read at runtime can be freely manipulated by the end user. Programs should therefore validate it with the same care as any other user input, while programs running under an elevated security privilege should ensure that they cannot have any of their functions configured by unprivileged users. As a counterexample, early shared-library implementations allowed hostile users to configure the search path so as to have privileged programs load system libraries of their own making. These libraries would then be used to manipulate the privileged program, bypassing security restrictions.

Exercise 6.12   Configure a program from the book's CD-ROM to compile and run in a supported environment. Examine the configuration process output files and manually verify four different configuration options.

Exercise 6.13   Read the source code of a configuration script, explaining how two different configuration options are determined.

Exercise 6.14   Compare the runtime configuration mechanisms we examined in terms of the provided functionality and usability.

Exercise 6.15   Earlier versions of Microsoft Windows supported runtime configuration through *initialization files* located in the Windows directory using a .ini extension. These were ASCII files, divided into sections, containing rows of key/value elements. Compare this scheme against the current registry-based realization.

6.5 Revision Control

We can envisage the source code of a system spanning space and time. Code, organized in the form of files and directories, covers the space, while the same code elements also evolve over time. A *revision control system* allows you to view and control this time element by tracking the code's evolution, tagging important occasions, and chronicling the rationale behind changes. In this section we detail how to use a revision control system to comprehend the code's temporal elements. A number of systems, such as SCCS, RCS, CVS, and Visual Source Safe are currently in use. Most of them have similar capabilities; we will base our examples on CVS since it is widely used in the open-source code community.

Before delving into the specifics of working with projects under revision control, it is useful to get an overall picture of how revisions are tracked in a typical development process. A revision control system keeps all historical information about files in a central *repository*. The history of each file is kept in identifiable versions, typically using automatically generated version numbers such as 3.9.2.11, and, often, associated tags (for example, R4.3-STABLE-p1) selected by developers to mark a milestone in the system's development. Before a project's release, version milestones are used to mark development objectives (for example, provision of specified functionality, clean compilation, successful regression testing); after the release, versions typically track evolutionary changes and bug fixes. When a developer has finished work on a file version she or he will *commit* or *check in* the file to the repository. The revision control system keeps full details about all file versions (most systems economize on space by storing the differences between versions) as well as metadata about every commit operation (typically date, time, developer name, and a change comment). Some development models allow developers to *lock* a file while they are working on it, thus prohibiting simultaneous changes. Other systems provide a way to reconcile conflicting changes after these have occurred. Sometimes development work on a given file may be *split* into two different *branches* (for example, a stable branch and a maintenance branch); later two branches may be *joined* again. To coordinate the release of complete systems consisting of numerous files, many systems provide a way to *tag* a set of files with a symbolic name identifying the system's version the file belongs to. It is thus possible to identify the version of each file that made up a complete system.

You can see an example of a file version tree and the associated symbolic names in Figure 6.12. The dashed arrow lines represent a UML *trace* dependency, indicating that the node pointed to by the arrow is a historical ancestor of the node at the arrow's tail. As an example, version 1.1.1.2 of the file cat.c is an ancestor of versions 1.9 and 1.1.1.3; correspondingly, version 1.9 is based on versions 1.8 and 1.1.1.2. The tagged values appearing within braces indicate the symbolic version name that was used for a particular release of the complete BSD system. Thus, we can see that the BSD *lite-2* distribution included version 1.1.1.3 of cat.c.

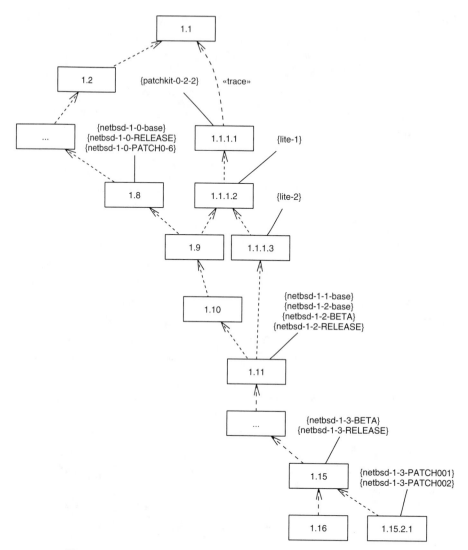

Figure 6.12 Revision tree and symbolic names for the file cat.c.

When examining code, you want to ensure that you are indeed reading the most current version. A revision control system provides a way to obtain an up-to-date version of the source code from its repository. Under CVS, for example, you would issue the command

```
cvs update -d -P
```

to obtain the latest version of each file from the complete source tree you are working on. The -d flag specifies to create directories that exist in the repository but are missing from the working directory, and the -P flag to remove directories that become empty after being updated.

Sometimes you do not want to examine the latest version of the source code—which may be in development flux—but a stable version used for a particular release. You can obtain the release you want to work on by using its symbolic tag. As an example, you would use the following CVS command to obtain the version of all files comprising the *sed* stream editor that correspond to the netbsd-1-2 release of NetBSD.

```
cvs co -rnetbsd-1-2 basesrc/usr.bin/sed
```

You can also request a particular version of a given file by using a command like the following.

```
cvs co -r1.17 basesrc/usr.bin/sed/compile.c
```

An important function of a revision control system is to help its users identify the file they are working on. This is achieved by embedding inside the source file *keywords* in a specific format. When the system retrieves the file from a repository, it will append to each keyword the respective data such as the file's version, name, or complete path. The following are some expanded keywords appearing in the source inside comments and strings.[22]

```
/* $NetBSD: cat.c,v 1.15 1997/07/20 04:34:33 thorpej Exp $ */
[...]
#ifndef lint
#if 0
static char sccsid[] = "@(#)cat.c 8.2 (Berkeley) 4/27/95";
#else
__RCSID("$NetBSD: cat.c,v 1.15 1997/07/20 04:34:33 thorpej Exp $");
#endif
#endif /* not lint */
```

Table 6.4 shows a list of the most commonly used keyword tags in three different common revision control systems. Keywords may appear in comments—typically at

---

[22] netbsdsrc/bin/cat/cat.c:1–51

Table 6.4 File Identification Tags Used in Revision Control Systems

Keyword	Contents
RCS and CVS	
$Author$	Login name of the user who checked in the revision
$Date$	Date and time the revision was checked in
$Header$	Path name, revision, date, time, author, state, locker
Id	Same as $Header$; file name without a path
$Locker$	Login name of the user who locked the revision
Log	Messages supplied at check-in, preceded by a header
$Name$	Symbolic name used to check out the revision
$RCSfile$	Name of the RCS file without a path
$Revision$	Revision number assigned to the revision
$Source$	Full path name of the RCS file
$State$	State assigned to the revision
SCCS	
%M%	Module name
%R%	Release
%L%	Level
%B%	Branch
%S%	Sequence
%I%	Release, level, branch, and sequence
%D% / %H%	Date of the current get
%T%	Time of the current get
%E% / %G%	Date the newest applied delta was created
%U%	Time the newest applied delta was created
%F% / %P%	SCCS file/full path name
%Y%	Module type
%C%	Current line number in the file
%Z%	The four-character string @(#) used by *what*
%W%	Shorthand for %Z%%M%*tab*%I%
%A%	Shorthand for %Z%%Y% %M% %I%%Z%
Visual Source Safe (VSS)	
$Archive:$	VSS archive file location
$Author:$	User who last changed the file
$Date:$	Date and time of the last check-in
$Header:$	Shorthand for Logfile, Revision, Date, Author
$History:$	File history, in VSS format
$JustDate:$	Date, without the time addendum
$Log:$	File history, in RCS format
$Logfile:$	Same as $Archive:$
$Modtime:$	Date and time of the last modification
$NoKeywords:$	No keyword expansion for keywords that follow
$Revision:$	VSS version number
$Workfile:$	File name

the file's head—to aid the reader of the source code or inside strings so that they are compiled and appear in the executable file. Revision control systems offer commands that examine the data inside a source, object, or executable file and display the keywords found. The command that recognizes CVS, RCS, and Visual Source Safe keywords is called *ident*.

```
$ ident cat.c
cat.c:
     $NetBSD: cat.c,v 1.28 2001/09/16 12:12:13 wiz Exp $
     $NetBSD: cat.c,v 1.28 2001/09/16 12:12:13 wiz Exp $
```

The corresponding command used with the SCCS system is *what*.

```
$ what cat.c
cat.c:
         Copyright (c) 1989, 1993
         cat.c   8.2 (Berkeley) 4/27/95
```

You can use commands that display executable file revision identification keywords to match an executable with its source code. In large programs you can thus obtain a list of all source code, including libraries, used to build an executable file.

```
$ ident mail
Mail:
     $NetBSD: crt0.c,v 1.9 1999/07/02 15:53:55 simonb Exp $
     $NetBSD: version.c,v 1.5 1997/10/19 05:04:07 lukem Exp $
     $NetBSD: aux.c,v 1.10 1998/12/19 16:30:52 christos Exp $
     $NetBSD: cmd1.c,v 1.13 2000/02/10 12:34:42 tron Exp $
     $NetBSD: cmd2.c,v 1.10 2000/02/10 12:34:43 tron Exp $
     $NetBSD: cmd3.c,v 1.11 1999/02/09 04:51:30 dean Exp $
     $NetBSD: cmdtab.c,v 1.8 1997/10/19 05:03:08 lukem Exp $
     $NetBSD: collect.c,v 1.20 2000/02/10 12:34:43 tron Exp $
     $NetBSD: dotlock.c,v 1.4 1998/07/06 06:51:55 mrg Exp $
     $NetBSD: edit.c,v 1.7 1997/11/25 17:58:17 bad Exp $
     $NetBSD: fio.c,v 1.12 1998/12/19 16:32:34 christos Exp $
     $NetBSD: getname.c,v 1.6 1998/07/26 22:07:27 mycroft Exp $
     $NetBSD: head.c,v 1.8 1998/12/19 16:32:52 christos Exp $
     $NetBSD: v7.local.c,v 1.10 1998/07/26 22:07:27 mycroft Exp $
     $NetBSD: lex.c,v 1.14 2000/01/21 17:08:35 mycroft Exp $
     $NetBSD: list.c,v 1.9 1998/12/19 16:33:24 christos Exp $
     $NetBSD: main.c,v 1.10 1999/02/09 04:51:30 dean Exp $
```

```
$NetBSD: names.c,v 1.8 1998/12/19 16:33:40 christos Exp $
$NetBSD: popen.c,v 1.9 1998/12/19 16:34:04 christos Exp $
$NetBSD: quit.c,v 1.11 2000/02/10 12:34:43 tron Exp $
$NetBSD: send.c,v 1.11 2000/02/10 12:34:44 tron Exp $
$NetBSD: strings.c,v 1.6 1997/10/19 05:03:54 lukem Exp $
$NetBSD: temp.c,v 1.7 1998/07/26 22:07:27 mycroft Exp $
$NetBSD: tty.c,v 1.11 1999/01/06 15:53:39 kleink Exp $
$NetBSD: vars.c,v 1.6 1998/10/08 17:36:56 wsanchez Exp $
```

Revision control systems keep metadata about every revision. This data can provide extremely useful information when examining a system's source code. You can obtain a full list of all revision metadata by using a command like the following.

```
cvs log cat.c
```

An annotated excerpt of the obtained data appears in Figure 6.13. In Section 8.2 we outline some heuristics you can apply on the change log data to obtain useful

```
RCS file: /cvsroot/basesrc/bin/cat/cat.c,v          — Repository file path
Working file: cat.c
head: 1.28                                           — Head of the tree
branch:
locks: strict                                        — Locking policy
access list:
symbolic names:                                      — File versions and corresponding symbolic names
    netbsd-1-5-PATCH002: 1.23
    [...]
    netbsd-1-5: 1.23.0.4
    [...]
    netbsd-1-2-BETA: 1.11
    netbsd-1-2-base: 1.11
    netbsd-1-2: 1.11.0.6
    [...]
keyword substitution: kv
total revisions: 33;    selected revisions: 33
description:
----------------------------
revision 1.28                                        — Revision 1.28 changes
date: 2001/09/16 12:12:13;  author: wiz;  state: Exp;  lines: +6 -4
Some KNF, via patch by Petri Koistinen in private mail.
----------------------------
revision 1.27                                        — Revision 1.27 changes
date: 2001/07/29 22:40:57;  author: wiz;  state: Exp;  lines: +6 -6
Some style improvements. [Nearly] #13592 by Petri Koistinen.   — 1 Bug id
[...]
----------------------------
revision 1.15.2.1                                    — Tree branch
date: 1998/02/08 21:45:36;  author: mellon;  state: Exp;  lines: +18 -9
Pull up 1.16 and 1.17 (kleink)
```

Figure 6.13 Sample RCS/CVS log output.

details. Some of the change comments may reference a particular numeric code (Figure 6.13:1). This code typically identifies a problem described in a bug tracking database such as GNATS, Bugzilla, or the SourceForge Bug Tracker. Using the bug-tracking code number, you can locate the particular issue in the database to see a full description of the problem, often including instructions for reproducing it and the way it was resolved.

You can also apply tools to massive log data output to obtain consolidated results. As an example, say you want to know which of the files in a project has undergone the largest number of revisions (sometimes indicating the location of possible trouble spots). You can massage the output of cvs log with the *awk* Unix-based text-processing tool to create a list of file names and version numbers, and then sort that list numerically in reverse order according to the secondary version number. The top files in the list are those with the highest revision number.

```
$ cvs log sed |
> awk '/^Working/ {w = $3}/^head:/{print $2, w}'|
> sort -n -t . +1 -r |
> head
1.30 sed/process.c
1.20 sed/compile.c
1.14 sed/sed.1
1.10 sed/main.c
1.8 sed/Makefile
1.7 sed/defs.h
1.6 sed/misc.c
1.6 sed/extern.h
1.4 sed/POSIX
```

You can also use the revision control system version repository to identify how particular changes were implemented. Consider the following log entry that appears for version 1.13 of cat.c.

```
revision 1.13
date: 1997/04/27 18:34:33;  author: kleink;  state: Exp;  lines: +8 -3
Indicate file handling failures by exit codes >0; fixes PR/3538 from
David Eckhardt <davide@piper.nectar.cs.cmu.edu>.
```

To see exactly how file-handling failures are now indicated you can issue a command to examine (in context—see Section 10.4) the differences between version 1.12 and version 1.13.

```
$ cvs diff -c -r1.12 -r1.13 basesrc/bin/cat/cat.c
Index: basesrc/bin/cat/cat.c
=====================================================================
RCS file: /cvsroot/basesrc/bin/cat/cat.c,v
retrieving revision 1.12
retrieving revision 1.13
diff -c -r1.12 -r1.13
[...]
***************
*** 136,141 ****
--- 136,142 ----
                           fp = stdin;
          else if ((fp = fopen(*argv, "r")) == NULL) {
                           warn("%s", *argv);
+                          rval = 1;
                           ++argv;
                           continue;
          }
```

As the above snippet indicates, a line was added to set the `rval` flag (presumably indicating the command's return value) when the file open command fails.

Exercise 6.16   How do you track revision histories in your environment? If you are not using a revision control system, consider adopting one.

Exercise 6.17   Explain how an executable file might contain different identification tags from some source files at hand. How would you solve such a problem?

Exercise 6.18   A number of open-source projects keep CVS-based revision control repositories open for read-only access to the public. Locate such a project and create a local copy of it on your machine. Using the command cvs log, examine the log of a given file (preferably one that contains branches) and match symbolic tags to file versions. Explain how branches were used to manage successive releases.

6.6 Project-Specific Tools

Large projects often have unique problems and matching resources to construct specialized tools as part of the implementation process. Custom-built tools are used for many different aspects of the software development process including configuration, build process management, code generation, testing, and documentation. In the following paragraphs we provide some representative examples of tools used for each task.

The configuration of an operating system kernel is a particularly complex task since it involves creating a customized kernel to match a specific hardware configuration by selecting among hundreds of device drivers and software options, many of them interdependent. The NetBSD kernel configuration is handled by *config*[23]—a tool that reads a configuration describing the system options and creates a description of I/O devices that may be attached to the system and a makefile for building the particular kernel. The input of *config* is of the following form.[24]

```
# CPU options
options       CPU_SA110  # Support the SA110 core

# Architecture options
options       OFW        # Enable common Open Firmware bits
options       SHARK      # We are a Shark

# File systems
file-system FFS          # UFS
file-system MFS          # memory file system
file-system NFS          # Network file system
[...]
# Open Firmware devices
ofbus*        at root
ofbus*        at ofbus?
ofrtc*        at ofisa?
```

Based on such input, *config* will generate a makefile that contains only the files that are to be compiled for the particular configuration and the file ioconf.c, which defines system structures for the selected devices, such as the following.

```
/* file systems */
extern struct vfsops ffs_vfsops;
extern struct vfsops mfs_vfsops;
extern struct vfsops nfs_vfsops;
[...]

struct vfsops *vfs_list_initial[] = {
        &ffs_vfsops,
        &mfs_vfsops,
```

---

[23] netbsdsrc/usr.sbin/config
[24] netbsdsrc/sys/arch/arm32/conf/GENERIC

```
      &nfs_vfsops,
      [...]
      NULL,
};
```

Specialized tools are also often employed to manage the build process, especially when the project is ported across many different platforms, rendering unfeasible the use of platform-specific tools. As an example, the X Window System uses *imake*,[25] a custom-built makefile preprocessor, to manage the build process. *imake* is used to generate makefiles from a template, a set of C preprocessor macro functions, and a per-directory input file. It is used to keep machine dependencies (such as compiler options, alternate command names, and special make rules) separate from the descriptions of the various items to be built. Thus a system-wide configuration file is used to tailor more than 500 separate makefiles. In addition, the architects of the X Window System could not rely on the existence of a particular dependency generator for C include files. They therefore devised a project specific generator, *makedepend*.[26]

By far the most common use of project-specific tools involves the generation of specialized code. A tool is thus used to dynamically create software code as part of the build process. In most cases the code is in the same language as the rest of the system (C, for example), and it is seldom sophisticated, typically comprising lookup tables or simple `switch` statements. Tools are used to construct the code at buildtime to avoid the overhead of performing the equivalent operation at runtime. In this way the resulting code is often more efficient and consumes less memory. The input to code generation tools can be another file representing in textual form the specifications for the code to generate, a simple domain-specific language, or even parts of the system's source code. Consider the example of the IBM 3270 terminal emulator. Comprising 77 files, the emulator is a project of modest size. It uses, however, four different tools to create appropriate mappings between the IBM characters and keyboard codes and the corresponding ones found on Unix workstations. Figure 6.14 depicts the way these tools are used during the build process. Two different tools, `mkastods`[27] and `mkdstoas`,[28] create mappings from ASCII to EBCDIC (IBM-specific) display characters and vice versa. The output files of these tools, `asc_disp.out` and `disp_asc.out`, are then included in the C file `disp_asc.c`[29] that is compiled as part of the `tn3270`

---

[25] XFree86-3.3/xc/config/imake
[26] XFree86-3.3/xc/config/makedepend
[27] netbsdsrc/usr.bin/tn3270/tools/mkastods/mkastods.c
[28] netbsdsrc/usr.bin/tn3270/tools/mkdstoas/mkdstoas.c
[29] netbsdsrc/usr.bin/tn3270/api/disp_asc.c

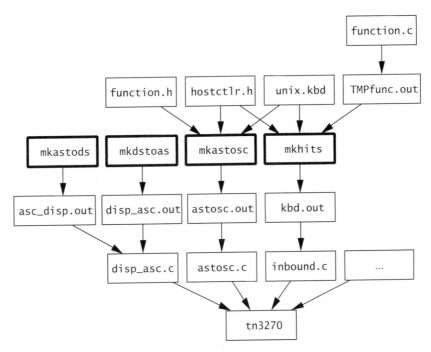

Figure 6.14 Tools used in building the IBM 3270 terminal emulator.

terminal emulator executable. Similarly, mkastosc[30] is used to create a mapping from ASCII codes to IBM keyboard scan codes and mkhits[31] to create a mapping from scan codes and shift-key state to IBM 3270 functions and characters. Both tools generate code by processing the Unix keyboard definition file unix.kbd,[32] the IBM 3270 command file hostctlr.h,[33] and the editing function definition files function.h[34] and function.c[35] (preprocessed as TMPfunc.out). The code these tools generate (astosc.out and kbd.out) is then included in C files (astosc.c[36] and inbound.c[37]) in the form of an array of structure definitions used for lookup tables. As an example,

[30] netbsdsrc/usr.bin/tn3270/tools/mkastosc/mkastosc.c
[31] netbsdsrc/usr.bin/tn3270/tools/mkhits/mkhits.c
[32] netbsdsrc/usr.bin/tn3270/ctlr/unix.kbd
[33] netbsdsrc/usr.bin/tn3270/ctlr/hostctlr.h
[34] netbsdsrc/usr.bin/tn3270/ctlr/function.h
[35] netbsdsrc/usr.bin/tn3270/ctlr/function.c
[36] netbsdsrc/usr.bin/tn3270/api/astosc.c
[37] netbsdsrc/usr.bin/tn3270/ctlr/inbound.c

`kbd.out` will contain key mappings of the following type.

```
struct hits hits[] = {
    { 0, {  {undefined}, {undefined}, {undefined}, {undefined}
    } },
    [...]
    { 70, { /* 0x05 */
            { FCN_ATTN },
            { undefined },
            { FCN_AID, AID_TREQ },
            { undefined },
    } },
    { 65, { /* 0x06 */
            { FCN_AID, AID_CLEAR },
            { undefined },
            { FCN_TEST },
            { undefined },
    } },
```

Project-specific tools are also often employed for handling a product's regression tests. An interesting example is the test suite used in the implementation of the Perl language. The suite comprises more than 270 test cases. A driver program TEST[38] is used to run each test and report the result. Interestingly, the test driver is also written in Perl, with particular care taken to avoid constructs that might fail during testing.

Finally, custom tools are also often used to automate the generation of a project's documentation. The *javadoc* program, now distributed as a general-purpose tool with the Java SDK, most probably started its life as a tool to create the documentation for the Java API. *javadoc* parses the declarations and documentation comments in a set of Java source files and produces a set of HTML pages describing the classes, inner classes, interfaces, constructors, methods, and fields. You can see a representative example of Java code with *javadoc*-specific comments in Figure 6.15.[39]

The Perl distribution, brought to us by a team of avid tool builders, also contains a set of tools based on the *pod* (plain old documentation) markup language that are used to create documentation in a number of different formats. The *pod* tools[40] can create output in LaTeX, Unix manual page, plain text, and HTML format. In common with *javadoc* they have also outgrown their original niche to become general-purpose documentation tools. One other area of documentation often managed by custom tools

---

[38] perl/t/TEST
[39] hsqldb/src/org/hsqldb/jdbcPreparedStatement.java:837–851
[40] perl/pod

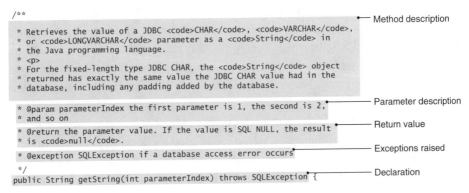

```
/**
 * Retrieves the value of a JDBC <code>CHAR</code>, <code>VARCHAR</code>,
 * or <code>LONGVARCHAR</code> parameter as a <code>String</code> in
 * the Java programming language.
 * <p>
 * For the fixed-length type JDBC CHAR, the <code>String</code> object
 * returned has exactly the same value the JDBC CHAR value had in the
 * database, including any padding added by the database.
 * @param parameterIndex the first parameter is 1, the second is 2,
 * and so on
 * @return the parameter value. If the value is SQL NULL, the result
 * is <code>null</code>.
 * @exception SQLException if a database access error occurs
 */
public String getString(int parameterIndex) throws SQLException {
```

- Method description
- Parameter description
- Return value
- Exceptions raised
- Declaration

Figure 6.15 *javadoc* comments embedded in a Java file.

is error messages. These are typically sown through large areas of the program code. Some projects develop a tool to locate the error messages in the code (by searching, for example, for calls to the function that creates them) and to produce orderly end-user documentation—often by using specially formatted comments that appear next to the message.

Exercise 6.19 Examine the kernel configuration program *config*[41] in the book's CD-ROM and document the aspects of the system it can configure.

Exercise 6.20 How is an installation process specified in your favorite integrated development environment? Discuss the advantages and shortcomings of the employed approach.

Exercise 6.21 Propose a way to locate code generation tools in the book's CD-ROM. Locate five such tools and explain the purposes they serve.

Exercise 6.22 Examine the Perl automated test processor TEST[42] and a test case, for example, array.t.[43] Explain how a test case should be written and how it is processed during regression testing.

Exercise 6.23 Convert your curriculum vitae into Perl *pod* format. Using Perl's *pod* processing tools, convert it into HTML and plain text. Comment on the usability of this approach.

6.7 Testing

Well-engineered projects contain provisions for testing all or a subset of their functionality. The provisions might be part of a deliberate plan to verify the system's

---

[41] netbsdsrc/usr.sbin/config
[42] perl/t/TEST
[43] perl/t/op/array.t

operation, or they may be remnants of less formal testing activities conducted by the system's developers during its implementation. As part of the source code reading activity, you should first be able to recognize and reason about test code and test cases, and then use testing artifacts as an aid for understanding the rest of the code. In the following paragraphs, we examine a number of different types of test code you will encounter.

The simplest type of code used for testing is a statement that generates *logging* or *debugging* output. Such statements are typically used by developers to test whether the program's operation agrees with their expectations. You can use a program's debugging output to help you understand crucial parts of a program's control flow and data elements. Moreover, the places where a tracing statement is located typically mark important parts of an algorithm's function. In most programs the debugging information typically goes to the program's standard output stream or into a file.[44]

```
#ifdef DEBUG
    if (trace == NULL)
        trace = fopen("bgtrace", "w");
    fprintf(trace, "\nRoll:  %d %d%s\n", D0, D1, race ? " (race)" : "");
    fflush(trace);
#endif
```

Notice in the above example how the DEBUG macro is used to control whether the specific code part will be compiled into the final executable. Production versions of a system are typically compiled without defining the DEBUG macro, so that the tracing code and the output it generates are omitted.

Programs running in the background (for example, Unix daemons or Microsoft Windows services) need a more sophisticated way to generate trace information, especially if multiple instances or threads of the same program are running at the same time. In Unix systems the syslog library function is used to append the information into the appropriate system log.[45]

```
syslog(LOG_DEBUG, "Successful lookup: %d , %d : %s\n",
    lport, fport, pwp->pw_name);
```

Under Microsoft Windows the function used to generate an equivalent type of log message is ReportEvent, while Java programs often use the freely available *log4j* library to organize and manage the efficient generation of logging messages.

---

[44] netbsdsrc/games/backgammon/backgammon/move.c:380–385
[45] netbsdsrc/libexec/identd/parse.c:372–373

Too much tracing information can obscure vital messages or slow down the operation of a program to the point of uselessness. For this reason programs often define an integer called the *debug level*, which is used to filter the generated messages.[46]

```
if (debug > 4)
    printf("systime: offset %s\n", lfptoa(now, 6));
```

In the above example the message will appear only when the debug level is above 4; a higher debug level signifies a more verbose program. A program option, signal, or configuration flag is used to change a program's debug level. In languages supporting exceptions, such as Ada, C++, C#, and Java, you will often find debug messages as part of the exception-handling code.[47]

```
try {
    if (servlet != null) {
        wrapper.deallocate(servlet);
    }
} catch (Throwable e) {
    log(sm.getString("standardWrapper.deallocateException",
                     wrapper.getName()), e);
```

The tracing statements we examined can generate copious output, but in most cases they fail to tell us whether that output is correct or not. Only in rare cases will a debugging statement display the correct expected value.[48]

```
printf("free %u bytes @%lx, should be <=%u\n",
    size, (u_long)ptr, a->size);
```

A more proactive approach has the program code test various conditions that should be true while the program is executing. These conditions, called *assertions*, are essentially statements specifying an expected outcome if the program works in the way its developer thought it would. A number of language constructs and libraries are designed to allow the testing of assertions with a minimum of clutter and the automatic generation of debugging output (and often the termination of the program) when an assertion fails. Assertions are used to verify steps in the operation of an algorithm, parameters received by a function, a program's flow of control, properties

---

[46]netbsdsrc/lib/libntp/systime.c:216–217
[47]jt4/catalina/src/share/org/apache/catalina/core/StandardWrapperValve.java:295–301
[48]netbsdsrc/sys/arch/powerpc/stand/ofwboot/alloc.c:222–223

of the underlying hardware, and the results of test cases. The C and C++ libraries use the `assert` facility for this purpose.

The following code excerpt illustrates the use of assertions to verify the operation of a regular expression pattern-matching algorithm.[49]

```
if (dp != NULL)
    break;
/* uh-oh... we couldn't find a subexpression-level match */
assert(g->backrefs);    /* must be back references doing it */
assert(g->nplus == 0 || m->lastpos != NULL);
```

In the above example, almost 100 lines within the execution of the pattern-matching function, the algorithm fails to find a subexpression-level match, probably due to the existence of back references. The programmer specifies in the form of assertions the values he expects the variables should have in such a case. Another 50 lines of code follow; the assertions are used in this case to checkpoint the algorithm's operation. You can use algorithm verification assertions to confirm your understanding of an algorithm's operation or as a point to start your reasoning.

Assertions are also often used to check the value of arguments received by a function.[50]

```
void
pmap_zero_page(register vm_offset_t phys)
{
    [...]
    assert(phys != vm_page_fictitious_addr);
```

A similar type of assertion is also sometimes used to verify a function's return value.[51]

```
static char *
aalloc(int size, int align)
{
  [...]
  assert(p > &last);
  assert(p <= (char *) RAMSIZE);
  return top = p;
}
```

Often function argument and result assertions document a function's preconditions and postconditions.

---

[49] netbsdsrc/lib/libc/regex/engine.c:244–249

[50] netbsdsrc/sys/arch/alpha/alpha/pmap.c:2402–2410

[51] netbsdsrc/sys/arch/i386/netboot/ne2100.c:2402–2410

An assertion statement with a false constant argument is used to mark a program's point that should normally not be reachable by its control flow.[52]

```
switch (mappad) {
case BitmapFormatImageRectMin:
    [...]
case BitmapFormatImageRectMaxWidth:
    [...]
case BitmapFormatImageRectMax:
    [...]
    break;
default:
    assert(0);
}
```

In the above example the `assert` statement indicates that `mappad` should match one of the `case` constants.

Assert statements are also used to verify properties of the underlying hardware or compilation process. The following excerpt verifies that integers occupy at least four bytes of storage.[53]

```
assert(sizeof(int) >= 4);
```

Finally, assertions are also sometimes used to implement complete test cases. The `main` function of the following C program consists entirely of calls to the functions under test and corresponding `assert` statements.[54]

```
int
main()
{
    assert(fpgetround() == FP_RN);
    assert(FLT_ROUNDS == 1);
    assert(fpsetround(FP_RP) == FP_RN);
    [...]
    assert(fpsetround(FP_RN) == FP_RZ);
    assert(fpgetround() == FP_RN);
    assert(FLT_ROUNDS == 1);
    exit(0);
}
```

---

[52] XFree86-3.3/xc/lib/font/Speedo/spglyph.c:84–120
[53] netbsdsrc/usr.sbin/amd/amd/amd.c:319
[54] netbsdsrc/regress/lib/libc/ieeefp/round/round.c:13–44

You can use assertions that test complete functions as specification statements for each given function.

When examining code, keep in mind that the expression within an `assert` macro is typically not compiled when the program is compiled as a "production" release, that is, with the macro `NDEBUG` set to 1. In this case assertions with side effects (such as the call to `fpsetround` in the example above) will not behave as you might expect.

Java programs often organize assertions into complete test cases using Kent Beck's and Erich Gamma's *JUnit* framework. *JUnit* supports the initialization of test data, the definition of test cases, their organization into a test suite, and the collection of the test results. It also provides a GUI tool, *TestRunner*, for executing the test cases. You can see the most pertinent parts of a *JUnit* test setup abstracted in Figure 6.16.[55,56] Test cases are organized into a class derived from the `TestCase` class. Fields inside the class are used to hold data needed between different test cases (Figure 6.16:1). A method called `setUp` is responsible for initializing the field values, while the `tearDown` method is responsible for tearing down the support erected for the specific test case. Test cases are written as separate methods with a name beginning with `test`. Inside each test case you will find many different types of `assert` methods used for verifying the obtained results. A number of test cases implemented inside a class can be collected into a *test suite* method named `suite`; in our case (Figure 6.16:2) the suite's constructor collects from the class all public methods with a name starting with `test`.

When a testing framework is not available, testing is often performed by a custom-made *test harness* program that executes the test cases. In Java programs it is common to add a `main` method inside a Java class and use it for testing the class as a unit.[57]

```
public static void main(String[] args) {
    String format = "yyyy-MM-dd HH:mm:ss.SSS";
    if (args.length > 0)
        format = args[0];
    SimpleDateFormat sdf = new SimpleDateFormat(format);
    FastDateFormat fdf = new FastDateFormat(sdf);
    Date d = new Date();
```

[55] jt4/catalina/src/test/org/apache/naming/resources/BaseDirContextTestCase.java
[56] jt4/catalina/src/test/org/apache/naming/resources/WARDirContextTestCase.java
[57] jt4/jasper/src/share/org/apache/jasper/util/FastDateFormat.java:128–139

```
public abstract class BaseDirContextTestCase extends TestCase {          ── JUnit base class
    [...]
    protected DirContext context = null;                                 ┃ Test fixture state
    [...]
}

public class WARDirContextTestCase extends BaseDirContextTestCase {

                                                                         ── Initialize test case state
    public void setUp() {
        context = new WARDirContext();
        ((WARDirContext) context).setDocBase(docBase);
    }

                                                                         ┃ How to run all unit tests
    public static Test suite() {
        return (new TestSuite(WARDirContextTestCase.class));
    }

                                                                         ── Test clean-up
    public void tearDown() {
        context = null;
    }

                                                                         ── Test case 1
    public void testGetAttributesWebInf() {
        [...]
        JarFile jarFile = new JarFile(docBase);
        assertNotNull("Created JarFile for " + docBase, jarFile);
        JarEntry jarEntry =
            (JarEntry) jarFile.getEntry("WEB-INF");
        assertNotNull("Created JarEntry for WEB-INF", jarEntry);
        [...]
    }

                                                                         ── Test case 2
    public void testGetAttributesWebXml() {
        [...]
    }
}
```

Figure 6.16 Using the *JUnit* test framework.

```
d.setTime(1);
System.out.println(fdf.format(d) + "\t" + sdf.format(d));
d.setTime(20);
System.out.println(fdf.format(d) + "\t" + sdf.format(d));
d.setTime(500);
System.out.println(fdf.format(d) + "\t" + sdf.format(d));
[...]
}
```

You will sometimes find the same effect achieved in C/C++ programs by having the test code appear in a module inside a conditionally compiled block controlled by the definition of the DEBUG preprocessor macro.[58]

```
#ifdef DEBUG
main()
    {
    int fd;

    makedata();                    /* make the test data */
    fd = open ("data", O_RDWR);
    process_test_data(fd);
    close(fd);
    }
[...]
#endif /* DEBUG */
```

Often the test programs are designed to be run interactively, as is the case with the *vttest* VT-100 terminal emulator test program.[59] However, a more productive form of testing involves testing a program's results against output known to be correct. A *regression test*, usually based on the manually verified results of earlier runs, is often executed after a program's implementation is modified to ensure that no part of the program was accidentally broken. A regression test typically consists of a test harness to execute the test cases, the input for each test case, the expected result, and a framework to execute all cases in a sequence. The regression tests for the execve program execution Unix system call is a typical example. A tiny driver program is used to execute different types of programs and print the result.[60]

```
int
main(int argc, char *argv[])
{ [...]
    if (execve(argv[1], &argv[1], NULL) == -1) {
        printf("%s\n", strerror(errno));
        exit(1);
    }
}
```

---

[58] XFree86-3.3/xc/programs/Xserver/hw/hp/input/drivers/hp7lc2k.c:355–406
[59] netbsdsrc/sys/arch/bebox/isa/pcvt/Util/vttest
[60] netbsdsrc/regress/sys/kern/execve/doexec.c:38–52

For each type of program (test case) to be executed, such as the following:[61]

```
#! /foo/bar/baz

echo foo
```

a separate file contains the expected correct result.[62]

```
No such file or directory
```

Finally, a `Makefile` rule is used to run all regression tests in sequence.[63]

```
regress:    test-empty test-nonexist \
    test-nonexistshell test-devnullscript test-badinterplen \
    test-goodscript test-scriptarg test-scriptarg-nospace \
    test-goodaout test-truncaout

test-empty: ${PROG} ${TD}/empty
    ${RP} ${TD}/empty | diff - ${OD}/empty
```

When reading source code, remember that test cases can be a partial substitute for functional specifications. In addition, you can use test case input data to dry-run source code sequences.

Exercise 6.24 Match the debugging output generated when running a program from the book's CD-ROM to the actual source code that generates it.

Exercise 6.25 Locate two different test cases in the book's CD-ROM and explain how their execution is (or could be) automated.

Exercise 6.26 Using as your guide the test cases in the `execve` regression test, derive the "Errors" section of the respective manual page. Compare the results you obtained against the actual manual page.[64]

---

[61] netbsdsrc/regress/sys/kern/execve/tests/nonexistshell:1–3
[62] netbsdsrc/regress/sys/kern/execve/good/nonexistshell:1–3
[63] netbsdsrc/regress/sys/kern/execve/Makefile:15–21
[64] doc/execve.pdf

Exercise 6.27   The Perl bug reporting documentation[65] suggests that

> A good test case has most of these attributes: fewest possible number of lines; few dependencies on external commands, modules, or libraries; runs on most platforms unimpeded; and is self-documenting.

Locate test cases in the book's CD-ROM and judge them against the above standard.

Further Reading

You can read the design and rationale behind the original *make* program in Feldman [Fel79]; you can find an in-depth treatment of *make* and its variants in two other sources [OT91, DE96]. The use of specialized tools in the implementation of the Haskell language is described in Spinellis [Spi93] and for managing error messages in Douglas [Dou90]. Specialized tools are also often used to implement domain-specific languages [Spi99b, Ram97, FNP97, Spi01, KS97, SG97a, SG97b, Cre97]. The two original articles on the revision control systems we discussed are Rochkind [Roc75], covering SCCS, and Tichy [Tic82], covering RCS; a more recent and accessible reference is Bolinger et al. [BBL95], while an annotated list of tools can be found in Hunt and Thomas [HT00, p. 271]. CVS is covered in two references [C+01, BF01]. The GNU *autoconf* tool is discussed in Vaughan et al. [VETL00]. You can read more on the process of configuration and revision management in Humphrey [Hum89, pp. 113–135, 225–246]. Testing methods and management are detailed in Kaner et al. [KFN99], while the testing of Java programs with *JUnit* is described in Beck and Gamma [BG98].

---

[65] perl/utils/perlbug.PL:1015–1017

Coding Standards and Conventions

The laws of nature are but the mathematical thoughts of God.

—Euclid

Significant coding efforts, or projects undertaken within the framework of large organized endeavors such as GNU and BSD, are likely to adopt a set of coding standards, guidelines, or conventions. Computer languages and programming systems offer programmers considerable leeway on how to express a given algorithm. Coding standards provide additional stylistic guidance aiming to increase the code's robustness, readability, and maintainability. When reading code, standards and conventions provide you additional guidance on the meaning of particular code elements, thereby increasing the effectiveness of your endeavor. In this chapter we examine some typical items prescribed in coding standard documents. To make our discussion concrete we examine our examples in the context of three commonly used coding standards: the GNU coding standards adopted by hundreds of project GNU packages and the Linux operating system; the BSD (kernel) style guide used by the BSD family of operating systems such as FreeBSD, NetBSD, and OpenBSD as well as in projects like *apache* and Perl; and the Java Code Conventions that are applied to most Java code. In addition, we will present the Hungarian naming notation that is commonly used for naming identifiers in the Microsoft Windows world.

Exercise 7.1 Identify the coding standards that apply in your organization. In the form of a table, compare their coverage against two other commonly used standards.

7.1 File Names and Organization

Most standards specify how files should be named and what extensions are to be used. As an example, you may not have realized that the customary .h suffix in the

C header files is merely a matter of style and is not prescribed by any language or compiler requirement. You can take file name and suffix conventions into account to optimize your searches through the source code. A number of file names and extensions are common across different projects and development platforms; we list them in Tables 7.1 and 7.2.

Furthermore, many style guides recommend how different program items are to be ordered in a source file. As an example, the BSD style guide specifies the precise order of include statements: kernel include files, followed by /usr include files, followed by user include files. Similarly, the Java code conventions specify that the order of elements in Java classes shall be as follows:

1. Class variables

2. Instance variables

3. Constructors

4. Methods

In addition, the Java conventions also specify that variables and methods shall be defined in the order of `private`, `protected`, and `public`. Knowing the file organization followed by a given code base allows you to browse efficiently through the source code.

Exercise 7.2   Discuss the advantages and disadvantages of defining and declaring code elements in a strictly prescribed order. How do modern integrated development environments affect your view?

Table 7.1 Common File Names

File Name	Contents
README	Project overview
MANIFEST	List of project files with brief explanations
INSTALL	Installation instructions
LICENSE or Copying	Licensing information
TODO	Wish list for future extensions
NEWS	Documentation on user-visible changes
ChangeLog or Changes	Code change summary
configure	Platform configuration script
Makefile	Build specification
Makefile.SH	Shell script producing the above
config.h	Platform configuration definitions
config_h.SH	Shell script producing the above
version.h or patchlevel.h	Project release version

Table 7.2 Common File Extensions

File Extension	Contents
.digit .man	Unix manual page source
.encoding	Text in a particular encoding (e.g., .utf8)
.language-code	Text in a particular language (e.g., .de for German)
.a, .lib	Library collection of object files
.asm, .s	Assembly language source (Microsoft DOS/Windows, Unix)
.asp, .cgi, .jsp, .psp	Web server–executed source
.awk	*awk* (language) source
.bas, .frm	Microsoft Visual Basic source
.bat, .cmd, .com	MS-DOS/NT, OS/2 *Rexx*, VMS commands
.bmp, .xbm, .png	Microsoft Windows, X Window System, portable bitmap file
.c	C source
.C, .cc, .cpp, .cxx	C++ source
.cs	C# source
.class	Java compiled file
.csh, .sh	Unix *csh*, *sh* (Bourne) shell source
.def	Microsoft Windows or OS/2 executable or shared library definition
.dll, .so	Shared object library (Microsoft Windows, Unix)
.dsp, .dsw, .vbp	Microsoft Developer Studio project and workspace file
.dvi	Documentation in *troff* or *TeX* device-independent output
.el	*Emacs* Lisp source
.eqn, .pic, .tbl	Equations, pictures, tables to be typeset by *eqn*, *pic*, *tbl*
.gz, .Z, .bz2	File compressed with *gzip*, *compress*, *bzip2*
.h	C or C++ header file
.hpp	C++ header file
.ico, .icon	Microsoft Windows, X Window System icon
.idl	Interface definition file
.info	Documentation generated by GNU *Texinfo*
.jar, .shar, .tar	File collection in Java, Unix shell, tape archive format
.java	Java source code
.jcl	IBM JCL instructions
.l	*lex* (lexical analyzer generator) source
.m4	*m4* (macro processor) code
.mak, .mk	Makefile (also often without any extension)
.mif	Documentation exported by FrameMaker
.mm, .me	Documentation using *troff mm*, *me* macros
.nr, .roff	Documentation in plain *troff* format
.o, .obj	Object file
.ok	Local additions to the spell-check dictionary
.pl, .pm, .pod	Perl, module source, documentation

(continued)

Table 7.2 Common File Extensions (continued)

File Extension	Contents
.ps	Postscript source, or formatted documentation
.py	Python source
.rb	Ruby source
.rc, .res	Microsoft Windows resource, compiled resource script
.sed	*sed* (stream editor) source
.t, .test	Test file
.tcl	Tcl/Tk source
.tex, .texi	Documentation in *TeX* or *LaTeX*, GNU *Texinfo* format
.y	*yacc* (parser generator) source

7.2 Indentation

Programs written in modern block structured languages use indentation to emphasize the nesting level of each block. Style guides often specify the amount and type of whitespace to use for indenting blocks. As an example, the Java code conventions specify the use of 4 space units and allow the use of 8-character-wide tabs, while the BSD style guide specifies the use of an 8-character-wide tab. The specification of whether tabs are allowed and their precise width is quite important. There are two different ways to indent a block of code: you can use a number of space characters or a tab. Unfortunately, a number of editors overload the *tab key* to indent by a given amount using spaces, while other editors also provide an option for specifying the number of spaces that the *tab character* (ASCII code 9) will generate. A mismatch between the tab settings used for composing the original program and the settings used for reading it will result in a code appearance that is at best confusing, at worst unreadable. Problems appear when tabs are used for indenting elements after some initial code (for example, comments and variable declarations) and when a mixture of tabs and spaces is used for indenting the code (some editors automatically substitute tab characters for a certain number of spaces). The excerpts in Figure 7.1.[1] illustrate how Java code formatted with tabs and spaces will appear when the tab setting is (erroneously) set to 4 instead of 8.

When reading code, ensure that the tab setting of your editor or printer matches the style guide specifications of the code you are reading. Elements that do not line up correctly indicate a wrong setting. If you cannot locate a style guide for the project you

---

[1] hsqldb/src/org/hsqldb/DatabaseInformation.java:143–444

```
 for (int i = 0; i < tTable.size(); i++) {
Table table = (Table) tTable.elementAt(i);
 [...]
for (int j = 0; j < columns; j++) {
    Object o[] = t.getNewRow();
    [...]

     if (table.getColumnIsNullable(j)) {
    nullable = DatabaseMetaData.columnNullable;
    } else {
    nullable = DatabaseMetaData.columnNoNulls;
    }
    [...]
    t.insert(o, null);
}
}
[...]
o[2] = new Integer(0);          // precision
 [...]
o[9] = new Boolean(false);          // unsigned
```

1 Wrong indentation

1 Wrong indentation

2 Comments do not line up

2

Figure 7.1 Wrong tab settings used in Java code.

are examining, try to experiment with some common settings. In addition, source files sometimes include in a comment the formatting settings used for composing them. These settings are specified in a format that some editors, such as *Emacs* and *vim*, can parse to automatically configure their editing session. Even if your editor does not support this functionality, you can read these values (typically located at the file's top or bottom) to manually set your editor's parameters. The following comment block is a typical example.[2]

```
/*
 * Local Variables:
 * tab-width: 4
 * c-indent-level: 4
 * c-argdecl-indent: 4
 * c-continued-statement-offset: 4
 * c-continued-brace-offset: -4
 * c-label-offset: -4
 * c-brace-offset: 0
 * End:
 */
```

Most style guides specify precisely how program elements are to be indented so as to reflect the program's block structure. You can use the indentation of a code block to quickly grasp its overall structure. More importantly, most style guides also specify

[2]netbsdsrc/usr.sbin/bootpd/hash.c:415–425

the indentation rules for statements that span more than one line. Knowing these rules allows you to quickly distinguish continuation lines from statements within a control block. As an example, knowing that the BSD style guides specify the indentation of continuation lines at 4 spaces and the control block elements at 8 allows you to correctly interpret that in the following code the sequence fp = fdp ... belongs to the if clause, without having to match the corresponding parentheses.[3]

```
if ((u_int)fd >= fdp->fd_nfiles ||
    (fp = fdp->fd_ofiles[fd]) == NULL)
        return (EBADF);
```

Exercise 7.3   Propose methods to identify the correct tab settings for a source code file.

7.3 Formatting

All coding standards specify the way declarations and each specific statement are to be formatted. The specification involves the distribution of whitespace and line breaks. You will notice two different schools of thought regarding the placement of braces. GNU, Linux, and many Windows programs tend to put braces in separate, often indented, lines.[4]

```
if (ia->ia_maddr != MADDRUNK)
{
    sc->pPacketPagePhys = ia->ia_maddr;
}
```

BSD and Java programs open the brace at the same line as the statement and use its indentation level for the closing brace.[5]

```
if ((cp = strchr(*argv, ':')) != NULL) {
    *cp++ = '\0';
    a_gid(cp);
}
```

Both variants can be quite readable if used consistently. The BSD/Java variant has the advantage of consuming slightly less vertical space, resulting in code blocks that are

---

[3]netbsdsrc/sys/kern/kern_descrip.c:786–788
[4]netbsdsrc/sys/arch/arm32/isa/if_cs_isa.c:521–524
[5]netbsdsrc/usr.sbin/chown/chown.c:158–161

more likely to fit in a single page. What is clearly a sign of trouble is the *inconsistent* formatting of code. Consider the following excerpt.[6]

```
xpupil.y = Xy(w->eyes.pupil[0].x, w->eyes.pupil[0].y, &w->eyes.t);
xnewpupil.x =  Xx(newpupil[0].x, newpupil[0].y, &w->eyes.t);
xnewpupil.y =  Xy(newpupil[0].x, newpupil[0].y, &w->eyes.t);
if (!XPointEqual (xpupil, xnewpupil)) {
```

Notice the different amounts of whitespace used after the = operator and the inconsistent use of space after a function name. Inconsistently formatted code should immediately raise your defenses. If the programmer who wrote the code does not have the discipline to get the formatting right, it is very likely that other more serious errors will abound. Other explanations for the inconsistencies also point to trouble spots. The code could have been the result of integrating elements from different code bases. Again, if the integrators did not coordinate the code's formatting (in many cases it could have been trivially fixed by using a code-formatting tool like *indent*), there is a possibility that they also failed to address more important integration issues. The inconsistencies could also have been the result of multiple programmers working on the same piece of code. In this case the formatting conflicts reveal a badly coordinated team or a series of programmers who didn't respect the work of their predecessors. Caveat emptor.

Style guides also specify the formatting and contents of comments. Despite what is being taught in undergraduate programming courses, the comment contents are not exclusively addressed to humans.

- Comments starting with the /*- sequence direct the formatting program *indent* to refrain from reformatting their contents. Such comments are likely to be carefully formatted (containing, for example, an ASCII drawing of a data structure) and therefore liable to get ruined if their contents are reformatted.

- Java comments starting with the /** sequence are processed by the *javadoc* tool to automatically generate source code documentation. Inside such comments *javadoc* keywords begin with a @ character (see Figure 6.15 on page 215).

- A comment containing the word FALLTHROUGH indicates to code verification programs such as *lint* that the programmer intentionally did not add a break statement at the end of a switch case code.[7]

---

[6]XFree86-3.3/contrib/programs/xeyes/Eyes.c:378–381
[7]netbsdsrc/bin/date/date.c:162–168

```
    case 10:                    /* yy */
        lt->tm_year = ATOI2(p);
        if (lt->tm_year < 69)        /* hack for 2000 ;-} */
            lt->tm_year += 100;
        /* FALLTHROUGH */
    case 8:                     /* mm */
        lt->tm_mon = ATOI2(p);
```

- Similarly, a comment containing the word NOTREACHED indicates that the program control flow will never reach the particular point and therefore it would be wrong to flag some warnings. As an example, in the following excerpt the NOTREACHED comment avoids a warning to the effect that the function does not return a value at its end.[8]

```
size_t
strcspn(const char *s1, const char *s2)
{
    register const char *p, *spanp;
    register char c, sc;

    /*
     * Stop as soon as we find any character from s2.  Note
     * that there must be a NUL in s2; it suffices to stop
     * when we find that, too.
     */
    for (p = s1;;) {
        c = *p++;
        spanp = s2;
        do {
            if ((sc = *spanp++) == c)
                return (p - 1 - s1);
        } while (sc != 0);
    }
    /* NOTREACHED */
}
```

- Comment elements of the form $Identifier$ or %Letter% are likely to be revision control system tags. These are automatically replaced as files are

---

[8]netbsdsrc/lib/libc/string/strcspn.c:53–74

processed by a revision control system to match specific file attributes. We discuss these in detail in Section 6.5.

Finally, some special comment words are specified by coding standards so as to be easily searchable and identifiable by all implementers. The identifier XXX is traditionally used to flag code that is incorrect but works (most of the time).[9]

```
/* XXX is this correct? */
v_evaluate(vq, s, FALSE);
```

The sequence FIXME flags code that is wrong and needs fixing.[10]

```
switch (*regparse++) {
/* FIXME: these chars only have meaning at beg/end of pat? */
case '^':
```

The sequence TODO is used to identify places for future enhancements.[11]

```
/*
 * TODO - sort output
 */
int
aliascmd(argc, argv)
```

Some editors, such as *vim*, smartly flag these comments with a special color to draw your attention to them. When examining code pay special attention to code sequences flagged with XXX, FIXME, and TODO: errors may lurk in them.

Exercise 7.4 Devise a guideline that prescribes under what circumstances the formatting of an imported piece of code should be changed to conform to the local coding standards. Take into account code quality, readability, maintenance, revision control, and future integration issues.

---

[9]netbsdsrc/bin/ksh/var.c:372–373
[10]netbsdsrc/lib/libcompat/regexp/regexp.c:483–485
[11]netbsdsrc/bin/sh/alias.c:200–204

7.4 Naming Conventions

An important part of most coding standards is devoted to the naming of identifiers. Guidelines for identifier names range from the succinct ("Choose variable names that won't be confused" [KP78, p. 15]) to the elaborate (you will read about the Hungarian notation later on). You will encounter three different ways for composing variable, class, and function identifiers.

1. **Use of capitalization.** Each new word in an identifier is capitalized. Two representative examples are the `SetErrorMode`[12] C Windows API function and the `RandomAccessFile`[13] Java class. This capitalization method is recommended by most Java and Windows coding conventions. The first character may or may not be capitalized depending on additional rules.

2. **Separation of words by underscores.** Each additional word in an identifier is separated by the previous one by an underscore (for example, `exponent_is_negative`[14]). This method is prevalent in code with a Unix influence and is recommended by the GNU coding standards.

3. **Initials.** Under this scheme the initials of each word are merged to construct a new identifier. As an example, `splbio`[15] stands for "set processor (interrupt) level (for) buffered input output." The GNU coding standards recommend against using this naming method except for very few commonly used identifiers; in the BSD world the method is endorsed by its use for documented interfaces. This method is also combined with the removal of word endings or vowels, for example, `rt_refcnt`[16]; also consider the standard C function `strcmp`.

All three coding standards agree on how to name constants: constants are named using uppercase characters, with words separated by underscores. Keep in mind that this uppercase naming convention can lead to conflicts with macros, which are named following the same scheme. In modern C and C++ programs integral constants should be defined using `enum` declarations. When the name of an `enum`-defined constant clashes with that of a macro, the resultant compiler error will in most cases be confusing since it will result from the `enum` value being replaced with the macro's replacement sequence.

---

[12]apache/src/os/win32/util_win32.c:529
[13]hsqldb/src/org/hsqldb/Cache.java:50
[14]apache/src/ap/ap_snprintf.c:569
[15]netbsdsrc/sys/kern/vfs_subr.c:410
[16]netbsdsrc/sys/netinet/if_arp.c:608

In addition, in programs that follow the Java coding conventions, package names always start from a top-level domain name (for example, `org.`, `com.sun.`), class and interface names start with an uppercase letter, and methods and variables start with a lowercase letter. This convention allows you to immediately distinguish between references to class (static) and instance variables and methods. As an example, the call `Library.register(hAlias);`[17] calls the class method `register` of the class `Library`, while the call `name.equals(".")`[18] calls the instance method `equals` of the object `name`.

In programs in the Windows world you will often encounter identifiers with difficult-to-pronounce names that appear to be composed using an elaborate scheme. You can actually decode the identifier names to obtain useful information. As an example, the variable name `cwSz` is probably used to denote the number of words in a zero-terminated string. The encoding scheme used is called the *Hungarian naming notation* after the country of origin of its developer, Charles Simonyi. . The premises behind the development of this notation are sound: identifier names should be easily remembered by programmers, have a suggestive value for others who read the code, be consistent with names of similar identifiers, and be swiftly decided. Unfortunately, the notation is more often than not misused, embedding implementation-dependent information in what should be opaque identifier names.

The basic element of all identifiers is their *tag*, a short identifier indicating an element's type. Programmers are supposed to invent new tag names for each data structure or data type used in the program. The tag can be prefixed by one or more type construction identifiers to denote composite types (for example, pointer to *X* or array of *X*) and suffixed by a *base name*, used to distinguish different elements of the same type, and by a *qualifier*, used to denote one of some common standard differentiations. We list some common primitive type tags, type constructions, and name qualifiers in Table 7.3. As an example, if `Point` is a tag used to denote elements representing points on the screen, `rgPoint` uses a prefix to indicate an array of such points, `pPointFirst` uses a prefix and a qualifier to indicate a pointer to the first element of the array, and `PointTop` and `PointBottom` use base names to differentiate among points presumably representing a shape.

The Hungarian notation is used not only in C and C++ identifiers. Programs written in Visual Basic, either in its stand-alone version or in one of its Visual Basic for Applications incarnations, often name identifiers using the Hungarian notation.

---

[17] hsqldb/src/org/hsqldb/Database.java:82
[18] hsqldb/src/org/hsqldb/Database.java:92

Table 7.3 Hungarian Notation Primitive Types, Type Constructions, and Name Qualifiers

Construct	Meaning
Primitive Types	
f or b	Flag (Boolean) primitive type
dw	Double word (32-bit-wide) with arbitrary contents
w	Word with arbitrary contents (typically unsigned)
b	Byte with arbitrary contents
ch	Character
sz	Pointer to the first character of a null-terminated string
h	Handle of a heap-allocated object
fn	Function
i	Integer
l	Long integer (32-bit-wide)
n	Short integer (16-bit-wide)
Type Constructions	
pX	Pointer to X
dX	Difference between two instances of X
cX	Count of instances of type X
mpXY	Array (map) of Ys indexed by X
rg$X$	Array (range) of Xs
iX	Index to array rg$X$
cb$X$	Size of instances of X in bytes
cw$X$	Size of instances of X in words
Name Qualifiers	
XFirst	First element of an ordered set of type X values
XLast	Last element of an ordered set of type X values that includes XLast
XNext	Next element of an ordered set of type X values
XPrev	Previous element of an ordered set of type X values
XLim	The upper limit of a range of X values that does not include XLim
XMac	The current upper limit, as opposed to the constant or allocated limit of the range
XNil	A special *Nil* value of type X, such as NULL, 0, or -1
XT	A temporary value of type X

Visual Basic offers a rich repertoire of built-in types and programmable GUI controls. The tags for the most common types and controls have been standardized to the names appearing in Table 7.4. When reading code that deals with the user interface of a GUI application, all user-interface controls of a form are often manipulated in the same code module. In a moderately sophisticated application tens of controls are globally

Table 7.4 Hungarian Notation for Common Visual Basic and Microsoft Access Types and Controls

Tag	Type
Primitive Types	
cur	Currency
time	Time
date	Date
dt	Date and time combined
qry	Database query
tbl	Database table
Common Controls	
frm	Form
mnu	Form menu
cmd	Command button
chk	Check button
opt	Radio button
lbl	Text label
txt	Text edit box
pb	Picture box
pic	Picture
lst	List box
cbo	Combo box
tmr	Timer

visible in that code part. The Hungarian notation prefix type tags appearing in front of the name of a user-interface control will help you determine its role.

Exercise 7.5   Some argue that the Hungarian naming conventions duplicate work that is performed by a type-checking compiler. Discuss.

7.5 Programming Practices

Many coding guidelines contain explicit rules for writing portable software. Be aware, however, that different programming standards may have incompatible notions of what constitutes a portable construct. This is particularly true for efforts whose main agenda is not the widest possible portability. As an example, GNU and Microsoft coding guidelines center their portability concerns on processor architectural differences and assume that the particular software will run on top of a GNU, Linux, or Microsoft operating system. Such a narrow portability definition, stemming no doubt from valid practical considerations, may have additional implications: the GNU coding standards explicitly state that the GNU project does not support 16-bit architectures. When inspecting code for portability and using a given coding standard as a guide, take care to understand the extent and limits of a standard's portability requirements.

Coding guidelines often also specify how applications are to be coded to ensure a correct or consistent user interface. A particularly pertinent example involves the parsing of command-line options. The BSD and GNU guidelines specify that programs with a command-line interface should correspondingly use getopt[19] and getopt_long to parse program options. Consider the following ad hoc code that parses command-line arguments.[20]

```
while (argc > 1 && argv[1][0] == '-') {
    switch(argv[1][1]) {
    [...]
    case 's':
        sflag = 1;
        break;
    default:
        usage();
    }
    argc--; argv++;
}
nfiles = argc - 1;
```

Compare the code above with the alternative standard expression using the library function getopt.[21]

```
while ((ch = getopt(argc, argv, "mo:ps:tx")) != -1)
    switch(ch) {
    [...]
    case 'x':
        if (!domd5)
            requiremd5("-x");
        MDTestSuite();
        nomd5stdin = 1;
        break;
    case '?':
```

---

[19]The getopt manual page appears in Figure 2.4 on page 29.
[20]netbsdsrc/usr.bin/checknr/checknr.c:209–259
[21]netbsdsrc/usr.bin/cksum/cksum.c:102–155

```
    default:
        usage();
    }
argc -= optind;
argv += optind;
```

Apart from being easier to understand, the `getopt` version appears in exactly the same form in all C programs that use it, establishing in your mind a precise usage pattern and immediate alertness to any deviation. We have seen tens of different ingenious ad hoc argument parsing code sequences; each one of them requires renewed effort to understand and verify. The advantages of standardized user-interface routines are even more pronounced in GUI applications. Various Microsoft guidelines recommend that programs use Windows-supplied interface controls such as the file, color, and font dialog boxes, instead of rolling their own. In all cases, when GUI functionality is implemented using an appropriate programming construct, the correct adoption of a given user-interface specification can be trivially verified by code inspection.

Exercise 7.6   Create an itemized list of programming practices that can help code readability. Try, where possible, to reference existing examples.

7.6 Process Standards

A software system is more than its code elements. Consequently many coding guidelines diverge into other fields of the development process, including documentation and the organization of the build and release process.

As a minimum, many guidelines prescribe standard documents and formats for writing them. End-user documentation is typically the best organized since it is often closely tied to the application or the release process. Microsoft Windows applications typically include a help file, GNU projects provide a *Texinfo* manual, and traditional Unix applications supply standardized manual pages. We discuss how documentation can help you read code in Section 8.2.

As we commented in Section 6.3, there is no universally standardized way to specify and execute a build process, making it difficult to understand the particulars of each different build mechanism. Many guidelines will help you here by establishing precise rules on how the build process is organized. The rules are often based on particular tools or standardized macros; once you get acquainted with these you can swiftly understand the build process of any project that follows the given guidelines.

ⓘ

To appreciate the difference a standardized build process can make in the complexity of the corresponding descriptions, compare the 18-line makefile[22] used for compiling the 64 files of the NetBSD network time protocol (NTP) library against the makefile template[23] of 40 handcrafted and 37 automatically generated lines used for compiling the 12 files of the *apache* support library.

The release process is also frequently precisely prescribed, typically to conform to the requirements of the application installation process. Standardized software distribution formats, such as the one used by the Microsoft Windows installer, or the Red Hat Linux RPM format, impose stringent rules on the types of files that comprise the distribution, versioning, installation directories, and user-controlled options. When examining a system's release process, you can often use as a baseline the requirements of the corresponding distribution format.

Exercise 7.7   Identify the process standards that apply in your organization. Explain what software elements (files, directories) have to be examined in order to verify that a system conforms to those standards.

Further Reading

Important coding conventions include the Indian Hill style guide [CEK+], the GNU Coding Standards [S+01], the FreeBSD kernel source file style guide [Fre95], and the Java Code Conventions [Sun99a]. You can also find coding advice in the classic book by Kernighan and Plauger [KP78], the more recent book by Kernighan and Pike [KP99], and in a series of articles by Spencer [Spe88, SC92, Spe93]. The Hungarian variable-coding notation was first described in Simonyi's Ph.D. thesis [Sim76]; a more accessible and readable version is his later work [Sim99].

---

[22] netbsdsrc/lib/libntp/Makefile
[23] apache/src/ap/Makefile.tmpl

8

Documentation

Documentation is like sex: when it is good, it is very, very good; and when it is bad, it is better than nothing.

—Dick Brandon

Any nontrivial software development project is likely to be accompanied by various formal or incidental documentation elements. In the following sections we present typical types of documentation you will encounter when examining projects, provide specific examples of how these can help you understand software code, examine some classes of documentation errors, and outline common open-source documentation formats. Take advantage of any documentation you find to supplement your code-reading effort. To paraphrase the aphorism advocating the use of your library: an hour of code reading can save you a minute of reading the documentation.

8.1 Documentation Types

A traditionally engineered project will generate over its development process a number of different documents. When these are properly maintained they can really help you understand the rationale, design, and implementation of a system. Although there is enormous variation of the types of documentation produced by different projects, the following paragraphs outline some representative documents you might encounter.

The *system specification document* details the objectives of the system, its functional requirements, management and technical constraints, and cost and schedule parameters. Use the system specification document to understand the environment where the code you are reading will operate. You will read the same function-plotting code from a different perspective if it is used within a screen saver rather than as part of a nuclear reactor control system.

The *software requirements specification* provides a high-level description of the user requirements and the overall system architecture, detailing the functional and nonfunctional requirements such as processing, external interfaces, logical database schemas, and design constraints. The same document may also include a description of the anticipated system evolution dynamics due to the changing software and hardware environment and user needs. Use the software requirements specification as a benchmark against which to read and evaluate the code.

In the *design specification* you will find the description of the system's architecture, data, and code structures, as well as the interfaces between the different modules. Object-oriented designs feature the system's basic classes and public methods. Detailed design specifications typically also include specific information on each module (or class), such as the processing it performs, a description of the provided interface, and its relationship to other modules or classes used. In addition you will find descriptions of the data structures employed and the applicable database schemas. You can use a system's design specification as a road map to the code structure and as a guide to specific code elements.

A system's *test specification* contains a test plan, specific test procedures, and actual test results. Each test procedure details the modules it tests (providing you with an idea of which modules are used to process a particular input) and the test case data. The test specification document provides you with data you can use to dry-run the code you are reading.

Finally, what is collectively called *user documentation* comprises a number of different documents, including a functional description, installation instructions, an introductory guide, a reference manual, and an administrator manual. A big advantage of the user documentation is that this is often the only documentation you are likely to get your hands on. When you are dealing with an unknown system, the functional description and the user guide can provide you with important background information to better understand the context of the code you are reading. You can employ the user reference manual to rapidly obtain background information on presentation and application logic code components and the administrator manual to find details on interfaces, file formats, and error messages you encounter in the code.

Exercise 8.1   Select three large projects from the book's CD-ROM and classify the available documentation.

Exercise 8.2   Comment on the applicability of the documentation types we described in open-source development efforts.

8.2 Reading Documentation

If you doubt that useful documentation actually does exist, here are some concrete examples of how you can make documentation work for you.

Documentation provides you with a shortcut for obtaining an overview of the system or for understanding the code that provides a particular feature. Consider the implementation of the Berkeley Unix *fast file system*. The file system's description in the system's manager manual comprises 14 typeset pages describing the system's organization, parameterization, layout policies, performance, and functional enhancements. Reading the text[1,2] requires a lot less effort than examining the 4,586 lines of source code that make up the system.[3] Even when examining small code fragments, their functioning becomes clearer once you understand their purpose by reading the documentation. Try to understand the following fragment:[4]

```
line = gobble = 0;
for (prev = '\n'; (ch = getc(fp)) != EOF; prev = ch) {
    if (prev == '\n') {
        if (ch == '\n') {
            if (sflag) {
                if (!gobble && putchar(ch) == EOF)
                    break;
                gobble = 1;
                continue;
            }
            [...]
        }
    }
    gobble = 0;
    [...]
}
```

---

[1] netbsdsrc/share/doc/smm/05.fastfs
[2] doc/ffs.pdf
[3] netbsdsrc/sys/ufs/ffs
[4] netbsdsrc/bin/cat/cat.c:159–207

before, and after, reading the documentation regarding the *cat* command's -s flag that sets the sflag identifier.[5,6]

-s Squeeze multiple adjacent empty lines, causing the output to be single spaced.

Documentation provides you with specifications against which to inspect the code. You can use the functional specification as a starting point. In many cases, the code supports a particular product or interfacing standard, so even if you cannot find a functional specification for the specific system, you can use the corresponding standard as your guide. Consider the task of inspecting the *apache* Web server compliance regarding the HTTP protocol. In the *apache* source code you will find the following sequence.[7]

```
switch (*method) {
    case 'H':
        if (strcmp(method, "HEAD") == 0)
            return M_GET; /* see header_only in request_rec */
        break;
    case 'G':
        if (strcmp(method, "GET") == 0)
            return M_GET;
        break;
    case 'P':
        if (strcmp(method, "POST") == 0)
            return M_POST;
        if (strcmp(method, "PUT") == 0)
            return M_PUT;
        if (strcmp(method, "PATCH") == 0)
            return M_PATCH;
```

You can easily verify the completeness of the implemented commands, as well as the existence of extensions, by checking them against the HTTP protocol specification document, RFC-2068.[8]

---

[5] netbsdsrc/bin/cat/cat.1
[6] doc/cat.pdf
[7] apache/src/main/http_protocol.c:749–764
[8] doc/rfc2068.txt:1913–1923

The Method token indicates the method to be performed on the
resource identified by the Request-URI. The method is
case-sensitive.

```
Method        = "OPTIONS"              ; Section 9.2
              | "GET"                  ; Section 9.3
              | "HEAD"                 ; Section 9.4
              | "POST"                 ; Section 9.5
              | "PUT"                  ; Section 9.6
              | "DELETE"               ; Section 9.7
              | "TRACE"                ; Section 9.8
              | extension-method
```

Documentation often mirrors and therefore reveals the underlying system structure. A representative example is provided by the system manager's manual of the *sendmail* mail-transfer agent.[9,10] Have a look at the system's source code files.[11]

```
arpadate.c, clock.c, collect.c, conf.c, convtime.c, daemon.c, deliver.c,
domain.c, envelope.c, err.c, headers.c, macro.c, main.c, map.c, mci.c,
mime.c, parseaddr.c, queue.c, readcf.c, recipient.c, safefile.c,
savemail.c, srvrsmtp.c, stab.c, stats.c, sysexits.c, trace.c, udb.c,
usersmtp.c, util.c, version.c
```

Table 8.1 shows how readily many of them match by simple inspection with particular headings of the documentation.

Documentation helps you understand complicated algorithms and data structures. Sophisticated algorithms tend to be difficult to follow and understand; when they are transcribed into efficient code they can become impenetrable. Sometimes the code's documentation will provide details of the algorithm used, or, more often, a comment in the code will direct you to an appropriate published reference.[12]

```
* This algorithm is from Knuth vol. 2 (2nd ed),
* section 4.3.3, p. 278.
```

---

[9] netbsdsrc/usr.sbin/sendmail/doc/intro
[10] doc/sendmail.pdf
[11] netbsdsrc/usr.sbin/sendmail/src
[12] netbsdsrc/lib/libc/quad/muldi3.c:86

Table 8.1 Source Files Corresponding to *sendmail* Documentation Headings

Documentation Heading		Source File(s)
2.5.	Configuration file	readcf.c
3.3.1.	Aliasing	alias.c
3.4.	Message collection	collect.c
3.5.	Message delivery	deliver.c
3.6.	Queued messages	queue.c
3.7.	Configuration	conf.c
3.7.1.	Macros	macro.c
3.7.2.	Header declarations	headers.c, envelope.c
3.7.4.	Address rewriting rules	parseaddr.c

A textual description of an algorithm can make the difference between an opaque piece of code and the chance to understand it. Consider the task of comprehending the following code.[13]

```
for (arcp = memp->parents ; arcp ; arcp = arcp->arc_parentlist) {
    [...]
    if ( headp -> npropcall ) {
        headp -> propfraction += parentp -> propfraction
                * ( ( (double) arcp -> arc_count )
                / ( (double) headp -> npropcall ) );
    }
}
```

Now try to map the code to the following algorithm's description.[14, 15]

Let C_e be the number of calls to some routine, e, and C_e^r be the number of calls from a caller r to a callee e. Since we are assuming each call to a routine takes the average amount of time for all calls to that routine, the caller is accountable for C_e^r/C_e of the time spent by the callee. Let the S_e be the *selftime* of a routine, e. The selftime of a routine can be determined from the timing information gathered during profiled program execution. The total time, T_r, we wish to account to a routine r is then given by the recurrence equation:

$$T_r = S_r + \sum_{r \ calls \ e} T_e \times \frac{C_e^r}{C_e}$$

where $r \ calls \ e$ is a relation showing all routines e called by a routine r.

Documentation often elucidates the meaning of source code identifiers. Consider the following macro definition and its associated terse comment.[16]

---

[13] netbsdsrc/usr.bin/gprof/arcs.c:930–950

[14] netbsdsrc/usr.bin/gprof/PSD.doc/postp.me:71–90

[15] doc/gprof.pdf:p. 4

[16] netbsdsrc/sys/netinet/tcp_fsm.h:50

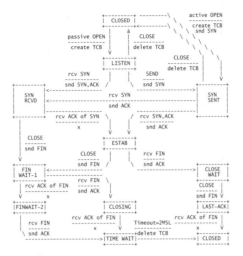

Figure 8.1 TCP connection diagram.

```
#define TCPS_ESTABLISHED 4 /* established */
```

The macro definition is part of the TCP/IP networking code. A search for the word ESTABLISHED in the corresponding documentation (RFC-2068) reveals the following description.[17]

> ESTABLISHED—represents an open connection, data received can be delivered to the user. The normal state for the data transfer phase of the connection.

Even more helpfully, the same RFC document contains an elaborate ASCII drawing that details how the TCP protocol is modeled as a finite state machine and the exact transitions between its different states (Figure 8.1). Examining the TCP source code without the corresponding state diagram at hand would be foolish indeed.

Documentation can provide the rationale behind nonfunctional requirements. The following code excerpt is from the source code of the domain name system (DNS) server.[18]

```
if (newdp->d_cred > dp->d_cred) {
    /* better credibility.
     * remove the old datum.
     */
    goto delete;
}
```

---

[17] doc/rfc793.txt:p. 21
[18] netbsdsrc/usr.sbin/named/named/db_update.c:447–452

Similar decisions regarding the "credibility" of data appear over the whole source code file. The DNS functional specification does not define the notion of data credibility or dictate specific behavior regarding data from different sources. However, a set of documents in the application's doc directory[19] outline a number of security problems associated with the DNS, and one specifically discusses how cache entries are tagged with a "credibility" level to update cached data based on its quality.[20, 21]

5.1. Cache Tagging

BIND now maintains for each cached RR a "credibility" level showing whether the data came from a zone, an authoritative answer, an authority section, or additional data section. When a more credible RRset comes in, the old one is completely wiped out. Older BINDs blindly aggregated data from all sources, paying no attention to the maxim that some sources are better than others.

Thus, the rationale behind a nonfunctional requirement—security—is elaborated in the documentation, allowing you to follow its implementation in the source code.

Furthermore, in a system's documentation you can often find the designer's thinking; the goals, purpose, and intent of the system requirements, architecture, and implementation; and rejected alternatives and reasons for their rejection. As a representative example, consider how Pike and Thompson reasoned about adopting the UTF Unicode representation over the 16-bit alternative in the Plan 9 operating system [PT93].

Unicode defines an adequate character set but an unreasonable representation. The Unicode standard states that all characters are 16 bits wide and are communicated in 16-bit units. . . . To adopt Unicode, we would have had to convert all text going into and out of Plan 9 between ASCII and Unicode, which cannot be done. Within a single program, in command of all its input and output, it is possible to define characters as 16–bit quantities; in the context of a networked system with hundreds of applications on diverse machines by different manufacturers, it is impossible.

. . .

The UTF encoding has several good properties. By far the most important is that a byte in the ASCII range 0–127 represents itself in UTF. Thus UTF is backward compatible with ASCII.

---

[19] netbsdsrc/usr.sbin/named/doc
[20] netbsdsrc/usr.sbin/named/doc/misc/vixie-security.ps
[21] doc/vixie-security.pdf:p. 5

Documentation explains internal programming interfaces. Large systems are typically divided into smaller subsystems interoperating through precisely defined interfaces. In addition, nontrivial collections of data are often organized as an abstract data type or a class with a similarly well-defined interface. The following examples are some typical types of API documentation you may encounter.

- The developer documentation of the Hypersonic SQL database engine *hsqldb*.[22] The documentation, automatically generated from the annotated Java source code using the *Together ControlCenter* system, can be read by using an HTML browser. It provides in a frame view a UML depiction of all classes, a tree structure of the package hierarchy, and a summary and detail view of each class's fields, constructors, and methods.

- The description of Perl's internal functions and data representation formats in the, aptly named, *perlguts* manual page.[23,24] You can see the first page of the documentation in Figure 8.2. Notice the disclaimer in the "Description" section; because documentation is seldom tested and stressed in the way the actual program code is, it can often be erroneous, incomplete, or out of date.

- The documentation of the FreeBSD functions and macros used for managing networking code memory.[25,26] In fact, the entire ninth section of the FreeBSD and NetBSD manual contains over 100 entries related to the internal operation of the system kernel, describing function interfaces and variables of use to the system and device driver programmer.

Documentation provides test cases and examples of actual use. Often, the source code or the functional documentation of a system will provide no clue as to how the system will actually be used. The *tcpdump* program supports an elaborate syntax for specifying the precise network packets you wish to examine. However, without actual examples of its use, it is difficult to understand what the source code is trying to accomplish; test cases provide you with material to dry-run the source code. Thankfully, the program's manual page—in common with most Unix manual pages—provides ten different typical use scenarios such as the following.[27,28]

---

[22] hsqldb/dev-docs/hsqldb/index.html
[23] perl/pod/perlguts.pod
[24] doc/perlguts.pdf
[25] netbsdsrc/share/man/man9/mbuf.9
[26] doc/mbuf.pdf
[27] netbsdsrc/usr.sbin/tcpdump/tcpdump.8
[28] doc/tcpdump.pdf:p. 6

PERLGUTS(1) User Contributed Perl Documentation PERLGUTS(1)

NAME

perlguts – Perl's Internal Functions

DESCRIPTION

This document attempts to describe some of the internal functions of the Perl executable. It is far from complete and probably contains many errors. Please refer any questions or comments to the author below.

Variables

Datatypes

Perl has three typedefs that handle Perl's three main data types:

```
SV  Scalar Value
AV  Array Value
HV  Hash Value
```

Each typedef has specific routines that manipulate the various data types.

What is an "IV"?

Perl uses a special typedef IV which is a simple integer type that is guaranteed to be large enough to hold a pointer (as well as an integer).

Perl also uses two special typedefs, I32 and I16, which will always be at least 32-bits and 16-bits long, respectively.

Working with SVs

An SV can be created and loaded with one command. There are four types of values that can be loaded: an integer value (IV), a double (NV), a string, (PV), and another scalar (SV).

The six routines are:

```
SV*  newSViv(IV);
SV*  newSVnv(double);
SV*  newSVpv(char*, int);
SV*  newSVpvn(char*, int);
SV*  newSVpvf(const char*, ...);
SV*  newSVsv(SV*);
```

To change the value of an *already-existing* SV, there are seven routines:

```
void  sv_setiv(SV*, IV);
void  sv_setuv(SV*, UV);
void  sv_setnv(SV*, double);
void  sv_setpv(SV*, const char*);
void  sv_setpvn(SV*, const char*, int)
void  sv_setpvf(SV*, const char*, ...);
void  sv_setpvfn(SV*, const char*, STRLEN, va_list *, SV **, I32, bool);
void  sv_setsv(SV*, SV*);
```

Notice that you can choose to specify the length of the string to be assigned by using `sv_setpvn`, `newSVpvn`, or `newSVpv`, or you may allow Perl to calculate the length by using `sv_setpv` or by specifying 0 as the second argument to `newSVpv`. Be warned, though, that Perl will determine the string's length by using `strlen`, which depends on the string terminating with a NUL character.

The arguments of `sv_setpvf` are processed like `sprintf`, and the formatted output becomes the value.

`sv_setpvfn` is an analogue of `vsprintf`, but it allows you to specify either a pointer to a variable argument list or the address and length of an array of SVs. The last argument points to a boolean; on return, if that boolean is true, then locale-specific information has been used to format the string, and the string's contents are therefore untrustworthy (see the *perlsec* manpage). This pointer may be NULL if that

2/May/1999 perl 5.005, patch 03 1

Figure 8.2 The first page of the *perlguts* manual.

To print all ftp traffic through internet gateway *snup*: (note that the expression is quoted to prevent the shell from (mis-)interpreting the parentheses):

```
tcpdump 'gateway snup and (port ftp or ftp-data)'
```

To print the start and end packets (the SYN and FIN packets) of each TCP conversation that involves a non-local host.

```
tcpdump 'tcp[13] & 3 != 0 and not src and dst net localnet'
```

Documentation often describes known implementation problems and bugs. Sometimes you may find yourself toiling for hours over a specific part of the source code to understand how, despite appearances, it correctly handles a given input. By reading the documentation you might well find that the specific situation you are examining is in fact *not* handled at all by the system and is a documented bug. The Unix manual pages, with remarkable and commendable candor, often contain a section titled "Bugs" to document exactly such cases. In fact, in this section you will find comments regarding an implementation's design or interface limitations:[29,30]

> *At* and *batch* as presently implemented are not suitable when users are competing for resources. If this is the case for your site, you might want to consider another batch system, such as *nqs*.

caveats regarding its use:[31,32]

> Because of the shell language mechanism used to perform output redirection, the command "cat file1 file2 > file1" will cause the original data in file1 to be destroyed! This is performed by the shell before *cat* is run.

humor:[33,34]

> There is no conversion specification for the phase of the moon.

---

[29] netbsdsrc/usr.bin/at/at.1
[30] doc/at.pdf
[31] netbsdsrc/bin/cat/cat.1
[32] doc/cat.pdf
[33] netbsdsrc/lib/libc/time/strftime.3
[34] doc/strftime.pdf

as well as actual bugs:[35,36]

> Recognition of *functions*, *subroutines* and *procedures* for FORTRAN and Pascal is done in a very simpleminded way. No attempt is made to deal with block structure; if you have two Pascal procedures in different blocks with the same name you lose.

Shortcomings and outright bugs of the development or execution environment can be a devilish source of problems. These are sometimes documented in a vendor's customer support system or in the fix list accompanying a product patch, not the most obvious places to search when a program behaves in an unexpected way. Fortunately, known environment deficiencies are typically documented in the source code; the code is the obvious place where a programmer can vent some of the frustration the problem caused by castigating or trashing the responsible vendor.[37]

```
// The following function is not inline, to avoid build (template
// instantiation) problems with Sun C++ 4.2 patch 104631-07/SunOS 5.6.
```

Change documentation can indicate trouble spots. The source code of many systems includes some form of maintenance documentation. At the very least, this includes a description of the changes made in every release, either in the form of the revision control system log entries we describe in Section 6.5 or in a simple text file—typically named ChangeLog—where change comments are ordered in chronological order. An examination of the change log will often reveal areas where repetitive, sometimes conflicting, changes are made or similar fixes are applied to different parts of the source code. The first type of changes can sometimes indicate fundamental design defficiencies that maintainers try to fix with a series of patches. The following entries in the ChangeLog of the Linux *smbfs* (Windows network filesystem) code are a typical example.

```
2001-09-17 Urban [...]
  * proc.c: Go back to the interruptible sleep as reconnects
    seem to handle it now.
[...]
2001-07-09 Jochen  [...]
  * proc.c, ioctl.c: Allow smbmount to signal failure to reconnect
    with a NULL argument to SMB_IOC_NEWCONN (speeds up error
    detection).
[...]
```

---

[35] netbsdsrc/usr.bin/ctags/ctags.1
[36] doc/ctags.pdf
[37] ace/TAO/tao/Sequence_T.cpp:130–131

```
2001-04-21 Urban  [...]
  * dir.c, proc.c: replace tests on conn_pid with tests on state
    to fix smbmount reconnect on smb_retry timeout and up the
    timeout to 30s.
[...]
2000-08-14 Urban [...]
  * proc.c: don't do interruptable_sleep in smb_retry to avoid
    signal problem/race.
[...]
1999-11-16 Andrew [...]
  * proc.c: don't sleep every time with win95 on a FINDNEXT
```

It is clear that the code in the file proc.c is susceptible to subtle timing problems and signal race conditions. (In all fairness to the *smbfs* developers, the underlying protocol was for a long time undocumented and is extremely complicated, with the numerous implementations behaving in different and incompatible ways.)

In contrast, similar fixes applied to different parts of the source code indicate an easily made error or oversight that could conceivably exist in other places as well. Such changes are exemplified by the following entries in the *vi* editor source.

```
1.65 -> 1.66 (05/18/96)
  + Send the appropriate TI/TE sequence in the curses screen
    whenever entering ex/vi mode.  This means that :shell now
    shows the correct screen when using xterm alternate screens.
[...]
1.63 -> 1.64 (05/08/96)
  + Fix bug where TI/TE still weren't working -- I didn't put
    in the translation strings for BSD style curses.
[...]
1.62 -> 1.63 (04/29/96)
  + Fix bug where nvi under BSD style curses wasn't sending
    TI/TE termcap strings when suspending the process.
```

These entries indicate that in all cases where *vi* starts or finishes performing command-line-oriented actions, the appropriate cursor addressing commands (TI/TE) must be sent to the terminal. When you encounter such entries while inspecting code, you should react by thinking about similar cases that might have been overlooked. In the case above, you should think of other possible editor commands that work in a command-line mode (such as compilation within the editor environment) and inspect the relevant functions, looking for the code that correctly handles the changes in the screen mode.

Exercise 8.3   Present an overview of the source organization of the *apache* Web server by examining the provided documentation.

Exercise 8.4   How can the formalized structure of the Unix manual pages be used to automate the construction of simple test cases?

Exercise 8.5   Map the table of contents of the BSD Unix description [LMKQ88] against the top two levels of the source tree available in the book's CD-ROM.

Exercise 8.6   Locate one instance of a published algorithm reference in the book's CD-ROM. Map the published version of the algorithm against its implementation.

Exercise 8.7   Identify two instances of state transitions in the TCP implementation in the book's CD-ROM and the corresponding changes in the TCP state transition diagram.[38]

Exercise 8.8   Locate in the book's CD-ROM three examples where the documented Perl internal interfaces are being used.

Exercise 8.9   Categorize and tabulate the types of problems described in the "Bugs" section of the Unix manual pages and sort them according to their frequency. Discuss the results you obtained.

Exercise 8.10   Search for the words "buffer overflow" in the revision control system change log of a large application. Plot the frequency of occurrences against time.

Exercise 8.11   Devise a simple process or tool to visualize the frequency of changes on specific files or file areas using the database of a revision control system.

8.3 Documentation Problems

When reading documentation, keep in mind that documentation may often provide a misleading view of the source code. The two different cases of misrepresentation you will encounter are *undocumented features* and an *idealized presentation*.

Features implemented in the source code may intentionally not be documented for a number of different (some of them defensible) reasons. A feature may not be documented because it may be

- Not officially supported
- Provided only as a support mechanism for suitably trained engineers

---

[38]doc/rfc793.txt:p. 21

- Experimental or intended for a future release
- Used by the product's vendor to gain an advantage over the competition
- Badly implemented
- A security threat
- Intended only for a subset of the users or product versions
- A Trojan horse, time bomb, or back door

Features are also sometimes not documented out of pure oversight, especially when they are added late in the product development cycle. As an example, the -C flag, which allows the specification of a configuration file, is not documented in the manual page of the *apropos* command;[39,40] this is probably an oversight. When reading code you should be wary of undocumented features. Classify each instance as justified, careless, or malicious, and accordingly decide whether the code or the documentation should be fixed.

The second sin encountered in the way documentation describes source code is an idealized presentation of the system. Documentation occasionally does not describe the system as implemented but as it should have been or will be implemented. The intention behind such discrepancies is often honorable: the documentation author may write end-user documentation based on a functional specification and the sincere hope that the system will be implemented as specified. On other occasions, architectural design documentation is not updated when structural changes are hastily implemented in the rush toward a software release. In both cases, the message conveyed to you, the code reader, is to lower the level of trust you place on the documentation.

Documentation can also be occasionally inconsistent with itself since, unlike the source code, it cannot be easily verified by the compiler or by regression tests. As an example, the NetBSD manual page of the *last* command documents a -T option in the command description but not in the synopsis.[41,42] Again, an abundance of such problems (not the case in the example we presented) may be a sign of documentation sloppily written or reviewed that should be read with an open mind.

There are also cases where the documentation may use an idiomatic language— to say the least. We counted about 40 different instances of the word *grok* in the book's CD-ROM. If you are not familiar with the word, the fault does not lie with your

---

[39] netbsdsrc/usr.bin/apropos/apropos.1
[40] doc/apropos.pdf
[41] netbsdsrc/usr.bin/last/last.1
[42] doc/last.pdf

knowledge of modern English. *Grok* appears in Robert A. Heinlein's science-fiction novel *Stranger in a Strange Land* [Hei61] as the Martian word meaning literally "to drink" and metaphorically "to be one with." In source code documentation the word *grok* typically means "to understand."[43]

```
// For linkers that cant grok long names.
#define ACE_Cleanup_Strategy ACLE
```

If unknown or idiosyncratically used words hinder your understanding of the code, try looking them up in the documentation's glossary (if it exists), *The New Hacker's Dictionary* [Ray96], or on a Web search engine.

Exercise 8.12   The book's CD-ROM contains over 40 references to undocumented behavior. Locate them and discuss the most common observed cause of documentation discrepancies.

8.4 Additional Documentation Sources

When looking for source code documentation, consider nontraditional sources such as comments, standards, publications, test cases, mailing lists, newsgroups, revision logs, issue-tracking databases, marketing material, and the source code itself. When investigating a large body of code, it is natural to miss documentation embedded in comments in the quest for more formal sources such as requirements and design documents. Yet source code comments are often better maintained than the corresponding formal documents and often hide gems of information, sometimes even including elaborate ASCII diagrams. As an example, the diagrams in Figure 8.3 and the formal mathematical proof in Figure 8.4[44] are all excerpts from actual source code comments. The ASCII diagrams depict the block structure of an audio interface hardware[45] (top left), the logical channel reshuffling procedure in X.25 networking code[46] (top right), the *m4* macro processor stack-based data structure[47] (bottom left), and the page format employed in the hashed *db* database implementation[48] (bottom right). However, keep in mind that elaborate diagrams such as these are rarely kept up-to-date when the code changes.

---

[43] ace/ace/Cleanup_Strategies_T.h:24–25
[44] netbsdsrc/sys/kern/kern_synch.c:102–135
[45] netbsdsrc/sys/dev/ic/cs4231reg.h:44–75
[46] netbsdsrc/sys/netccitt/pk_subr.c:567–591
[47] netbsdsrc/usr.bin/m4/mdef.h:155–174
[48] netbsdsrc/lib/libc/db/hash/page.h:48–59

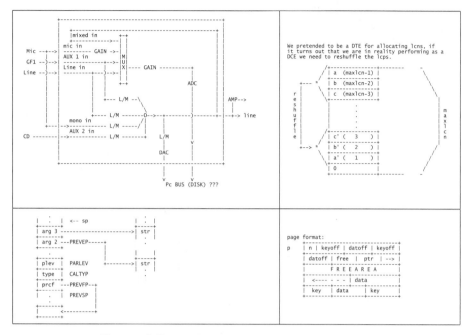

Figure 8.3 ASCII drawings in source code comments.

Always view documentation with a critical mind. Since documentation is never executed and rarely tested or formally reviewed to the extent code is, it can often be misleading or outright wrong. As an example, consider some of the problems[49] of the comment in Figure 8.4.

- It inexplicably uses the symbol ~= the first three times to indicate "approximately equal to" and thereafter uses =~.

- It uses both loadavg and loadav to refer to the same quantity. The surrounding code, not shown in the figure, uses loadav and a structure field named ldavg!

- The approximations are very sloppy and there is no justification that they are close enough. For example, the result of the division 5/2.3 is approximated as 2. This has the effect of replacing the constant .1 in the original equation with 0.08, a 20% error. The comment does not justify the correctness of this approximation.

---

[49]Contributed by Guy Steele.

```
* We wish to prove that the system's computation of decay
* will always fulfill the equation:
*  decay ** (5 * loadavg) ~= .1
*
* If we compute b as:
*  b = 2 * loadavg
* then
*  decay = b / (b + 1)
*
* We now need to prove two things:
* 1) Given factor ** (5 * loadavg) ~= .1, prove factor == b/(b+1)
* 2) Given b/(b+1) ** power ~= .1, prove power == (5 * loadavg)
*
* Facts:
*         For x close to zero, exp(x) =~ 1 + x, since
*             exp(x) = 0! + x**1/1! + x**2/2! + ... .
*             therefore exp(-1/b) =~ 1 - (1/b) = (b-1)/b.
*         For x close to zero, ln(1+x) =~ x, since
*             ln(1+x) = x - x**2/2 + x**3/3 - ...      -1<x<1
*             therefore ln(b/(b+1)) = ln(1 - 1/(b+1)) =~ -1/(b+1).
*         ln(.1) =~ -2.30
*
* Proof of (1):
*     Solve (factor)**(power) =~ .1 given power (5*loadav):
* solving for factor,
*        ln(factor) =~ (-2.30/5*loadav), or
*        factor =~ exp(-1/((5/2.30)*loadav)) =~ exp(-1/(2*loadav)) =
*            exp(-1/b) =~ (b-1)/b =~ b/(b+1).                          QED
*
* Proof of (2):
*     Solve (factor)**(power) =~ .1 given factor == (b/(b+1)):
* solving for power,
*        power*ln(b/(b+1)) =~ -2.30, or
*        power =~ 2.3 * (b + 1) = 4.6*loadav + 2.3 =~ 5*loadav.   QED
```

Figure 8.4 A mathematical proof in a source code comment.

- The approximations used for exp(x) and ln(1+x) depend on x being "close to zero," but there is no explanation of how close is close enough and no evidence or explanation provided to justify the assumption that x will indeed be close enough to zero in the actual application at hand. (A little analysis shows that for x to be "close to zero," loadavg needs to be "large," but there is no discussion of this, either.)

- Before the proofs, the comment methodically lays out two useful "facts" about approximations on which the proofs rely. This is good. But the proofs also rely on a third fact about approximations that is *not* laid out ahead of time: (b-1)/ b =~b/(b+1) if b is "large enough." The QED line of the first proof simply pulls a fast one.

- Finally, the comment is actually much more verbose than it needs to be because the two proofs are redundant! They prove essentially the same mathematical fact from two different directions.

A nontraditional documentation element, intimately bound to the source code, is the revision control system. This repository contains a detailed history of the source code's evolution and, often, comments justifying each change. In Section 6.5 we examine how you can benefit from using such a system when reading code. Associated with a revision control system is also often an issue-tracking database. There you will find details of bug reports, change requests, and other maintenance documentation. When these originate from inside the development organization, they may provide background on design and implementation issues related to the code you are reading.

The tautology may appear to be an oxymoron, but the source code can sometimes be its own documentation. Apart from the obvious case of self-documenting code, sometimes you can read code between the lines as a specification, even if the actual code does not implement the underlying intention of what the code should actually do. Consider the following (trivial) shell-script excerpt.[50]

```
for file in $* ; do echo $file":" ; done
```

The code will display each one of the space-separated arguments appearing in the $* list on a separate line. It is obvious, however, from the loop structure that the *intention* of the code is to display each file name in the $* list on a separate line. Although the file variable should more appropriately have been named filename, and the code will not work correctly when file names contain whitespace, you can still read the code as the specification of what it should do, rather than what it actually claims it does.

Finally, you can often find additional documentation on the periphery or outside the development organization. *Standards documents* can be treated as the functional specification for software that implements a specific standard (for example, an MP3 player). Similarly, you can often find a description of a given design, system, algorithm, or implementation in *journal or conference publications*. If verification and validation

---

[50]netbsdsrc/usr.bin/lorder/lorder.sh:82

are handled by a separate test group, you can use their *test cases* as a substitute or a supplement of a functional specification. When desperate, even *marketing material* can provide you with an (inflated) list of a system's features. And you can always search the Web for discussions, unofficial information, FAQ pages, and user experiences; archived newsgroups and mailing lists may sometimes reveal the rationale behind the design of the code you are reading. When the code is open-source, a particularly effective search strategy is to use three or four nonword identifiers from the code part you are reading (for example, bbp, indouble, addch) as search terms in a major search engine. Open-source code also provides you with the option to contact the code's original author. Try not to abuse this privilege, and be sure to give something back to the community for any help you receive in this way. Remember: most open-source projects are developed and maintained by (typically overworked) volunteers.

Exercise 8.13   Create an annotated list of documentation sources for the *apache* Web server or Perl. Categorize the sources based on the type of information they provide. Strive for wide coverage of areas (for example, specifications, design, user documentation) rather than completeness.

8.5 Common Open-Source Documentation Formats

You will encounter documentation in two different flavors: binary files generated and read using a proprietary product such as Microsoft Word or Adobe FrameMaker, and text files containing structure and formatting commands in the form of a *markup language*. The most common documentation formats you will encounter when dealing with open-source software are the following.

troff   The *troff* document formatting system is typically used in conjunction with the traditional *man* or the new BSD *mdoc* macros to create Unix manual pages. Other descriptive parts of the Unix manuals are also typeset in *troff*. Document formatting commands appear either at the beginning of a line starting with a dot (.) or are preceded with a backslash. You can see a part of a Unix manual page formatted using the *mdoc* macros in Figure 8.5[51] and the most common *troff* commands and *man* and *mdoc* macros in Table 8.2.

Texinfo   The *Texinfo* macros are processed by the *TeX* document formatting system. They are used to create on-line and printed documentation for many projects

---

[51] netbsdsrc/usr.bin/cut/cut.1:1–66

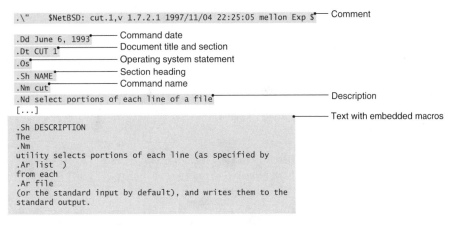

Figure 8.5 Documentation in *mdoc* format.

implemented under the GNU effort. *Texinfo* commands start with an @ character and can have arguments inside braces or following on the same line. You can see a sample *Texinfo* file in Figure 8.6[52] and the most common *Texinfo* commands in Table 8.3.

DocBook   *DocBook* is an XML/SGML application adopted, among other uses, in the FreeBSD documentation project. As you would expect, *DocBook* tags are denoted by *<tag>* sequences; their names are typically self-explanatory.

javadoc   The *javadoc* application will process Java source code suitably annotated with specially marked comments to generate documentation in a number of different formats. *javadoc* comments start with a /** sequence and can contain tags marked with an @ sign. Tags that are embedded in text appear inside braces. You can see a summary of the *javadoc* commands in Table 8.4 and Java code with embedded *javadoc* comments in Figure 6.15 on page 215.

Doxygen   *Doxygen*[53] is a documentation system for source code written in C++, Java, IDL, and C. It can generate an on-line documentation browser (in HTML) and an off-line reference manual (in *LaTeX*) from a set of suitably annotated source code files. It can also generate output in RTF, Postscript, hyperlinked PDF, and Unix *man* pages.

---

[52]netbsdsrc/usr.sbin/amd/doc/am-utils.texi:383–395
[53]http://www.stack.nl/d̃imitri/doxygen/

Table 8.2 Common *troff* Commands and *Man* and *mdoc* Line Macros

Macro	Function
troff	
.\"	Comment.
.br	Line break.
man	
.B	Typeset in boldface.
.BI	Alternate bold and italic fonts.
.BR	Alternate bold and roman fonts.
.I	Set in italic font.
.IP	Start indented paragraph.
.IR	Alternate italic and roman fonts.
.RB	Alternate roman and bold fonts.
.SH	Section heading.
.TH	Title section.
mdoc	
.Ar	Command-line argument.
.Bl	Begin list.
.Dd	Specify document date as month, day, year.
.Dt	Specify document title, section, volume.
.Dv	Defined variable.
.Ic	Interactive command.
.It	List item.
.Nm	Command name.
.Op	Option.
.Os	Specify operating system, version, release.
.Pa	Path or file name.
.Sh	Section heading.
.Xr	Manual page cross-reference.

```
@node Filesystems and Volumes, Volume Naming, Fundamentals, Overview
```
— Node definition

```
@comment node-name,  next,  previous,  up
@section Filesystems and Volumes
```
— Comment
— New section
— Concept index terms

```
@cindex Filesystem
@cindex Volume
@cindex Fileserver
@cindex sublink
```

— Text marked with Texinfo commands

```
@i{Amd} views the world as a set of fileservers, each containing one or
more filesystems where each filesystem contains one or more
@dfn{volumes}.  Here the term @dfn{volume} is used to refer to a
coherent set of files such as a user's home directory or a @TeX{}
distribution.@refill
```

Figure 8.6 Documentation in *Texinfo* format.

Table 8.3 Common *Texinfo* Commands

Command	Function
@c	The rest of the line is a comment.
@cindex	Add an entry to the index of concepts.
@code {*sample*}	*Sample* is a program element.
@emph {*text*}	*Text* appears emphasized.
@end *environment*	Set the end of an environment.
@example	Begin a (code) example.
@file {*name*}	Mark a file or directory name.
@item	Begin an itemized or enumerated paragraph.
@node *name, next, prev, up*	Define a hypertext node.
@pxref {*node name*}, @xref	Create a cross-reference.
@samp {*text*}	*Text* is a code fragment.
@section *title*	Start a new section.
@strong {*text*}	*Text* appears emphasized (bold).
@var {*name*}	Name is a metasyntactic variable.

Table 8.4 The *javadoc* Tags

Command	Function
@author	Used to indicate authors.
{@docRoot}	Relative path to generated document from root.
@deprecated	Add comment indicating a deprecated feature.
@exception or @throws	Indicate exceptions a method throws.
{@link}	Add a link to another Java element.
@param	Specify a method's parameter.
@return	Specify return type.
@see	Add a link in the "*see also*" heading.
@serial	Indicate a default serializable field.
@serialData	Specify type and order of serial data.
@serialField	Document field as serializable.
@since	Indicate first release supporting a feature.
@version	Version of software supporting a class or member.

Documentation based on markup languages such as *TeX*, *troff*, or XML is typically more tightly integrated with the source code since it is often maintained using a revision control system, automatically manipulated or generated using text-processing tools, and fully integrated into the product build process. An even tighter level of integration with the source code is achieved when the documentation is part of the source, as is the case in the CWEB system and the *javadoc* comments often used in Java source code.

Table 8.5 Unix Reference Manual Sections

Section	Contents
1	General commands (tools and utilities)
2	Operating system calls
3	C and other language libraries
4	Special files and hardware support
5	File formats
6	On-line games
7	Miscellaneous information pages
8	System maintenance and operation commands
9	Kernel internals

When reading documentation for a large system, familiarize yourself with the documentation's overall structure and conventions. For example, you may have noticed that the Java platform API documentation is organized around packages and a flat list of classes or that the Unix manual pages are typically structured around the numbered sections appearing in Table 8.5.

When confronted with voluminous documentation, you can improve your reading productivity by employing tools or by typesetting the text on a high-quality output device such as a laser printer. Many of the tools we examine in Chapter 10 can be used on the source code of markup-based documentation. Applying the tools on the source code allows you to search for markup commands as well as proper text. As an example, we used the following shell command to create a list containing invocations of the getopt argument parsing function call and the corresponding flag documentation of each Unix command.

```
(
  find . -name '*.c' -print | xargs grep getopt
  find . -name '*.1' -print | xargs egrep '^\.(Op|Fl)'
) | sort -u
```

We used the above command to find discrepancies between the documentation and implementation of Unix tools. The first *find* pipeline searches all C source code files for calls to the getopt function; these typically contain a list of arguments a program accepts. The second *find* pipeline searches in all manual pages for lines containing descriptions of an option or flag; they are marked with a macro sequence, .Op or .Fl. Since the output of the two *grep*-based searches begins with the file name where the particular pattern was encountered, sorting them generates a correctly merged list of documented options and the corresponding `getopt` parsed arguments with entries such as the following.

```
cut.1:.Fl b Ar list
cut.1:.Fl c Ar list
cut.1:.Fl f Ar list
cut.1:.Op Ar
cut.1:.Op Fl d Ar delim
cut.1:.Op Fl n
cut.1:.Op Fl s
cut.c:while ((ch = getopt(argc, argv, "b:c:d:f:sn")) != -1)
```

It is not widely known that some documentation formats we habitually struggle to read on 75 dpi (dots per inch) computer screens can be easily formatted for output on a 1,200 dpi laser printer. This is how you can typeset high-quality output from some common documentation formats.

Unix Manual Pages   Some versions of the *man* command support a -t flag to produce device-independent or Postscript output; on other systems you can directly typeset a manual page into Postscript by using a sequence such as one of the following.

```
gunzip -c /usr/share/man/man1/ls.1.gz | groff -Tps -man
troff -Tpsc /usr/share/man/man1/ls.1 | psdit
```

javadoc Comments   Apart from the standard *javadoc* HTML output format, a number of *doclets* (customized *javadoc* back-ends) can be used in conjunction with *javadoc* to create documentation in MIF (Adobe FrameMaker Interchange Format), RTF (Microsoft Rich Text Format), *LaTeX*, and *DocBook* formats.

Texinfo Documents   You can typeset the *Texinfo* file by running the *TeX* program on the `.texi` source file (*not* the processed `.info` file).

DocBook Files   Use the *Jade* or *OpenJade* packages in conjunction with the *DocBook* style sheets to export the text in formats such as RTF or *TeX*.

Exercise 8.14   Compare the documentation formats we described on usability, readability, features provided, and amenability to automated processing by ad hoc tools.

Exercise 8.15   Locate and typeset on a high-quality output device each of the different documentation formats available in the book's CD-ROM in your local environment. Discuss the difficulties you encountered.

Further Reading

The practice of *literate programming* refers to programs with embedded documentation regarding their operation [Knu92]. You can find many examples of literate programs in old columns in the *Communications of the ACM* [BKM86, Han87, Jac87, Ham88, WL89]. Douglas [Dou90] describes how a set of project-specific tools were used to manage error messages. The original *troff* and its device-independent successor *ditroff* are described in two references [Oss79, Ker82], while a more accessible reference is Gehani [Geh87] and the online documentation of various macro packages. The CWEB literate programming system is described in Knuth and Levy [KL93], *TeX* in Knuth [Knu89], *LaTeX* in Lamport [Lam94], *DocBook* in Walsh and Muellner [WM99], and the application of *DocBook* in the Linux documentation project in Komarinski et al. [KGM01].

9

Architecture

The physician can bury his mistakes, but the architect can only advise his client to plant vines.

—Frank Lloyd Wright

Discerning a system's architecture from its source code base can be difficult. However, after recognizing important architectural elements, you will find it a lot easier to navigate through the system, comprehend its structure and properties, and plan for new addition, modification, and restructuring activities. This happens because once you abstract an architectural feature, you immediately share a semantically rich vocabulary with its creators. In addition, an understanding of a system's architecture will guide you toward the types of interactions, communication patterns, and code structures to expect.

Starting with a top-down view, we first examine how subsystems are typically organized to form a larger system (Section 9.1) and how a system's units are typically controlled (Section 9.2). When examining a system, its overall structure may not be readily apparent or may not even exist at the level of detail you are dealing with. Therefore, in Section 9.3 we complement our description with a bottom-up overview of the numerous element-packaging approaches you are likely to encounter.

Architecture is said to be an old man's art: experienced designers are more likely to have seen in practice how particular designs address specific problems and which architectural solutions can be combined to form a functional and coherent whole. In Section 9.4 we present how successful designs are typically disseminated to be used again and the forms through which you will encounter architecture reuse when reading existing code.

9.1 System Structures

Many of the systems we examine follow a simple "main program and subroutine" structure. Others adopt a more sophisticated architectural structure for organizing their constituent subsystems. Common, nontrivial structures can be categorized into a small number of distinct architectural styles: centralized repository, data-flow, object-oriented, or layered. Orthogonal to those styles lies often a hierarchical structure used for taming the complexity of large systems. We examine each style individually; however, keep in mind that one system can (and in nontrivial cases does) exhibit many different styles simultaneously. Different architectural styles can appear by looking at the same system in a different way, by examining different parts of the system, or by employing different levels of decomposition.

9.1.1 Centralized Repository and Distributed Approaches

A centralized repository architectural model relies on a central process or data structure acting as a control or information hub for the system. In larger-scale systems the coordination role can be distributed across several hub processes. You will find centralized repository architectures employed when several semiautonomous processes need to cooperate to access shared information or resources. Examples in this category include window managers,[1,2] file[3] and print[4] servers, and network resource management applications.[5] Centralized repository architectures are also the basis for many collaborative applications such as the World Wide Web, on-line messaging, player games, and revision control systems like CVS and RCS.

As a typical small-scale example, consider the description of the method used for connecting two independent Unix *talk* processes in a one-to-one on-line chat session.[6]

> The talk server acts [as] a repository of invitations, responding to requests by clients wishing to rendezvous for the purpose of holding a conversation. In normal operation, a client, the caller, initiates a rendezvous by sending a CTL_MSG to the server of type LOOK_UP. This causes the server to search its invitation tables to check if an invitation currently exists for the caller (to speak to the callee specified in the message). If the lookup fails, the caller then sends

[1] XFree86-3.3/xc/programs/Xserver
[2] netbsdsrc/usr.bin/window
[3] netbsdsrc/usr.sbin/nfsd
[4] netbsdsrc/usr.sbin/lpr/lpd
[5] netbsdsrc/usr.sbin/dhcp
[6] netbsdsrc/include/protocols/talkd.h:44–56

an ANNOUNCE message causing the server to broadcast an announcement on the callee's login ports requesting contact. When the callee responds, the local server uses the recorded invitation to respond with the appropriate rendezvous address and the caller and callee client programs establish a stream connection through which the conversation takes place.

When the centralized repository and the applications that access it operate as independent processes, the architectural model is also often referred to as a *client-server model*. An important extra-functional property promoted by systems adhering to the client-server model is *integrability*, allowing different clients and servers to seamlessly interlink in a larger environment. You may have noticed that the *talk* daemon protocol of the previous paragraph has its C header file located in a system-wide header directory `include/protocols` rather than in the application's source code directory. This fact constitutes an implicit promise to allow other clients and servers to interoperate as long as they follow the protocol's conventions. Other header files residing in the same directory specify the *dump* backup format,[7] the *routed* routing information protocol exchanges,[8] the *timed* time synchronization mechanism,[9] and the *rwhod* local area network user information messages.[10] These specifications are shared by clients and servers but depend on an operating system–specific header. Applications expected to operate in a heterogeneous environment typically have their communication protocol standardized and published. In the case of Internet protocols these descriptions are publicly available from the Network Information Center in the form of the modestly named RFC (Request for Comments) documents.[11] Examples of important protocols documented as RFCs include IP (RFC-791), TCP (RFC-793), SMTP (RFC-821), FTP (RFC-959), POP-3 (RFC-1939), and HTTP (RFC-2068).

A number of centralized repository schemes are implemented by using a relational database as the data store. Clients access the database either directly by using its data manipulation language (typically SQL) or through a separate server process offering higher-level, task-oriented services. You will find the two approaches referred to as *two-tier* and *three-tier architectures*, respectively. In some cases a separate intermediate server is used as a *transaction monitor* providing a centralized transaction collection point that typically offers resiliency, redundancy, load distribution, and message sequencing.

Centralized repositories are also often used even when there is no requirement for the data persistency offered by a database. In this case the repository typically serves

---

[7] netbsdsrc/include/protocols/dumprestore.h
[8] netbsdsrc/include/protocols/routed.h
[9] netbsdsrc/include/protocols/timed.h
[10] netbsdsrc/include/protocols/rwhod.h
[11] ftp://ftp.internic.net/rfc

```
API_EXPORT(int) ap_set_byterange(request_rec *r)
{
    [...]
    else if (ranges == 1) {
        [...]
        ap_table_setn(r->headers_out, "Content-Length",     ━━ ❶ Blackboard write
            ap_psprintf(r->pool, "%ld", one_end - one_start + 1));      "Content-Length"
        [...]
    } else {
        [...]
        ap_table_setn(r->headers_out, "Content-Length",     ━━ ❶
            ap_psprintf(r->pool, "%ld", length));
        [...]
    }
}
[...]
API_EXPORT(int) ap_set_keepalive(request_rec *r)
{
    [...]
    if ((r->connection->keepalive != -1) &&
        ((r->status == HTTP_NOT_MODIFIED) ||
         (r->status == HTTP_NO_CONTENT) ||
         r->header_only ||
         ap_table_get(r->headers_out, "Content-Length") ||   ━━ Blackboard read "Content Length"
         [...]
        ) {
        [...]
        ap_table_setn(r->headers_out, "Keep-Alive",     ━━ Blackboard write "Keep-Alive"
            ap_psprintf(r->pool, "timeout=%d",
                        r->server->keep_alive_timeout));
    [...]
}
```

Figure 9.1 A blackboard in the *apache* Web server.

the role of a communications hub for a number of different code elements. By accessing the repository, unrelated code blocks can pass information between them without the expense of structuring the program to accommodate the data flow. Such a repository is termed a *blackboard system*. It typically stores loosely structured data as key/value pairs, with communicating code blocks using a common key-naming convention to exchange information. Blackboards may allow other code to *read* a key's data, *write* data for a given key, *remove* an entry, and *notify* other entities when a given entry appears or changes. When the blackboard is used to coordinate different processes, you will find a shared memory area or a file used to access the common information. In cases where the processes are located in different systems, a central server and a request-reply mechanism are often used to remotely access the blackboard.

A blackboard is used in the *apache* Web server to decouple the processing of the request and reply headers and, more importantly, as a mechanism that allows the tens of different add-in modules supported to seamlessly cooperate with the server proper. In Figure 9.1[12] you can see how two phases of the server's default page handler pass between them information concerning a page's content length. The `ap_set_byterange`

---

[12] apache/src/main/http_protocol.c:276–510

function is called from the main page handler function (`default_handler`[13]) to check a client request's HTTP `Range` header. This is a mechanism by which a Web client can request a page to be sent in multiple parts, consequently affecting the length of each part. When the server sends the HTTP header back to the client, it needs to establish whether the connection will be maintained after the page is transmitted and then set the appropriate header field. This can be done only if there is a defined page content length; otherwise the connection has to be terminated to signify that there is no more data. Thus, `ap_set_keepalive` checks the `Content-Length` blackboard entry to see whether other procedures (like `ap_set_byterange`) have already given it a value.

An important element of distributed architectures is the underlying communication protocol. The client-server and blackboard protocols we examined up to now were ad hoc designs optimized for a particular application domain. A more general approach involves the use of a *remote procedure call* or a *remote method invocation* abstraction. This allows client code to call a procedure on a remote server and receive a result. As you might expect, this exercise requires considerable coordination between the client and the server, as well as a fair amount of support infrastructure termed *middleware*. In a nutshell, the most common middleware architectures you will encounter are the following.

- CORBA (Common Object Request Broker Architecture) is an architecture- and language-neutral specification for transparent communication between applications and application objects. It is defined and supported by the Object Management Group (OMG), a nonprofit trade association of over 700 software developers, vendors, and end-users. In CORBA-based systems you will find an object request broker (ORB) mediating to forward a client's request to the appropriate object implementation.

- DCOM (Distributed Component Object Model) is an object-oriented architecture designed to promote interoperability of software objects in a distributed, heterogeneous environment. Defined by Microsoft, it mainly targets Windows systems. Its evolution is the Microsoft .NET architecture.

- RMI (Remote Method Invocation) is a Java-specific technology supporting the seamless remote invocation on objects in different Java virtual machines.

- Sun's RPC (Remote Procedure Call) is an architecture- and language-neutral message-passing protocol that Sun Microsystems and others use to call

---

[13] apache/src/main/http_core.c:3696

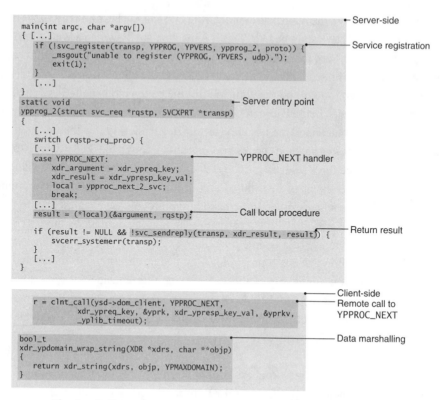

Figure 9.2 Remote procedure calls in the yp/NIS implementation.

remote procedures over different network infrastructures. A number of higher-level domain-specific protocols like the NIS (Network Information System) distributed host configuration database and the NFS (Network File System) are built on top of Sun's RPC specification.

Programs using one of the object-oriented middleware systems (CORBA, DCOM, or RMI) define the server-side methods in classes extending appropriate middleware-specific base classes. On the client side a different class is responsible for locating the server on the network and providing the corresponding *stub* methods for redirecting the calls to the server. Under Sun RPC an API allows the server to register RPC procedures and the client to call the server procedures (Figure 9.2[14–16]). All the

[14] netbsdsrc/usr.sbin/ypserv/ypserv/ypserv.c:125–399
[15] netbsdsrc/lib/libc/yp/yp_first.c:166–168
[16] netbsdsrc/lib/libc/yp/xdryp.c:130–136

systems we outlined, apart from RMI, have to deal with different data representations across processor architectures. This problem is solved by marshalling data types into an architecture-neutral format used for communicating between arbitrary hosts. Marshalling can occur either transparently (CORBA, DCOM) by describing the interfaces in an *interface definition language* (IDL) that is compiled into the appropriate marshalling code or explicitly (Sun RPC) by calling data-transformation functions.

9.1.2 Data-Flow Architectures

You will often find data-flow (or pipes-and-filters) architectures adopted when processing can be modeled, designed, and implemented as a series of data transformations. Consider the creation of a database containing a short description for each entry documented in a Unix manual page. As an example, the entry for the `getopt` function (whose manual page appears in Section 2.3) will be:

```
getopt (3) - get option character from command line argument list
```

This task can be modeled as a number of discrete steps:

1. Find all manual pages.
2. Remove duplicate entries. (When a single manual page documents multiple commands, it appears linked through different file names.)
3. Extract the appropriate entries.
4. Catenate them into a database.
5. Install the database in its final location.

Each of these steps receives input from the previous one and produces output that its successor will process.

Although data-flow architectures may appear restrictive, they offer a number of advantages. First of all, data-flow architectures often model real processes and the way people actually work. In addition, a realization of a system designed by using a data-flow architecture can be implemented either sequentially or concurrently. Finally, the implemented data transformations can be easily reused; the success of Unix as a rapid application prototyping and development environment stems exactly from the aggressive reuse of its many *filter* programs. Data-flow architectures are often employed in automatic data-processing batch-oriented environments, especially on platforms that efficiently support data-transformation tools. On the other hand,

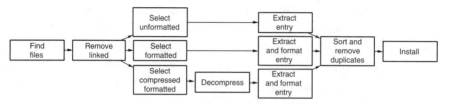

Figure 9.3 Data-flow diagram for creating manual page descriptions.

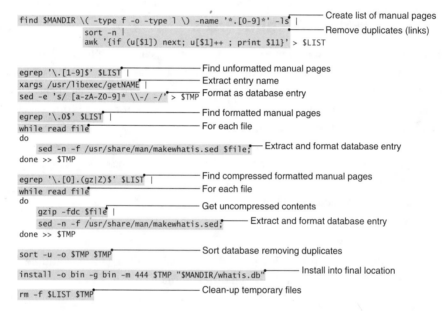

```
find $MANDIR \( -type f -o -type l \) -name '*.[0-9]*' -ls |      ——— Create list of manual pages
        sort -n |                                                  ——— Remove duplicates (links)
        awk '{if (u[$1]) next; u[$1]++ ; print $11}' > $LIST

egrep '\.[1-9]$' $LIST |                         ——— Find unformatted manual pages
xargs /usr/libexec/getNAME |                     ——— Extract entry name
sed -e 's/ [a-zA-Z0-9]* \\-/ -/' > $TMP          Format as database entry

egrep '\.0$' $LIST |                             ——— Find formatted manual pages
while read file                                  ——— For each file
do
        sed -n -f /usr/share/man/makewhatis.sed $file;  ——— Extract and format database entry
done >> $TMP

egrep '\.[0].(gz|Z)$' $LIST |                    ——— Find compressed formatted manual pages
while read file                                  ——— For each file
do
        gzip -fdc $file |                        ——— Get uncompressed contents
        sed -n -f /usr/share/man/makewhatis.sed; ——— Extract and format database entry
done >> $TMP

sort -u -o $TMP $TMP                             ——— Sort database removing duplicates

install -o bin -g bin -m 444 $TMP "$MANDIR/whatis.db"  ——— Install into final location

rm -f $LIST $TMP                                 ——— Clean-up temporary files
```

Figure 9.4 The filter-based implementation of the *makewhatis* command.

data-flow architectures are not well suited for designing reactive systems such as GUI front ends and real-time applications.

A telltale sign of a data-flow architecture is the use of temporary files or pipelines for communicating between different processes. The implementation of the *makewhatis* command, which creates the manual page database outlined in Figure 9.3,[17] is a typical example (Figure 9.4). A pipeline first creates a file containing a list of all unique manual pages installed on the system. The resulting file is then processed by three different pipelines, one for each different type of manual page found: unformatted manual pages (*troff* source code), formatted pages (text with embedded control

---

[17] netbsdsrc/libexec/makewhatis/makewhatis.sh:20–39

characters), and compressed formatted pages. The results of the three pipelines are appended into a single file, which is in turn processed by *sort* to remove remaining duplicate entries (occurring, for example, when a manual page exists in formatted and unformatted form).

To understand the functioning of a system based on a data-flow architecture you need to comprehend two things: its processes and the data that flows between them. Processes are typically data transformations. Try to understand each transformation in isolation, thinking about its input and output data. If the processes in the system you are examining communicate by using pipelines, it may be worth temporarily redirecting the data contents of a pipeline into a file and examining its contents. The Unix tool *tee* allows you to set up such a tap. When temporary files are used, simply eliminate commands that remove these files at the end of the processing cycle. In business applications, data often consists of line-oriented records with separate fields either occupying a fixed-width space or separated by a special character. Data, however, can also consist of fixed-width records or application-specific objects, or it can follow the conventions of a particular binary stream, as is the case, for example, in the *netpbm* image-processing and the *sox* sound-manipulation tools. To understand the structure of a whole system, it may be helpful to draw a *data-flow diagram*, such as the one illustrated in Figure 9.3. If you are lucky, such diagrams will be included in the system's design documentation.

9.1.3 Object-Oriented Structures

Systems that adopt an object-oriented structure base their designs on interacting objects that locally maintain their own states. The system's architecture is defined by the relationships between different classes or objects and the ways objects interact. Real-world systems can consist of hundreds of different classes. As an example, the Cocoon XML publishing framework source code[18] contains more than 500 Java classes. Establishing order out of such a system can be a difficult task indeed. Fortunately you can rely on a standardized notation and vocabulary, the *Unified Modeling Language* (UML), to express a system's model or read its existing documentation. In addition, a number of UML-based tools allow you to *reverse engineer* salient elements of the architecture and express them in UML notation.

UML is used to model different perspectives during a system's lifetime. These span from the conceptual model of the world to the abstract software specification

---

[18]cocoon/src

RequestFilterValve
-static final info: String = "org.apache.catalina.valves.RequestFilterValve/1.0"
#allow: String = null
#deny: String = null
+getAllow(): String
+setAllow(allow: String): void
+getDeny(): String
+setDeny(deny: String): void
+getInfo(): String
+*invoke(request:): void*
#precalculate(list: String): RE[]
#process(property: String, request:): void

Figure 9.5 A class representation in UML.

model to the concrete actual implementation model. UML, suffering from a slight case of notational overload, offers no less than nine different diagrams for expressing these views. When examining the code of an actual system, you will typically model its structure in terms of a class or object diagram and its internal interactions in terms of a sequence or a collaboration diagram. The basic building elements in most UML diagrams are classes; Figure 9.5 illustrates how the `RequestFilterValve`[19] class could appear in a UML model. The three parts of the box contain the *class name*, its *attributes* (properties), and its *operations* (methods). The class name appears in italics to denote that the specific class is abstract (it has been defined using the `abstract` keyword and cannot therefore be used to directly instantiate objects). Attributes and operations are adorned with the symbols + to denote a member defined as `public` (one that all methods can access), - to denote a member defined as `private` (one accessible only within the class's methods), and # to denote a member defined as `protected` (one accessible only from the methods of the class and its derived classes). In addition, members defined as `static` (referring to the class and not its individual objects) appear underlined; `abstract` members appear in italics. Do not let the syntax of the individual member definitions distract you; when using UML to reverse engineer an existing system, the syntax will typically follow the system's implementation language. Models such as the ones we examine in this section apply to all languages that support objects, including C++, C#, Eiffel, Java, Perl, Python, Ruby, Smalltalk,

---

[19] jt4/catalina/src/share/org/apache/catalina/valves/RequestFilterValve.java

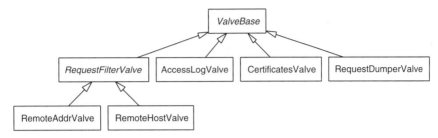

Figure 9.6 Simple generalization relationships.

and Visual Basic .NET. When depicting a system's architecture, you will often hide parts of a class description (its attributes and operations), thus gaining room to depict relationships among numerous classes.

A UML class diagram shows a set of classes, interfaces, collaborations, and relationships. It can be useful for understanding the structural aspects of a system's architecture. As an example, the diagram in Figure 9.6 illustrates the class hierarchy of the valves[20] package in the Tomcat servlet container: the ValveBase abstract class is used as a base to derive six other classes. The arrows connecting the classes are the UML notation for expressing a *generalization relationship* (inheritance in our case): the fact that the specialized class (for example, RemoteAddrValve) shares the structure and behavior of the generalized class (RequestFilterValve). Thus the particular relationship expresses the following Java code.[21]

```
public final class RemoteAddrValve
    extends RequestFilterValve {
```

Relationships between classes can quickly become more complicated. In object-oriented languages that support *multiple inheritance*, such as C++, Eiffel, and Perl, you can have a specialized class inheriting from multiple parent classes. In addition, there are cases where a class does not inherit functionality from another class but enters a contractual relationship to implement one or more specific *interfaces*. This is the case for some of the functions appearing in the example discussed in Section 9.1.4. Java explicitly supports such relationships through the interface keyword and classes defined with an implements declaration. You can model such cases by using the UML *realization relationship* to indicate that the classifier located at

---

[20]jt4/catalina/src/share/org/apache/catalina/valves
[21]jt4/catalina/src/share/org/apache/catalina/valves/RemoteAddrValve.java:83–84

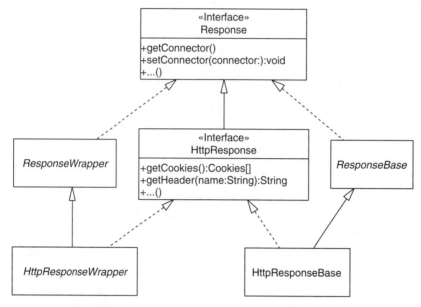

Figure 9.7 Realization and generalization relationships.

the arrow's head specifies a contract that the classifier at the arrow's tail guarantees to carry out. You can see a class structure involving both realization and generalization relationships in Figure 9.7. The model, depicting some of the classes participating in the Tomcat `connector` package,[22] contains two interfaces, `Response` and its specialization `HttpResponse`, and four classes. The `ResponseWrapper` and `ResponseBase` classes implement the `Response` interface, while the `HttpResponseWrapper` and `HttpResponseBase` classes implement the `HttpResponse` interface and also inherit the functionality of `ResponseWrapper` and `ResponseBase`. Although these relationships appear straightforward in the model, discerning the structure directly from the Java source code definitions dispersed in six different files and two directories could have been tricky. It is therefore worthwhile to use diagrams to model the relationships in object-oriented architectures.

Although drawing diagrams by hand on a whiteboard or paper will help you understand a system's structure, you can also benefit from numerous tools that can build models by reverse engineering existing code. All the UML diagrams we examined were initially generated using the open-source ArgoUML[23] modeling tool. You can often

---

[22] jt4/catalina/src/share/org/apache/catalina/connector
[23] http://www.argouml.org

import source code into a modeling tool to reverse engineer a system's architecture. The version of ArgoUML we used can import Java code and identify generalization and realization relationships between classes. Commercial modeling tools like the Rational Rose and the Together ControlCenter support the import of more programming languages and can detect and display in your model additional relationships like associations between classes. These tools also offer the ability to perform *round-trip engineering modeling*, whereby changes to the code are reflected to the model and vice versa.

9.1.4 Layered Architectures

Systems with a multitude of alternative peer subsystems are often organized following a layered architecture. In such an architecture, each separate layer presents a well-defined interface to its upper layer and communicates using a different but standard interface with its lower layer. Within such a framework each layer can be implemented by using different technologies or approaches without affecting the architectural integrity of the whole. Computer networks and operating systems typically follow such an approach: a network's physical layer does not affect and is not affected by the format of the data passing over it; user applications do not concern themselves with the particulars of the hardware devices they communicate with. Layered architectures are typically implemented by stacking software components with standardized interfaces. In a sense each layer presents a *virtual machine interface* to the layers above it. In many cases you will recognize such an architecture by stumbling across the specification or documentation of these interface layers.

An important rule of layered architectures is that lower layers cannot use upper layers—usage (not calling, but usage) flows down. If everything used everything, then the layers could not be easily replaced or abstracted. As an example, a network's physical layer implementation (for example, Ethernet or SONET) cannot make assumptions about the upper-level protocols (for example, TCP/IP) that will run on top of it. This guarantees that other upper-level protocols (for example, UDP/IP or NETBIOS) can be implemented on top of Ethernet without having to modify the Ethernet's implementation. As a further example, code generated with different Java compilers will run on any same-standard Java Virtual Machine. The implication of this rule when you are examining a layered architecture is that a system's layer can view lower layers as abstract entities and (as long as the layer is satisfying its requirements) does not care how upper layers will use it.

For a concrete illustration of a relatively sophisticated layered architecture, brace yourself as we examine how a simple `fwrite` request in a C program running on

	Function name	Layer	Role
↓	`fwrite`	`stdio` library	User-space buffering
↓	`write`	System call	POSIX interface
	User / kernel-space boundary		
↓	`sys_write`	Kernel entry point	Argument processing
↓	`vn_write`	Vnode	Adapt to vnode interface
↓	`VOP_WRITE`	Vnode switch	Multiple interfaces
↓	`ext2fs_write`	File system	Data structure
↓	`bwrite`	Kernel buffer cache	Kernel-space buffering
↓	`VOP_STRATEGY`	Vnode switch	Multiple interfaces
↓	`ufs_strategy`	Block	Logical blocks
↓	`VOP_STRATEGY`	Vnode switch	Multiple interfaces
↓	`spec_strategy`	Device switch	Multiple devices
	`sdstrategy`	Asynchronous operations	I/O queues
	Synchronous / asynchronous code boundary		
	`scsipi_done`	SCSI interface	Queuing and process notification
↑	`aha_done`	Device commands	Result processing
↑	`aha_finish_ccbs`	Command control blocks	Result processing
↑	`aha_intr`	Device interrupt	Message box handling
↑	`INTR`	System interrupt	Interrupt processing

Figure 9.8 A file write operation: from a user program to the device.

a NetBSD operating system ends up as a Linux filesystem–specific bit pattern on a SCSI disk connected on an Adaptec controller. We illustrate the different functions called to service this request, the layer each function represents, and the layer's role in Figure 9.8. When the program is executing as a user process the `fwrite`[24] function provides the `stdio` library buffering, while the `write`[25] system call handles the standard POSIX system call interface. When the system call reaches the kernel, the sequence `sys_write`[26] → `vn_write`[27] → `VOP_WRITE`[28] decodes the system call and directs

---

[24]netbsdsrc/lib/libc/stdio/fwrite.c:56–59
[25]netbsdsrc/sys/kern/syscalls.master:52–53
[26]netbsdsrc/sys/kern/sys_generic.c:228–286
[27]netbsdsrc/sys/kern/vfs_vnops.c:370–394
[28]netbsdsrc/sys/kern/vnode_if.src:98–103

it to the appropriate filesystem–specific function, `ext2fs_write`[29] (the Linux *ext2* filesystem in this case). From that point the sequence `bwrite`[30] → `VOP_STRATEGY`[31] → `ufs_strategy`[32] writes the block in the appropriate logical position of the device, while the sequence `VOP_STRATEGY`[33] → `spec_strategy`[34] → `sdstrategy`[35] directs the request for queued processing to a specific device (a SCSI disk in this example). The completion of the hardware request is in our case propagated upward from the device to a notification function using interrupts; these layers do not interact directly with the layers above but are synchronized using a `sleep`/wakeup interface. Thus, a device interrupt, signaling the completion of the command, is first processed by `INTR`,[36] then propagated to the device-specific function (`aha_intr`),[37] to the function that processes the SCSI-specific control blocks (`aha_finish_ccbs`),[38] to the function that processes the command result (`aha_done`),[39] and finally to the function that will notify the waiting process and queue new requests (`scsipi_done`).[40]

A layer interface can consist of either a family of complementary functions supporting a specific concept or a series of interchangeable functions supporting different underlying implementations of an abstract interface. As an example, in the code we examined, the `write` system call forms a part of the operating system call interface layer (a concept) together with other functions such as `read`, `open`, `close`, `fork`, and `exec`. Similarly `bwrite` supports the kernel buffer interface[41] together with the functions `bremfree`, `bufinit`, `bio_doread`, `bread`, `brelse`, `biowait`, and `biodone`. On the other hand, `ext2fs_write` supports a concrete implementation of a filesystem write (an abstract interface specification) in parallel with `msdosfs_write`,[42] `nfsspec_write`,[43] `union_write`,[44] and `ufsspec_write`.[45] Similarly `aha_intr` handles the

[29] netbsdsrc/sys/ufs/ext2fs/ext2fs_readwrite.c:169–298
[30] netbsdsrc/sys/kern/vfs_bio.c:297–350
[31] netbsdsrc/sys/kern/vnode_if.src:228–230
[32] netbsdsrc/sys/ufs/ufs/ufs_vnops.c:1616–1651
[33] netbsdsrc/sys/kern/vnode_if.src:228–230
[34] netbsdsrc/sys/miscfs/specfs/spec_vnops.c:479–489
[35] netbsdsrc/sys/dev/scsipi/sd.c:429–492
[36] netbsdsrc/sys/arch/i386/isa/vector.s:148–200
[37] netbsdsrc/sys/dev/ic/aha.c:464–508
[38] netbsdsrc/sys/dev/ic/aha.c:374–459
[39] netbsdsrc/sys/dev/ic/aha.c:836–921
[40] netbsdsrc/sys/dev/scsipi/scsipi_base.c:266–346
[41] netbsdsrc/sys/kern/vfs_bio.c
[42] netbsdsrc/sys/msdosfs/msdosfs_vnops.c:501
[43] netbsdsrc/sys/nfs/nfs_vnops.c:3194
[44] netbsdsrc/sys/miscfs/union/union_vnops.c:917
[45] netbsdsrc/sys/ufs/ufs/ufs_vnops.c:1707

device-specific interrupts in concert with asc_intr,[46] fxp_intr,[47] ncr_intr,[48] pcic_intr,[49] px_intr,[50] sbdsp_intr,[51] and many others. In the example we presented, some of the layers exist just to multiplex or demultiplex different layer interfaces, depending on the specific request. This functionality is implemented by using arrays of function pointers such as the following.[52]

```
struct vnodeopv_entry_desc ext2fs_vnodeop_entries[] = {
    { &vop_default_desc, vn_default_error },
    { &vop_lookup_desc, ext2fs_lookup },    /* lookup */
    { &vop_create_desc, ext2fs_create },    /* create */
    [...]
    { &vop_update_desc, ext2fs_update },    /* update */
    { &vop_bwrite_desc, vn_bwrite },        /* bwrite */
    { (struct vnodeop_desc*)NULL, (int(*) __P((void*)))NULL }
};
```

You will find that systems implemented in object-oriented languages directly express layer interface multiplexing operations by using virtual method calls.

9.1.5 Hierarchies

A central element in both building and understanding complex architectures is the notion of *hierarchical decomposition*. Hierarchies are often used to tame complexity by separating concerns in a structured and easy-to-navigate manner. Hierarchical decomposition is often orthogonal to other architectural aspects of the system; the architecture can be defined in a hierarchical manner, or one or more distinct hierarchies can cross-cut and permeate a different architectural structure. It is important to appreciate that a system can be organized across various axes using different and distinct hierarchical decomposition models. For a concrete example, look at the layers depicted in Figure 9.8 (page 280)—involving clearly a hierarchical decomposition of concerns—and compare them against the directory structure that contains the underlying functions. The two do not match because they involve two different hierarchical

---

[46] netbsdsrc/sys/dev/tc/asc.c:824
[47] netbsdsrc/sys/dev/pci/if_fxp.c:908
[48] netbsdsrc/sys/dev/pci/ncr.c:4240
[49] netbsdsrc/sys/dev/ic/i82365.c:467
[50] netbsdsrc/sys/dev/tc/px.c:153
[51] netbsdsrc/sys/dev/isa/sbdsp.c:1481
[52] netbsdsrc/sys/ufs/ext2fs/ext2fs_vnops.c:1389–1433

models, one concerned with the control and data flow across the system, the other with the organization of the source code.

When examining a system's architecture, you will discern hierarchical structures in the following instances:

- The source layout in directories
- The static or dynamic procedure call graph
- The `namespace` (in C++), `package` (in Ada, Java, Perl), or identifier names
- Class and interface inheritance
- The naming of structured blackboard entries
- Inner classes or nested procedures
- Navigation within heterogeneous data structures and object associations

Be open to accepting the architecture's different—and possibly conflicting—methods of hierarchical decomposition as different views of the same scene; a tree-like diagram will help you model any hierarchy you encounter.

9.1.6 Slicing

A valuable conceptual tool for deriving details about a program's structure is *slicing*. Informally, you can think of a *program slice* as the parts of a program that can affect variable values computed at a specific program location. Thus, the *slicing criterion* (a specification of the parts that will make up the slice) is a set of variables and a program location. You can see an illustration of the technique in action in Figure 9.9.[53] The original code (Figure 9.9:2) is sliced with respect to the variable `charct` and the program point indicated in Figure 9.9:1, as shown in Figure 9.9:3, and also with respect to the variable `linect` and the same program point, as shown in Figure 9.9:4. The value of slicing as an analysis and program comprehension technique is that it brings together a program's data and control dependencies: the flow of data and the order of statement execution. Slicing thus allows you to restructure the strict hierarchical decomposition of a large program by grouping nonsequential sets of statements. By slicing a large body of code on a key result variable you can eliminate nonessential information and, hopefully, reverse engineer the underlying design or algorithm. Slicing will also provide you with a measure of module *cohesion*: the degree of relatedness among

---

[53] netbsdsrc/usr.bin/wc/wc.c:202–225

```
while ((len = read(fd, buf, MAXBSIZE)) > 0) {          ——2 Original code
    charct += len;
    for (C = buf; len--; ++C) {
        if (isspace(*C)) {
            gotsp = 1;
            if (*C == '\n') {
                ++linect;
            }
        } else {
            if (gotsp) {
                gotsp = 0;
                ++wordct;
            }
        }
    }
}                  ——1 Slicing point
```

```
while ((len = read(fd, buf, MAXBSIZE)) > 0) {          ——3 Slice on the variable charct
    charct += len;
}
```

```
while ((len = read(fd, buf, MAXBSIZE)) > 0) {          ——4 Slice on the variable linect
    for (C = buf; len--; ++C) {
        if (isspace(*C)) {
            if (*C == '\n') {
                ++linect;
            }
        }
    }
}
```

Figure 9.9 Examples of program slicing.

processing elements within a module. A high level of cohesion within a module justifies the initial architectural design that brought its elements together; a low level of cohesion indicates that there is room to regroup module elements that were only coincidentally brought together. To identify a module's cohesion you can create a series of module slices based on its different output variables. The intersections (the common code lines) of these slices indicate processing element relationships; their size is a measure of the module's cohesion. Using the same procedure across modules you can also measure *coupling*: the degree of interrelatedness between modules. A high level of coupling indicates code that is difficult to understand and change; in such a case slices can be used to uncover how different modules relate to each other.

Exercise 9.1   Describe how you can determine the database schema in the relational database system you are using. Devise a simple tool that will convert the schema into a nicely formatted report.

Exercise 9.2   Global variables are supposed to hinder code readability. How does a blackboard approach differ?

Exercise 9.3 Not many open-source projects use middleware. Discuss why.

Exercise 9.4 Locate applications based on a data-flow architecture in the book's CD-ROM. What was your search strategy?

Exercise 9.5 Download the GNU *tar* program[54] and show in the form of a data-flow diagram how the program handles remote backups, compression, and fixed block I/O.

Exercise 9.6 Use a UML modeling tool to reverse engineer the structure of an object-oriented application from the book's CD-ROM.

Exercise 9.7 Identify how the OSI network layers correspond to the actual implementation of the NetBSD networking code.

Exercise 9.8 Can slicing techniques help you comprehend object-oriented programs? Discuss how the Law of Demeter (see the Further Reading section) affects the applicability of program slicing.

9.2 Control Models

A system's control model describes how its constituent subsystems interact with each other. In common with the system structures we examined in the previous section, many systems adopt a simple, centralized, single-threaded *call and return* control model. In addition, some of the system structures we examined are implicitly based on a specific control model: in a data-flow structure subsystems are controlled by the flow of data, and in an object-oriented structure control is typically coordinated through method invocations. Other common, nontrivial control models can be event-driven, be based on a system manager, or revolve around state transitions.

9.2.1 Event-Driven Systems

In many systems control decisions are made by responding to externally generated events. You will find that systems based on an *event-driven architecture* span the full range of possible software abstractions: from low-level interrupt-driven assembly code handler routines and process scheduling to the implementation of high-level GUI structures and relational database triggers. The implementation of event-driven

---

[54]http://www.gnu.org/software/tar

systems can take a number of different forms. Events can be broadcast to a set of event listeners[55]

```
for (int i = 0; i < list.length; i++)
    ((ContainerListener) list[i]).containerEvent(event);
```

or, as is often the case with hardware interrupts, invoke a single handler routine. In addition, some applications are structured around an event loop that polls for events and directs the processing[56]

```
while (XtAppPending(appCtx))
    XtAppProcessEvent(appCtx, XtIMAll);
```

while others may be integrated within a framework where event-processing routines can register to handle specific events, as illustrated in Figure 9.10.[57–59]

The fact that an event can be sent to an application without any prior arrangement makes events particularly well suited to modern GUI-based environments where events are used to channel the data generated by the different input devices, the window manager, and the operating system to the numerous executing applications. Typically such events include those generated by the keyboard, mouse movements, receipt of the application focus, menu selections, scrollbar movements, button presses, the power management system, and interprocess communication. Explicitly handling these events can render an application's structure quite complicated, as illustrated in Figure 9.11.[60] For this reason, a number of GUI application frameworks such as the Microsoft Foundation Classes (MFC), the Java Abstract Windowing Toolkit (AWT) and Swing libraries, and the X Window System–based Xt and Motif toolkits provide facilities for registering handlers for specific events. Internally each toolkit contains an event loop that retrieves events from the underlying GUI system and an event pump that distributes events to the registered handlers. As an example, the following methods are automatically invoked for the corresponding events by the system's event manager.[61]

```
public class TabResults extends TabSpawnable
implements Runnable, MouseListener, ActionListener, ListSelectionListener {
```

[55] jt4/catalina/src/share/org/apache/catalina/core/ContainerBase.java:1330–1331
[56] XFree86-3.3/contrib/programs/xfontsel/xfontsel.c:1331
[57] XFree86-3.3/contrib/programs/xman/Xman.ad:67–78
[58] XFree86-3.3/contrib/programs/xman/main.c:119–221
[59] XFree86-3.3/contrib/programs/xman/handler.c:643–652
[60] demogl/CPP/DemoGL/dgl_dllstartupdialog.cpp:86–554
[61] argouml/org/argouml/ui/ProjectBrowser.java:46–160

```
*help*Paned.manualPage.translations:#override \        ● Keyboard accelerator definitions
    [...]                                                  (Xman.ad)
    Ctrl<Key>d: GotoPage(Directory) \n\
    Ctrl<Key>m: GotoPage(ManualPage) \n\
    Ctrl<Key>v: ShowVersion()
```

```
XtActionsRec xman_actions[] = {                        ● Event action table
  {"GotoPage",          GotoPage},                       (main.c)
  {"Quit",              Quit},
  [...]
  {"SaveFormattedPage", SaveFormattedPage},
  {"ShowVersion",       ShowVersion},
};
```

```
void
main(int argc, char **argv)
{
  XtAppContext app_con;

  [...]
                                                                      ● Create application context
  initial_widget = XtAppInitialize(&app_con, "Xman", xman_options,
          XtNumber(xman_options), &argc, argv,
          fallback_resources, NULL, ZERO);

  [...]
  XtAppAddActions(app_con, xman_actions, XtNumber(xman_actions));  ── Register event actions
  [...]
  XtAppMainLoop(app_con);                              ── Start the event loop
}
```

```
                                                       ● Event action function to
void                                                     show the application's version
ShowVersion(w, event, params, num_params)                (handler.c)
Widget w;
XEvent * event;
String * params;
Cardinal * num_params;
{
  ManpageGlobals * man_globals = GetGlobals(w);
  ChangeLabel(man_globals->label, XMAN_VERSION);
}
```

Figure 9.10 Implicit event registration and handling in Xt.

```
[...]
/////////////////////////////////////////////////////////////////
// MouseListener implementation

public void mousePressed(MouseEvent me) { }
public void mouseReleased(MouseEvent me) { }
public void mouseClicked(MouseEvent me) {
  if (me.getClickCount() >= 2) myDoubleClick(me.getSource());
}
```

Object-oriented systems often add one other interesting twist to the event-handling structure by organizing events around classes. Class-based event handling confers two distinct advantages to the application.

```
BOOL CALLBACK
StartupDlgMsgHandler(HWND hWnd, UINT iMsg, WPARAM wParam, LPARAM lParam)          ┃1 Event parameters
{                                                                                     (typeless)
    [...]
    switch (iMsg)
    {
                                                        ●────── Initialize dialog box
    case WM_INITDIALOG:
    {
        // Get pointer to startupdat structure
        pStartupDat=m_gpDemoDat->GetStartupDat();

        [...]                                           ─────── 263 more lines
        return TRUE;
    }; break;

                                                        ●── Left mouse button pressed
    case WM_LBUTTONDOWN:
    {       [...]
        PostMessage(hWnd,WM_NCLBUTTONDOWN,HTCAPTION,NULL);
        return FALSE;
    }; break;

                                    ●── Handle scrollbar event
    case WM_HSCROLL:
    {       [...]
        switch(LOWORD(wParam))●── Handle different scrollbar subevents
        {
            case SB_THUMBTRACK:
            case SB_ENDSCROLL:
            case SB_LINELEFT:
            case SB_LINERIGHT:
            case SB_PAGELEFT:
            case SB_PAGERIGHT:
            {       [...]
            }; break;
        }
        return FALSE;
    }; break;

                                        ●── Handle commands
    case WM_COMMAND:
    {       [...]
        switch(HIWORD(wParam))          ●── Handle command parameters
        {
            case EN_SETFOCUS:
            [...]
            case CBN_SELCHANGE:
            [...]
            case BN_CLICKED:
            {
                switch(LOWORD(wParam))   ●── Handle command buttons
                {
                    case IDC_BTNSTART:
                    [...]                ─── 86 more lines
                    case IDC_BTNCANCEL:
                    case IDCANCEL: [...]
                    case IDC_BTNABOUT: [...]
                    case IDC_RDBSNDYES:
                    case IDC_RDBSNDNO: [...]
                }
            };break;
        }
        return TRUE;
    }; break;

        default:  [...]
    }
}
```

Figure 9.11 Explicit handling of Microsoft Windows messages.

1. Events can carry additional information with them in the form of the object properties, obviating the problem of typeless, generic event parameters, for example, as they are found in the Microsoft Windows SDK (Figure 9.11:1).

2. Subclassing and inheritance can be used to establish an event hierarchy that can also drive event dispatch policies.

The following code excerpt illustrates a simple use of these concepts.[62]

```
public abstract class ArgoEvent extends EventObject
implements ArgoEventTypes {

    protected int _eventType = 0;

    public ArgoEvent(int eventType, Object src) {
        super(src);
        _eventType = eventType;
    }
}
```

The above `ArgoEvent` class extends the Java `EventObject` and is in turn extended by the `ArgoModuleEvent`[63] and `ArgoNotationEvent`[64] classes.

9.2.2 System Manager

Systems that require the (pseudo-)concurrent execution of multiple processes often adopt a *system managercontrol model*. A single system component acts as a centralized manager, starting, stopping, and coordinating the execution of other system processes and tasks. This is the model used in the BSD Unix kernel for scheduling the swapping of processes. Although normally processes are periodically scheduled in a round-robin fashion based on their dynamically adjusted priorities, there are extreme cases where this procedure is not sufficient. When a process is completely inactive, the system is running low on memory, or the memory pool is becoming fragmented, the system will swap the complete image of a process to the disk. This is the task of the process scheduler, acting as a Unix system's central manager (excerpted in Figure 9.12).[65] The system's kernel, after performing all the start-up activities such as the scheduling

---

[62] argouml/org/argouml/application/events/ArgoEvent.java:34–42
[63] argouml/org/argouml/application/events/ArgoModuleEvent.java
[64] argouml/org/argouml/application/events/ArgoNotationEvent.java
[65] netbsdsrc/sys/vm/vm_glue.c:350–419

```
void
scheduler()
{
loop:
```
                                                                            Find a process to swap-in
```
        pp = NULL;
        ppri = INT_MIN;
        for (p = allproc.lh_first; p != 0; p = p->p_list.le_next) {
            if (p->p_stat == SRUN && (p->p_flag & P_INMEM) == 0) {
                pri = p->p_swtime + p->p_slptime
                    - (p->p_nice - NZERO) * 8;
                if (pri > ppri) {
                    pp = p;
                    ppri = pri;
                }
            }
        }
```

                                                                    Nothing to do
                                                                    Sleep allowing interrupt-driven tasks to run
```
        if ((p = pp) == NULL) {
            tsleep((caddr_t)&proc0, PVM, "scheduler", 0);
            goto loop;
        }
```

                                                                    There is space to bring a process in memory
```
        if (cnt.v_free_count > atop(USPACE)) {
            swapin(p);
            goto loop;
        }
```

                                                        No space available
                                                        Wait for the pageout daemon to create space
```
        (void) splhigh();
        VM_WAIT;
        (void) spl0();

        goto loop;
}
```

Figure 9.12 The BSD Unix swap process scheduler.

of the event-driven periodic process-control tasks, calls the scheduler, entering its infinite loop.[66]

```
void
main(void *framep)
{
    [...]
    /* Kick off timeout driven events by calling first time. */
    roundrobin(NULL);
    schedcpu(NULL);
    [...]
    /* The scheduler is an infinite loop. */
    scheduler();
    /* NOTREACHED */
}
```

---

[66]netbsdsrc/sys/kern/init_main.c:166–424

The system we described is actually a hybrid of two control models. An event-driven system coordinates normal process activity, while the more robust process manager model we examined above is used as a fail-over mechanism for extreme situations. Many real-world systems adopt the best parts of multiple architectures. When dealing with such a system, do not seek in vain for the all-encompassing architectural picture; locate, recognize, and appreciate each different architectural style as a separate yet interrelated entity.

9.2.3 State Transition

A *state transition model* manages a system's flow of control by manipulating data: the system's state. The state data determines where execution control will be directed, and changes to the state data are used to redirect the execution target. Systems (or, more often, subsystems) that adopt the state transition control model are typically modeled and structured in the form of a *state machine*. A state machine is defined by a finite set of states it can be in and the rules for performing processing and transitioning from one state to another. Two special states, the *initial state* and the *final state*, specify the machine's start point and termination condition, respectively. You will find state machines typically implemented as a loop around a `switch` statement. The `switch` statement branches according to the state of the machine; each `case` statement performs processing for a specific state, changes the state, and returns control to the top of the state machine. You can see a typical example of a state machine in Figure 9.13[67] and its respective UML state transition diagram in Figure 9.14. The specific state machine is used for recognizing the names of shell variables; these can consist of a single letter (PS_VAR1 state), of letters and digits (PS_IDENT state), or entirely of digits (PS_NUMBER state). The PS_SAW_HASH state is used to allow special handling of variables starting with a single # character. The variable `state` is used to hold the machine's state. It starts from PS_INITIAL (shown as a filled circle in the UML diagram) and terminates the function when its value becomes PS_END (the filled circle surrounded by the unfilled circle in the UML diagram).

You will find state machines used to implement simple reactive systems (user interfaces, thermostat and motor controls, and process automation applications), virtual machines, interpreters, regular expression pattern matchers, and lexical analyzers. A state transition diagram will often help you untangle a state machine's operation.

Exercise 9.9 Describe how the handling of the Microsoft Windows SDK API messages illustrated in Figure 9.11 could be organized using an object-oriented structure.

---

[67]netbsdsrc/bin/ksh/lex.c:1124–1194

```
static char *
get_brace_var(XString *wsp, char *wp)
{
    enum parse_state {
                PS_INITIAL, PS_SAW_HASH, PS_IDENT,           ——— States
                PS_NUMBER, PS_VAR1, PS_END
            }
        state;                                               ——— State variable
    char c;

    state = PS_INITIAL;                                      ——— Start state
    while (1) {
        c = getsc();
        /* State machine to figure out where the variable part ends. */
        switch (state) {
            case PS_INITIAL:
                [...]
            case PS_SAW_HASH:                              •——— State transition rules
                if (letter(c))
                    state = PS_IDENT;
                else if (digit(c))
                    state = PS_NUMBER;
                else if (ctype(c, C_VAR1))
                    state = PS_VAR1;
                else
                    state = PS_END;

                break; [...]
            case PS_VAR1:                                   •——— Final state
                state = PS_END;
                break;
        }
                                                           •——— Terminate when final state is reached
        if (state == PS_END) {
            [...]
            break;
        }
    [...] }
    return wp;
}
```

Figure 9.13 Code for a state machine.

Exercise 9.10   Trace the handling of the automatic power management (APM) events in the book's CD-ROM.

Exercise 9.11   Locate thread-based applications and describe the control model they use.

Exercise 9.12   How are state transition control models typically implemented in the code found in the book's CD-ROM? Suggest how the code of such models could be organized to continue to be readable as the system gets more complicated.

9.3 Element Packaging

The bottom-up counterpart of a system's top-down architectural structure involves the way individual elements of the system are packaged. When dealing with a large body of code, it is important to understand the mechanisms employed to decompose it into separate units.

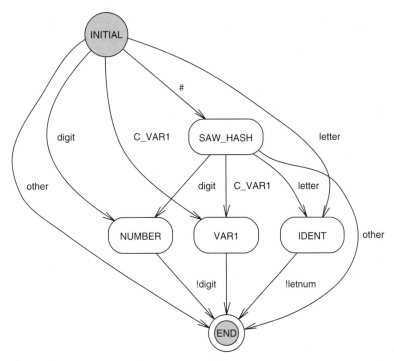

Figure 9.14 UML state transition diagram for a state machine.

9.3.1 Modules

The most common decomposition element you will encounter is probably a *module*: a separately named and addressable component that provides services to other modules. Although our definition encompasses many different decomposition elements such as objects and filters, keep in mind that we will describe those more specific entities separately and will use the term *module* only when none of the other cases apply. Modules typically interact with other modules through procedure calls and data sharing. A module's physical boundary is in most cases a single file, files organized in a directory, or a collection of files with a unique prefix. In addition, in languages that allow the nested definition of procedures (for example, Pascal) you will find modules implemented as globally visible procedures. While a similar method can also be used to group multiple modules into a single file using the C++ `namespace` functionality or the Modula `module` abstraction, this is seldom done in practice. However, these facilities, as we shall see in Section 9.3.2, are often used to group functionality implemented in a number of files into a single module.

```
static char * const fmt[] = {                    •————————— Local data and definitions
#define   DEC    0
    "%ld",
#define   SDEC   1
    "%+ld",
[...]
};
```

```
/*                                               •————— Public function
 * v_increment -- [count]#[#+-]
 *    Increment/decrement a keyword number.
 *
 * PUBLIC: int v_increment __P((SCR *, VICMD *));
 */
int
v_increment(SCR *sp, VICMD *vp)
{
    [...]
}
```

```
static void                                      •————— Local function
inc_err(SCR *sp, enum nresult nret)
{
    [...]
}
```

Figure 9.15 An *nvi* editor module.

A typical system organized around the file/module equivalence concept is the BSD *nvi* editor.[68] Each one of the 113 files that comprise it defines one or more public functions or data elements served by some private (`static`) functions (Figure 9.15[69]).

The BSD *window* package[70] (a text-based windowing interface) is a system that uses a prefix file-naming convention to construct modules out of a file group. Some readily apparent modules and the corresponding file names appear below.

- **Keyboard command handling:** `cmd.c`, `cmd1.c`, `cmd2.c`, `cmd3.c`, `cmd4.c`, `cmd5.c`, `cmd6.c`, `cmd7.c`.

- **Command-line processing:** `lcmd.c`, `lcmd.h`, `lcmd1.c`, `lcmd2.c`.

- **Parser:** `parser.h`, `parser1.c`, `parser2.c`, `parser3.c`, `parser4.c`, `parser5.c`.

- **Terminal driver:** `tt.h`, `ttf100.c`, `ttgeneric.c`, `tth19.c`, `tth29.c`, `ttinit.c`, `ttoutput.c`, `tttermcap.c`, `tttvi925.c`, `ttwyse60.c`, `ttwyse75.c`, `ttzapple.c`, `ttzentec.c`.

---

[68] netbsdsrc/usr.bin/vi
[69] netbsdsrc/usr.bin/vi/vi/v_increment.c:31–267
[70] netbsdsrc/usr.bin/window

Table 9.1 NetBSD Kernel Directories and Corresponding Modules

Directory	Module
ddb	Kernel debugger
isofs/cd9660	ISO CD filesystem
msdosfs	MS-DOS filesystem
netatalk	AppleTalk networking
netccitt	CCITT networking
netinet	Internet networking
nfs	Network filesystem
vm	Virtual memory support
ufs/mfs	Memory-based filesystem
ufs/lfs	Log-structured filesystem
ufs/ffs	"Fast" filesystem

- **Window system:** `ww.h`, `wwadd.c`, `wwalloc.c`, `wwbox.c`, `wwchild.c`, `wwclose.c`, `wwclreol.c`, `wwclreos.c`, `wwcursor.c`, `wwdata.c`, `wwdelchar.c`, `wwdelete.c`, `wwdelline.c`, `wwdump.c`, `wwend.c`, `wwenviron.c`, `wwerror.c`, `wwflush.c`, `wwframe.c`, `wwgets.c`, `wwinit.c`, `wwinschar.c`, `wwinsline.c`, `wwiomux.c`, `wwlabel.c`, `wwmisc.c`, `wwmove.c`, `wwopen.c`, `wwprintf.c`, `wwpty.c`, `wwputc.c`, `wwputs.c`, `wwredraw.c`, `wwredrawwin.c`, `wwrint.c`, `wwscroll.c`, `wwsize.c`, `wwspawn.c`, `wwsuspend.c`, `wwterminfo.c`, `wwtty.c`, `wwunframe.c`, `wwupdate.c`, `wwwrite.c`.

Thus, 75 files of the system are grouped into five different modules. The remaining 25 files probably represent separate modules, in many cases grouped as a header file providing the public interface and a C file providing the corresponding implementation (`char.c`/`char.h`, `string.c`/`string.h`, `var.c`/`var.h`, `xx.c`/`xx.h`). It is worth commenting here that, although the window system and terminal driver file names are reasonable, the naming convention used for the keyboard command handling, command-line processing, and parser file names leaves a lot of room for improvement.

Finally, the BSD kernel[71] is an example of a system that groups modules in separate directories. Table 9.1 shows some representative directories. Note, however, that some functionality is further subdivided by using a common file prefix. As an example, the files in the `netinet` directory use the `if_`, `in_`, `ip_`, `tcp_`, and `udp_` prefixes to denote the respective part of the networking protocol stack they address. In addition, while a

---

[71]netbsdsrc/sys

module typically will be stored in a single directory, the reverse is not true: directories are often used to group together many related modules that do not neccessarily form a larger whole.

9.3.2 Namespaces

An important concept of a module is the principle of *information hiding*, prescribing that all information related to a module should be private to it unless it is specifically declared to be public. In C modules implemented as a single file you will find that global identifiers are declared with the `static` keyword to limit their visibility to a single compilation unit (file).[72]

```
static int zlast = -1;
static void islogin(void);
static void reexecute(struct command *);
```

However, this technique does not prevent identifiers used in header files from leaking to the files that include them. As an example, in the C and C++ language a `typedef` or a preprocessor macro definition in a header file may result in a clash when another file defines a global function or variable with the same name. Although some cases can be solved by renaming the offending identifier in the program being developed, others, where two different existing modules clash with each other, can be difficult to solve since they may not fall under the developer's control. Consider the (contrived) example of compiling the following code.

```
#include "libz/zutil.h"
#include "libc/regex/utils.h"
```

The two header files included[73, 74] both define a `uch` identifier, thus creating the following error.

```
libc/regex/utils.h:46: redefinition of `uch'
libz/zutil.h:36: `uch' previously declared here
```

This problem of *namespace pollution* is solved in a number of ad hoc ways in the C language; other languages like Ada, C++, Eiffel, Java, Perl, and the Modula

---

[72] netbsdsrc/bin/csh/func.c:64–66
[73] netbsdsrc/lib/libz/zutil.h
[74] netbsdsrc/lib/libc/regex/utils.h

family provide specific constructs for combatting this problem. A common solution for curbing the namespace pollution, without the need for additional language-provided facilities, involves prefixing identifiers with a certain unique prefix. Notice how in the example below all type, function, and macro identifiers of the `rnd.h` header file[75] are prefixed with an `rnd` prefix.

```
void  rnd_attach_source(rndsource_element_t *, char *, u_int32_t);
void  rnd_detach_source(rndsource_element_t *);
[...]
#define RND_MAXSTATCOUNT    10  /* 10 sources at once max */
[...]
typedef struct {
    u_int32_t    start;
    u_int32_t    count;
    rndsource_t source[RND_MAXSTATCOUNT];
} rndstat_t;
```

In fact, the prefix method of identifier isolation is officially sanctioned by the ANSI C standard by reserving all identifiers starting with an underscore character (_) for use by the language implementation. When reading a library header you will notice that all identifiers start with an underscore, thus being kept separated from any identifiers a user might define.[76]

```
struct __sbuf {
    unsigned char *_base;
    int _size;
};
```

Although in the above example the `_base` and `_size` structure tags belong—according to ANSI C—in a separate namespace (that of the `_sbuf` structure tags), they still need to be prefixed with an underscore since they might clash with macro definitions.

To avoid the problems we described above you will find that modern C++ programs often make use of the `namespace` functionality. A logical group of program entities comprising a module is defined or declared within a `namespace` block (Figure 9.16:2).[77,78] These identifiers can then be used in other scopes either by

---

[75] netbsdsrc/sys/sys/rnd.h:134–178

[76] netbsdsrc/include/stdio.h:82–85

[77] OpenCL/include/skipjack.h:11–34

[78] OpenCL/checks/block.cpp:36–139

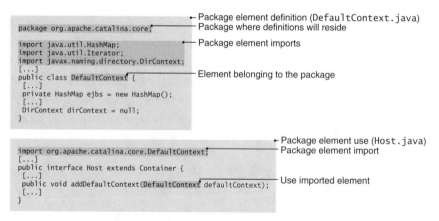

Figure 9.16 Namespace definition and use in C++.

Figure 9.17 Package definition and use in Java.

explicitly prefixing the (declared) identifier name with the correct namespace (Figure 9.16:1) or by importing all identifiers declared within a namespace by means of a using directive (Figure 9.16:3). The second method makes the imported namespace's identifiers available for use without any prefix (Figure 9.16:4).

Java provides a similar solution to the namespace pollution problem through the package keyword. As illustrated in Figure 9.17,[79,80] the package keyword is used to specify that the code that follows it will define its classes and interfaces as part

---

[79]jt4/catalina/src/share/org/apache/catalina/core/DefaultContext.java:65–1241
[80]jt4/catalina/src/share/org/apache/catalina/Host.java

of the named package and can also access all types contained within the package. Correspondingly, the `import` statement is used to make classes of the given package available with an abbreviated name in the context in which it appears. Since fully qualified class names are always accessible in Java, the Java community has adopted the convention of qualifying all package names by a prefix based on the Internet domain or the company name of the package's producer.[81-84]

```
package org.argouml.cognitive.critics;
package org.hsqldb;
package org.apache.cocoon.components.sax;
import ru.novosoft.uml.foundation.core.*;
```

The analogous facility in Ada is very similar, based on the corresponding `package` and `use` keywords. The only difference is that Ada packages must be explicitly imported using a `with` keyword. Similarly, Modula-3 uses `INTERFACE` and `MODULE` declarations to define namespaces for interfaces and implementations, and the `FROM ... IMPORT` and `IMPORT ... AS` statements to introduce names into a local context. Finally, Perl also provides a namespace facility through the `package` and `use` keywords. However, Perl programmers can configure the way identifiers are made visible; in most cases the `Exporter` module is used to specify a list of identifiers to export.[85]

```
package CPAN;
[...]
use Config ();
use Cwd ();
use DirHandle;
use Exporter ();
[...]
@EXPORT = qw(
        autobundle bundle expand force get cvs_import
        install make readme recompile shell test clean
        );
```

[81] argouml/org/argouml/cognitive/critics/Critic.java:29
[82] hsqldb/src/org/hsqldb/WebServer.java:36
[83] cocoon/src/java/org/apache/cocoon/components/sax/XMLByteStreamCompiler.java:8
[84] argouml/org/argouml/ui/ActionGoToEdit.java:33
[85] perl/lib/CPAN.pm:2–66

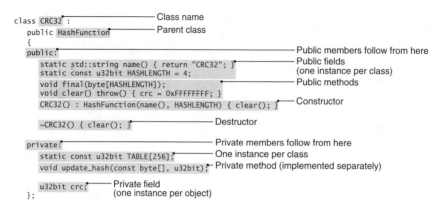

Figure 9.18 Declaration of a C++ class for the CRC algorithm.

9.3.3 Objects

An *object* is a runtime entity that provides an access mechanism to the data it encapsulates. In pure object-based systems, computation is performed by objects sending and receiving *messages* or invoking *methods* of other objects. Similar objects have their behavior abstracted in the form of a *class*, while often related classes are organized into an *inheritance hierarchy*.

In object-based languages you will recognize the definition of an object class by the use of the corresponding language keyword: `class` in C++, C#, Eiffel, and Java, `object` in Modula-3, `package` in Ada-95, and `bless` in Perl. In addition, object-oriented and object-based languages associated with an integrated programming environment such as Smalltalk and Visual Basic provide support for object definition and inspection through a built-in object or *class browser* facility. Finally, even in languages that do not provide explicit support for creating objects, it is possible to define objects by grouping together in a structure the data elements and functions used to process those elements.

Fields and Methods

You can see a representative C++ class definition in Figure 9.18[86] and a Java class definition in Figure 9.19.[87] Every class is defined with a name, used later for declaring, defining, and creating objects of that class. Classes participating in an inheritance hierarchy also declare their parent class or classes. Java allows a class to inherit

---

[86] OpenCL/include/crc32.h:16–31

[87] cocoon/src/java/org/apache/cocoon/util/PostInputStream.java:20–255

```
public class PostInputStream                 Class name
    extends InputStream {                    Parent class
    [...]
    public static final String CLASS =       Public field (one instance per class)
        PostInputStream.class.getName();
    private InputStream m_inputStream = null; Private fields
    private int m_contentLen = 0;            (one instance per object)
    [...]
                                             Constructor
    public PostInputStream() {
        super();                             Invoke parent class method
    }

    [...]
                                             Protected method
    protected void init(final InputStream input,
        final int len) throws IllegalArgumentException {
        [...]
        this.m_inputStream = input;          Field access using this
        this.m_contentLen = len;
    }

    [...]
                                             Public method
    public InputStream getInputStream() {
        return( m_inputStream );             Direct field access
    }
}
```

Figure 9.19 The Java class for the input stream of an HTTP post operation.

from only a single class, but a class can use the `implements` keyword to signify that it will implement the functionality of a number of classes. A class typically encapsulates a number of *member variables* or *fields*, or *attributes* that store object-related information and some *member functions* or *methods* that act on the object's fields. Every member function is invoked in conjunction with a particular object[88]

```
hash_input.final(input_hash);
```

and can therefore directly access the particular object's fields and call other methods related to that object. As an example, the following method implementation accesses the object's `crc` field (defined in Figure 9.18) and calls the object's `clear()` method.

```
void CRC32::final(byte output[HASHLENGTH])
    {
    crc ^= 0xFFFFFFFF;
    for(u32bit j = 0; j != HASHLENGTH; j++)
        output[j] = get_byte(j, crc);
    clear();
    }
```

---

[88] OpenCL/checks/block.cpp:121

Both C++ and Java provide the this keyword to explicitly address a method's underlying object for reasons of clarity or to disambiguate naming collisions.

Constructors and Destructors

Since objects can come into life and disappear in a number of different ways (as global or local variables, as dynamically created data structure elements, or as temporary entities) one can define a special function termed a *constructor* to be called whenever an object is created and a corresponding *destructor* or *finalizer* to be called just before an object is destroyed. Constructors are defined in C++ and Java as methods named after the class; C++ destructors use again the class's name prefixed by a tilde (~) character; the corresponding Java method is simply named finalize. Object constructors are often used to allocate the resources associated with an object and initialize its state. Destructors are typically used to free the resources an object has appropriated during its lifetime. In the following example an event listener is associated with the object when it is constructed and removed once the object ceases to exist.[89]

```
public abstract class FigEdgeModelElement [...] { [...]

  public FigEdgeModelElement() {
    _name = new FigText(10, 30, 90, 20);
    _name.setFont(LABEL_FONT);
    [...]
    ArgoEventPump.addListener(ArgoEvent.ANY_NOTATION_EVENT, this);
  } [...]

  public void finalize() {
    ArgoEventPump.removeListener(ArgoEvent.ANY_NOTATION_EVENT, this);
  } [...]
}
```

In the C++ language memory allocated for an object via the new operator must be explicitly freed by using the delete operator. (Java performs this garbage collection

---

[89] argouml/org/argouml/uml/diagram/ui/FigEdgeModelElement.java:63–458

task automatically.) Therefore, C++ destructors are also used for freeing memory allocated during the object's lifetime.[90]

```
isockunix::isockunix (const sockunixbuf& sb)
  : ios (new sockunixbuf (sb))
{}

isockunix::~isockunix ()
{
  delete ios::rdbuf ();
}
```

In C++ programs a lack of symmetry between the memory allocated via new in the object's constructor and the memory disposed via delete in the object's destructor can be a sign of a memory leak situation that must be corrected. In addition, in C++, since the system-provided object-copying mechanism will result in the same dynamically allocated memory block being shared by two objects with a resultant potential of duplicate deletion, a *copy constructor* (a constructor taking as its only argument its object's reference) must be provided to handle this situation in a graceful manner. Typically this involves either sharing the object and keeping track of reference counts (shallow copy) or performing a complete (deep) copy of the object's contents.

Object and Class Members

There are cases where data or processing is related to the entire class and not the individual objects. Such *class methods* or *class fields* are represented in C++ and Java by prefixing them with the static keyword. Notice that class methods cannot access object methods or fields since they are not invoked in conjunction with a specific object. Object methods, however, can always access class methods and fields. Object methods often use class fields for storing data that controls the operation of all methods (such as a lookup table or a dictionary) or for maintaining state information about the class's operation (for example, a counter for assigning a unique identifier to each object). The following example illustrates such a case.[91,92]

---

[90] socket/sockunix.C:75–82
[91] ace/TAO/tests/Param_Test/any.h:27–97
[92] ace/TAO/tests/Param_Test/any.cpp:115–119

```
class Test_Any {
public: [...]
  int reset_parameters (void); [...]
private: [...]
  static size_t counter; [...]
};

int
Test_Any::reset_parameters (void)
{ [...]
  CORBA::ULong index = (counter++ % Test_Any::ANY_LAST_TEST_ITEM);
```

Visibility

A class definition, apart from setting up a container for object data and specifying shared methods for processing that data, also serves as an information-hiding mechanism. Members (fields and methods) can be declared as `private` to signify that they can be accessed only from within their class's methods, as `public` to denote that they can be accessed from anywhere in the program (through objects or as global functions for class methods), and as `protected` to limit their visibility to the methods of their class and to the subclasses derived from it. You'll find that in well-designed classes all fields are declared as private with access to them provided through public *access methods*. These methods, often named after the property name with a corresponding `get` or `set` prefix or suffix attached to it, are so common that languages like C# and Visual Basic contain intrinsic support for them. Hiding the fields behind access methods allows the separation between the interface to some functionality (provided by the access methods) and the corresponding implementation. The separation allows the trivial addition of functionality related to the update or (less frequently) the access of a particular field. The example below contains the access methods for the `bAutoCommit` private field.[93]

```
public class jdbcConnection implements Connection { [...]
    private boolean          bAutoCommit; [...]

    public void setAutoCommit(boolean autoCommit) throws SQLException {
        bAutoCommit = autoCommit;
        execute("SET AUTOCOMMIT " + (bAutoCommit ? "TRUE" : "FALSE"));
    } [...]

    public boolean getAutoCommit() {
```

---

[93] hsqldb/src/org/hsqldb/jdbcConnection.java:76–997

```
        if (Trace.TRACE) {
            Trace.trace();
        }
        return bAutoCommit;
    } [...]
}
```

You will find access methods also commonly used to restrict the type of access provided to fields. The following code provides a get method, but no corresponding set method, creating in effect a field with read-only access.[94]

```
public class jdbcDatabaseMetaData implements DatabaseMetaData {
    private jdbcConnection cConnection; [...]
    public Connection getConnection() {
    if (Trace.TRACE) {
        Trace.trace();
        return cConnection;
    }
}
```

Finally, in C++ private methods are sometimes used, in conjunction with operator overloading, to completely prohibit the application of some operators on a particular object. The following example bars the use of the assignment operator on the underlying objects.[95]

```
private:
    // = Disallow these operations.
    ACE_UNIMPLEMENTED_FUNC (void operator= (const ACE_Future_Set<T> &))
```

Sometimes functions, individual methods, or all methods of an entire class may need to access another class's private members. When, in C++, you see a function, method, or class being declared in another class by using the friend keyword, this provides the former complete access to the latter's private members. In the following example, main can access chatters and all other private members of the Chatter class.[96]

---

[94] hsqldb/src/org/hsqldb/jdbcDatabaseMetaData.java:61–2970
[95] ace/ace/Future_Set.h:81–83
[96] qtchat/src/0.9.7/core/chatter.h:36–124

```
class Chatter : public QListBoxItem { [...]
    private:
        static ChatterRef *chatters[MAX_NUM_CHATTERS];
        [...]
        friend int main(int, char *argv[]); // to destroy chatters[]
};
```

When you encounter friend declarations, pause to question the actual design reason for overriding the class's encapsulation.

Polymorphism

An important feature associated with objects belonging to inheritance hierarchies is the ability of objects belonging to a derived class to be used as objects of the parent class. In some cases the parent class only provides common functionality and the interface the derived classes are expected to provide; no objects of the parent class are to be created. Such parent classes have the methods that subclasses are expected to provide declared as *abstract* by using the abstract keyword in Java or the = 0 definition in C++. Every time a method of a base-class object (or object pointer or reference in C++) is used, the system will dynamically dispatch the call to the appropriate derived-class method. Thus, at runtime the same method call will result in different methods being called according to the type of the underlying object. Consider the example in Figure 9.20.[97–101] All algorithms (subclasses of Algorithm) are expected to provide a clear method, and all classes that implement a hash function (a way to compress a large message into a representative signature) are expected to provide a final method. These methods are declared virtual in the parent class to indicate that they will be provided by derived classes. You can see the respective declarations and one implementation of the (trivial) CRC implementation of clear in the declarations of the MD2 and CRC24 classes—both are subclasses of HashFunction. The function derive, which creates a cryptographic key using the OpenPGP S2K algorithm, varies its function according to the OpenPGP_S2K class's hash member. This can be set to point to objects belonging to any HashFunction subclass. When the clear and final methods are called from the code, the calls will be dynamically dispatched to the appropriate class methods.

---

[97] OpenCL/include/opencl.h:19–105
[98] OpenCL/include/md2.h:13–28
[99] OpenCL/include/crc24.h:16–29
[100] OpenCL/include/pgp_s2k.h:13–22
[101] OpenCL/src/pgp_s2k.cpp:13–59

```
class Algorithm {
    public:
        virtual void clear() throw() = 0;————————— Abstract method implemented by
    [...] };                                        all Algorithm-derived classes

                                                ——— Satisfies the Algorithm interface
class HashFunction : public Algorithm {
    public:
        virtual void final(byte[]) = 0;————————— Abstract method implemented by
    [...] };                                        all HashFunction-derived classes

                                                ——— Satisfies HashFunction interface
class MD2 : public HashFunction {
    public:
        void final(byte[HASHLENGTH]);——————————— Methods with class-specific implementations
        void clear() throw();
    [...] };

                                                ——— Satisfies HashFunction interface
class CRC24 : public HashFunction {
    public:
        void final(byte[HASHLENGTH]);
        void clear() throw() { crc = 0xB704CE; }—— Methods with class-specific implementations
    [...] private: [...]
        u32bit crc;
    };

class OpenPGP_S2K : public S2K {
    [...] private:
        HashFunction* hash;——————————————————————— Pointer to a HashFunction object
    };                                              Can point to MD2, CRC24, or other objects

SymmetricKey OpenPGP_S2K::derive(const std::string& pw, u32bit keylen) const
    { [...]
    hash->clear();————————————————————————————————— Call appropriate derived class function
    while(keylen > generated)
        {
        [...]
        hash->final(hash_buf);————————————————————— Call appropriate derived class function
        }
    return SymmetricKey(key, key.size());
    }
```

Figure 9.20 Runtime polymorphism in C++.

Operator Overloading

The C++ language allows programmers to redefine the meaning of the standard language operators by means of *operator overloading methods*. This feature is often misused by novice programmers creating code that uses operators in counterintuitive ways. In practice, you will find that operator overloading is used either sparingly to enhance the usability of a particular class or overreachingly to endow a class implementing a number-like entity with the full functionality associated with the built-in arithmetic types. Overloaded operators are defined by means of a method or a `friend` function named with the `operator` keyword followed by the actual operator symbol or data type. Operator functions implemented as `friend` functions receive all their operands as arguments, whereas those implemented as methods will access the first operand as the method's underlying object.

The most popular reasons for selectively overloading specific operators are the following.

- Further overload the shift operators (<< and >>) to allow formatted input and output of new data types.[102]

```
ostream& operator << (ostream& o, smtp& s)
{
  char buf [1024];
  int  cont = 1;
  while (cont) {
    cont = s.get_response (buf, 1024);
    o << buf << endl;
  }
  return o;
}
```

- Provide comparison operators so that library functions requiring comparable objects will work.[103]

```
ACE_INLINE int
ACE_Addr::operator == (const ACE_Addr &sap) const
{
  return (sap.addr_type_ == this->addr_type_ &&
    sap.addr_size_ == this->addr_size_   );
}
```

- Make smart, pointer-like objects behave intuitively by overloading the assignment and dereference operators.[104]

```
  * @brief A smart pointer stored in the in-memory object database
  * ACE_ODB.  The pointee (if any) is deleted when reassigned.  */
class ACE_Export ACE_Dumpable_Ptr
{
public:
  ACE_Dumpable_Ptr (const ACE_Dumpable *dumper = 0);
```

---

[102] socket/smtp.C:156–165
[103] ace/ace/Addr.i:19–24
[104] ace/ace/Dump.h:90–104

```
    const ACE_Dumpable *operator->() const;
    void operator= (const ACE_Dumpable *dumper) const;
private:
    /// "Real" pointer to the underlying abstract base class
    /// pointer that does the real work.
    const ACE_Dumpable *dumper_;
};
```

- Provide strings with the assignment and concatenation operators supported
  in symbol-processing languages like Basic, *awk*, and Perl.[105]

```
// concatenation.
const CStdString&   operator+=(const CStdString& str);
```

When operator overloading is used to create new arithmetic types (such as complex numbers, fractions, large integers, matrices, or multiple precision floating-point numbers), the designer's goal is to support all arithmetic operators. Figure 9.21[106] illustrates declarations for a class of objects supporting unlimited-width integer arithmetic that never overflows. Notice the multitude of declarations used to support all reasonable operations and conversions.

Classes in Perl

As we illustrate in Figure 9.22,[107] most Perl object-oriented operations are based on small extensions to the imperative language syntax. In contrast to C++ and Java, Perl supports objects and classes by providing, by means of the bless keyword, a way to declare that a given variable (scalar, array, hash, subroutine) is an object belonging to a class. The reference is often assigned to a variable named self and used similarly to the C++ and Java this pseudo-variable. Encapsulation is provided by using the existing package mechanism, while methods are simply subroutines that, when called, receive a reference to the invoking object. A constructor is just a package subroutine, typically named new, that returns an element "blessed" to belong to the given class. From that point onward the blessed element can be used to call methods of the class that blessed it.[108]

---

[105] demogl/Include/Misc/StdString.h:363–364
[106] purenum/integer.h:79–199
[107] perl/lib/DirHandle.pm:1–64
[108] ace/bin/pippen.pl:157–160

```
class Integer
{
public: [...]
    // conversion operators
    inline operator bool() const;
    inline operator signed int() const;
    inline operator unsigned int() const;
    inline operator float() const;
    inline operator double() const;
    inline operator long double() const;


    // unary math operators (members)
    inline Integer &operator++();        // prefix
    inline Integer operator++(int);      // postfix
    inline Integer &operator--();        // prefix
    inline Integer operator--(int);      // postfix


    // binary math operators (members)
    inline Integer &operator=(const Integer &);
    inline Integer &operator=(const atom &);
    inline Integer &operator=(const satom &);
    inline Integer &operator+=(const Integer &); [...]
    inline Integer &operator-=(const Integer &); [...]
    inline Integer &operator*=(const Integer &); [...]
    inline Integer &operator/=(const Integer &); [...]
    inline Integer &operator%=(const Integer &); [...]


    // friends: unary math operators (global functions)
    friend Integer operator~(const Integer &);
    friend bool operator!(const Integer &);
    friend Integer operator-(const Integer &);
    friend Integer operator+(const Integer &);


    // friends: binary math operators (global functions)
    friend Integer operator+(const Integer &, const Integer &);
    friend Integer operator+(const Integer &, const atom &);
    friend Integer operator+(const atom &, const Integer &);
    friend Integer operator+(const Integer &, const satom &);
    friend Integer operator+(const satom &, const Integer &);
    friend Integer operator-(const Integer &, const Integer &); [...]
    friend Integer operator*(const Integer &, const Integer &); [...]
    friend Integer operator/(const Integer &, const Integer &); [...]
    friend Integer operator%(const Integer &, const Integer &); [...]
    friend bool operator==(const Integer &, const Integer &); [...]
    friend bool operator!=(const Integer &, const Integer &); [...]
    friend bool operator>(const Integer &, const Integer &); [...]
    friend bool operator>=(const Integer &, const Integer &); [...]
    friend bool operator<(const Integer &, const Integer &); [...]
    friend bool operator<=(const Integer &, const Integer &); [...]
    friend bool operator&&(const Integer &, const Integer &); [...]
    friend bool operator||(const Integer &, const Integer &); [...]
```

Annotations:
- Convert between types
- Unary operator members (operand accessible via `this->`)
- Assignment for different types
- Sample of assignment variants
- Unary operator `friend` functions (operand is the function's argument)
- Binary + for different types
- Sample of other binary operators

Figure 9.21 Operator overloading in C++.

```
my $dh = new DirHandle ($target);
if (defined $dh) {
    foreach my $entry ($dh->read ()) {
```

A destructor is a subroutine named DESTROY. Perl does not provide explicit support for creating object fields. Fields are typically implemented as elements of a

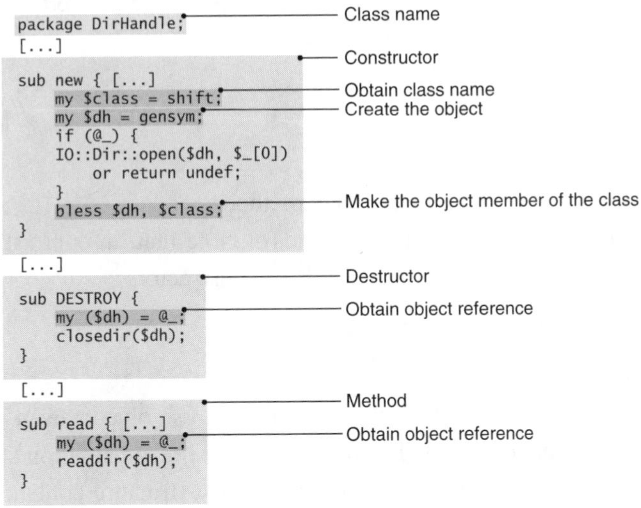

Figure 9.22 Declaration of a Perl directory access class.

blessed hash. In the following example[109] the variables `Handle`, `File`, and `Queue` are thus used as member variables by blessing the hash containing them in the `load` constructor and accessing them through the object reference in the `find` method.

```
sub load
{
  [...]
  bless {Handle => $handle, File => $file, Queue => 'SESSION' },
    "OS2::DLL::$file";
}

sub find
{
    my $self   = shift;
    my $file   = $self->{File};
    my $handle = $self->{Handle};
```

Inheritance in Perl is also provided through a very simple mechanism. A class will signify its participation in an inheritance hierarchy by setting the ISA array to

---

[109]perl/os2/OS2/REXX/DLL/DLL.pm:47–48

contain the names of the classes from which its methods are derived.[110]

```
package IO::Socket;
[...]
@ISA = qw(IO::Handle);
```

The above code merely signifies that calls to methods not defined in IO::Socket will call the corresponding methods in IO::Handle. Note that, in contrast to C++ and Java, there is no implicit inheritance of fields or constructors.

Classes in C

As we noted earlier, it is also possible to define and use objects even in languages that do not directly support them. The most common implementation style you will encounter in C code has each object represented by a structure containing its fields as structure members and its methods as function pointers, as in the following code excerpts.[111,112]

```
typedef struct {
    char *name;                 /* name of format */
    int bsz;                    /* default block size. */
    int hsz;                    /* Header size in bytes. */
    int hlk;                    /* does archive store hard links info? */
    int (*id)(char *, int)      /* checks if a buffer is a valid header */
    int (*st_rd)(void);         /* initialize routine for read. */
    int (*rd)(ARCHD *, char *); /* read header routine. */
    [...]
    int (*options)(void);       /* process format specific options (-o) */

} FSUB;

FSUB fsub[] = {
/* 0: OLD BINARY CPIO */
    { "bcpio", 5120, sizeof(HD_BCPIO), 1, 0, 0, 1, bcpio_id, cpio_strd,
      bcpio_rd, bcpio_endrd, cpio_stwr, bcpio_wr, cpio_endwr, NULL,
      cpio_subtrail, rd_wrfile, wr_rdfile, bad_opt },
    [...]
```

---

[110] perl/ext/IO/lib/IO/Socket.pm:7–24
[111] netbsdsrc/bin/pax/pax.h:140–218
[112] netbsdsrc/bin/pax/options.c:99–129

```
/* 5: POSIX USTAR */
    { "ustar", 10240, BLKMULT, 0, 1, BLKMULT, 0, ustar_id, ustar_strd,
    ustar_rd, tar_endrd, ustar_stwr, ustar_wr, tar_endwr, tar_trail,
    NULL, rd_wrfile, wr_rdfile, bad_opt }
};
```

Note that in the above example objects carry a complete copy of all method pointers   ⊡
and that methods have no direct relationship with the underlying object data. More
elaborate schemes substitute the function pointers with a pointer to a separate per-class
method pointer structure and adopt a specific convention for passing an object pointer
to each method. This is the case in the code presented in Figure 9.23.[113–117] In fact, the
C code explicitly implements many of the features found in object-oriented languages.
The v_op pointer (Figure 9.23:1) that is associated with every object, pointing to a
shared table of pointers to the corresponding methods (Figure 9.23:3), is internally
implemented by most object-based system compilers and termed a *virtual function
table* or *vtbl*. Also, the pointer to the object passed to every method in VOP_RECLAIM
(Figure 9.23:2) and retrieved in the method body (Figure 9.23:4) is also implicitly
passed to object methods and available in the body through the this pseudo-variable
in object-based systems. Although the implementation effort appears extreme, similar
approaches are also used in other systems such as the X Window System Xt toolkit.[118]
However, hopefully you will agree that object-oriented languages provide a more
readable approach to the same functionality.

9.3.4 Generic Implementations

A *generic implementation* of a data structure or an algorithm is designed to work
on elements of arbitrary data types. You will find that generic implementations are
realized either at compile time through macro substitution and language-supported
facilities such as the C++ templates and the Ada generic packages or at runtime by
using element and function pointers or object polymorphism. We will expand on
these possibilities by reference to a simple function that returns the minimum of

---

[113] netbsdsrc/sys/sys/vnode.h:71–341
[114] netbsdsrc/sys/kern/vnode_if.src:208–210
[115] netbsdsrc/sys/kern/vnode_if.c:467–481
[116] netbsdsrc/sys/sys/vnode_if.h:663–676
[117] netbsdsrc/sys/ufs/ffs/ffs_vnops.c:69–257
[118] XFree86-3.3/xc/lib/Xt

```
struct vnode {
    [...]
    int    (**v_op)  _P((void *));    /* vnode operations vector */
    [...]
    enum  vtagtype v_tag;             /* type of underlying data */
    void   *v_data;                   /* private data for fs */
};
```
— Object structure (vnode.h)

1 Pointer to method table

— Fields

```
struct vnodeop_desc {
    int  vdesc_offset;    /* offset in vector--first for speed */
    char *vdesc_name;     /* a readable name for debugging */
    int  vdesc_flags;     /* VDESC_* flags */
    [...]
};
```
— Method table entry (vnode.h)

```
#define VOCALL(OPSV,OFF,AP) (( *((OPSV)[(OFF)])) (AP))
#define VCALL(VP,OFF,AP) VOCALL((VP)->v_op,(OFF),(AP))
#define VDESC(OP) (& __CONCAT(OP,_desc))
#define VOFFSET(OP) (VDESC(OP)->vdesc_offset)
```
— Method call support (vnode.h)

```
vop_reclaim {
    IN struct vnode *vp;
};
```
— Method declaration (vnode.src; generates vnode_if.h, vnode_if.c)

```
int vop_reclaim_vp_offsets[] = {
    VOPARG_OFFSETOF(struct vop_reclaim_args,a_vp),
    VDESC_NO_OFFSET
};
struct vnodeop_desc vop_reclaim_desc = {
    0,
    "vop_reclaim",
    0,
    vop_reclaim_vp_offsets,
    [...]
};
```
— Method-related data (vnode_if.c)

```
struct vop_reclaim_args {
    struct vnodeop_desc *a_desc;
    struct vnode *a_vp;
};

static _inline int VOP_RECLAIM(struct vnode *vp)
{
    struct vop_reclaim_args a;
    a.a_desc = VDESC(vop_reclaim);
    a.a_vp = vp;
    return (VCALL(vp, VOFFSET(vop_reclaim), &a));
}
```
— Automatically generated call stub
— Method arguments (vnode_if.h)

2 VOP_RECLAIM method call (vnode_if.h)

```
struct vnodeopv_entry_desc ffs_vnodeop_entries[] = {
    { &vop_default_desc, vn_default_error },
    { &vop_lookup_desc, ufs_lookup },    /* lookup */
    { &vop_create_desc, ufs_create },    /* create */
    [...]
    { &vop_reclaim_desc, ffs_reclaim },  /* reclaim */
    [...]
    { (struct vnodeop_desc*)NULL, (int(*) _P((void*)))NULL }
};
```
3 Actual method table (ffs_fnops.c)

```
int
ffs_reclaim(void *v)
{
    struct vop_reclaim_args /* {
        struct vnode *a_vp;
    } */ *ap = v;
    register struct vnode *vp = ap->a_vp;
    [...]
    vp->v_data = NULL;
    return (0);
}
```
— ffs::ffs_reclaim method implementation (ffs_fnops.c)

4 Obtain object pointer

— Field access
```

**Figure 9.23** An object class with a shared method table implemented in C.
```

two elements. It is common to see simple generic functions implemented as a preprocessor macro in C and C++ programs.[119]

```
#  define ace_min(a,b)        (((b) > (a)) ? (a) : (b))
```

The body of the `ace_min` macro will be textually expanded wherever it is used to
contain the actual elements that were specified as its arguments. This textual expansion
allows the `min` function to work on any arguments that can be compared using the >
operator. It is also efficient since it obviates the function call overhead. On the other
hand, its two arguments may be evaluated twice; if the evaluation of any argument
has an associated side effect (for example, an argument is passed to `min` with a
postincrement operator applied to it), this side effect (perhaps surprisingly for the
programmer) will occur twice. In addition, the code of nested macro expansions can
quickly expand to unreasonable size and complexity. The following example illustrates
a simple expression[120]

```
ACE_MIN (ACE_THR_PRI_FIFO_MAX,
         ACE_MAX (ACE_THR_PRI_FIFO_MIN, priority))
```

and its resultant expansion.

```
((((((((ACE_THR_PRI_FIFO_MIN)) > ((priority))) ?
((ACE_THR_PRI_FIFO_MIN)) : ((priority))))) >
((ACE_THR_PRI_FIFO_MAX))) ? ((ACE_THR_PRI_FIFO_MAX)) :
((((((ACE_THR_PRI_FIFO_MIN)) > ((priority))) ?
((ACE_THR_PRI_FIFO_MIN)) : ((priority))))))
```

Since a compiler typically reports macro definitions that result in erroneous code
at the place they are used, rather than the place they are defined, macro errors can
be difficult to trace and correct. Running the program through the C preprocessor is
often a good strategy to adopt when debugging macro errors.

In C++ programs you will find generic implementation of code concretely expressed through the `template` mechanism.[121]

---

[119] ace/ace/Min_Max.h:62
[120] ace/ace/OS.cpp:3089–3090
[121] ace/ace/Min_Max.h:25–30

```
template <class T>
inline const T &
ace_min (const T &t1, const T &t2)
{
   return t2 > t1 ? t1 : t2;
}
```

In the above example, the ace_min function is defined to take as arguments two const element references of the nonspecified type T and return as a result one of those elements. Concrete instances of the functions are instantiated as the program is being compiled to satisfy specific uses of the function. Thus, because in the code the type of the priority variable is long, the compiler will automatically generate an internal function like the following.

```
inline const long &
ace_min (const long &t1, const long &t2)
{
   return t2 > t1 ? t1 : t2;
}
```

In common with macro substitutions, many current implementations of the C++ template mechanism also lead to excessive executable code sizes and inscrutable error messages, but at least the underlying language facilities provide the necessary groundwork for realizing more programmer-friendly translation tools.

In object-oriented languages *polymorphic functions* can be realized by dynamically calling the appropriate object methods at runtime. The following example is an attempt to implement a generic, object-oriented min function.[122]

```
static Object min(Object a, Object b, int type) throws SQLException {
    if (a == null) { return b; }
    if (b == null) { return a; }
    if (compare(a, b, type) < 0) {
        return a;
    }
    return b;
}
```

---

[122]hsqldb/src/org/hsqldb/Column.java:769–783

However, this particular code just pushes the problem to the compare function, which in this case explicitly checks the types of the arguments passed to it.[123]

```
static int compare(Object a, Object b, int type) throws SQLException {
int i = 0;
[...]
switch (type) {
[...]
case INTEGER:
    int ai = ((Integer) a).intValue();
    int bi = ((Integer) b).intValue();

    return (ai > bi) ? 1 : (bi > ai ? -1 : 0);
```

This implementation style is inflexible, error prone (the compiler cannot detect missing type cases), and inefficient. The recommended object-oriented approach to this problem is to derive all objects for which min is to be applied from a class or an interface that supports a lessThan method and to modify the code in min to read as follows.

```
if (a.lessThan(b))
    return a;
else
    return b;
```

As a concrete example, the following code works by calling the object's toString method, which yields a result appropriate to the type of the underlying object.[124]

```
boolean compare(Object o) { [...]
    String s = o.toString();
    if (bIgnoreCase) { s = s.toUpperCase(); }
    return compareAt(s, 0, 0, s.length());
}
```

Finally, as you might expect, generic implementations based on runtime calls are also often written in C by representing elements through void pointers (which can point to any value) and processing functions through function pointers. The following implementation of a sequential array search function is a typical example.[125]

---

[123] hsqldb/src/org/hsqldb/Column.java:825–852
[124] hsqldb/src/org/hsqldb/Like.java:97–109
[125] netbsdsrc/lib/libcompat/4.3/lsearch.c:50–101

```
typedef int (*cmp_fn_t) (const void *, const void *);

static void *
linear_base(const void *key, const void *base,
    size_t *nelp, size_t width, cmp_fn_t compar, int add_flag)
{
    register const char *element, *end;
    end = (const char *)base + *nelp * width;
    for (element = base; element < end; element += width)
        if (!compar(element, key))          /* key found */
            return((void *)element);
    if (!add_flag)                          /* key not found */
        return(NULL);
[...]
}
```

The above function searches an array of *nelp width-sized elements starting at base for the element pointed to by key. The comparison function compar is passed pointers to the key and each successive element to determine when a particular key is found. Notice how the two important factors about the array elements, their size and the way to determine equality, are explicitly passed as arguments to the function. In the other examples we have examined, both are automatically derived by the compiler from the underlying types.

Writing a generic implementation of a particular concept requires substantial intellectual effort. For this reason you'll find generic implementations used mostly in cases where considerable advantages will be gained by the implementation's extensive reuse. Typical examples of this category are (1) *containers* (often implemented as the abstract data types we examine in Section 9.3.5), (2) associated algorithms such as searching, sorting, and other operations on sets and ordered ranges, and (3) generalized numeric algorithms.

9.3.5 Abstract Data Types

An *abstract data type* (ADT) is a data structure encapsulation mechanism. It relies on many of the aspects we have described so far: encapsulation, the separation of interface and implementation, and, often, a generic realization. In addition, the ADT's interface is sometimes described through a formal algebraic specification in terms of relationships between its operations; for example, the C++ standard template library (STL) documentation prescribes that for a sequential container a.resize(n) ⇒ a.size() == n. A basic characteristic of an ADT is that the interface to the data it represents remains independent of the underlying data format. As a typical example, consider the BSD dbopen database access methods.[126] A call to dbopen returns a pointer to a DB element. This in turn provides access to the functions get, put, del, and seq, used respectively for retrieving, adding, deleting, and sequentially processing the database's records. The same interface is used for accessing a number of different data organization methods based on B+ trees, extended linear hashing, an in-memory pool, and fixed- or variable-length record files.

ADTs are often used to encapsulate commonly used data organization schemes (such as trees, lists, or stacks) or to hide a data type's implementation details from its user. Examples of the first case include the BSD dbopen interface we already examined; the BSD queue macros[127] which abstract singly linked lists, singly linked tail queues, lists, tail queues, and circular queues; the Java java.util Hashtable, Vector, and Stack classes; and the C++ STL containers. For an example of ADTs used to hide the details of the underlying implementation, consider the POSIX directory access functions: opendir, readdir, telldir, seekdir, and closedir. In the early days of Unix, programs that needed to obtain a list of files in a directory would simply open the file containing the directory's contents (for example, /usr/include) and interpret the file's contents according to the known way directory structures were stored on disk. This approach meant that after any changes to the format of the directory data (for example, an increase of the allowed file name length) all programs that depended on it would have to be adjusted to conform to the new structure. The directory access functions present a directory's contents as an ADT, thereby shielding implementations from such changes.

9.3.6 Libraries

A *library* is an organized collection of modules that share a common purpose. In many cases libraries are packaged as a single file containing a set of precompiled modules in object code format. Consequently, a library is often accompanied with detailed documentation regarding its interface and, where required, elements that allow its integration with other code such as header files, definition files, or import library stubs. You will find that libraries are employed for a number of different purposes: to reuse source and object code, to organize module collections, to structure and optimize the build process, and to load application features on demand.

---

[126]netbsdsrc/lib/libc/db
[127]netbsdsrc/sys/sys/queue.h

Code Reuse

Stable and efficient code that is of general utility can be efficiently shared with others once it is packaged in library form and appropriately documented. Furthermore, libraries, which require a nontrivial amount of effort to package their elements and document their interfaces, send a strong positive signal to other programmers regarding their utility, stability, ease of use, and likely level of support. Therefore, code packaged in library form is more easily adopted than, for example, objects distributed in source code form. As an example, the NetBSD system includes more than ten different libraries in its distribution covering, among other aspects, cryptography,[128] screen cursor addressing,[129] command-line editing,[130] kernel data access,[131] and network packet capturing.[132]

Encapsulation

A library conveniently integrates into a single package a multitude of object files without explicitly revealing its internal composition. As an example, the NetBSD C library[133] consists of more than 600 compiled C files, providing both public interfaces such as bsearch[134] and internally used functions such as __errno().[135] Thus a library packages a large set of interrelated files into a coherent whole.

Structure

Libraries are often used to structure large systems into manageable units. Consider the directory structure of the *rayshade* ray-tracing renderer[136] illustrated in Figure 9.24. Apart from the four files located in the rayshade/rayshade directory the program is built by combining eight different libraries. The libshade library contains the program operation and the scene description modules, while the libray library is composed of six other libraries that provide the ray-tracing functionality: libimage (image-loading functions), libcommo (common mathematical functions), liblight (light sources), libobj (object definitions), libsurf (surface properties), and libtext (textures).

---

[128] netbsdsrc/lib/libcrypt
[129] netbsdsrc/lib/libcurses
[130] netbsdsrc/lib/libedit
[131] netbsdsrc/lib/libkvm
[132] netbsdsrc/lib/libpcap
[133] netbsdsrc/lib/libc
[134] netbsdsrc/lib/libc/stdlib/bsearch.c
[135] netbsdsrc/lib/libc/gen/_errno.c
[136] http://graphics.stanford.edu/~cek/rayshade/

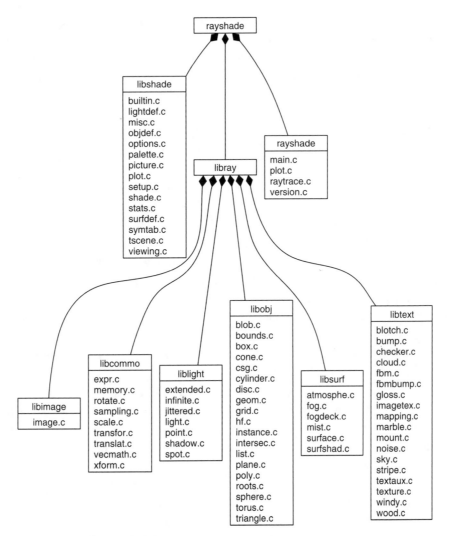

Figure 9.24 The library-structured *rayshade* program.

Optimization of the Build Process

Libraries are also often used to reduce the complexity and increase the efficiency of the build process. Instead of linking hundreds of object files, the build process is often organized so as to link large object file collections in the form of a library. Libraries are often more efficiently structured than is an equivalent collection of object files, thereby reducing the link time. You may counter that the problem is merely transferred to the building of the actual libraries, but this is not the case due to the locality of

[i]   reference exhibited in most software development efforts. Large parts of the code may be relatively stable over the lifetime of a system; these are often efficiently packaged into a library. As an example, important parts of the *apache* Web server are separately compiled and then linked in the form of libraries. These include the *expat* XML parser toolkit,[137] the *sdbm* hashed database library,[138] and the *regex* package.[139]

Reduction of Code Size

In many systems the appropriate use of libraries can lead to a reduction of the space a program occupies both when stored on a disk and while it is executing. *Shared libraries* (also called *dynamic shared objects* under many flavors of Unix and *dynamic link libraries* or DLLs under Microsoft Windows) allow a single instance of machine code or data to be shared by multiple programs. The library providing the corresponding code is stored in a globally known place; programs that require it link with it once they are loaded, thus reducing their size. Most operating systems also arrange for a single copy of the library to be loaded in memory and shared by multiple programs, thereby reducing the combined memory footprint of the programs using the particular

[i]   library. As an example, under Linux the size of the X Window System shared library is almost 1MB; this is 1MB saved for every program stored on disk and for every client loaded in memory. However, since shared libraries exist independently of the

▲   program that uses them, there are often cases where a library's version may fail to match the library version the program was originally linked against. In such cases, at best the program or the dynamic linker may detect the problem and terminate the execution with an error message; at worst the program may exhibit subtle bugs that cannot be reproduced on different installations. Under the Windows environment this situation is aptly named "DLL hell."

Dynamic Linking

Finally, libraries are often used to simplify the configuration of large systems by postponing it from the buildtime to the actual system execution. A system built in this way typically incorporates into its main body only the most general core functionality. All additional features required are dynamically linked as libraries during the system's execution. This approach keeps the base system lean without affecting the functionality it offers. The kernel modules of NetBSD[140] and Linux, as well as the dynamic

---

[137] apache/src/lib/expat-lite
[138] apache/src/lib/sdbm
[139] apache/src/regex
[140] netbsdsrc/sys/kern/kern_lkm.c

module loading mechanisms of *apache*[141] and Perl,[142] are prime examples of this approach. Under Microsoft Windows DLLs are also often used for the dynamic setup of localized application versions. In addition, dynamic linking decouples elements of the development process, allowing separate teams to work completely independently, submitting as deliverables updated versions of the compiled library.

9.3.7 Processes and Filters

In cases where the functionality that a package will provide is well defined, the associated interfaces are extremely stable, and the communication requirements are either simple or have an overhead that cannot be avoided, a *process* is used to encapsulate the corresponding functionality. You will find that large and distributed systems are often implemented as a number of cooperating processes, often communicating by using the mechanisms we described in Section 9.1.1.

As an encapsulation mechanism, a process has a number of advantages. First of all, a process acts as a fault isolation barrier. For example, a stray pointer in one process cannot directly affect the memory contents of another. In addition, a process allows us to independently examine and manage the resources it uses. Through operating system management tools such as the Microsoft Windows task manager and the Unix *ps* command we can directly view a process's memory and CPU utilization, network connections, open files, threads, and other resources. Some distributed systems (such as the *apache* Web server) are even structured in a way that allows throughput increases to be realized by running multiple instances of a single process. In multiprocessor systems, multiple processes—in common with multiple threads—will automatically distribute the processing load among CPUs.

Finally, a process, being an independently compiled entity, simplifies the build procedures of a large system by lessening team coordination requirements and reducing the impact of build errors across the project.

As a concrete example, consider the process structure of the GNU compiler collection[143] and associated back-end tools (*as*, *ld*) illustrated in Figure 9.25. A compilation sequence is typically invoked by running a *compiler driver* such as the traditional Unix C compiler interface *cc* or the GNU C++ front-end *g++*. The driver examines the command-line arguments and separately compiles each source file specified by running a number of processes: the preprocessor *cpp*, the compiler proper, the assembler,

---

[141] apache/src/modules/standard/mod_so.c
[142] perl/ext/DynaLoader/dlutils.c
[143] http://www.gnu.org/software/gcc

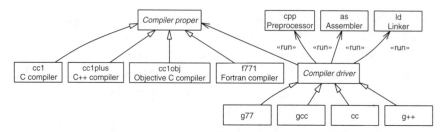

Figure 9.25 The process structure of the GNU compiler system.

and the linker. The processes communicate with each other through intermediate files or pipelines. The GNU compiler collection supports a number of different languages; each one is implemented as a different compiler-proper process that typically takes as input a preprocessed source file and produces as output the compiled result in assembly language. Each one of the processes we described is separately maintained, and many have an independent release schedule. Most changes typically affect only a single process: a new Fortran language feature will require only an updated *f771* executable, a new type of executable might affect only the linker. Only when an interface change occurs (for example, the addition of a new debugging tag) must the release of multiple executables be coordinated.

A *filter* is a special type of process that interacts with others through data flow from its input to its output. In Section 9.1.2 we describe how filters can be combined to construct larger systems. Many types of programs can be viewed and operated as filters if they follow some simple rules, which you can verify from the program's documentation, operation, and source code. First, you should ensure that the program runs synchronously and not in the background; Unix daemon-style programs and Microsoft Windows services and nonconsole applications do not qualify. In addition, the process should be able to receive data from its standard input (the keyboard or another redirected source), send its results to its standard output (the screen or a redirected target), and operate without any user intervention. If the program has an interactive user interface, its operation should be optional and there should be an option to disable it. Finally, the program should follow standard conventions for its input and output. Many useful filters operate on simple textual data where each line is regarded as a single record; in some cases space-separated items are also interpreted as individual fields. Elaborately formatted output with items spanning an arbitrary number of lines is difficult for other filter programs to use. Similarly, decorative headers, copyright messages, and output that relies on the existence of a screen should be avoided or made optional. The beauty of the filter-packaging abstraction is that simple programs that perform a single processing function are also often effective reusable filters.

9.3.8 Components

A software *component* is a typically self-contained unit of program composition with documented and well-defined interfaces. Components can in most cases be deployed without access to the original developers and are often distributed and used by third parties. In common with objects, components encapsulate state, allow access to it through separately described interfaces, and support modular design based on separation of concerns. However, components differ from objects in a number of ways: they can be implemented in different languages, they are often packaged in binary containers, they can encapsulate multiple objects, and they are typically more robustly packaged than objects. A number of development environments provide support for the seamless integration of new components into the environment's framework. Component-packaging technologies you are likely to encounter include CORBA, ActiveX, and JavaBeans.

You can see a simple JavaBean component and its use in a Java server page illustrated in Figures 9.26[144] and 9.27.[145] The bean implements a simple number-guessing game. As you can see, it uses a standard naming convention for providing access to its data fields (often termed *properties* in the context of components). Java development environments can use Java's *reflection* functionality to examine the bean's internal structure and expose it appropriately to the component-using developer. If a bean's designer does not find this default behavior sufficient, she or he can always provide custom methods for differentiating it. Keep in mind that the amount of support code a component developer has to write differs radically between various component technologies and programming environments. For example, you will find that ActiveX components can be written in Visual Basic with minimal support code, while the same components when implemented in C++ require more complex code structures, even when they use Microsoft's Active Template Library (ATL).

9.3.9 Data Repositories

In some cases, you will see decomposition centered around pure data repositories. These can be simple files, directory hierarchies, structured documents, or even complete databases. For example, recent versions of Microsoft Windows store user information as a tree under the `Documents and Settings` directory containing elements such as `Cookies`, `Desktop`, `Favorites`, `My Documents`, and `Start Menu`. Unix systems store many types of configuration data in flat text files. For example, the file `/etc/inetd.conf` specifies the Internet services supported by a given host.

---

[144]jt4/webapps/examples/WEB-INF/classes/num/NumberGuessBean.java:66–119
[145]jt4/webapps/examples/jsp/num/numguess.jsp:10–27

```
public class NumberGuessBean {

    int answer;                              ●———— Internal component state
    boolean success;
    String hint;
    int numGuesses;


    public NumberGuessBean() {               ●——————————————— Component initialization
      reset();
    }


    public void reset() {                    ●— Method
      answer = Math.abs(new Random().nextInt() % 100) + 1;
      success = false;
      numGuesses = 0;
    }


    public void setGuess(String guess) {     ┃1 Set property access function
      numGuesses++;
      int g;
      [...] g = Integer.parseInt(guess); [...]
      if (g == answer) {
        success = true;
      } else if (g == -1) {
        hint = "a number next time";
      } else if (g < answer) {
        hint = "higher";
      } else if (g > answer) {
        hint = "lower";
      }
    }


    public boolean getSuccess() {            ┃2 Get property access functions
      return success;
    }
    public String getHint() {
      return "" + hint;
    }
    public int getNumGuesses() {
      return numGuesses;
    }

}
```

Figure 9.26 A simple JavaBean servlet component.

```
<%@ page import = "num.NumberGuessBean" %>              ●—— Use component
<jsp:useBean id="numguess" class="num.NumberGuessBean" scope="session"/>

<jsp:setProperty name="numguess" property="*"/>        ——— Component methods to set bean properties
<html>                                                      from the form element values
<head><title>Number Guess</title></head>
<body bgcolor="white">
<font size=4>
<% if (numguess.getSuccess()) { %>                     ┃1 Access component property
  Congratulations!  You got it.
                                                        ┃1
And after just <%= numguess.getNumGuesses() %> tries.<p>

<% numguess.reset(); %>                                ——— Call component method
Care to <a href="numguess.jsp">try again</a>?
```

Figure 9.27 Using a JavaBean in a Java server page.

Relational databases are used as a centralized repository for data that can be structured in the form of records and fields; the Microsoft Internet Information Server log file is maintained by using this method. Complex data is also often stored in a structured file accessed by using representation assumptions shared between different applications (this is the method used for the revision repository of the RCS revision control system). Although many such files are structured in a proprietary format, XML is increasingly employed as a common underlying representation schema.

In many cases, you can decipher the structure of a text-based data repository by browsing through the data stored in it. Consider the Unix Internet daemon (*inetd*) configuration file.[146]

```
ftp    stream tcp nowait root /usr/libexec/ftpd ftpd -ll
telnet stream tcp nowait root /usr/libexec/telnetd telnetd
[...]
ntalk  dgram udp wait nobody.tty /usr/libexec/ntalkd ntalkd
```

By looking at the entries you can discern that each line contains a service name, the networking protocol used, whether the daemon should wait for the program's completion, the identity under which the service runs, and the way the service is to be invoked. In addition, most Unix file formats are documented in Section 5 of the on-line manual. Microsoft also documents some of the file formats used by its applications in the Microsoft Developer Network Library (MSDN).[147] Sometimes you can increase your insight by adding, modifying, or removing entries from the repository to observe the changes in the program's behavior.

You will have to use a different approach when working to get behind the structure of data stored in a relational database. Database data is stored in a binary format and is manipulated using a query language; therefore there is often no easily discernable correspondence between a program's source code and the underlying database files. However, all databases offer facilities for examining the database *schema*: a high-level description of the database's contents in terms of the employed data model. Relational database systems typically store information about each table and its columns in a separate database, often referred to as the *data dictionary*. You can examine a relational database's schema by performing queries on the tables of the data dictionary or by using database-specific SQL commands such as `show table`.

---

[146]netbsdsrc/etc/inetd.conf:7–18

[147]http://msdn.microsoft.com

Exercise 9.13 Discuss how namespace management issues can affect the reuse of code and outline how the global function identifier namespace is occupied by the standard C library.

Exercise 9.14 Locate in the book's CD-ROM four useful modules that could be reused in other situations. For each one, describe the most appropriate packaging mechanism.

Exercise 9.15 Find code written in an object-oriented language you are not familiar with, and locate in it the basic constructs for dealing with classes, objects, methods, fields, visibility, inheritance, and polymorphism. If you are a polyglot, draw a table describing how the above features are syntactically handled in the languages you know.

Exercise 9.16 Locate in the book's CD-ROM code instances that would benefit from the use of a generic implementation.

Exercise 9.17 Provide an approximate count of the number of linked-list implementations you can find in the book's CD-ROM.

Exercise 9.18 Locate instances of operator overloading and classify their use. How can you recognize that a given operator is overloaded?

Exercise 9.19 Search the Web for popular sites containing code libraries. Find in the book's CD-ROM corresponding code that could have been implemented using those libraries.

Exercise 9.20 Component software vendors often provide a chart of their wares ordered by component popularity. Find such a chart and discuss its composition.

Exercise 9.21 Locate a PC running Microsoft Windows and explore its registry (the database storing the system's configuration) through the *regedit* command. Without using other information sources, document its structure.

9.4 Architecture Reuse

Many systems are designed following established architectures. *Frameworks* and *code wizards* are two mechanisms through which architectures are reused at the code level. At a higher level of abstraction, *design patterns* and various *domain-specific archi-tectures* prescribe architectural elements that can be tailored to satisfy a considerable number of diverse requirements. Reading code that reuses an existing architecture can be challenging because its implementers often consider the underlying architecture known and not worth documenting or commenting. Furthermore, reusable architec-tures, having to satisfy a diverse set of applications, tend to be more complicated than tailor-made, application-specific structures. On the other hand, you can be sure that the application you are examining does follow an architectural style, which in most cases is carefully structured, has been successfully used in other contexts, and is documented (somewhere). After recognizing a reused architectural element, look up its original description to gain additional insight on the way it is used or abused.

9.4.1 Frameworks

You will often see large system designs implementing or relying on organized collections of classes serving a common goal, such as the provision of a GUI front end or a communication facility. These class collections and their associated interfaces are typically termed a *framework*. In contrast to a single class, which is a fine-grain design abstraction, a framework has room for enough structural material (classes) to allow the expression of sophisticated architectures. As an example, the Adaptive Communication Environment (ACE) that you can find in the book's CD-ROM[148] contains frameworks supporting reactive and proactive I/O, the dynamic configuration of objects, the modular integration of hierarchically related communication services, various types of higher-level concurrency, control and synchronization patterns, the dynamic allocation of shared and local memory, and CORBA integration. Each one of these frameworks consists of multiple classes designed to harmoniously work together, providing you with a subsystem architecture you can readily reuse in other systems.

One particular class of framework architectures you will often encounter concerns the implementation of GUI application front ends.[149] The provision of a consistent user interface that correctly handles keyboard and mouse input, windowing system events, and the coordination of multiple input and output widgets (controls) can be a fiendishly difficult task. Systems like the Microsoft Foundation Classes (MFC), the Java Abstract Windowing Toolkit (AWT) and Swing libraries, and the X Window System–based Xt and Motif toolkits typically implement a Model-View-Controller (MVC) framework. User and environment input events are received and processed by the controller classes. The processing updates the application's model of the world and generates appropriate view modification messages. The application's view can always be regenerated by querying the model state.

Despite the help that a framework provides, you will often find that applications built using a framework are anything but simple. As an example, a simple application to display a message box on the screen[150] adds up to more than 800 lines of code under Xt. This level of complexity can be explained by the fact that frameworks, typically designed to build large and sophisticated applications, impose their own

---

[148]ace/ace
[149]vcf/src
[150]XFree86-3.3/contrib/programs/xmessage

all-encompassing and necessarily intricate views on the systems that use them. Notable exceptions are frameworks packaged in the form of a domain-specific language such as Tcl/Tk and Visual Basic (both often used to create GUI applications) or *awk* and Perl (often applied to report-generation tasks).

When examining in depth an application built on top of a framework, the best course of action is to begin by studying the framework itself. Many frameworks come with a bare-bones application that follows the framework conventions without adding any major functionality. The message box Xt application is one example, the NetBSD null filesystem implementation[151] is another; the most common example you will encounter, however, is likely to be a humble "hello world" program. Study the example carefully, build it, and try to modify it. These actions will significantly ease the framework's initial steep learning curve and will help you discern code that is functional from code that merely satisfies the framework's requirements.

9.4.2 Code Wizards

The steep learning curve of many framework architectures has bred a class of tools termed *code wizards*. These present the application developer with a series of questions or selections and then generate canned code that satisfies the user's stated requirements. Limit your expectations when reading wizard-generated code and you will not be disappointed. The code you will be examining was created by programmers who trusted the wizard's judgment more than their own and was subsequently modified based on a probably limited understanding of the underlying code structures.

A typical feature of wizard-generated code is comments written by the wizard and directed toward the application customizer.[152]

```
BEGIN_MESSAGE_MAP(CServerApp, CWinApp)
    //{{AFX_MSG_MAP(CServerApp)
    ON_COMMAND(ID_APP_ABOUT, OnAppAbout)
        // NOTE - the ClassWizard will add and remove mapping macros here.
        //      DO NOT EDIT what you see in these blocks of generated code!
    //}}AFX_MSG_MAP
    // Standard file based document commands
    ON_COMMAND(ID_FILE_NEW, CWinApp::OnFileNew)
    ON_COMMAND(ID_FILE_OPEN, CWinApp::OnFileOpen)
```

---

[151] netbsdsrc/sys/miscfs/nullfs
[152] ace/TAO/examples/mfc/server.cpp:26–110

```
    // Standard print setup command
    ON_COMMAND(ID_FILE_PRINT_SETUP, CWinApp::OnFilePrintSetup)
END_MESSAGE_MAP()
[...]
CServerApp::CServerApp()
{
  // TODO: add construction code here,
  // Place all significant initialization in InitInstance
}
```

One other problem associated with wizard-generated code is that most wizards cannot modify the code they generated once it has been customized. Therefore, the only way to change the initial options given to the wizard is often to regenerate the code from scratch. You can sometimes save some of the effort by viewing the file difference between the wizard-generated code (with the options you assume were used) and the code at hand. In some cases you can even reapply those changes (generated in the form of a *context diff*—see Section 10.4) to new wizard code generated with different options; as in the common disclaimer, your mileage may vary.

9.4.3 Design Patterns

Probably the most general-purpose way in which an architectural form can be reused is a *design pattern*. The notion of design patterns has its origins in the seminal work of architect Christopher Alexander, who outlines how the relationship between recurring problems and their respective solutions establishes patterns as follows [AIS+77].

> Each pattern describes a problem which occurs over and over again in our environment, and then describes the core of the solution to that problem, in such a way that you can use this solution a million times over, without ever doing it the same way twice.

Twenty years later these ideas were cross-pollinated into the field of reusable object-oriented software design. Design patterns offer a convenient way to capture, document, organize, and disseminate existing knowledge from a given area in a consistent and accessible format. Patterns differ from algorithms and data structures in that the concepts they describe cannot be coded and used as a subroutine or an object class. Patterns also differ from frameworks, as they do not describe the structure of a complete system: interrelated patterns are typically used together to solve a general design problem in a given context. You will often find patterns described through a fairly standard outline consisting of the following items:

- A pattern name such as *Singleton* or *Reactor* used to identify the pattern
- An illustration of its structure using a UML diagram
- A classification of the pattern as, for example, creational, behavioral, or structural
- An illustration of the design problem that provides the motivation to use the pattern
- An outline of the situations where the pattern can be applied
- An outline of the pattern's participants
- A description of how the pattern supports its objectives
- Examples of and prescriptive guidelines for the pattern's implementation

We can get the flavor of how patterns are used in typical code by examining the realization of the *Singleton pattern*. The Singleton pattern is used in cases where the designer needs to ensure that only a single instance of a given object will ever be created. One solution would be to store the instance in a global variable. However, this approach does not preclude other instances from being instantiated and used, it pollutes the program's namespace, and it hinders class extensions through subclassing. The Singleton pattern solves the problem by having a class variable (declared as `static` in Java and C++) store a unique instance of a single object, providing a method for returning that unique instance (and creating it if needed), and protecting the class's constructor from external access. Figures 9.28[153] and 9.29[154] illustrate the use of the same pattern in two different cases. They differ in many aspects: they are coded in different languages, they are used to protect different underlying classes, the C++ implementation is generic, and they are used in two dissimilar systems. Yet the pattern's defining aspects, the class unique instance variable and accessor method, and the protected constructor are readily apparent. Learn a few basic design patterns and you will find that the way you view code architectures will change: your vision and vocabulary will extend to recognize and describe many commonly used forms. Failing that, when you read that a given piece of code follows a specific pattern, try to read the pattern's description as a shortcut for understanding the code's design.

The reuse of architectural designs often predates their description in the form of patterns. In fact, most pattern descriptions contain references to previous known uses of

---

[153] cocoon/src/java/org/apache/cocoon/components/renderer/ExtendableRendererFactory.java:26–81
[154] ace/TAO/tao/TAO_Singleton.h:83–112

```
public class ExtendableRendererFactory implements RendererFactory {

    protected final static RendererFactory singleton =          Unique instance field
        new ExtendableRendererFactory();

                                                                 Protected constructor
    private ExtendableRendererFactory() {
        // Add the default renderers which come with Apache FOP.
        addRenderer("application/pdf", PDFRenderer.class);
        addRenderer("application/postscript", PSRenderer.class);
        addRenderer("application/vnd.hp-PCL", PCLRenderer.class);
    }

                                                                 Unique instance accessor method

    public final static
        RendererFactory getRendererFactoryImplementation() {
            return singleton;
    }

    [...]
}
```

Figure 9.28 Use of a Singleton pattern in Java document renderer.

```
template <class TYPE, class ACE_LOCK>
class TAO_Singleton : public ACE_Cleanup
{
public: [...]
    static TYPE *instance (void);                    Unique instance accessor method
    [...]
protected: [...]
    TAO_Singleton (void);                            Protected constructor
    [...]
    static TAO_Singleton<TYPE, ACE_LOCK> *singleton_;  Unique instance field
    [...]
}
```

Figure 9.29 A C++ Singleton template.

the given pattern. You will therefore often encounter frequently used patterns without explicit references to their names. As an example, the synchronous/asynchronous code boundary illustrated earlier in Figure 9.8 (page 280) is a standard device driver design used from the earliest versions of Unix and carried over to MS-DOS and Microsoft Windows; only in 1995 was it formally described as a design pattern and termed the *Half-Sync/Half-Async pattern*. Therefore, try to understand architectures in terms of the underlying patterns, even if the patterns are not explicitly mentioned in the code.

9.4.4 Domain-Specific Architectures

The structure of some application categories has over the years stabilized into an almost universally adopted *domain-specific architecture*. As an example, most applications that process a computer language, be it a configuration file or a programming language, typically divide the task into the process of organizing characters into *tokens* (*lexical analysis*) and the assembly of tokens into larger structures (*parsing*).

```
int parse_statement (cfile, group, type, host_decl, declaration)
{ [...]                                          ┌── Fetch token
    switch (next_token (&val, cfile)) {

                                                 ── Process token
        case HOST:
            [...]
        case GROUP:
            [...]
```

Figure 9.30 Reading the DHCP daemon configuration file.

```
int db_load(filename, in_origin, zp, def_domain)
{ [...]                                           ── Fetch token
    while ((c = gettoken(fp, filename)) != EOF) {

                                                  ── Process token
        switch (c) {
        case INCLUDE:
            [...]
        case ORIGIN:
            [...]
```

Figure 9.31 Reading the DNS specifications.

```
static void
infile(const char *name)
{ [...]
    if (fgets(buf, (int) sizeof buf, fp) != buf)
        break; [...]
    fields = getfields(buf);                      ── Convert line into tokens
    [...]
    lp = byword(fields[0], line_codes);           ── Fetch token
    [...]
                                                  ── Process token
    switch ((int) (lp->l_value)) {
        case LC_RULE:
            [...]
        case LC_ZONE:
            [...]
```

Figure 9.32 Compiling a time-zone file.

In Figures 9.30,[155] 9.31,[156] 9.32,[157] and 9.33[158] you can see how the same architecture (a lexical analyzer providing tokens to a parser) is used in four different applications. Subdomains of this area have even more specialized architectures: compilers typically follow the lexical analysis and parsing with distinct source code semantic analysis, optimization, and code generation phases; most interpreters convert the parsed code into an internal parse tree or bytecode representation and then process the program with a state-based or virtual machine.

---

[155] netbsdsrc/usr.sbin/dhcp/server/confpars.c:167–192

[156] netbsdsrc/usr.sbin/named/named/db_load.c:164–277

[157] netbsdsrc/lib/libc/time/zic.c:773–829

[158] hsqldb/src/org/hsqldb/Parser.java:503–533

```
private Select parseSelect() throws SQLException {
    [...]
    String token = tTokenizer.getString();          Fetch token
    [...]                                            Process token

    if (token.equals("DISTINCT")) {
        [...]
    } else if( token.equals("LIMIT")) {
        [...]
```

Figure 9.33 Parsing an SQL SELECT statement.

```
top:                                                 Get program start
    cp = prog;
redirect:                                            Is an instruction available?
    while (cp != NULL) {
        [...]                                        Select instruction-specific action
        switch (cp->code) {                          Instruction code
        case 'a':                                    Processing statements

            if (appendx >= appendnum)
                appends = xrealloc(appends,
                    sizeof(struct s_appends) *
                    (appendnum *= 2));
            appends[appendx].type = AP_STRING;
            appends[appendx].s = cp->t;
            appends[appendx].len = strlen(cp->t);
            appendx++;
            break;
                                                     Branch instruction
                                                     fetch new code pointer and continue
        case 'b':
            cp = cp->u.c;
            goto redirect;

        case 'c':
            [...]
        case 'd':
            [...]
        case 'D':
            [...]                                    Quit instruction

        case 'q':
            if (!nflag && !pd)
                OUT(ps)
            flush_appends();
            exit(0);
                                                     Process code for
                                                     eight more instruction codes follows
        [...]
    }                                                Fetch next instruction
    cp = cp->next;
} /* for all cp */
```

Figure 9.34 The *sed* command interpreter.

In Figure 9.34[159] you can see how the *sed* (stream editor) command interpreter is structured around a loop that continuously fetches instruction codes and acts on the contents of each instruction. The parsed program is internally stored as a linked list with each element containing an instruction code and associated parameters.

----

[159]netbsdsrc/usr.bin/sed/process.c:105–257

The cp variable is part of the *interpreter state*, always pointing to the instruction being executed. A number of variables such as appendx hold the *program state*. Most interpreters you will encounter follow a similar processing architecture built around a state machine whose operation depends on the interpreter's current state, the program instruction, and the program state.

One other class of domain-specific architectures you may come across is termed *reference architectures*. In many cases, reference architectures prescribe a notional structure for an application domain, which is not neccessarily followed by the concrete implementations. The Open Systems Interconnection (OSI) conceptual architecture is such an example. The OSI architecture specifies that networking systems are to be decomposed into a stack of seven network layers: application, presentation, session, transport, network, data link, and physical. You will often hear and read arguments concerning functionality related to particular layers.[160]

```
* DUMB!! Until the mount protocol works on iso transport, we must
* supply both an iso and an inet address for the host.
```

However, you will rarely encounter software implementations with a structure that matches the seven layers prescribed by the ISO model. Concerns about efficiency, historical practice, and conflicting interoperability requirements often result in implementations where different ISO layers are handled by the same software module or where different subsystems cooperate to service a single layer. As an example, the session layer does not typically apply to TCP/IP networks, while BSD Unix systems typically split the handling of routing between a simple kernel module[161] and more sophisticated user-mode programs like *route*[162] and *routed*.[163]

Exercise 9.22 Find a program in the book's CD-ROM that is built on top of a framework. (How will you search for it?) Measure the lines of code that perform processing and compare their size against that of those needed to satisfy the framework's requirements.

Exercise 9.23 Use a code wizard to create an application. Examine the resultant code and identify parts that could have been abstracted by using mechanisms other than automatic code generation.

Exercise 9.24 The ACE communication framework[164] uses many different patterns: *Acceptor, Active Object, Adapter, Asynchronous Completion Token, Component Configurator,*

---

[160] netbsdsrc/sbin/mount_nfs/mount_nfs.c:577–578
[161] netbsdsrc/sys/net/route.c
[162] netbsdsrc/sbin/route
[163] netbsdsrc/sbin/routed
[164] ace/ace

Connector, Decorator, Double Checked Locking, Extension Interface, External Polymorphism, Half-Sync/Half-Async, Interceptor, Iterator, Leader/Followers, Monitor Object, Object Lifetime Manager, Observer, Proactor, Reactor, Scoped Locking, Service Configurator, Singleton, Strategized Locking, Strategy Bridge, Thread-per Request, Thread-per Session, Thread-Safe Interface, Thread Pool, Visitor, and *Wrapper Facade.* For each pattern, locate the corresponding code and, with reference to the pattern's documentation, identify in the code the pattern's distinguishing features.

Exercise 9.25   Download the source code of the GNU C compiler[165] and identify how parts of its code fit into a typical compiler architecture.

Exercise 9.26   Discuss how parts of the NetBSD networking code[166−169] correspond to the ISO network stack.

Further Reading

Several references discuss software architectures [Sha95, SG96, BCK98, BHH99] and design patterns [CS95, GHJV95, BMR+96, SSRB00]. An overview of client-server computing can be found in Sinha [Sin92], while a detailed examination of many widely deployed Internet client-server applications can be found in Comer and Stevens [CS96]. Blackboard systems are concisely described in Hunt and Thomas [HT00, pp. 155–170]. The middleware specifications we outlined are described in references about CORBA [Obj02, Sie99], DCOM [Mic95], Java RMI [Sun99b], and Sun RPC [Sun88a, Sun88b]. The Unix system provides a number of facilities for supporting data-flow architectures: see Kernighan and Pike [KP84] and, for a description of how these are applied in the document preparation domain, Kernighan [Ker89]. The pipes-and-filters data-flow architecture is described as a design pattern in Meunier [Meu95]. The Unified Modeling Language we used to model object-oriented architectures is defined in Rumbaugh et al. [RJB99] and described in Booch et al. [BRJ99]; the article by Daniels [Dan02] succinctly describes how to use the various UML diagrams in practice. The ArgoUML tool we used is presented in Robbins and Redmiles [RR00]. The concept of layering was first used as a design principle in Dijkstra's implementation of the THE operating system and has been instrumental to the development of operating systems [Org72], computer networks [DZ83], and the Java portability layer [LY97]. However, you should also study the seminal paper describing the end-to-end arguments on system design [SRC84] as well as another detailing

---

[165] http://www.gnu.org/software/gcc
[166] netbsdsrc/sys/net
[167] netbsdsrc/sys/netinet
[168] netbsdsrc/sys/netiso
[169] netbsdsrc/sys/netnatm

architectural considerations that affect the traditionally layered networking protocols [CT90]. Slicing was initially described by Weiser [Wei82]; you can read how slicing can help the understanding and reverse engineering of code in subsequent works [BE93, JR94, WHGT99]. The concepts of coupling and cohesion were defined by Constantine and Yourdon [CY79]; the relationship between slices and cohesion is analyzed in Ott and Thuss [OT89]. The Law of Demeter is described in Lieberherr and Holland [LH89] and also in Hunt and Thomas [HT00, pp. 140–142]. You can read more about the BSD Unix kernel process management in Leffler et al. [LMKQ88, pp. 69–165]. Common event-centered architectures are described in pattern form in Ran [Ran95]; event demultiplexing in Schmidt [Sch95].

The element-packaging approaches we described in Section 9.3 are based on the structural property model found in Shaw and Garlan [SG95]. You can read more about modularity in Meyer [Mey00] and in the timeless work by Parnas [Par72]. A handy reference covering object-oriented languages is Salus [Sal98]; for particular languages the canonical references are Stroustrup [Str97] for C++, Microsoft [Mic01] for C#, Arnold and Gosling [AG00] for Java, Conway [Con00] for object-oriented Perl, and Goldberg [Gol80] for Smalltalk. You can find more details on how objects are internally implemented in Ellis and Stroustrup [ES90]. Abstraction methods and approaches are discussed in Plauger [Pla93, pp. 177–209], and generic programming within the framework of C++ in two other sources [Aus98, Ale01]. You can read more about component-based software development in several references [BW98, Szy98, Wil99, SR00]. Experience reports, applications, and problems encountered using domain-specific frameworks can be found in works by Fayad et al. [FJ99, FJS99a, FJS99b]. A method for framework documentation using patterns is presented in Johnson [Joh92].

A number of books cover patterns and pattern languages [GHJV95, BMR⁺96, Ris00, Tic98, Vli98]. You will also find many interesting articles in the proceedings of the *International Conference on Pattern Languages of Programming* and the *European Conference on Pattern Languages of Programming* [CS95, CKV96, MRB97, HFR99]. The Adaptive Communication Environment (ACE) that you can find in the book's CD-ROM[170] is described in detail in Schmidt et al. [SSRB00]. If the subject interests you, you will also enjoy Alexander's work in architectural patterns [Ale64, AIS⁺77].

The canonical reference for the architecture of the language processors we examined is Aho et al. [ASU85]. Other areas where domain-specific architectures have evolved are operating systems [Tan97], computer networks [Com00, CS98], and client-server systems [DCS98].

---

[170]ace/ace

10

Code-Reading Tools

Give us the tools and we will finish the job.

—Winston Churchill

When reading code you are most of the time fortunate enough to have the code accessible on-line. This means you can process the source code with *tools* to enhance your reading efficiency and understanding. The following are typical tasks you might want to perform on a body of code.

- Identify the declaration of a particular entity to determine the type of a function, variable, method, template, or interface.
- Locate where a particular entity is defined, for example, find the body of a function or class.
- Go through the places where an entity is used.
- List deviations from coding standards.
- Discover code structures that might help you understand a given fragment.
- Find comments explaining a particular feature.
- Check for common errors.
- View the code structure.
- Understand how the code interacts with its environment.

In this chapter we describe tools you can use to automate the above tasks and perform them in the most efficient manner. In addition, modeling tools can often help you reverse engineer a system's architecture, while a number of documentation tools can automatically create project documentation from specially formated source code. (You can read more about the use of such tools in Section 9.1.3 and Section 8.5, respectively.) Many of the tools and examples in this chapter are based on the Unix environment and its tool family. If your tools do not match the Unix facilities, check this chapter's last section for advice on how to obtain compatible tools. We examine tools based on increasing levels of affinity between the source code and its execution. We start with tools that operate on source code at a lexical level (that is, they process characters without parsing the program structure), continue with tools based on code parsing and compilation, and finish with an overview of tools that depend on the code execution.

10.1 Regular Expressions

The tools that operate on source code at a lexical level are powerful and often underestimated. They can be used on any programming language or platform, operate without a need to preprocess or compile files, handle a wide variety of tasks, execute swiftly, and handle arbitrary amounts of program text. Using such tools, you can efficiently search for patterns in a large code file or across many files. These tools are by their nature imprecise; however, their use can save you time and yield results that might escape casual manual browsing.

The power and flexibility of many lexical tools come from the use of *regular expressions*. You can think of a regular expression as a recipe for matching character strings. A regular expression is composed from a sequence of characters. Most characters match only with themselves, but some characters, called *meta-characters*, have special meaning. You create regular expressions by using a combination of regular characters and meta-characters to specify a recipe for matching the exact code items you may be looking for. We list the most common regular expression building blocks in Table 10.1.

Most program editors provide a command for searching a text string using a regular expression. Table 10.2 contains the specific commands for some popular editors. The regular expression syntax outlined in Table 10.1 is the same across most editors; it is supported in its exact form by *vi*, *Emacs*, and *Epsilon*. Most editors extend the regular expression syntax with additional facilities; some use a slightly different syntax. As an example, the BRIEF editor uses ? to match any character, % to match the beginning of a line, ~ to denote a nonmatching character class, and + to express one or more matches of the preceding regular expression. Consult your editor's documentation to learn the complete regular expression syntax it supports.

Table 10.1 Common Regular Expression Building Blocks

Character	Matches
.	Any character
[abc]	Any of the characters a, b, or c (character class)
[ˆabc]	All characters except for a, b, and c
a*	Zero or more occurrences of a
\m	The (meta-character) m
ˆ	Beginning of a line
$	End of a line
\<	Beginning of a word
\>	End of a word

Table 10.2 Regular Expression Search Commands in Popular Editors

Editor	Forward Search Command	Backward Search Command
BRIEF[a]	Search Forward	Search Backward
Emacs	C-M-s[b] isearch-forward-regexp	C-M-r isearch-backward-regexp
Epsilon	C-A-s[c] regex-search	C-A-R reverse-regex-search
vi	/	?
Visual Studio	FindRegExpr	FindRegExprPrev

[a] After performing a regular expressions toggle.
[b] Control-Meta-s.
[c] Control-Alt-s.

Given an editor that supports regular expressions and basic knowledge of their syntax, you can use them to efficiently browse large code files. To avoid accidentally changing the file contents, make sure that you do not have write permission on the files, or use the editor in a read-only mode (for example, vi -R for the *vi* editor).

In Figure 10.1[1] we provide some examples of the types of searches you can perform using regular expressions. Often you can locate particular program elements by taking advantage of the programming style used by the programmer. A common case concerns looking for a function definition (Figure 10.1:1). Most programming style guides specify that function definitions are to be written with the function name starting on a separate line. You can therefore locate a function definition by using a regular expression search of the type ˆ*function name*. This regular expression will

---

[1] netbsdsrc/sys/arch/sparc/fpu/fpu_sqrt.c:189–300

```
struct fpn *
fpu_sqrt(fe)                        1 ^fpu_sqrt
    struct fpemu *fe;               2 \<fe\>
{                                                  3 \.*x
    register struct fpn *x = &fe->fe_f1;
    register u_int bit, q, tt;
    register u_int x0, x1, x2, x3;
    register u_int y0, y1, y2, y3;            4 [xyd][0-3]
    register u_int d0, d1, d2, d3;
    [...]

#define    DOUBLE_X { \
    FPU_ADDS(x3, x3, x3); FPU_ADDCS(x2, x2, x2); \         \\$
    FPU_ADDCS(x1, x1, x1); FPU_ADDC(x0, x0, x0); \
}
    [...]
        q = bit;
        x0 -= bit;              5 x0.*bit
    [...]
    t1 = bit;                   6 t1.*[^=]=[^=]
```

Figure 10.1 Regular expression matches.

match all lines that start with *function name*. Such an expression will also match functions with a name that starts with the same character sequence as the function name you specified. You can always amend the corresponding regular expression to have it match the function name as a complete word: `^function name\>`.

In practice, you will find that a simple regular expression specification works well enough for locating the text you are looking for and that you need to give a more specific expression only in cases where the original expression generates too many false-positive matches. In some cases you will also find that you can get away with specifying only a part of the string you are looking for. In other cases, when you are looking for a variable with a short name that appears in many different contexts, you will find that you need to explicitly specify word delimiters ($\<$, $\>$) around it (Figure 10.1:2). Unfortunately, many regular expression meta-characters are also used by programming languages. You will therefore have to remember to escape them (using a backslash) when you are searching for program elements that contain them (Figure 10.1:3). Regular expression character classes are useful for searching for all variables with a name that follows a specific pattern (Figure 10.1:4), while character classes with negation can be used to avoid false-positive matches. As an example, the expression in Figure 10.1:6 locates assignments to t1 (locating where a variable is modified is often crucial for understanding code) without matching lines where t1 appears on the left of the equality operator (==). The zero-or-more matches (*) meta-character is often used in conjunction with the match-any meta-character (.) symbol to specify an arbitrary amount of unknown text (.*). When such an expression is given, the regular expression matching code, instead of greedily matching all characters until the end of the line, will try to match only enough characters to create a match for the whole regular expression (including the part of the pattern after the `.*`). In Figure 10.1:5 we use this feature to locate all lines that contain the variable x0 followed by the variable `bit`.

Exercise 10.1   Learn the regular expression syntax provided by the editor you are using. Experiment with any additional features it provides. Try to express the additional features using only the meta-characters we have described. Comment on the relative merits of a rich regular expression syntax versus the cost of learning it.

Exercise 10.2   Write regular expressions to locate integers, floating-point numbers, and a given word within a character string. Where would you use such expressions?

Exercise 10.3   Write regular expressions to locate violations from the style guide used in the source code you are reading.

10.2 The Editor as a Code Browser

Some editors (for example, *Emacs* and *vi*) use regular expression searches in conjunction with an index file to allow you to efficiently locate various definitions in source code. You first create an index file using the *ctags* tool applied on all source files that interest you. The index file, named `tags`, contains a sorted set of the definitions found in the source files. For the C language the definitions recognized include functions, #defines, and, optionally, typedefs, structs, unions, and enums. Each line of the `tags` file contains the name of the entity recognized, the file it was found in, and a regular expression pattern for locating that entity within the file. The following lines are part of the output of `tags` run on the source code of *sed* .[2,3]

```
NEEDSP   process.c      /^#define       NEEDSP(reqlen)    \\$/
compile_addr    compile.c       /^compile_addr(p, a)$/
e_args  defs.h  /^enum e_args {$/
s_addr  defs.h  /^struct s_addr {$/
```

The use of regular expressions instead of line numbers keeps the `tags` file current even after lines are inserted or removed in the source file. While browsing the source code, a special command (`^]` in *vi*, `M-.` in *Emacs*) scans the entity name under the cursor and transfers you to the point where that entity is defined. Thus, by using the tags facility you can quickly view the definitions of new entities you encounter.

---

[2] netbsdsrc/usr.bin/sed
[3] Unless otherwise noted, all examples in this chapter use the same set of source files.

```
@ARGV = (<*.frm>,<*.bas>,<*.ctl>);                    Visual Basic source files
                                                       Go through all lines of all files
while (<>) {
    chop;
    if (/Begin\s+[^ ]+\s+(\w+)/) {                     Is this a control?
        push(@lines, "$1\t$ARGV\t?$_?\n");             Add tag line to the tags array
    } elsif (/(Sub|Function)\s+(\w+)/) {               Is this a subroutine or function?
        push(@lines, "$2\t$ARGV\t?$_?\n");             Tag line containing entity name, filename, pattern
    }
}

open(T, '>tags') || die "tags: $!\n";                  Generate sorted tags file from the tags array
print T sort @lines;
```

Figure 10.2 Generating tags from Visual Basic source files.

By taking advantage of the plain format of the `tags` file you can easily write simple tools to create custom tag files for other source languages or specific applications.

The Perl program in Figure 10.2 will create a `tags` file from Microsoft Visual Basic source code, allowing you to browse Visual Basic source code using any editor that supports tags. The precise formatting of the Visual Basic source code files simplifies the program's operation. The program's main loop goes through all possible source files in the current directory and matches lines (using the Perl enhanced regular expression syntax) for lines that look like definitions of controls, subroutines, or functions. The array `lines` contains a list of all search patterns generated, so that when all input has been read it can be written in sorted form to the `tags` file. Although the program can be improved in numerous ways, it is, like most operations based on the lexical structure, good enough for most purposes.

A number of tools build upon the original *ctags* idea.

- The *idutils* indexing tools[4] create a database of program identifiers and their occurences within a set of files. Separate command-line tools can then be used to query the database for files containing an identifier, edit a set of files that satisfy a query, list the tokens within a file, or *grep* through the subset of files containing an identifier to output the lines where it occurs. *idutils* can be enhanced by user-supplied scanners; they are supported by a number of editors such as *Emacs* and newer variants of *vi* like *vim*. Compared to *ctags*, *idutils* handle a wider range of "identifiers" including literals and names of include files.

- The *exuberant ctags* indexing tools[5] enhance *ctags* by providing support for 23 different languages.

---

[4] http://www.gnu.org/directory/idutils.html
[5] http://ctags.sourceforge.net/

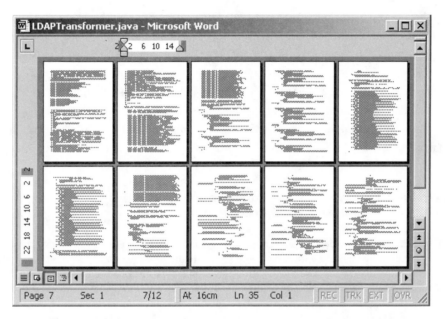

Figure 10.3 Bird's-eye view of source code using Microsoft Word.

When browsing large code files you can obtain a bird's-eye view of the source code structure by using an editor's outline view. The GNU *Emacs* editor provides the *selective display* command (C-x $—set-selective-display) to hide lines indented more than a certain number of columns. The command takes as a numerical argument the number of indented columns to hide; by using an appropriate number you can hide deeply nested source code. You can also use the *Emacs outline mode* (M-x outline-mode) and appropriate definitions for heading lines to quickly switch between a file's tree view and the corresponding node contents. The *vim* editor also supports the outline concept through the *folding* commands (for example, set foldenable, Zm, Zr, Zo, Zc.). These allow you to fold parts of the source file, thus obtaining an overview of the file's structure.

One other interesting way to look at a whole lot of source code quickly under Windows is to load it into Microsoft Word and then set the zoom factor to 10%. Each page of code will appear at about the size of a postage stamp, and you can get a surprising amount of information about the code's structure from the shape of the lines. For example, in Figure 10.3[6] you can discern the initial import statements, method blocks, and heavily indented code.

---

[6]cocoon/src/java/org/apache/cocoon/transformation/LDAPTransformer.java

You can also use your editor to detect matching parentheses, brackets, and braces. The appropriate commands are again different for each editor. *Emacs* provides a series of list commands: C-M-u (backward-up-list) moves up and backward in list structure, C-M-d (down-list) moves down and forward, C-M-m (forward-list) moves forward, and C-M-p (backward-list) moves backward. The *vi* editor provides the % command that will move the cursor to the matching bracketing element. Finally, in the Microsoft Visual Studio IDE you can use the LevelUp and LevelDown commands to navigate across different levels and the GoToMatchBrace and GoToMatchBrace-Extend commands to detect or select text that matches a given brace.

Exercise 10.4   Learn about and experiment with the tags facility of the editor you are using. Can it be extended using external tools?

Exercise 10.5   To localize the output message catalog of the *vi* editor you need to copy the English base file and replace messages with strings in the new local language. Unfortunately, in order to identify the purpose of each message argument you need to search the source code for each message.[7] Write a custom tag tool to automate this process.

Exercise 10.6   Propose additional uses for the tags facility. Consider large bodies of code such as the Unix kernel.[8]

Exercise 10.7   Does the editor or programming environment you are using support viewing the outline of a source code file? Experiment with this feature using examples from the book's CD-ROM.

10.3 Code Searching with *grep*

Large projects are typically split into multiple files, sometimes organized in a directory structure. Searching through each file with an editor is not always practical; fortunately, there are tools that can automate this task. The parent of all tools used for searching through large bodies of code is *grep*, which gets its name from the *ed/ex* editor command that prints all lines matching a pattern (g/RE/p—globally through the file find lines that match the given regular expression and print them). *grep* takes as an argument a regular expression to look for and a list of files to search in. The files are typically specified using a wildcard pattern, for example, *.c *.h. Many of the

---

[7] netbsdsrc/usr.bin/vi/catalog/README:113–125
[8] netbsdsrc/sys

characters used in regular expressions also have a special meaning for the command-line shell, so it is better to enclose the regular expression in quotes. The following sequence displays the file and the line containing the definition for the function `strregerror` in the source code of *sed*.

```
$ grep '^strregerror' *.c
misc.c:strregerror(errcode, preg)
```

To find both the definition and all uses, we would simply use the name of the function as the regular expression.

```
$ grep strregerror *.c
compile.c:  err(COMPILE, "RE error: %s", strregerror(eval, *repp));
misc.c:strregerror(errcode, preg)
process.c: err(FATAL, "RE error: %s", strregerror(eval, defpreg));
```

grep need not be applied to program code. If you are not sure what exactly you are looking for and where to start searching, you can use *grep* to search through the code with a keyword in the hope that the word will be mentioned in a comment or be part of an identifier. To ensure that capitalization and the word's ending and derivatives do not overly restrict your search space, search using the word's stem, omitting its initial character. In the following example we are looking for code associated with the compilation process.

```
$ grep ompil *.c
[...]
compile.c:                 p = compile_re(p, &a->u.r);
main.c: * Linked list pointer to compilation units and pointer to
main.c: compile();
main.c: * Add a compilation unit to the linked list
```

You can also use *grep* to search through the output of other tools. For example, in a project with numerous source files you can use *grep* to search the file list for a file that might interest you.[9]

```
$ ls | grep undo
v_undo.c
```

---

[9]netbsdsrc/usr.bin/vi

Sometimes you do not want to read the code that contains a regular expression but are interested only in the files that contain it. The -1 option of *grep* will display (once) the name of every file that contains the given regular expression.

```
$ grep -1 xmalloc *.c *.h
compile.c
main.c
misc.c
extern.h
```

You can then use this output to automatically perform a specific task on all those files. Typical tasks might be editing each file to further scrutinize it or locking each file under a revision control system. In Unix-type shells you can accomplish this by enclosing the output of *grep* in backticks.

```
emacs `grep -1 xmalloc *.c`
```

In other environments (for example, Windows), you need to modify the output of *grep* by adding the invocation of an editor command in front of each line and saving the result to a batch file, which you then execute. You can perform this and a number of similar tasks by using *stream editing*. Stream editing refers to the automated modification of text streams by a sequence of commands you specify. Two tools commonly used for stream editing are *sed* and *Perl*. Although *sed* is specifically targeted toward stream editing, we will use Perl in our examples because of its more regular syntax and in-place editing capability. If you use stream editing in a production environment, it might be worthwhile to also learn *sed*, which can be more efficient for some tasks.

The most useful editing command is the substitution command (s), which is specified as follows.

s/*regular expression*/*replacement*/*flags*

The command will locate text matching the regular expression and replace it with the replacement text. In the replacement text you can use the special expression $n to indicate the nth parenthesized part of the regular expression (for example, $1 will match the first parenthesized part of the regular expression). The *flags* are single-character modifiers that change the command behavior. The most useful flag is g, which makes the substitution change all nonoverlapping occurences of the regular expression and not just the first one, as is the default behavior. When using Perl as a stream editor, you need to execute it with a -p command-line flag to indicate that it should execute a printing loop over its input and specify the substitution command as an argument to the -e command-line flag. You can provide more than one substitution command by separating them with a semicolon. You can also specify that Perl should edit a file in-place rather than work as a filter on its input by using the -i*backup-extension* flag. Refer to the Perl documentation for more details.

Returning to our problem of creating a batch file for editing the files that match a pattern, all you need to do is pipe the output of *grep* to Perl in order to substitute the beginning of each line with the edit command.

```
C:\> grep -l xmalloc *.c | perl -p -e 's/^/edit /' >cont.bat
C:\> cont
```

In a Unix-type shell you can pipe the output of *Perl* back into a shell for immediate processing.

```
grep -l OBSOLETE *.c | perl -p -e 's/^/gzip /' | sh
```

This code compresses all files containing the word OBSOLETE. You can even pipe the output into a shell loop to execute a number of commands for every matching file. As an example, the code in Figure 10.4 uses *grep* to locate all files that contain the word xmalloc and pipes the output into the do loop. The code in the loop will do the following.

- Read each file name as the $f variable.
- Check out each file from the RCS repository, locking it for modification.
- Change all occurrences of xmalloc to safe_malloc using the in-place editing feature of *Perl*.
- Check in the file in the RCS repository with an appropriate log message.

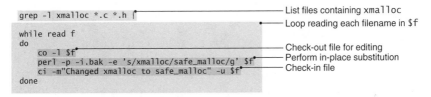

```
grep -l xmalloc *.c *.h |                                    List files containing xmalloc
                                                             Loop reading each filename in $f
while read f
do
    co -l $f                                                 Check-out file for editing
    perl -p -i.bak -e 's/xmalloc/safe_malloc/g' $f           Perform in-place substitution
    ci -m"Changed xmalloc to safe_malloc" -u $f              Check-in file
done
```

Figure 10.4 Changing an identifier name under RCS control.

▲

When automating tasks based on the output of *grep*, note that *grep* will *not* display
the name of the file where a match was found if only a single file was specified as
an argument. If your script depends on the existence of a file name, it will fail when

[i]   run on a single file. The GNU version of *grep* supports a switch -with-filename
to always display the file name; on other platforms you can program defensively by
specifying the system empty file (/dev/null under Unix, NUL under Windows) as an
extra argument to *grep*. This file will never match the pattern but will force *grep* to
always display the file name.

As with all tools that operate at a lexical level, a *grep*-based search will not

▲   always locate exactly the entities you are looking for. In particular, *grep* will get
confused by substitutions made by the C preprocessor, items that span more than one
line, comments, and strings. Fortunately, most of the time *grep* search specifications
result in *noise* (extraneous output) rather than *silence* (lines that should appear but
are missed). You can sometimes eliminate output noise by specifying a more exact
regular expression. For example, if you are looking for the uses of malloc, a naive
regular expression specification will result in the following output.

```
$ grep malloc *.c *.h
[...]
misc.c: if ((p = malloc(size)) == NULL)
misc.c:           return (xmalloc(size));
misc.c: oe = xmalloc(s);
extern.h:void    *xmalloc __P((u_int));
```

To eliminate the spurious xmalloc lines you could specify in the regular expression
that the first character should not be an x, as in [^x]malloc. Note, however, that this
regular expression will not match malloc at the beginning of a line because there is
no initial character to match the [^x] pattern. An alternative, very effective approach
requiring less mental effort is to filter the *grep* output to eliminate spurious matches.
For example, looking for uses of the code structure field will result in the following
output.

```
$ grep code *.c *.h
[...]
process.c: * This code is derived from software contributed to
process.c: * 1. Redistributions of source code must retain the
process.c:                switch (cp->code) {
process.c:              switch(cp->code) {
```

```
defs.h: * This code is derived from software contributed to
defs.h: * 1. Redistributions of source code must retain the
defs.h: char code;                              /* Command code */
```

The -v switch instructs *grep* to display only lines that do *not* match the given regular expression, that is, to filter out all lines that match the regular expression. Noticing that all spurious lines are block-comment lines starting with a *, we can eliminate them as follows.

```
$ grep code *.c *.h | grep -v "^ \*"
process.c:                      switch (cp->code) {
process.c:              switch(cp->code) {
defs.h: char code;                              /* Command code */
```

Using the command-line editing feature of your shell, you can apply this approach incrementally, gradually refining the output of *grep* with additional filters until you see exactly the output you want.

Sometimes a complicated and tedious code-reading task can be automated by combining a number of tools. Consider the task of locating in a project a subset of all identifiers containing an underline (for example, only those that are local to the project). Such a task could be specified as part of switching to a coding style that espouses formatting identifiers with mixed character case (for example, IdentifierFileName). The task can be performed semiautomatically in three steps.

1. Create a list of candidate identifiers.
2. Hand-edit the list to remove unsuitable identifiers (for example, library function names and type definitions).
3. Use the list as input for another search through the project files.

First we would locate all lines with such identifiers.

```
$ grep "[a-z0-9]_[a-z0-9]" *.c *.h
[...]
process.c:       size_t len;
process.c:       enum e_spflag spflag;
process.c:       size_t tlen;
process.c:       struct s_command *cp, *end;
```

[i]   Then we would isolate the identifiers by removing extraneous code. This can be done by specifying a Perl regular expression that matches the identifier, parenthesizing it by using the Perl construct (*expression*), and, for each line, printing the result of any such match ($1) after substituting the matched expression with an empty one.

[i]   This idiom will loop, printing all matched identifiers of each line.

```
$ grep "[a-z0-9]_[a-z0-9]" *.c *.h |
> perl -n -e 'while (s/\b(\w+_\w+)//) {print "$1\n"}'
[...]
rm_so
rm_eo
rm_eo
rm_so
rm_so
size_t
e_spflag
size_t
s_command
```

(The *Perl* regular expression construct \b indicates a word boundary, \w indicates word characters, and + indicates one or more matches; all these are just convenient shortcuts for simpler regular expressions.) We then want to make each identifier appear only

[i]   once in the output. This is typically accomplished by sorting the output (using the *sort* program) and then removing duplicate lines using the *uniq* program.

```
$ grep "[a-z0-9]_[a-z0-9]" *.c *.h |
> perl -n -e 'while (s/\b(\w+_\w+)//) {print "$1\n"}'
> sort |
> uniq >idlist
$ cat idlist
add_compunit
add_file
cmd_fmts
compile_addr
compile_ccl
compile_delimited
```

After hand-editing the list to remove identifiers that are outside the project scope (for example, members of the C library), we have a newline-separated list of identifiers to search for in our project files. For this task we can use *fgrep*, a relative of *grep*. *fgrep* searches only for fixed strings (not regular expressions) in files but can receive as an argument a newline-separated list of fixed strings to match against. The algorithm used by *fgrep* is optimized for performing such searches; the string list can easily contain hundreds of elements. Therefore *fgrep* is useful for searching source code against precomputed lists of fixed strings. In our case, having saved the hand-tuned list of identifiers in the idlist file, we can search all files for such identifiers.

```
$ fgrep -f idlist *.c
compile.c:       struct  labhash *lh_next;
compile.c:       u_int   lh_hash;
compile.c:       struct  s_command *lh_cmd;
compile.c:       int     lh_ref;
[...]
```

When the project source spans multiple directories, a number of different approaches can be employed. One approach for searching in a simple two-level directory structure is to run *grep* with a suitable file wildcard pattern.[10]

```
$ grep isblank */*.c
ex/ex_write.c:           for (++p; *p && isblank(*p); ++p);
ex/ex_write.c:           for (p += 2; *p && isblank(*p); ++p);
vi/getc.c:        if (csp->cs_flags != 0 || !isblank(csp->cs_ch))
```

In addition, some shells (such as *zsh*) allow you to specify a recursive search by a pattern like the following.

```
**/*.c
```

In cases of deep, nontrivial directory hierarchies the best approach is to create a list of files you want to search for using the *find* command and pipe the result to the *xargs* command, specifying as its argument *grep* and the relevant regular expression.[11]

```
$ find . -name '*.c' -print | xargs grep 'rmdir('
./nfs/nfs_serv.c:nfsrv_rmdir(nfsd, slp, procp, mrq)
./ufs/ext2fs/ext2fs_vnops.c:ext2fs_rmdir(v)
./ufs/lfs/lfs_vnops.c:lfs_rmdir(v)
./ufs/lfs/lfs_vnops.c:        ret = ufs_rmdir(ap);
./ufs/ufs/ufs_vnops.c:ufs_rmdir(v)
[...]
```

---

[10]netbsdsrc/usr.bin/vi
[11]netbsdsrc/sys

The *find* command will traverse the specified directory hierarchy and print files that match a given condition (here the file with a name matching the pattern *.c). The *xargs* command takes as its argument a command name and a set of initial arguments, reads additional arguments from its standard input, and then executes the command one or more times with any initial arguments followed by the arguments read from its standard input. In our case *xargs* runs *grep*, giving it as file arguments the output of *find*, that is, all .c files found under the current directory (.). Using this scheme *grep* can process an arbitrary number of files without being constrained by the system's limitation on the size of the command-line arguments. If your Windows-based environment does not support the above constructs, you have to be more creative and dynamically construct a temporary batch file containing the required commands.

We end this discussion of *grep*-style tools with advice on three useful *grep* command-line switches.

- Search through all comments and through the code of languages with case-insensitive identifiers (for example, Basic) using case-insensitive pattern matching (grep -i).

- Regular expressions that start with a dash will confuse *grep* into interpreting them as a switch. To avoid this problem, specify the particular regular expression by using the -e switch.

- Create checklists of files and line numbers that match a given regular expression by using the *grep* -n command-line switch.

When the volume of data you want to search using *grep* becomes prohibitively large, you may have to investigate alternative approaches. We discuss tools that create tag databases for popular editors in Section 10.2. In addition, if source code editing and browsing is not your first concern, you can consider using a general-purpose indexing tool like *Glimpse*.[12]

Exercise 10.8   Often programmers identify code parts that need further attention by using a special marker such as XXX or FIXME. Search for, count, and examine such instances in the source code tree.

---

[12]http://webglimpse.org/

Exercise 10.9   The task of locating underline-separated identifiers involved hand-editing the output list to remove identifiers that are part of the system libraries (for example, `size_t`). Propose a way to automate this task, taking into account that the identifiers used by system libraries are all declared in include files that you can process.

Exercise 10.10   The system call declarations in this book's Unix source distribution are generated from a single file.[13] Locate the definition of the first 20 system calls in the source tree. Automate this task as much as possible.

Exercise 10.11   Write a shell script or a batch file that uses *grep*, regular expressions, and other tools to list coding standard violations in a set of source files. Document the violations caught and the type of spurious noise that can be expected.

10.4 Locating File Differences

A temptingly easy way to reuse code is to create a copy of the respective source code and modify it as needed. There are many problems with this mode of code reuse; one of them is that two diverging versions of the code base are created. Another common situation where you will find two different versions of a source code file is when you are examining the evolution of a body of code. In both cases you will end up with two slightly different versions of a source code file. One way to compare them is to print both on fanfold paper and lay the listings side by side, looking for differences. A more efficient way is to use a tool. The *diff* program will compare two different files or directories and list lines that must be changed to bring the two files into agreement.

The *diff* tool can output the file differences in a number of ways. Some output formats are terse and are optimized for use by other programs such as *ed*, RCS, or CVS. One of the formats, the *context diff*, is particularly user-friendly: it displays the differences between the two files in the context of the lines that surround them. The -g option of *diff* specifies this output format; other tools such as CVS and RCS (see Section 6.5) also support this option when comparing different source versions. Lines that are different between the two files are marked with a !, lines that are added are marked with a +, and deleted lines are predictably marked with a -. Figure 10.5 contains an example of the output of *diff*. The two compared files are different instances of driver code for a specific network card; one file is part of the operating system network interface,[14] and the other is used for stand-alone booting over the network.[15]

---

[13] netbsdsrc/sys/kern/syscalls.master
[14] netbsdsrc/sys/arch/i386/stand/lib/netif/wd80x3.c:364–382
[15] netbsdsrc/sys/arch/i386/netboot/wd80x3.c:331–346

```
*** stand/lib/netif/wd80x3.c Wed Jan 07 02:45:48 1998          Files a and b being compared
--- netboot/wd80x3.c Tue Mar 18 01:23:53 1997
[...]
                                                                File a
***************
*** 364,382 ****                        Lines in file a
    * available. If there is, its contents is returned in a
    * pkt structure, otherwise a nil pointer is returned.
    */
! int                                   Lines changed
! EtherReceive(pkt, maxlen)
! char *pkt;
! int maxlen;
! {
     u_char pageno, curpage, nextpage;
     int dpreg = dpc.dc_reg;
     dphdr_t dph;
     u_long addr;

     if (inb(dpreg + DP_RSR) & RSR_PRX) {
-    int len;                           Lines removed from file a
-
     /* get current page numbers */
     pageno = inb(dpreg + DP_BNRY) + 1;
     if (pageno == dpc.dc_pstop)
                                                                File b
--- 331,346 ----                        Respective lines in file b
    * available. If there is, its contents is returned in a
    * pkt structure, otherwise a nil pointer is returned.
    */
! packet_t *                            Lines changed
! EtherReceive(void) {
     u_char pageno, curpage, nextpage;
     int dpreg = dpc.dc_reg;
+    packet_t *pkt;                     Line added in file b
     dphdr_t dph;
     u_long addr;

+    pkt = (packet_t *)0;               Line added in file b
     if (inb(dpreg + DP_RSR) & RSR_PRX) {
     /* get current page numbers */
     pageno = inb(dpreg + DP_BNRY) + 1;
     if (pageno == dpc.dc_pstop)

***************                          Start of next file difference block
*** 385,414 ****
[...]
```

Figure 10.5 Comparing files: output of the *diff*-c command.

The *diff* program works at the lexical level, comparing the files line by line. It can thus compare files written in any programming language that provides a way to save the source files as plain text. Sometimes supposedly clever program editors and other similar tools gratuitously change the formatting of a program, causing *diff* to emit extraneous output. You can use the *diff* -b flag to make the file comparison algorithm ignore trailing blanks, the -w flag to ignore all whitespace differences, and the -i flag to make the file comparison case insensitive.

Displaying differences between files is one of the few programming tasks that are more efficiently performed in a graphical environment. The Microsoft Visual Studio development environment contains a program called *windiff* that displays file or directory differences in a graphical way. Similar programs (*xxdiff*, *xdiff*, *gtkdiff*) run under the X Window System.

Exercise 10.12   Propose a simple way to calculate a "measure of similarity" metric for two different files. Apply this metric to files in the source collection that share the same file name and create a list of files that could benefit from a structured approach toward code reuse.

Exercise 10.13   A number of tools support the organized control of file revisions. If you are using such a tool, examine how you can display the differences between different file versions. Is there a way to display the differing lines in context?

10.5 Roll Your Own Tool

Sometimes none of the tools at your disposal will handle a mundane and obviously automatable code-reading task. Do not be afraid to create your own code-reading tools. The Unix shell with its tools and modern interpreted programming languages such as Perl, Python, Ruby, and Visual Basic are particularly suited for creating customized code-reading tools. Each environment has its own particular strengths.

- **The Unix shell** provides a plethora of tools such as *sed*, *awk*, *sort*, *uniq*, and *diff* that can be incrementally combined to obtain the required functionality.

- **Perl, Python, and Ruby** have strong support for strings, regular expressions, and associative arrays, simplifying many code-parsing tasks that can be achieved at a lexical level.

- **Visual Basic** can access through its object model code that is not normally available to text-based tools. Examples include Microsoft Access validation functions and recursive walks through deep object hierarchies.

Consider one particular example, the location of code lines with an indentation that does not match that of the surrounding code. Such code can be misleading at best and is often an indication of an important program bug. When we wanted to look in the existing source code base for examples of such code (see Section 2.3), none of the tools at our disposal could perform such a task, so we proceeded to roll our own. Figure 10.6 contains the implementation we used. As you can see, the tool depends on lexical heuristics and makes a number of assumptions about the code. It detects suspect code by locating two consecutive indented lines that follow an `if`, `while`, or `for` statement that does not end with an opening brace. The tool can get confused by reserved words and tokens inside comments or strings, statements that span more

```
#!/usr/bin/perl
use File::Find;                              Process all files in the tree specified
find(\&process, $ARGV[0]);

sub process
{
    return unless -f;                        Process only C files
    return unless (/\.c$/i);
    open(IN, $fname = $_) || die "Unable to open $_:$!\n";
    while (<IN>) {                           For every source code line
        chop;
        if (/^(\t+)(if|for|while)/ && !/\{/) {    Is it an if/for/while without a brace?
            $tab = $1;
            $n = <IN>;                       Get the next two lines
            $n1 = <IN>;

                                             Are they ; –terminated plain statements
            if ($n =~ m/^$tab\t.*;/ &&       starting with an additional tab?
                $n1 =~ m/^$tab\t.*;/ &&
                $n !~ m/\t(if|for|while|switch)/) {

                print "$File::Find::name\n$_\n$n$n1\n";    Then we found a problem.
            }                                Print the file location and the lines.
        }
    }
}
```

Figure 10.6 Locating code blocks with incorrect indentation.

than one line, and the use of whitespace instead of tabs. However, its 23 lines of code were written in less than an hour by gradually improving on the original idea until we could live with the signal-to-noise ratio of its output. (One of the previous versions did not handle the very common occurrence of the first line introducing a new braced block.) The way we implemented our indentation verification tool is applicable to the development of similar tools.

Cunningham [Cun01] describes how he wrote two 40-line CGI Perl scripts to summarize and amplify large Java source code collections. Both scripts create HTML output so that a Web browser can be used to navigate over megabyte-large source collections. You can see an example of the summarization tool's output[16] in Figure 10.7. The summarization script condenses each Java method into a single line consisting of the {};" characters that occur in the method's body. This method's *signature* can reveal a surprising amount of information; the size and structure of the method are readily apparent from the line's length and the placement of braces. Hyperlinks allow you to navigate to each particular method to examine it in detail, but in practice the tool's strength lies in its ability to succinctly visualize huge code collections.

The rules we follow when building tools can be summarized as follows.

- Exploit the capabilities of modern rapid-prototyping languages.
- Start with a simple design, gradually improving it as needed.

---

[16]jt4/catalina/src/share/org/apache/catalina

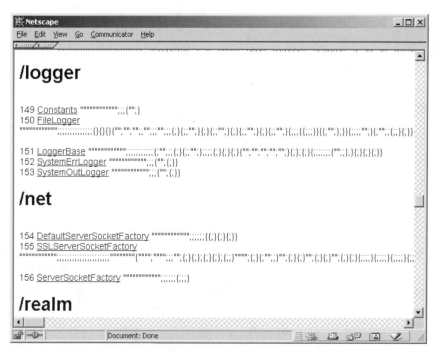

Figure 10.7 A signature survey of Java code.

- Use heuristics that exploit the lexical structure of the code.
- Tolerate some output noise or silence (extraneous or missing output), but remember to take into consideration this noise or silence when using the tool.
- Use other tools to preprocess your input or postprocess your output.

Exercise 10.14   Identify code-reading tasks that can benefit by use of a custom-built tool. Briefly describe how each such tool could be built. Implement one of the tools you described.

Exercise 10.15   A *pretty-printer* typesets source code in a way that makes it easy to read (see Section 10.7). Typically, different fonts or font styles are used for comments, variables, and reserved words. Implement a simple pretty-printer for the language of your choice based on lexical heuristics. To typeset the output you can use Postscript or drive another program: under Unix you can output *LaTeX* or *troff* commands; under Windows you can output RTF (rich text format) code or drive Microsoft Word using OLE automation.

Exercise 10.16   Write a tool that indexes source code files to simplify their browsing. The index entries can be function definitions and declarations. You can present the index as an alphabetically sorted list or an HTML page with hypertext links.

10.6 The Compiler as a Code-Reading Tool

The one tool that performs the definite analysis of your code is its compiler. The compiler is more than a translator from source code into object code; you can use it to examine the program at various levels of detail. Here are six ways to tap a compiler for information about the program.

1. Generate warning messages.
2. Tweak the code to generate error messages.
3. Generate program listings.
4. Obtain the preprocessor output.
5. Examine the generated symbolic (assembly) code.
6. Work through the final object code.

These ways do not apply to all compilers and languages, but some of them are likely to help you better understand the code you are dealing with.

 A number of legal (syntactically correct) program constructs can lead to questionable or plainly wrong program behavior. Some of them can be detected by the compiler and can be flagged through *warning messages*. Examples include:

- Expressions that may behave differently depending on the underlying architecture, leading to portability problems
- Implicit type casts and conversions between different but compatible types
- The use of a constant in place of a conditional expression in `if` or `while` statements
- Functions that do not return a value although they should
- Variable declarations that mask other variables with the same name
- Missing enumeration members or extraneous values in a `switch` statement
- Unknown `#pragma` options
- Unreferenced variables, structure members, or labels
- Failing to initialize a `const` declared object

Many compilers provide an option to increase or decrease the severity of warnings that will be displayed or to treat warnings as errors. When reading code, make the compiler your friend: specify the appropriate level of compiler warnings and carefully evaluate the results. If you have control over a body of code, your goal should be to

make the program compile without any warnings. Choose a compiler warning level
compatible with local coding practices or the quality of the code you are maintaining
(or are trying to achieve) and correct or modify questionable constructs until all warning messages are eliminated. Sometimes the generation of these warning messages is
delegated to another specialized tool. Many of these tools go by the name of *lint* after
Steve Johnson's original Unix program that was designed to remove residual "lint"
from code.

You can also use your compiler to locate all places where a variable, method,
type, or class is used. Simply rename the corresponding declaration or definition of
the identifier you want to search for, and perform a full compilation cycle. The errors
specifying that the given identifier is now undefined will indicate the place where the
identifier is used. However, keep in mind that some compilers will issue only one
error message for each undefined identifier and that in languages that allow you to
overload function definitions you need to rename all definitions or declarations of a
given identifier. You can also employ a similar strategy to detect the files that link
against a given identifier. In this case you keep the identifier declaration but remove
its definition. All object files that depend on the given identifier will then report
unresolved references during the program's link phase.

Some compilers, mainly those that have been developed in a culture not influenced
by the Unix environment, have options to generate elaborate listings of the compiled
code. These listings are often accompanied by indices of variable and function definitions, statistics, and summaries about individual code blocks. When you do not have
access to *grep*-style tools (Section 10.3) or an integrated development environment
with code-browsing capabilities (Section 10.7), you can use these indices to navigate
through large bodies of code. As an example, in Figure 10.8 you can see the symbol
listing generated by the Microsoft Macro Assembler.

The C programming language draws heavily on the support of the C preprocessor for a number of language features such as separate and conditional compilation,
the definition of constants and inline code, and the handling of comments. The C
preprocessor is also often used (or abused) to create additional control structures, provide object-oriented constructs, and support template-based (generic) programming.
Since the implementation of these nonstandard language features is entirely dependent on the creativity or perversion of the program's author, the resulting programs
can sometimes appear unreadable. Many of the winning programs in the International
Obfuscated C Code Contest (IOCCC) depend to a large extent on the C preprocessor.
Your C compiler can help you fight back against such programs. Most compilers have
an option (often -E) that passes the program source through the preprocessor and
outputs the resulting code. You can then read the code to understand how a particular

```
Microsoft (R) Macro Assembler Version 5.10B       11/2/2
winclip.c                                         Symbols-1
Symbols:

              N a m e              Type   Value  Attr
[...]
_argc$ . . . . . . . . . . . . .   NUMBER 0008
_argv$ . . . . . . . . . . . . .   NUMBER 000C
[...]
_error . . . . . . . . . . . . .   N PROC 091D   _TEXT    Length = 0065
_exit  . . . . . . . . . . . .     L NEAR 0000   External
_fileno  . . . . . . . . . . .     L NEAR 0000   External
_fname$  . . . . . . . . . . .     NUMBER -0004
_fname$22039 . . . . . . . . .     NUMBER -1030
_fopen . . . . . . . . . . . .     L NEAR 0000   External
_fprintf . . . . . . . . . . .     L NEAR 0000   External
_fread . . . . . . . . . . . .     L NEAR 0000   External
_fwprintf  . . . . . . . . . .     L NEAR 0000   External
```

Figure 10.8 Symbol listing generated by the Microsoft Macro Assembler.

macro expands, or why a constant #defined in a library include file generates an obscure error message in code that appears legitimate. Keep in mind that it will be difficult to navigate through the preprocessed code: included header files, expanded macros and constants, and removed comments all conspire to make your life difficult. The best strategy is to target a unique C identifier (variable, label, or function name) that you know appears first near the place you want to examine and then use the editor to search for that identifier in the preprocessed code.

To definitely understand how the compiler treats a particular piece of code, look at the generated symbolic (assembly) code. Although you can do this by disassembling the generated code, you will obtain more readable code by instructing the compiler to generate it for you. Most compilers will create symbolic code either as an intermediate step before object code generation or as a debugging aid for programmers and the compiler builders. Unix compilers use the -S option for this purpose; the corresponding Visual C/C++ switch is /Fa. Reading the generated symbolic code to understand what a piece of code does is an extreme measure. Some cases where it might be warranted are the following:

- To understand how an implementation-defined operation (for example, a type cast) is actually performed

- To see how compiler optimizations affect the resulting code
- To convince yourself that the compiler correctly translates a piece of code, or (rarely) to find a compiler bug
- To verify that hardware-specific code written in C actually performs the operations you expect
- To learn how a particular construct can be written in symbolic code

A final way to use your compiler as a tool for reading code is to compile a program into object code. At this level the interesting information you can obtain is mainly the public (`extern`) and private (`static`) symbols defined in each file. Many programming environments provide tools for examining the symbols defined, exported, and used in object files (*nm* under Unix, *dumpbin* under Windows). By running such a tool on a compiled file, you can find out where a particular symbol is defined and which files actually use it. Figures 10.9 and 10.10 contain representative symbol definitions

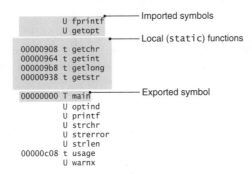

Figure 10.9 Object code symbols (Unix *nm*).

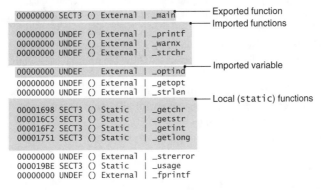

Figure 10.10 Object code symbols (Windows *dumpbin*).

from the object file generated by compiling the `printf` command.[17] Contrary to the fuzzy results generated by *grep*-type searches, the results you obtain by examining object files are extremely accurate. The compilation process guarantees that all the effects of header includes, conditional compilation, macro definitions, and compiler optimizations are taken into account and accurately reflected in the file's import and export list. The same process also ensures that you will not get confused by identifier names appearing in strings, comments, labels, or enumerations. Note, however, that inlined functions can under certain circumstances be entirely omitted from an object file.

One complication arises from the use of identifier *name mangling* used by most C++ compilers in order to support function overloading and type checking across files. These compilers append to externally visible identifiers (typically methods and function names) a sequence of characters that encode their type or rewrite identifiers in their entirety. As an example, the public method `setItem`[18] of the class `MenuItem` will be encoded as `?setItemMenuItemQAEHPBDHZ` by the Microsoft C/C++ compiler and as `_setItem__8MenuItemPCci` by the GNU C compiler. In most cases you will still be able to read the function names, but you may need to discard or decode the decorating type information.

Exercise 10.17 Provide (or, better yet, locate) code examples for some of the compiler warnings discussed in this section. Can your compiler detect them? Are there legitimate reasons for using such code?

Exercise 10.18 Many warnings generated by C compilers would be treated as errors in other strongly typed languages. Find a list of warnings that your C compiler generates and mark those that identify code with legitimate uses. See how many of them are detected in other languages.

Exercise 10.19 Propose and document a policy regarding the handling of warnings for your site. How does this policy affect code readability? Consider the cases where extraneous code may be needed to silence a particular compiler warning.

Exercise 10.20 Run some of the winning IOCCC entries[19] through the C preprocessor and try to understand how the program works and how the original obfuscation was achieved.

Exercise 10.21 Compile a program (with compiler optimizations disabled) and read the generated symbolic code. Repeat this process with all optimizations enabled. Describe how arguments are passed between functions in each case.

---

[17] netbsdsrc/usr.bin/printf/printf.c
[18] qtchat/src/0.9.7/Tree/Menu.cc:23–33
[19] http://www.ioccc.org

Exercise 10.22   Write a tool that, given a set of object files, displays for each file a list of symbols that could have been defined as `static`. *Hint:* You do not need to parse the object file; use an existing tool to do this work for you.

10.7 Code Browsers and Beautifiers

A number of tools are explicitly designed to support source code browsing. Typical facilities provided by browsers include the display of the following.

- **Definitions:** Locate where an entity is defined.
- **References:** Go through all places where an entity is used.
- **A call graph:** List the functions called by a given function.
- **A caller graph:** List the functions calling a given function.
- **A file outline:** List the functions, variables, types, and macros defined in a file.

Browsers for object-oriented languages like Smalltalk, C++, and Java provide additional facilities for examining classes. Given a class name you can obtain

- Where the class is defined
- The locations where the class is referenced
- The classes derived from this class
- The base classes for this class
- Its public, protected, and private methods and fields

Figure 10.11 presents the derived class view for the *groff*[20] node class and details of the `ligature_node` class members, properties, definition, and references.

We provide pointers for some well-known open-source browsers in the following paragraphs.

- The *cscope* tool[21] is a Unix-based source code browser with a textual interface. It is designed for parsing C, but its parser is flexible enough to be useful for C++ and Java. *cscope* can be integrated with a number of editors like *Emacs*, *nvi*, and *vim*.

---

[20]http://www.gnu.org/software/groff/
[21]http://cscope.sourceforge.net/

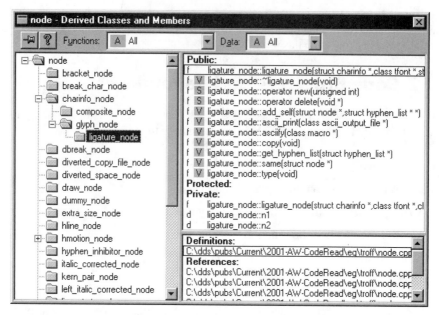

Figure 10.11 Microsoft Visual Studio source browser on *troff* classes.

- The *cbrowser* tool[22] is a graphical C/C++ source code searching and browsing tool and a hierarchical function call viewer. It is built on top of *cscope*.
- The *Source-Navigator*[23] provides browsing capabilities for a number of languages including C, C++, Java, Tcl, FORTRAN, and COBOL.
- The LXR browser[24] (Figure 10.12) provides a Web-based cross reference of large code collections.

In addition, source browsing facilities are also provided by most IDEs. When working on a large multifile project it may be worthwhile to load it as a project into an IDE—even if you do not intend to use the IDE for development—to benefit from its source code browsing functionality.

If source browsers can navigate you through large collections of source code, beautifiers and pretty-printers can help you disentangle the code details. Beautifiers

---

[22]http://cbrowser.sourceforge.net/

[23]http://sources.redhat.com/sourcenav/

[24]http://lxr.linux.no/

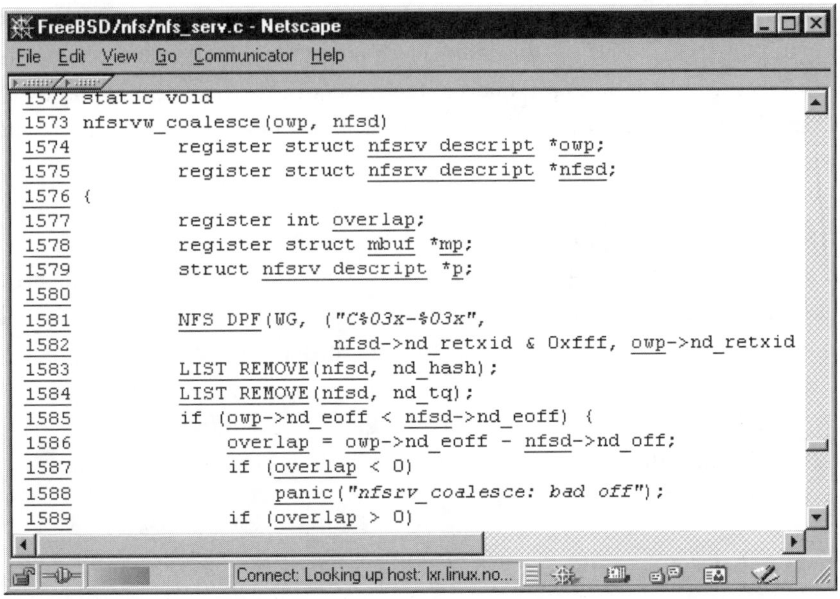

Figure 10.12 Sample output from the LXR Web-based source browser.

like the Unix programs *cb* (C beautify) and *indent* reformat a source code file to follow specific code formatting conventions. These programs can handle indentation, the placement of braces, whitespace around operators and keywords, declarations, and line breaks. You can set command-line options and create configuration files to tune the program's behavior to the local formatting conventions. Resist the temptation to beautify foreign code to your coding standards; gratuitous formatting changes create divergent code bases and hinder organized maintenance. Nowadays most code is written by competent professionals and follows a set of formatting conventions. Beautifiers operate mechanically and will often destroy careful handcrafted formatting created to provide additional hints for understanding the code. However, some legitimate cases where a beautifier will help remain. Use a beautifier to

- Fix code that is written truly inconsistently without following *any* formatting standards
- Adopt orphaned code for maintenance
- Create a temporary version of the code to help you decipher it
- Integrate code under the common roof of a larger project

A pretty-printer will neatly typeset program source code to make it more readable. One common style—used by the Unix *vgrind* program—will place comments in italics, set keywords in boldface, and list the name of the current function down the right margin of each page. Figure 10.13 contains parts of the *rmdir* program[25] typeset by using *vgrind*.

When reading code on-line you can use the syntax coloring features of many modern editors and IDEs to make different language elements stand out. Keep in mind that editors and pretty-printers often allow you to specify the key elements of a language's syntax so that you can adapt them to any language you are working on.

In some cases you may have to resort to more specialized tools. One common case concerns C declarations: the combined use of prefix and postfix operators to declare a type can make some declarations appear daunting and inscrutable. The open-source *cdecl*[26] program will translate such declarations into plain English. Consider the following definition.[27]

```
int (*elf_probe_funcs[])() = {
    [...]
};
```

A simple copy-paste operation of the definition into *cdecl* will immediately provide you with a clear explanation.

```
cdecl> explain int (*elf_probe_funcs[])()
declare elf_probe_funcs as array of pointer to function returning int
```

You can also use the same program, under its *c++decl* guise, on C++ types.[28]

```
c++decl> explain const char *(Drwho_Node::*get_name)(void)
declare get_name as pointer to member of class Drwho_Node
function (void) returning pointer to const char
```

Exercise 10.23 Try your IDE source browser on the Unix kernel of the supplied source code base.[29] List and comment on the difficulties you encounter.

---

[25] netbsdsrc/bin/rmdir/rmdir.c:1–134

[26] ftp://metalab.unc.edu/pub/linux/devel/lang/c/cdecl-2.5.tar.gz

[27] netbsdsrc/sys/arch/mips/mips/elf.c:62–69

[28] ace/apps/drwho/PMC_Ruser.cpp:119

[29] netbsdsrc/sys

```
– –                                                              – –


rmdir.c                                                      rmdir.c


/*         $NetBSD: rmdir.c,v 1.14 1997/07/20 20:52:05 christos Exp $        */
/* [...] */
#include <err.h>
#include <errno.h>
#include <stdio.h>
#include <stdlib.h>
#include <string.h>
#include <locale.h>
#include <unistd.h>

int rm_path __P((char *));
void usage __P((void));
int main __P((int, char *[]));

int
main(argc, argv)                                                  main
        int argc;
        char *argv[];
{
        int ch, errors;
        int pflag;

        setlocale(LC_ALL, "");
        pflag = 0;
        while ((ch = getopt(argc, argv, "p")) != -1)
                switch(ch) {
                case 'p':
                        pflag = 1;
                        break;

                case '?':
                default:
                        usage();
                }
        argc -= optind;
        argv += optind;
        if (argc == 0)
                usage();
        for (errors = 0; *argv; argv++) {
                char *p;

                /* Delete trailing slashes, per POSIX. */
                p = *argv + strlen(*argv);
                while (--p > *argv && *p == '/')
                        ;
                *++p = '\0';
                if (rmdir(*argv) < 0) {
                        warn("%s", *argv);
                        errors = 1;
                } else if (pflag)
                        errors |= rm_path(*argv);
        }
        exit(errors);
}

/* [...] */

void
usage()                                                          usage
{

        (void)fprintf(stderr, "usage: rmdir [-p] directory ...\n");
        exit(1);
}


Apr 20 11:23 2001                                        Page 1 of rmdir.c
```

Figure 10.13 The source code of *rmdir* typeset by using *vgrind*.

Exercise 10.24   Can your IDE source browser cooperate with other tools? For example, can you search or otherwise process the results listed by the browser, or have the browser automatically create a report of where each function contained in a list you supply is defined? Propose a source browser design that provides this flexibility.

Exercise 10.25   Write a tool that reads a C source file and deduces its formatting conventions, generating the appropriate switches for *indent*.

Exercise 10.26   Format one of the example files by using a pretty-printer.

Exercise 10.27   See if your editor supports user-defined syntax coloring. Define syntax coloring for a language you use that the editor does not support.

Exercise 10.28   Integrate *cdecl* with your favorite IDE.

10.8 Runtime Tools

Often you can gain valuable insight on how the program operates by actually executing it. This is especially true for programs that lack adequate documentation or whose documentation is out-of-date. In this case, instead of trying to understand the code line by line, you can run the program on test data and observe its external behavior.

To obtain a more detailed picture you can examine how the program interacts with the operating system. Since all program resources are controlled by the operating system, observing this interaction will provide you with valuable insights concerning its functionality. Many operating system platforms support tools that can monitor and display all operating system calls made by the program. Such tools include *trace* for MS-DOS (Figure 10.14), API *Spy* for Microsoft Windows (Figure 10.15), and *strace*

```
20:53:05 27b5 30 27C5:00C2 get_version() = 7.10                          ● ── Program startup
20:53:05 27b5 4a 27C5:0137 realloc(27B5:0000, 0x11320) = ok
20:53:05 27b5 30 27C5:03AE get_version() = 7.10
20:53:05 27b5 35 27C5:01AD get_vector(0) = 1308:2610
20:53:05 27b5 25 27C5:01BF set_vector(0, 27C5:0178)
20:53:05 27b5 44 27C5:0254 ioctl(GET_DEV_INFO, 4) =
         CHARDEV: NOT_EOF LOCAL NO_IOCTL
[...]
20:53:05 27b5 44 27C5:0254 ioctl(GET_DEV_INFO, 0) =
         CHARDEV: STDIN STDOUT SPECIAL NOT_EOF LOCAL CAN_IOCTL

20:53:05 27b5 40 27C5:0FDA write(1, 28E7:1022, 5) = 5    "hello"          ● ── Actual execution
20:53:05 27b5 40 27C5:0FDA write(1, 28E7:0D6C, 1) = 1    " "
20:53:05 27b5 40 27C5:0FDA write(1, 28E7:1022, 5) = 5    "world"
20:53:05 27b5 40 27C5:0F80 write(1, 28E7:0B4C, 2) = 2    "\r\n"

20:53:05 27b5 25 27C5:030E set_vector(0, 1308:2610)                      ── Termination functions
20:53:05 27b5 4c 27C5:02F3 exit(0)
```

Figure 10.14 Output from the *trace* program under MS-DOS.

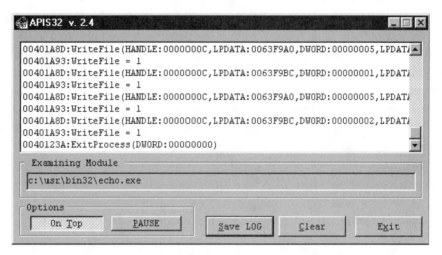

Figure 10.15 The Microsoft Windows API Spy program.

```
execve("/bin/echo", ["echo", "hello", "world"], [/* 22 vars */]) = 0     ← Program startup
brk(0)                                      = 0x804a668
[...]
getpid()                                    = 652
brk(0)                                      = 0x804a668
brk(0x804a808)                              = 0x804a808
[...]
open("/usr/share/locale/en_US/LC_MESSAGES/SYS_LC_MESSAGES", O_RDONLY) = 4
fstat(4, {st_mode=S_IFREG|0644, st_size=44, ...}) = 0
mmap(0, 44, PROT_READ, MAP_PRIVATE, 4, 0) = 0x40013000
close(4)                                    = 0
```
```
[...]
write(1, "hello world\n", 12)               = 12      ── Actual execution
munmap(0x40017000, 4096)                    = 0       ── Program termination
_exit(0)                                    = ?
```

Figure 10.16 Output from the *strace* program under Linux.

for Unix (Figure 10.16). The system call log will contain all files the program opens, the corresponding input and output data, system call return values (including errors), execution of other processes, signal handling, operations on the filesystem, and access to system databases. Since you do not need to prepare the programs for system call monitoring, you can use this procedure on programs even when you do not have access to the source code.

The operating system boundary is not the only place you can tap to monitor a program's operation. Two other sources are the network and the user interface. A number of programs like *tcpdump* and *WinDump* can monitor and display network packets. Restrict their monitoring to a given host and TCP port pair and you can obtain an accurate picture of a program's network operations. In this way you can observe a communication protocol while it is operating, instead of trying to deduce its functionality from the source code. Another class of programs let you examine the program at its user interface. *Xev* under the X Window System and *Spy++* under Microsoft Windows will monitor the events received by a window and display them in a human-readable form. Windows-based interactive programs are often coded around an event loop; you can match a particular user action to the underlying code by observing the events that the given action generates.

You can get a different level of detail by using an *execution profiler*. This facility, built into IDEs like the Microsoft Visual Studio or available in the form of the *gprof* tool under Unix, will monitor the program's execution and provide you with the corresponding profile. The profile typically lists the time the program spends on each function (and optionally its descendant functions). Most execution profilers can also calculate the program's dynamic *call graph*: the way functions call other functions at runtime. The amount of time spent in each routine can help you quickly pinpoint code areas that can benefit from optimizations. By using the call graph you can obtain a program structure chart and understand how routines interact with each other. If the test data is exhaustive you can even locate *dead code*: program code that is never executed. To activate the collection of profile data you usually need to compile your code with a suitable compiler option and link it with a special library. After the program terminates, a file will contain the profile data in a raw format. A report generator will then process this data to generate the final profile.

For an even finer-grained execution profile you can take advantage of a technique called *line counting* or *basic block coverage analysis*. Here a compile-time switch (-a in conjunction with -pg and -g for *gcc*) or an object code postprocessing procedure (*prep* in the Microsoft Visual Studio) creates code that will count the number of times each basic block is executed. Basic blocks are sequences of instructions with exactly one entry and one exit point; therefore, by counting the times each basic block is executed, you can propagate the results to individual source code lines. Look for lines that are never executed to find weaknesses in your test coverage and amend your test data. An examination of the times each line is executed can reveal how an algorithm works.

Consider the output example in Figure 10.17. This is a part of the *gprof* annotated listing generated by running the *wc*[30] character-, word-, and line-counting program on its source code. The *gprof* options -1, -A, and -x were used to generate

---

[30] netbsdsrc/usr.bin/wc/wc.c:201–228

```
   1 -> gotsp = 1;
 1,3,1 -> while ((len = read(fd, buf, MAXBSIZE)) > 0) {
   2 ->         charct += len;
2,6151,2 ->        for (C = buf; len--; ++C) {
 6149 ->             if (isspace(*C)) {
 1487 ->                 gotsp = 1;
 1487 ->                 if (*C == '\n') {
  269 ->                     ++linect;
                        }
 1487 ->             } else {
 4662 ->                 if (gotsp) {
  968 ->                     gotsp = 0;
  968 ->                     ++wordct;
                        }
                    }
                }
   2 -> }
   1 -> if (len == -1) {
##### ->         warn("%s", file);
##### ->         rval = 1;
```

1 While loop execution counts
1 For loop execution counts
2 Executed for each character
3 Executed for each line
4 Executed for each word
5 Lines never executed

Figure 10.17 Basic block count output from *gprof*.

the particular output. The source code consists of 269 lines, 968 words, and 6,149 characters. These numbers are respectively reflected in the number of times specific source code lines are executed (Figure 10.17:3, Figure 10.17:4, and Figure 10.17:2). Also interesting is the way loops are annotated: the three numbers at the beginning of the line (Figure 10.17:1) signify the number of times the loop was entered, the number of times the loop branched back to its beginning, and the number of times the loop exited, respectively. Note how the number of times the while loop branched back to its beginning (3) is reflected in the number of times its body was executed (2). Lines that are never executed are also specially marked (Figure 10.17:5), allowing you to identify parts of the program that were not exercised by the particular test input. At the time of this writing, the basic block profiling output generated by *gcc*-compiled code was not compatible with the data expected by *gprof*; a small Perl script (*bbconv.pl*—part of the *gprof* distribution) can be used to convert the data into the required format.

To explore every detail of the dynamic operation of a program you are examining, run it under a debugger. Although debuggers are primarily provided for finding program errors, they are also a very versatile tool for examining how a program works. The following list outlines the most useful debugger features for reading code.

- **Step-by-step program execution** allows you to follow the exact sequence of the program's operation for a given input. Most debuggers allow you to *step over* subroutine calls (when the particular routine does not interest you) or *step into* a call (when you want to examine the routine's operation).

- **Code breakpoints** give you the ability to stop the program when it reaches a particular point. You can use them to quickly jump to a place that interests you or to verify that a particular piece of code is or isn't executed.

- **Data breakpoints** can stop the program execution when a particular data item (for example, a variable) is read or modified. Using specialized hardware support available on modern processors, this under-appreciated feature lets you efficiently monitor how data is being accessed in your program.

- **Variable displays** provide you with a view of the variable values; use them to monitor how these change as the program operates.

- **A stack dump** provides you with a trace of the call history that led to the current execution point. The stack dump contains each routine and its arguments (starting from *main* in C and C++).

- **Structure browsing** allows you to collapse and expand structure members and follow pointers to examine, understand, and verify data structures.

Debuggers are another class of tools that benefit immensely from a graphical interface; if you are using a line-based debugger, consider switching to a graphical front end like *xxgdb*.

Exercise 10.29   Run a program under a system call monitor and reason about the operating system calls made. Noninteractive programs generally provide less noise than interactive ones.

Exercise 10.30   Obtain profile data for the execution of the *printf* program.[31] Using that data (and without looking at the source code), draw the program's structure chart (how routines call each other).

Exercise 10.31   Compile the quicksort implementation[32] with line-count profiling enabled. Write a small program to sort lines (this is called a *test harness*) and study the line execution counts when you give your program random data and data sorted in ascending or descending order. You can use the BSD Unix *jot* program to create sequences of random data elements and *sort* to sort them. Do the line execution numbers match your expectations?

Exercise 10.32   Create a quick-reference card outlining how each of the debugger features we described can be used in your programming environment.

---

[31] netbsdsrc/usr.bin/printf/printf.c
[32] netbsdsrc/lib/libc/stdlib/qsort.c:1–182

10.9 Nonsoftware Tools

We finish our discussion on tools you can use for reading code with some very powerful tools that are not based on fancy programmer productivity software.

Print on paper code you find hard to understand. A typical computer screen consists of about a million dots; a page from a laser printer can contain more than 30 million dots. This difference results in more information per page and less eyestrain. More importantly, you can take the printout to places where you can concentrate better than at your desk, and you can easily highlight code, draw lines, and write side notes. Use highlighters, colored pens, Post-it notes, and anything else that will help you annotate the code to make it understandable.

Draw diagrams to depict the code's operation. As the printout has allowed you to move away from your screen, you can now take out a piece of paper and draw diagrams for the parts you want to understand. Do not strive for perfect or even correct diagrams; anything goes as long as it helps you focus on the code you are reading. Some things you can draw include the following:

- Functions in little boxes with arrows to indicate function calls or flow of data
- Class hierarchies or diagrams of concrete object instances with properly filled-in properties
- Data structures (trees, lists, and so on) using arrows to indicate pointers
- Bit fields and corresponding masks in bit-mapped registers
- State transition diagrams using circles to indicate states and arrows to indicate state transitions
- Strings or arrays and corresponding indices or pointers
- Entity-relationship diagrams to understand how parts of a larger system fit together

Use a pencil when drawing and be prepared to revise your diagram as you gradually comprehend the program's operation.

You can always get a better understanding of a piece of code by explaining it to someone else. The act of articulating the program's operations to make them understandable to a third person forces you to think at a different pace and can bring forward details you may have glossed over. In addition, to properly explain the program you may need to draw on supplementary material such as books, diagrams, and printouts that you may have been too lazy to use when attempting to understand it on your own.

To understand complicated algorithms or subtle data structures, select a peaceful and quiet environment and concentrate deeply without drawing any help from computerized or mechanical aids. Dijkstra detailed in a lecture how people asked to reason about the derivation of a particular synchronization algorithm would invariably become confused the moment they grabbed a pencil or pen [Dij01]. Interruptions can be similarly distractive. Psychologists use the term *flow* to describe the condition of deep, nearly meditative involvement with a particular task, a condition often associated with an euphoric state of mind and obliviousness to the passage of time. This is the state you want to be in when examining complicated code. Unfortunately, you may need as many as 15 minutes to reach that state, and any interruption (telephone ring, arrival of new e-mail, a colleague asking for help) will bring you back to square one. Therefore, create an environment and work habits that let you work without interruptions when needed.

Exercise 10.33 Print out a copy of the topological sort tool[33] and explain the operation of the `tsort` function to a friend. For extra credit explain it to a nonprogrammer, a pet, or a bonsai tree.

Exercise 10.34 Repeat the exercise above after drawing appropriate diagrams.

Exercise 10.35 Measure the time intervals that pass without interruptions in your work environment. Calculate the resulting hours of flow and compare them to the total time you spend at work.

Tool Availability and Further Reading

As we indicated at the beginning of this chapter, many of the examples we provided are based on the Unix tool family. These are available under all flavors of Unix and recent versions of MacOS. Users of Microsoft Windows systems can also benefit from these tools: a number of efforts have been undertaken to provide the functionality of the Unix tools in the Windows environment. The UWIN port [Kor97] of the Unix tools and libraries supports all X/Open Release 4 headers, interfaces, and commands. *Cygwin*[34] [Noe98] is a full Win32 porting layer for Unix applications. It supports the GNU development tools and allows the effortless port of many Unix programs by supporting almost all POSIX.1/90 calls and other Unix version-specific functionality.

---

[33] netbsdsrc/usr.bin/tsort
[34] http://sources.redhat.com/cygwin/

OpenNt [Wal97], currently marketed as *Interix*,[35] is a complete porting and runtime environment that can be used to migrate application source, developed on traditional Unix systems, directly to Windows NT. Ported software includes many X11R5 clients and over 200 other utilities. In addition, Microsoft provides a package known as *Windows Services for Unix*[36] that includes most common Unix tools, and Mortice Kern Systems[37] market the more complete *MKS Toolkit*. If you are looking for a platform-independent IDE, you should also have a look at the *Eclipse* IDE.[38]

The *outwit*[39] tool suite [Spi00] complements these efforts by providing tools based on the Unix tool design principles that allow the processing of Windows application data with sophisticated data manipulation pipelines. The *outwit* tools offer access to the Windows clipboard, the registry, the event log, relational databases, document properties, and shell links.

Finally, if you cannot find ready-to-run tools for your environment, you can port and compile tools from the book's source code base. We fondly remember the productivity boost we received when we implemented a bare-bones version of *grep* on a 1970s-era Perkin-Elmer machine running OS/32.

The most complete reference on regular expressions is the book by Friedl and Oram [FO02]. For practical implementation details of lexical tools, read the articles by Aho and Corasick [AC75] and Hume [Hum88]. The theoretical basis of regular expression–based string searching is covered in Aho et al. [AHU74, ASU85]. Apart from *grep* and your editor, other strong tools for processing text are *sed* [McM79, DR97b], *awk* [AKW88, DR97a], the Unix shells [Bou79, KP84, Bli95, NR98], Perl [WCSP00, SCW01], and Python [Lut02]. Perl is one of the most versatile languages for writing small tools, and Schwartz et al. [SCW01] is the standard introductory text; a number of works [WCSP00, Sri97, CT98] target advanced users. When rolling your own code-reading tools, you can benefit from techniques used for the rapid development of domain-specific languages [Spi01]. The signature survey method and tools are described in Cunningham [Cun01], and if you are interested in visualization techniques, Tufte [Tuf83] is both a valuable reference and an interesting adornment for your coffee table. The *glimpse* tool is described in Manber and Wu [MW94]. A nice overview on the way typographical style affects program readability is Oman and Cook's work [OC90]. The original program checker, *lint*, was first documented

---

[35] http://www.interix.com/
[36] http://www.microsoft.com/windows/sfu
[37] http://www.mks.com/
[38] http://www.eclipse.org/
[39] http://www.dmst.aueb.gr/dds/sw/outwit

as a technical report [Joh77], then reproduced in the Unix programmer's manual [Joh79]. Common C problems and portability issues that your compiler should (but will not always) warn you about are detailed in three sources [Koe88, Hor90, RS90]. If perversely unreadable programs fascinate you, you can read more about them in the work by Libes [Lib93]. The operation of the *gprof* execution profiler is detailed in Graham et al. [GKM82, GKM83]. The design of a graphical debugger front end is described in Adams and Muchnick [AM86]. Currently, the standard notation for drawing various program-related diagrams is the UML [FS00, BRJ99, RJB99]. *Extreme programming* [Bec00] is a development process that actively encourages programmer interaction by promoting pair-based programming. The concept of flow in the context of productive work environments is described in two references [DL99, Bra86].

11

A Complete Example

For a successful technology, reality must take precedence over public relations, for nature cannot be fooled.

—Richard Phillips Feynman

Most examples we have encountered in this book so far deal with isolated instances of code we tried to understand. In this chapter we will examine, by means of a larger example, how code-reading and understanding skills are applied in practice. We set as our goal the enhancement of the *hsqldb* database to natively support a new SQL date/time function. The function we chose to add, PHASEOFMOON, returns the moon's phase on a given date as a number in the range 0–100, with 0 representing a new moon and 100 a full moon. At over 34,000 lines of Java source, *hsqldb* is not a trivial piece of code. Performing a minor modification, such as a bug fix or an extension, on a relatively large body of code is a task we are often given and one that almost always requires expert code-reading skills. In addition, we will employ code-reading techniques to locate and port an existing implementation of the algorithm and to debug the modifications we introduce.

What follows is the description of the whole process, structured as a personal journal (and therefore written as a first-person narrative), laid out in chronological order.

11.1 Overview

I start by examining the system's top-level directory to get a general feeling of the *hsqldb* distribution's structure. There is no README file, but a file titled index.htm[1] appears to be a promising start. Indeed, the file outlines the contents of all the top-level directories and provides me with a picture of the overall layout.

---

[1] hsqldb/index.html

My next step will be to compile the system from the source code and run it. The benefits of this step are numerous. First, I will understand the system's build process; since I will build the system multiple times while changing it, being able to control the build process will be essential. In addition, I will ensure that the source code I have on my hands can indeed be compiled, and thus I will not waste effort over a system that fails to build. The reasons behind a failed build process vary: corrupted source code; unsuitable compilation environment, compiler, or tools; missing libraries or components; invalid configuration. All of them, however, must be addressed early to minimize the risk of starting on a wrong path. Furthermore, running the system will hopefully provide me with a rough understanding of its functionality (remember, I want to minimize the reading of manuals as well as source code) and allow me to experiment with test cases that I will later use to verify my changes. Finally, a system that compiles and runs provides me with a dependable fixed starting point; any compile or runtime failures from this point onward will be my mistakes. Conversely, I will not blame my change for any problems I encounter during the initial build.

The `index.html` file provides a link documenting the system's build process. Running the `build.bat`[2] script results in what appears to be a clean build. To verify the build, I need to run the system. Another link on the `index.html` documentation section directs me to a copy of the *hsqldb* Web site.[3] By selectively browsing its contents I understand how the package works and its basic modes of operation. Inside the `bin` directory I now run the database manager (`run DatabaseManager`) and start my first interactive session. Since I will be adding a new date function, I read the SQL syntax documentation provided on the system's Web pages and experiment with a few relevant SQL commands.

```
create table test (d date);
insert into test values('2002-09-22')
select year(d) from test;
```

The last command shows on the result window one record with a single column containing, as expected, 2002.

11.2 Attack Plan

I now devise a plan for how to proceed. I will first search in the SQL documentation for functions with attributes and types similar to those of the function I wish to add. I will then model my function following the structure of those existing functions. To

---

[2] hsqldb/src/build.bat
[3] hsqldb/doc/internet/hSql.html

be able to efficiently use plain text-matching for searching through the code, I select a function with an uncommon name (DAYOFWEEK) as opposed to functions with names such as YEAR and HOUR.

I can now search for instances of that function to get a rough indication of the file(s) I will need to modify.

```
$ cd src/org/hsqldb
$ grep -i dayofweek *.java
Library.java:    [...], "DAYOFWEEK",
Library.java:    "org.hsqldb.Library.dayofweek", "DAYOFYEAR",
Library.java:    public static int dayofweek(java.sql.Date d) {
```

I edit the `Library.java` file and search for the DAYOFWEEK string. The first instance appears in the following context.[4]

```
final static String sTimeDate[] = {
    "CURDATE", "org.hsqldb.Library.curdate", "CURTIME",
    [...]
    "DAYOFMONTH", "org.hsqldb.Library.dayofmonth", "DAYOFWEEK",
    "org.hsqldb.Library.dayofweek", "DAYOFYEAR",
```

Apparently the array `sTimeDate` maps SQL functions to the corresponding Java implementations.

I repeat my search in a case-insensitive manner to locate instances of the dayofweek function. The second (and last) instance of the string is a static method definition.[5]

```
/**
 * Method declaration
 * @param d
 * @return
 */
public static int dayofweek(java.sql.Date d) {
    return getDateTimePart(d, Calendar.DAY_OF_WEEK);
}
```

---

[4]hsqldb/src/org/hsqldb/Library.java:85–89
[5]hsqldb/src/org/hsqldb/Library.java:814–824

As you can see, the method is not commented in any meaningful manner, but I feel I need to understand its functioning since I will model my new code on similar lines. Assuming that `getDateTimePart` is part of the Java library, I open the JDK documentation and read the details of the `Calendar` class. However, I find no references to a `getDateTimePart` method, so I continue my search in the *hsqldb* source code. I find it used in many different instances, and I also isolate its definition.[6]

```
private static int getDateTimePart(java.util.Date d, int part) {
    Calendar c = new GregorianCalendar();
    c.setTime(d);
    return c.get(part);
}
```

Again, the definition is preceded by an unfilled *javadoc* comment template; not terribly helpful. The function apparently creates `c` as an instance of the `Calendar` class, sets its value to the date passed, and returns an element of `Calendar`, as specified by the `part` parameter.

My task is to return a part related to the phase of the moon. I start by searching for the word "moon" in the documentation of the Java `Calendar` and `GregorianCalendar` classes. I do not find anything useful, and I continue reading the `GregorianCalendar` JDK notes for the class's architecture. The details on how the `GregorianCalendar` is implemented are fascinating; however, I end up realizing that I will require new code to calculate the phase of the moon.

11.3 Code Reuse

Not feeling a particular rush to reinvent the wheel, I decide to search for an existing implementation of the moon phase calculation algorithm. I could have searched the entire Web or an open-source software repository using a search engine, but I start closer to the material I have at hand by searching through the book's CD-ROM for the word "moon." I immediately realize I need to separate the chaff from the wheat.

```
$ find . -type -f -print | xargs grep -i moon
./netbsdsrc/games/battlestar/nightfile.c:
```

---

[6]hsqldb/src/org/hsqldb/Library.java:777–783

```
"Feather palms outlined by mellow moonlight and a silvery black
  ocean line\n\
./netbsdsrc/games/battlestar/nightfile.c:
  by a huge tropical moon stretches at least 30 meters inland.\n\
[...]
./netbsdsrc/games/hack/hack.main.c:
  pline("You are lucky! Full moon tonight.");
./netbsdsrc/games/pom/pom.c:
    * Phase of the Moon.  Calculates the current phase of the moon.
[...]
./netbsdsrc/lib/libc/stdlib/malloc.c:
    * a memory fault if the old area was tiny, and the moon
```

Among a large number of fictional references and satirical comments the code in pom.c[7] appears to be actually calculating the phase of the moon. A quick look in the NetBSD manual page confirms my hunch and also offers some light relief.

> The *pom* utility displays the current phase of the moon. Useful for selecting software completion target dates and predicting managerial behavior.

I continue reading the program's source code, intending to extract the phase of moon algorithm and port it to the *hsqldb* Java source. A comment lists a book that provides details of the algorithm.[8]

```
 * Based on routines from `Practical Astronomy with Your
 * Calculator', by Duffett-Smith.  Comments give the section
 * from the book [...]
```

A potentially useful fact; however, I will first try to extract meaning directly from the code.

The largest function in the file is the potm function, which appears to be a promising case.[9]

```
double
potm(days)
    double days;
```

---

[7] netbsdsrc/games/pom/pom.c
[8] netbsdsrc/games/pom/pom.c:54–55
[9] netbsdsrc/games/pom/pom.c:133–135

Again the function's comment (potm--return phase of the moon) is not very useful for purposes other than justifying the function's name. Given that I have no other clue about what the days argument represents, I locate the function's call to get a hint from its use.[10]

```
today = potm(days) + .5;
```

I then proceed to read backward to see how the value of the days variable is derived.[11]

```
struct timeval tp;
struct timezone tzp;
struct tm *GMT;
time_t tmpt;
double days, today, tomorrow;
int cnt;

if (gettimeofday(&tp,&tzp))
    err(1, "gettimeofday");
tmpt = tp.tv_sec;
GMT = gmtime(&tmpt);
days = (GMT->tm_yday + 1) + ((GMT->tm_hour +
    (GMT->tm_min / 60.0) + (GMT->tm_sec / 3600.0)) / 24.0);
for (cnt = EPOCH; cnt < GMT->tm_year; ++cnt)
    days += isleap(cnt) ? 366 : 365;
```

The code, apart from the EPOCH constant, mostly uses standard ANSI-C and POSIX functions. I therefore reason that I can reconstruct from equivalent information in Java a potm argument that works in the same way with no further need to understand what the days argument actually represents. I note that the code appears to be calculating the number of days from EPOCH to tp. I am not sure how and why the isleap function is being used, but I decide to deal with this problem later.

I proceed to search the source backward, looking for the EPOCH constant. The search reveals a number of constants that probably also need to be moved to the Java code.[12]

---

[10] netbsdsrc/games/pom/pom.c:104
[11] netbsdsrc/games/pom/pom.c:89–103
[12] netbsdsrc/games/pom/pom.c:70–77

```
#define PI        3.141592654
#define EPOCH     85
#define EPSILONg 279.611371 /* solar ecliptic long at EPOCH */
#define RHOg  282.680403 /* solar ecliptic long of perigee */
#define ECCEN 0.01671542 /* solar orbit eccentricity */
#define lzero 18.251907  /* lunar mean long at EPOCH */
#define Pzero 192.917585 /* lunar mean long of perigee at EPOCH */
#define Nzero 55.204723  /* lunar mean long of node at EPOCH */
```

I use the following regular expression–based replace operation in my editor (*vi*)[13]

```
:'a,'bs/#define^I\([^^I ]*\)[ ^I]*\(.*\)^I\(.*\)/^I\3^M^I
 private static final double \\1 = \\2;
```

to automatically transform most of the above preprocessor defines into Java constant definitions.

```
private static final double PI = 3.141592654;
private static final double EPOCH = 85;
/* solar ecliptic long at EPOCH */
private static final double EPSILONg = 279.611371;
/* solar ecliptic long of perigee at EPOCH */
private static final double RHOg = 282.680403;
/* solar orbit eccentricity */
private static final double ECCEN = 0.01671542;
/* lunar mean long at EPOCH */
private static final double lzero = 18.251907;
/* lunar mean long of perigee at EPOCH */
private static final double Pzero = 192.917585;
/* lunar mean long of node at EPOCH */
private static final double Nzero = 55.204723;
```

---

[13]Although the statement may appear like tty noise bursting from an old modem, its deconstruction is not overly difficult. All the statement does (take a deep breath) is: from the code point marked a to the code point marked b ('a, 'b), substitute (s/) #define, followed by a tab (^I), followed by the stored (\(...\)) string \1: anything but a tab or a space ([^^I]) repeated zero or more times (*), followed by a space or tab ([^I]), followed by the stored string \2 that can contain any character repeated zero or more times (.*), followed by a tab (^I), followed by the stored string \3 that can also contain any character repeated zero or more times, with (/) a tab, followed by the stored string \3 (the comment), followed by a newline (^M), followed by a tab and private static final double, followed by the stored string \1 (the constant name), followed by =, followed by the stored string \2 (the constant's value).

To see if isleap is a standard C function, I quickly compile a simple test program.

```
#include <time.h>
main() { int i = isleap(444); }
```

The function appears undefined, so apparently it is nonstandard; I therefore search for its definition in the files it includes.[14]

```
#define isleap(y) (((((y) % 4) == 0 && ((y) % 100) != 0) || \
                    ((y) % 400) == 0)
```

From its definition I see that the function takes a year as an argument and returns true if the year is a leap year. I search for the word "leap" in the Java GregorianCalendar class; I find it supported in the same form as the isLeapYear method.

I continue browsing the pom.c file looking for other functions I might need to port to the Java implementation. For each of the two functions found (dtor and adj360) I search the source to see where the corresponding function is used. Both functions are used inside potm and will therefore need to be ported.

I now shift my attention to understanding what is represented by the return value of the potm function. The code inside potm is totally opaque.[15]

```
return(50 * (1 - cos(dtor(D))));              /* sec 63 #3 */
```

However, the code sequence at the point where the function is called suggests that the phase is returned as a floating-point number with values 0–100 representing the moon's phase from a new to a full moon.[16]

```
if ((int)today == 100)
    (void)printf("Full\n");
else if (!(int)today)
    (void)printf("New\n");
```

Subsequent use of the value confirms the theory, since 50 apparently represents the moon's two quarter values (half-moons).[17]

```
if ((int)today == 50)
    (void)printf("%s\n", tomorrow > today ?
        "at the First Quarter" : "at the Last Quarter");
```

---

[14] netbsdsrc/include/tzfile.h:151
[15] netbsdsrc/games/pom/pom.c:163
[16] netbsdsrc/games/pom/pom.c:106–109
[17] netbsdsrc/games/pom/pom.c:112–114

The original pom.c[18] code displays the current phase of the moon. Since the new moonPhase method will calculate the phase of the moon on a date passed as its argument, I decide that the C code manipulating the current date should not be trivially ported to Java. I need to spend more effort to understand the meaning of the days variable. The first steps of the calculation[19]

```
days = (GMT->tm_yday + 1) + ((GMT->tm_hour +
    (GMT->tm_min / 60.0) + (GMT->tm_sec / 3600.0)) / 24.0);
for (cnt = EPOCH; cnt < GMT->tm_year; ++cnt)
    days += isleap(cnt) ? 366 : 365;
today = potm(days) + .5;
```

contain an expression part divided by 24 and additions of the 365 constant; both strongly indicate that days probably contains the number of days (including fractional parts) since EPOCH. If my understanding is correct, then the code can be rewritten in terms of the Java getTime difference between the Date object passed as the moonPhase method's argument and a Date object representing EPOCH.

```
GregorianCalendar e =
    new GregorianCalendar(EPOCH, Calendar.JANUARY, 1);
return potm((d.getTime() - e.getTime().getTime()) /
    1000.0 / 60.0 / 60.0 / 24.0);
```

However, a number of questions remain open and cannot be easily answered from the code: the issue of time zones and the consistent handling of leap years between the C and the Java approach. To answer these questions I decide that, instead of spending more time trying to understand the code, I will test my Java implementation against results obtained from the C version.

I proceed to transcribe the rest of the code into Java almost verbatim, without attempting to understand it. The adj360 function needs a bit more work since it receives an argument as a pointer. Reading the code in the function's body, I see that the pointer is used to pass an argument by reference and modify its value in the calling context.[20]

---

[18] netbsdsrc/games/pom/pom.c
[19] netbsdsrc/games/pom/pom.c:100–101
[20] netbsdsrc/games/pom/pom.c:181–192

```
void
adj360(double *deg;)
{
    for (;;)
        if (*deg < 0)
            *deg += 360;
        else if (*deg > 360)
            *deg -= 360;
        else
            break;
}
```

I can trivially modify the function and its calls via a source-to-source transformation by adding a `return` statement at the function's end; this is the only exit point for the function. The Java equivalent will thus be the following code.

```
private static double adj360(double deg)
{
    for (;;)
        if (deg < 0)
            deg += 360;
        else if (deg > 360)
            deg -= 360;
        else
            break;
    return (deg);
}
```

Calls to `sin` and `cos` also need to be prefixed by the Java `Math` prefix; similarly, I take the opportunity to use Java's definition of `Math.PI` to replace the C program's definition. The first draft of the moon phase algorithm transcribed into Java appears in Figure 11.1.

11.4 Testing and Debugging

I end my implementation of the `MoonPhase` class with the addition of a simple test harness to verify its correct operation.

```
public static void main(String args[]) {
    GregorianCalendar t = new GregorianCalendar(2002,
                             Calendar.SEPTEMBER, 30);
    System.out.println(moonPhase(t.getTime()));
}
```

```
import java.util.*;

class MoonPhase {
    private static final int EPOCH = 85;
    /* solar ecliptic long at EPOCH */
    private static final double EPSILONg = 279.611371;
    [...]                                                            ──────── Other constants

    public static double moonPhase(Date d) {                         ●── Driver function
        GregorianCalendar e = new GregorianCalendar(EPOCH, Calendar.JANUARY, 1);
        return potm((d.getTime() - e.getTime().getTime()) /
            1000.0 / 60.0 / 60.0 / 24.0);
    }

    public static void main(String args[]) {                         ●── Test harness
        GregorianCalendar t = new GregorianCalendar(2002, Calendar.SEPTEMBER, 30);
        System.out.println(moonPhase(t.getTime()));
    }

    private static double potm(double days) {
        [...]
        Ec = 360 / Math.PI * ECCEN * Math.sin(dtor(Msol));           ── Use Java Math

        [...]                                                        ── Almost verbatim copy of the
    }                                                                   original C source

    private static double dtor(double deg) {
        return(deg * Math.PI / 180);
    }

    private static double adj360(double deg)
    {
        [...]                                                        ── See text
    }
}
```

Figure 11.1 The moon phase algorithm transcribed into Java.

Testing the class with a few full-moon days (which I glean from my organizer's calendar) reveals that my initial implementation is not working correctly. The part most likely to be wrong is the code I completely reimplemented in Java.[21]

```
for (cnt = EPOCH; cnt < GMT->tm_year; ++cnt)
    days += isleap(cnt) ? 366 : 365;
```

In the above code EPOCH is compared against tm_year, so I can reasonably assume that both entities reference the same underlying quantities. A quick look in the manual page of the ctime function shows the following definition for tm_year.

```
int tm_year;    /* year - 1900 */
```

___

[21] netbsdsrc/games/pom/pom.c:102–103

Thus `tm_year` has an implicit constant offset of 1900. The corresponding documentation of the Java `Calendar` and `GregorianCalendar` classes does not indicate the use of such an offset; I therefore need to adjust `EPOCH` accordingly.

```
private static final int EPOCH = 1985;
```

Following that change, the Java and C code appear to produce compatible results, and I can therefore proceed to modify the *hsqldb* code. According to my understanding, the only change needed is to add a new entry in the `sTimeDate` array.

```
"org.hsqldb.MonnPhase.moonPhase", "PHASEOFMOON",
```

After rebuilding the source, I am ready to test the new function. I prepare a small SQL test script I will use from now on to test the program's operation.

```
create table test (d date);
insert into test values('2002-09-22')
select phaseofmoon(d) from test;
```

Running the above script I get my first error from *hsqldb*: "unexpected token: PHASEOFMOON." Apparently I need to better understand how *hsqldb* is extended. I begin by examining the compiled class files to ensure that my code got compiled. I find them in the directory `classes/org/hsqldb`; however, the directory contains no trace of a recompiled `Library` or the compiled `MoonPhase` class. Rereading the build script I am using, I discover that the compiled files are directly stored into a *jar* (Java archive) file. I therefore examine the *jar* file, looking for `MoonPhase`.

```
$ jar tvf hsqldb.jar | grep -i moon
  2061 Mon Sep 30 11:30:32 GMT+03:00 2002 org/hsqldb/MoonPhase.class
```

The compiled file is there, so the reason for the token not being recognized lies elsewhere.

I repeat my search for instances of `dayofweek` strings to see if I missed something, to no avail. However, while examining the code again I added

```
"org.hsqldb.MonnPhase.moonPhase", "PHASEOFMOON",
```

I notice a spelling error and correct it.

```
"org.hsqldb.MoonPhase.moonPhase", "PHASEOFMOON",
```

Nevertheless, after rebuilding *hsqldb* I still get the error "unexpected token: PHASEOFMOON."

I now search for the code that produces the error message.

```
$ grep "unexpected token" *.java
(no results)
$ grep unexpected *.java
(no results)
```

I reason that I probably overlooked some source code: code that contains the "unexpected token" error message and also the code I should have modified. A recursive directory search for other Java source files does not reveal anything interesting. I try a case-insensitive search; the message could get formatted in a weird way. This time I obtain a number of matches.

```
$ grep -i unexpected *.java
Access.java: throw Trace.error(Trace.UNEXPECTED_TOKEN, right);
Database.java: throw Trace.error(Trace.UNEXPECTED_TOKEN, sToken);
[...]
Function.java: Trace.check(i != -1, Trace.UNEXPECTED_TOKEN, function);
Parser.java: throw Trace.error(Trace.UNEXPECTED_TOKEN, token);
[...]
Tokenizer.java: throw Trace.error(Trace.UNEXPECTED_TOKEN, sToken);
[...]
Trace.java: UNEXPECTED_TOKEN = 10,
[...]
Trace.java: "37000 Unexpected token",
    "37000 Unexpected end of command",
```

It turns out that I was searching for the error message spelled incorrectly; in the application it was indeed spelled with an uppercase "U." As a side effect of my error, I find the references to the `Trace.UNEXPECTED_TOKEN` constant in the `Parser.java` and `Tokenizer.java` files. Judging by the file names, the `Parser` class handles the SQL grammar, while the `Tokenizer` class handles the lexical analysis; I reason that the error probably stems from the latter.

I quickly browse through the `Tokenizer.java` source to identify the problem. My eye first falls on a code sequence initializing a table with keywords. The editor I am using colors strings with a distinct color, so the whole block stands out.[22]

---

[22] hsqldb/src/org/hsqldb/Tokenizer.java:66–75

```
String keyword[] = {
  "AND", "ALL", "AVG", "BY", "BETWEEN", "COUNT", "CASEWHEN",
  "DISTINCT", "DISTINCT", "EXISTS", "EXCEPT", "FALSE", "FROM",
  "GROUP", "IF", "INTO", "IFNULL", "IS", "IN", "INTERSECT", "INNER",
  "LEFT", "LIKE", "MAX", "MIN", "NULL", "NOT", "ON", "ORDER", "OR",
  "OUTER", "PRIMARY", "SELECT", "SET", "SUM", "TO", "TRUE",
  "UNIQUE", "UNION", "VALUES", "WHERE", "CONVERT", "CAST",
  "CONCAT", "MINUS", "CALL"
};
```

Immediately below the array initialization I see that the strings are inserted into another structure.[23]

```
for (int i = 0; i < keyword.length; i++) {
    hKeyword.put(keyword[i], hKeyword);
}
```

I then search for hKeyword to see what else is included in that structure since most SQL function names are not there. I see that hKeyword is a Hashable instance, local to the class, used for identifying keywords in the wasName method. No other methods add elements to the hKeyword variable, and since it is local to the class, there is no need to further examine it. However, one use of hKeyword provides me with my next lead.[24]

```
return !hKeyword.containsKey(sToken);
```

I examine how sToken is used. However, it forms the heart of the lexical analyzer, and I abandon the exercise.

Having reached a dead end, I move my attention back to the Library.java source and examine how the array where I inserted the new function is used. I notice that the array is local to the class.[25]

```
final static String sTimeDate[] = {
```

Thus I need to examine only that specific file. My eyes then focus on the asymmetry between the last two lines.

---

[23]hsqldb/src/org/hsqldb/Tokenizer.java:76–78
[24]hsqldb/src/org/hsqldb/Tokenizer.java:192
[25]hsqldb/src/org/hsqldb/Library.java:85

```
"YEAR", "org.hsqldb.Library.year",
"org.hsqldb.MoonPhase.moonPhase", "PHASEOFMOON",
```

Obviously I inserted my definition in the wrong order. Earlier lines were formatted differently.[26]

```
"org.hsqldb.Library.dayofweek", "DAYOFYEAR",
"org.hsqldb.Library.dayofyear", "HOUR", "org.hsqldb.Library.hour",
```

I did not pay close attention to the exact wording of the constants, hence my error. If I were controlling the source I would reform at that initialization code into two distinct columns, from

```
"CURDATE", "org.hsqldb.Library.curdate", "CURTIME",
"org.hsqldb.Library.curtime", "DAYNAME", "org.hsqldb.Library.dayname",
"DAYOFMONTH", "org.hsqldb.Library.dayofmonth", "DAYOFWEEK",
"org.hsqldb.Library.dayofweek", "DAYOFYEAR",
"org.hsqldb.Library.dayofyear", "HOUR", "org.hsqldb.Library.hour",
[...]
```

into

```
"CURDATE",      "org.hsqldb.Library.curdate",
"CURTIME",      "org.hsqldb.Library.curtime",
"DAYNAME",      "org.hsqldb.Library.dayname",
"DAYOFMONTH",   "org.hsqldb.Library.dayofmonth",
"DAYOFWEEK",    "org.hsqldb.Library.dayofweek",
"DAYOFYEAR",    "org.hsqldb.Library.dayofyear",
"HOUR",         "org.hsqldb.Library.hour",
[...]
```

to avoid such problems in the future. I correct the error and recompile. This time I get not an error from the tokenizer but an exception:

"`java.lang.NoClassDefFoundError: org/hsqldb/MoonPhase` (wrong name: MoonPhase)."

I reason that the problem stems from an incorrect package specification. I therefore examine how `Library.java` is structured as a package[27]

---

[26]hsqldb/src/org/hsqldb/Library.java:89–90
[27]hsqldb/src/org/hsqldb/Library.java:36

```
package org.hsqldb;
```

and add the same specification to the `MoonPhase` class.

Retesting the *hsqlb* code with my test script results in a new error.

```
Wrong data type: java.util.Date in statement
  [select phaseofmoon(d) from test;]
```

Again I decide to start my code search bottom-up from the source of the error. Searching for the error message (this time paying attention to the correct capitalization of my search term), I quickly find its location.[28]

```
$ grep "Wrong data type" *.java
Trace.java:     [...], "37000 Wrong data type",
```

A few lines upward the corresponding constants are declared; searching for the word WRONG, I locate the one that interests me.[29]

```
WRONG_DATA_TYPE = 15,
```

Examining in the `Trace.java` code the relation between error constants and messages, I become disconcerted to see that the constants for indicating errors and the corresponding error messages are stored inside two different arrays and that no automatic mechanism (or even a comment) exists to keep them synchronized.[30]

```
final static int       DATABASE_ALREADY_IN_USE = 0,
            CONNECTION_IS_CLOSED = 1,
            CONNECTION_IS_BROKEN = 2,
            DATABASE_IS_SHUTDOWN = 3,
            COLUMN_COUNT_DOES_NOT_MATCH = 4,
[...]
private static String      sDescription[] = {
"08001 The database is already in use by another process",
"08003 Connection is closed", "08003 Connection is broken",
"08003 The database is shutdown",
"21S01 Column count does not match", "22012 Division by zero",
```

---

[28] hsqldb/src/org/hsqldb/Trace.java:108
[29] hsqldb/src/org/hsqldb/Trace.java:76
[30] hsqldb/src/org/hsqldb/Trace.java:63–103

I raise my defenses. Maybe the changes I made are encountering similar hidden interdependencies. I search for instances of the WRONG_DATA_TYPE constant in the code.

```
$ grep WRONG_DATA *.java
Column.java: Trace.check(i != null, Trace.WRONG_DATA_TYPE, type);
Column.java: throw Trace.error(Trace.WRONG_DATA_TYPE, type);
Expression.java: throw Trace.error(Trace.WRONG_DATA_TYPE);
jdbcResultSet.java: throw Trace.error(Trace.WRONG_DATA_TYPE, s);
Log.java: Trace.check(check, Trace.WRONG_DATABASE_FILE_VERSION);
Table.java: Trace.check(type == Column.INTEGER,
            Trace.WRONG_DATA_TYPE, name);
Trace.java: WRONG_DATA_TYPE = 15,
Trace.java: WRONG_DATABASE_FILE_VERSION = 29,
```

I have a quick look at each occurrence; they all appear quite complicated, and I fail to understand what each code instance is trying to accomplish. I therefore decide to try an alternative top-down approach: instead of focusing on the error, I will see how my function is called. Searching for sTimeDate in Library.java shows that it is "registered" into a hashable class by a public method.[31]

```
static void register(Hashtable h) {
register(h, sNumeric);
register(h, sString);
register(h, sTimeDate);
register(h, sSystem);
}
```

The method is in turn called in Database.java.[32]

```
Library.register(hAlias);
```

The name of the Hashable field (hAlias) strongly suggests that the SQL names are just aliases for the corresponding Java functions and that no further information is associated with them. I therefore reexamine the declaration of the function I am trying to emulate and notice that its argument is of type java.sql.Date[33]

```
public static int dayofweek(java.sql.Date d) {
```

---

[31] hsqldb/src/org/hsqldb/Library.java:109–114
[32] hsqldb/src/org/hsqldb/Database.java:82
[33] hsqldb/src/org/hsqldb/Library.java:823

whereas the argument of the new function was of type Date. I change the implementation of moonPhase accordingly.

```
public static double moonPhase(java.sql.Date d) {
```

I also fix the class's test harness that was invalidated by the change.

```
public static void main(String args[]) {
    java.sql.Date  d = new java.sql.Date(102,
                        Calendar.SEPTEMBER, 30);
    System.out.println(d);
    System.out.println(moonPhase(d));
}
```

The function now appears to work correctly, so I test it with additional data taken from a desk calendar.

```
create table test (d date);
insert into test values('1999-1-31');
insert into test values('2000-1-21');
insert into test values('2000-3-20');
insert into test values('2002-09-8');
insert into test values('2002-09-15');
insert into test values('2002-09-22');
insert into test values('2002-10-21');
select d, phaseofmoon(d) from test;
```

11.5 Documentation

"Are we done?" asks the impatient reader. Not quite—we also need to update the system's documentation. I employ the same strategy for locating the parts that need changing, searching for occurrences of the dayofweek string in the doc directory.

```
find . -type f -print  | xargs grep -li dayofweek
```

The results indicate that I will probably need to change two files.

```
./internet/hSqlSyntax.html
./src/org/hsqldb/Library.html
```

The first file contains a sorted list of the date/time functions.[34]

```
<b>Date / Time</b>
<br>CURDATE() (returns the current date)
<br>CURTIME() (returns the current time)
[...]
<br>WEEK(date) (returns the week of this year (1-53)
<br>YEAR(date) (returns the year)
```

I therefore add at the appropriate place a new entry.

```
<br>PHASEOFMOON(date) (returns the phase of the moon (0-100))
```

The location of the second file strongly suggests that it somehow mirrors the source code structure and could have been automatically generated by *javadoc*. I therefore check the beginning of the file (automatically generated files often start with a comment indicating the fact) and find the confirmation I am looking for.[35]

```
<!-- Generated by javadoc on Mon Apr 02 13:25:37 EDT 2001 -->
```

Finally, if I were maintaining the code in its original distribution, I would add a comment to the change log file[36] and update its version. If, on the other hand, the change were made for a project internal to an organization, I would add a README file in the source's root directory indicating the modifications I made.

11.6 Observations

Typical software evolution activities will require the understanding of code for a number of different purposes. In this chapter we read code to identify the Java source and documentation that needed changing, to find and port code we intended to reuse, and to understand and fix the errors in the new code we introduced. Notice how, in the context of software evolution, code reading is an opportunistic, goal-directed activity. In most cases, we simply cannot afford to read and understand the code of an entire software system. Any attempt to precisely analyze code will typically branch into numerous other classes, files, and modules and quickly overwhelm us; we

---

[34]hsqldb/doc/internet/hSqlSyntax.html:477–492
[35]hsqldb/doc/src/org/hsqldb/Library.html:5
[36]hsqldb/CHANGELOG.txt

therefore actively try to limit the extent of code we have to understand to the absolutely necessary minimum. Instead of striving for a global and complete understanding of the code, we try to find heuristic shortcuts (the book is full of such examples) and employ the build process and the execution of the running system to direct us to the code areas that require our attention. The *grep* tool and our editor's search functions are the tools of first choice and (often) our last resort. They allow us to quickly search over large code expanses, minimizing the code we need to analyze and understand. In many cases we may reach a dead end, encountering code that is very difficult to comprehend. To escape, we employ a breadth-first search strategy, attacking code-reading problems from multiple sides until one of them gives way.

Appendix A

Outline of the Code Provided

Life would be so much easier if we could just look at the source code.

—Dave Olson

Table A.1 outlines the code you can find in the book's CD-ROM. In the following paragraphs we let each package's developers speak for their own project.

ACE[1,2] is an open-source framework that provides many components and patterns for developing high-performance, distributed real-time and embedded systems. ACE provides powerful yet efficient abstractions for sockets, demultiplexing loops, threads, and synchronization primitives.

The Apache Project[3,4] is a collaborative software development effort aimed at creating a robust, commercial-grade, full-featured, and freely available source code implementation of an HTTP (Web) server.

ArgoUML[5,6] is a powerful yet easy-to-use interactive graphical software design environment that supports the design, development, and documentation of object-oriented software applications.

Apache Cocoon[7,8] is an XML publishing framework that raises the usage of XML and XSLT technologies for server applications to a new level. Designed for performance and scalability around pipelined SAX processing, Cocoon offers a flexible environment based on the separation of concerns between content, logic, and style. A centralized

---

[1]http://www.cs.wustl.edu/s̃chmidt/ACE.html
[2]ace
[3]http://httpd.apache.org/
[4]apache
[5]http://argouml.tigris.org/
[6]argouml
[7]http://xml.apache.org/cocoon/
[8]cocoon

Table A.1 Contents of the Book's CD-ROM

Directory	Original File	Language
ace	ACE-5.2+TAO-1.2.zip	C++
apache	apache_1.3.22	C
argouml	ArgoUML-0.9.5-src.tar.gz	Java
cocoon	cocoon-2.0.1-src.tar.gz	Java
demoGL	demogl_src_v131.zip demogl_docs_v131.zip	C++
doc	(Formatted documentation)	PDF
hsqldb	hsqldb_v.1.61, hsqldb_devdocs.zip	Java
jt4	jakarta-tomcat-4.0-src	Java
netbsdsrc	netBSD 1.5_ALPHA	C
OpenCL	OpenCL-0.7.6.tar.gz	C++
perl	perl-5.6.1	C
purenum	purenum.tar.gz	C++
qtchat	qtchat-0.9.7.tar.gz	C++
socket	socket++-1.11.tar.gz	C++
vcf	vcf.0.3.2.tar.gz	C++
XFree86-3.3	netBSD 1.5_ALPHA	C

configuration system and sophisticated caching top this all off and help you create, deploy, and maintain rock-solid XML server applications.

DemoGL[9,10] is an OpenGL-based, C++, Win32 execution platform for audio-visual effects. It allows the development of stand-alone executables or screensavers under the Microsoft Windows platform.

The HSQL Database Engine[11,12] (HSQLDB) is a relational database engine written in Java, with a Java database connectivity (JDBC) driver, supporting a subset of ANSI-92 SQL. It offers a small (about 100K), fast database engine with both in-memory and disk-based tables.

NetBSD[13,14] is a free, secure, and highly portable Unix-like operating system available for many platforms, from 64-bit AlphaServers and desktop systems to hand-held and embedded devices. Its clean design and advanced features make it excellent in both production and research environments, and it is user-supported with complete source.

---

[9] http://sourceforge.net/projects/demogl
[10] demogl
[11] http://hsqldb.sourceforge.net/
[12] hsqldb
[13] http://www.netbsd.org/
[14] netbsdsrc

OpenCL[15,16] is (or rather, is trying to be) a portable, easy-to-use, and efficient C++ class library for cryptography.

Perl[17-19] is a language optimized for scanning arbitrary text files, extracting information from those text files, and printing reports based on that information. It's also a good language for many system management tasks. The language is intended to be practical (easy to use, efficient, complete) rather than beautiful (tiny, elegant, minimal).

Purenum[20,21] is a C++ bignum library for programmers. Its unlimited-width `Integer` type works with all of the C++ math operators, but unlike the `int` type there can never be overflow errors. Division by zero and running out of memory are catchable exceptions. Optimized inline code is used, and the software `Integer` operations for single-width values run almost as quickly as hardware `int` operations do. An `Array` type provides for resizeable arrays of bignums.

QtChat[22,23] is a Yahoo! Chat client based on the Qt library. It includes such features as a plethora of autoignore options, highlighting, private messaging capability, and others.

The socket++[24,25] library defines a family of C++ classes that can be used more effectively for using sockets than directly calling the underlying low-level system functions. One distinct advantage of Socket++ is that it has the same interface as that of the `iostream` so that the users can perform type-safe input/output.

Tomcat 4[26,27] is the official Reference Implementation of the Servlet 2.3 and JavaServer Pages 1.2 technologies.

The Visual Component Framework[28,29] is a C++ framework designed as a completely cross-platform GUI framework. It was inspired by the ease of use of

---

[15]http://opencl.sourceforge.net/
[16]OpenCL
[17]http://www.perl.org
[18]http://www.cpan.org
[19]perl
[20]http://freshmeat.net/projects/purenum/
[21]purenum
[22]http://www.mindspring.com/abjenkins/qtchat/
[23]qtchat
[24]http://www.netsw.org/softeng/lang/c++/libs/socket++/
[25]socket
[26]http://jakarta.apache.org/tomcat/
[27]jt4
[28]http://vcf.sourceforge.net/
[29]vcf

environments like NEXTStep's Interface Builder, Java IDEs like JBuilder, Visual J++, and Borland's Delphi and the C++ Builder.

The X Window System[30,31] is a vendor-neutral, system-architecture neutral network-transparent window system and user interface standard. X runs on a wide range of computing and graphics machines.

We also provide in a separate directory[32] formatted pages of package documentation we refer to in the book's text.

---

[30]http://www.x.org/
[31]XFree86-3.3
[32]doc

Appendix B

Source Code Credits

*The world is divided into people who do things and people who get the credit.
Try, if you can, to belong to the first class. There's far less competition.*

—Dwight Morrow

The source code used in the book's examples has been graciously contributed to a number of open-source initiatives by the following individuals and organizations.

Rich $alz, AGE Logic, Inc., Eric Allman, Kenneth Almquist, the American Telephone and Telegraph Co., the Apache Software Foundation, Kenneth C. R. C. Arnold, Anselm Baird-Smith, Graham Barr, Berkeley Softworks, Jerry Berkman, Keith Bostic, Frans Bouma, Manuel Bouyer, Larry Bouzane, John H. Bradley, John Brezak, Brini, Mark Brinicombe, the University of British Columbia, the Regents of the University of California, Ralph Campbell, the Carnegie Mellon University, Scott Chasin, James Clark, Aniruddha Gokhale, J. T. Conklin, Donna Converse, Robert Paul Corbett, Gregory S. Couch, Jim Crafton, Charles D. Cranor, Ian F. Darwin, Christopher G. Demetriou, Peter Dettori, the Digital Equipment Corporation, Derek Dominish, Leendert van Doorn, Kinga Dziembowski, Julian Elischer, Peter Eriksson, the University of Erlangen-Nuremberg, Robert S. Fabry, Kevin Fall, Danno Ferrin, Michael Fischbein, Alessandro Forin, the Free Software Foundation, Inc., Thorsten Frueauf, Fujitsu Limited, Jim Fulton, John Gilmore, Eric Gisin, Michael Graff, Susan L. Graham, Bradley A. Grantham, Matthew Green, David Greenman, Jarle Greipsland, Neil M. Haller, Charles M. Hannum, the Hewlett-Packard Company, Hitachi, Ltd., Ken Hornstein, Steve Hotz, the HSQL Development Group, Conrad C. Huang, Jason Hunter, the Board of Trustees of the University of Illinois, the Imperial College of Science, Technology & Medicine, the International Business Machines Corp., the Internet Software Consortium, the Institute of Electrical and Electronics Engineers,

Inc., Van Jacobson, Mats O. Jansson, Anthony Jenkins, David Jones, William N. Joy, Andreas Kaiser, Philip R. Karn, Peter B. Kessler, Chris Kingsley, Steve Kirkendall, Thomas Koenig, John T. Kohl, Andreas Konig, Anant Kumar, the Lawrence Berkeley Laboratory, Joe O'Leary, Samuel J. Leffler, Dave Lemke, Ted Lemon, Craig Leres, Kim Letkeman, Jack Lloyd, the Mach Operating System project at Carnegie-Mellon University, Rick Macklem, Remy Maucherat, Stefano Mazzocchi, Steven McCanne, Craig R. McClanahan, Rob McCool, Peter McIlroy, Marshall Kirk McKusick, Eamonn McManus, Luke Mewburn, Paul Mockapetris, Andrew Moore, Rajiv Mordani, Thomas Mueller, Keith Muller, Mike Muuss, Ron Natalie, Philip A. Nelson, the NetBSD Foundation, Inc., Network Computing Devices, Inc., Novell, Inc., Mark Nudelman, Jeff Okamoto, Arthur David Olson, Joseph Orost, Keith Packard, Kirthika Parameswaran, David Parsons, Jan-Simon Pendry, Chris D. Peterson, Jochen Pohl, Paul Popelka, Harish Prabandham, Quadcap Software, Theo de Raadt, Mandar Raje, Michael Rendell, Asa Romberger, Mark Rosenstein, Gordon W. Ross, Guido van Rossum, Douglas C. Schmidt, Donn Seeley, Margo Seltzer, Roger L. Snyder, Wolfgang Solfrank, Solutions Design, Henry Spencer, Diomidis Spinellis, Davanum Srinivas, the Stichting Mathematisch Centrum, Timothy C. Stoehr, Sun Microsystems, Inc., Gnanasekaran Swaminathan, Ralph R. Swick, Robert S. Thau, Spencer Thomas, Jason R. Thorpe, TooLs GmbH, Chris Torek, TRW Financial Systems, John Tucker, the University of Utah, the Unix System Laboratories, Inc., Anil K. Vijendran, Lance Visser, Vixie Enterprises, Paul Vixie, the Vrije Universiteit Amsterdam, John S. Walden, Larry Wall, Sylvain Wallez, Edward Wang, the Washington University, Niklaus Wirth, John P. Wittkoski, James A. Woods, the X Consortium, Inc., Shawn Yarbrough, Ozan Yigit, Erez Zadok, Ilya Zakharevich, Carsten Ziegeler, and Christos Zoulas.

Appendix C

Referenced Source Files

There are no answers, only cross references

—Weiner's Law of Libraries

The following text lists in alphabetical order the complete path names of all source files that have been referenced in this book. The base name of each file (for example, `cat.c`) appears in the index.

Appendix D

Source Code Licenses

NB: This software will not save the world.

—Jim Crafton

D.1 ACE

The source code contained in the ace directory is copyrighted by Douglas C. Schmidt and his research group at Washington University and, unless otherwise noted, is distributed under the following license.

```
Copyright and Licensing Information for ACE(TM) and TAO(TM)

[1]ACE(TM) and [2]TAO(TM) are copyrighted by [3]Douglas C. Schmidt and
his [4]research group at [5]Washington University, Copyright (c)
1993-2001, all rights reserved. Since ACE and TAO are [6]open source,
[7]free software, you are free to use, modify, and distribute the ACE
and TAO source code and object code produced from the source, as long
as you include this copyright statement along with code built using
ACE and TAO.

In particular, you can use ACE and TAO in proprietary software and are
under no obligation to redistribute any of your source code that is
built using ACE and TAO. Note, however, that you may not do anything
to the ACE and TAO code, such as copyrighting it yourself or claiming
authorship of the ACE and TAO code, that will prevent ACE and TAO from
being distributed freely using an open source development model.

ACE and TAO are provided as is with no warranties of any kind,
including the warranties of design, merchantibility and fitness for a
particular purpose, noninfringement, or arising from a course of
dealing, usage or trade practice. Moreover, ACE and TAO are provided
with no support and without any obligation on the part of Washington
University, its employees, or students to assist in its use,
correction, modification, or enhancement. However, commercial support
for ACE and TAO are available from [8]Riverace and [9]OCI,
respectively. Moreover, both ACE and TAO are Y2K-compliant, as long as
the underlying OS platform is Y2K-compliant.

Washington University, its employees, and students shall have no
liability with respect to the infringement of copyrights, trade
```

secrets or any patents by ACE and TAO or any part thereof. Moreover,
in no event will Washington University, its employees, or students be
liable for any lost revenue or profits or other special, indirect and
consequential damages.

The [10]ACE and [11]TAO web sites are maintained by the [12]Center for
Distributed Object Computing of Washington University for the
development of open source software as part of the [13]open source
software community. By submitting comments, suggestions, code, code
snippets, techniques (including that of usage), and algorithms,
submitters acknowledge that they have the right to do so, that any
such submissions are given freely and unreservedly, and that they
waive any claims to copyright or ownership. In addition, submitters
acknowledge that any such submission might become part of the
copyright maintained on the overall body of code, which comprises the
[14]ACE and [15]TAO software. By making a submission, submitter agree
to these terms. Furthermore, submitters acknowledge that the
incorporation or modification of such submissions is entirely at the
discretion of the moderators of the open source ACE and TAO projects
or their designees.

The names ACE (TM), TAO(TM), and Washington University may not be used
to endorse or promote products or services derived from this source without
express written permission from Washington University. Further, products or
services derived from this source may not be called ACE(TM) or
TAO(TM), nor may the name Washington University appear in their names,
without express written permission from Washington University.

If you have any suggestions, additions, comments, or questions, please
let [16]me know.

[17]Douglas C. Schmidt

Back to the [18]ACE home page.

References

1. http://www.cs.wustl.edu/~schmidt/ACE.html
2. http://www.cs.wustl.edu/~schmidt/TAO.html
3. http://www.cs.wustl.edu/~schmidt/
4. http://www.cs.wustl.edu/~schmidt/ACE-members.html
5. http://www.wustl.edu/
6. http://www.opensource.org/
7. http://www.gnu.org/
8. http://www.riverace.com/
9. file://localhost/home/cs/faculty/schmidt/.www-docs/www.ociweb.com
10. http://www.cs.wustl.edu/~schmidt/ACE.html
11. http://www.cs.wustl.edu/~schmidt/TAO.html
12. http://www.cs.wustl.edu/~schmidt/doc-center.html
13. http://www.opensource.org/
14. http://www.cs.wustl.edu/~schmidt/ACE-obtain.html
15. http://www.cs.wustl.edu/~schmidt/TAO-obtain.html

16. `mailto:schmidt@cs.wustl.edu`
17. `http://www.cs.wustl.edu/~schmidt/`
18. `file://localhost/home/cs/faculty/schmidt/.www-docs/ACE.html`

D.2 Apache

The source code contained in the `apache`, `cocoon`, and `jt4` directories is copyrighted by the Apache Software Foundation and, unless otherwise noted, is distributed under the following license:

```
==============================================================================
                    The Apache Software License, Version 1.1
==============================================================================

Copyright (C) 1999-2002 The Apache Software Foundation. All rights reserved.

Redistribution and use in source and binary forms, with or without modifica-
tion, are permitted provided that the following conditions are met:

1. Redistributions of  source code must  retain the above copyright  notice,
   this list of conditions and the following disclaimer.

2. Redistributions in binary form must reproduce the above copyright notice,
   this list of conditions and the following disclaimer in the documentation
   and/or other materials provided with the distribution.

3. The end-user documentation included with the redistribution, if any, must
   include  the following  acknowledgment: "This product includes   software
   developed  by the  Apache Software Foundation  (http://www.apache.org/)."
   Alternately,  this  acknowledgment may  appear in the software itself,  if
   and wherever such third-party acknowledgments normally appear.

4. The names "Apache Cocoon" and  "Apache Software Foundation" must  not  be
   used to  endorse or promote  products derived from  this software without
   prior written permission. For written permission, please contact
   apache@apache.org.

5. Products  derived from this software may not  be called "Apache", nor may
    "Apache" appear  in their name,  without prior written permission  of the
   Apache Software Foundation.

THIS SOFTWARE IS PROVIDED "AS IS" AND ANY EXPRESSED OR IMPLIED WARRANTIES,
INCLUDING, BUT NOT LIMITED TO, THE IMPLIED WARRANTIES OF MERCHANTABILITY AND
FITNESS  FOR A PARTICULAR  PURPOSE ARE  DISCLAIMED. IN NO  EVENT SHALL  THE
APACHE SOFTWARE  FOUNDATION  OR ITS CONTRIBUTORS  BE LIABLE FOR  ANY DIRECT,
INDIRECT, INCIDENTAL, SPECIAL,  EXEMPLARY, OR CONSEQUENTIAL  DAMAGES (INCLU-
DING, BUT NOT LIMITED TO, PROCUREMENT  OF SUBSTITUTE GOODS OR SERVICES; LOSS
OF USE, DATA, OR  PROFITS; OR BUSINESS  INTERRUPTION) HOWEVER CAUSED AND ON
ANY  THEORY OF LIABILITY,  WHETHER  IN CONTRACT,  STRICT LIABILITY,  OR TORT
```

D.3 ArgoUML

The source code contained in the ArgoUML directory is copyrighted by the Regents
of the University of California and, unless otherwise noted, is distributed under the
following license.

D.4 DemoGL

The source code contained in the DemoGL directory is copyrighted by Solutions Design
and, unless otherwise noted, is distributed under the following license.

1. Redistributions of source code must retain the above copyright notice, this list of conditions and the following disclaimer.
2. Redistributions in binary form must reproduce the above copyright notice, this list of conditions and the following disclaimer in the documentation and/or other materials provided with the distribution.

THIS SOFTWARE IS PROVIDED BY SOLUTIONS DESIGN "AS IS" AND ANY EXPRESS OR IMPLIED WARRANTIES, INCLUDING, BUT NOT LIMITED TO, THE IMPLIED WARRANTIES OF MERCHANTABILITY AND FITNESS FOR A PARTICULAR PURPOSE ARE DISCLAIMED. IN NO EVENT SHALL SOLUTIONS DESIGN OR CONTRIBUTORS BE LIABLE FOR ANY DIRECT, INDIRECT, INCIDENTAL, SPECIAL, EXEMPLARY, OR CONSEQUENTIAL DAMAGES (INCLUDING, BUT NOT LIMITED TO, PROCUREMENT OF SUBSTITUTE GOODS OR SERVICES; LOSS OF USE, DATA, OR PROFITS; OR BUSINESS INTERRUPTION) HOWEVER CAUSED AND ON ANY THEORY OF LIABILITY, WHETHER IN CONTRACT, STRICT LIABILITY, OR TORT (INCLUDING NEGLIGENCE OR OTHERWISE) ARISING IN ANY WAY OUT OF THE USE OF THIS SOFTWARE, EVEN IF ADVISED OF THE POSSIBILITY OF SUCH DAMAGE.

The views and conclusions contained in the software and documentation are those of the authors and should not be interpreted as representing official policies, either expressed or implied, of Solutions Design.

D.5 hsqldb

The source code contained in the hsqldb directory is copyrighted by the HSQL Development Group and, unless otherwise noted, is distributed under the following license.

Copyright (c) 2001, The HSQL Development Group
All rights reserved.

Redistribution and use in source and binary forms, with or without modification, are permitted provided that the following conditions are met:

Redistributions of source code must retain the above copyright notice, this list of conditions and the following disclaimer.

Redistributions in binary form must reproduce the above copyright notice, this list of conditions and the following disclaimer in the documentation and/or other materials provided with the distribution.

Neither the name of the HSQL Development Group nor the names of its contributors may be used to endorse or promote products derived from this software without specific prior written permission.

THIS SOFTWARE IS PROVIDED BY THE COPYRIGHT HOLDERS AND CONTRIBUTORS "AS IS" AND ANY EXPRESS OR IMPLIED WARRANTIES, INCLUDING, BUT NOT LIMITED TO, THE IMPLIED WARRANTIES OF MERCHANTABILITY AND FITNESS FOR A PARTICULAR PURPOSE ARE DISCLAIMED. IN NO EVENT SHALL THE REGENTS OR CONTRIBUTORS BE LIABLE FOR ANY DIRECT, INDIRECT, INCIDENTAL, SPECIAL, EXEMPLARY, OR CONSEQUENTIAL DAMAGES (INCLUDING, BUT NOT LIMITED TO, PROCUREMENT OF SUBSTITUTE GOODS OR SERVICES; LOSS OF USE, DATA, OR PROFITS; OR BUSINESS INTERRUPTION) HOWEVER CAUSED AND ON ANY THEORY OF LIABILITY, WHETHER IN CONTRACT, STRICT LIABILITY, OR TORT

(INCLUDING NEGLIGENCE OR OTHERWISE) ARISING IN ANY WAY OUT OF THE USE OF THIS
SOFTWARE, EVEN IF ADVISED OF THE POSSIBILITY OF SUCH DAMAGE.

This package is based on HypersonicSQL, originally developed by Thomas Mueller.

D.6 NetBSD

All source code contained in the `netbsd` directory, unless otherwise noted, is copyrighted by the Regents of the University of California and is distributed under the following license.

Redistribution and use in source and binary forms, with or without
modification, are permitted provided that the following conditions
are met:

1. Redistributions of source code must retain the above copyright
   notice, this list of conditions and the following disclaimer.
2. Redistributions in binary form must reproduce the above copyright
   notice, this list of conditions and the following disclaimer in the
   documentation and/or other materials provided with the distribution.
3. All advertising materials mentioning features or use of this software
   must display the following acknowledgement:
This product includes software developed by the University of
California, Berkeley and its contributors.
4. Neither the name of the University nor the names of its contributors
   may be used to endorse or promote products derived from this software
   without specific prior written permission.

THIS SOFTWARE IS PROVIDED BY THE REGENTS AND CONTRIBUTORS "AS IS" AND
ANY EXPRESS OR IMPLIED WARRANTIES, INCLUDING, BUT NOT LIMITED TO, THE
IMPLIED WARRANTIES OF MERCHANTABILITY AND FITNESS FOR A PARTICULAR PURPOSE
ARE DISCLAIMED. IN NO EVENT SHALL THE REGENTS OR CONTRIBUTORS BE LIABLE
FOR ANY DIRECT, INDIRECT, INCIDENTAL, SPECIAL, EXEMPLARY, OR CONSEQUENTIAL
DAMAGES (INCLUDING, BUT NOT LIMITED TO, PROCUREMENT OF SUBSTITUTE GOODS
OR SERVICES; LOSS OF USE, DATA, OR PROFITS; OR BUSINESS INTERRUPTION)
HOWEVER CAUSED AND ON ANY THEORY OF LIABILITY, WHETHER IN CONTRACT, STRICT
LIABILITY, OR TORT (INCLUDING NEGLIGENCE OR OTHERWISE) ARISING IN ANY WAY
OUT OF THE USE OF THIS SOFTWARE, EVEN IF ADVISED OF THE POSSIBILITY OF
SUCH DAMAGE.

D.7 OpenCL

The source code contained in the `OpenCL` directory is copyrighted by the OpenCL Project and, unless otherwise noted, is distributed under the following license.

Copyright (C) 1999-2001 The OpenCL Project. All rights reserved.

Redistribution and use in source and binary forms, for any use, with or without
modification, is permitted provided that the following conditions are met:

1. Redistributions of source code must retain the above copyright notice, this list of conditions, and the following disclaimer.

2. Redistributions in binary form must reproduce the above copyright notice, this list of conditions, and the following disclaimer in the documentation and/or other materials provided with the distribution.

3. Products derived from this software may not be called "OpenCL" nor may "OpenCL" appear in their names without prior written permission of The OpenCL Project.

THIS SOFTWARE IS PROVIDED BY THE AUTHOR(S) "AS IS" AND ANY EXPRESS OR IMPLIED WARRANTIES, INCLUDING, BUT NOT LIMITED TO, THE IMPLIED WARRANTIES OF MERCHANTABILITY AND FITNESS FOR A PARTICULAR PURPOSE, ARE DISCLAIMED.

IN NO EVENT SHALL THE AUTHOR(S) OR CONTRIBUTOR(S) BE LIABLE FOR ANY DIRECT, INDIRECT, INCIDENTAL, SPECIAL, EXEMPLARY, OR CONSEQUENTIAL DAMAGES (INCLUDING, BUT NOT LIMITED TO, PROCUREMENT OF SUBSTITUTE GOODS OR SERVICES; LOSS OF USE, DATA, OR PROFITS; OR BUSINESS INTERRUPTION) HOWEVER CAUSED AND ON ANY THEORY OF LIABILITY, WHETHER IN CONTRACT, STRICT LIABILITY, OR TORT (INCLUDING NEGLIGENCE OR OTHERWISE) ARISING IN ANY WAY OUT OF THE USE OF THIS SOFTWARE, EVEN IF ADVISED OF THE POSSIBILITY OF SUCH DAMAGE.

D.8 Perl

The source code contained in the `perl` directory is copyrighted by Larry Wall and, unless otherwise noted, is distributed under the following license.

```
Perl Kit, Version 5.0

    Copyright 1989-2001, Larry Wall
All rights reserved.

This program is free software; you can redistribute it and/or modify
it under the terms of either:

a) the GNU General Public License as published by the Free
Software Foundation; either version 1, or (at your option) any
later version, or

b) the "Artistic License" which comes with this Kit.

This program is distributed in the hope that it will be useful,
but WITHOUT ANY WARRANTY; without even the implied warranty of
MERCHANTABILITY or FITNESS FOR A PARTICULAR PURPOSE.  See either
the GNU General Public License or the Artistic License for more details.

The "Artistic License"
```

Preamble

The intent of this document is to state the conditions under which a
Package may be copied, such that the Copyright Holder maintains some
semblance of artistic control over the development of the package,
while giving the users of the package the right to use and distribute
the Package in a more-or-less customary fashion, plus the right to make
reasonable modifications.

Definitions:

"Package" refers to the collection of files distributed by the
Copyright Holder, and derivatives of that collection of files
created through textual modification.

"Standard Version" refers to such a Package if it has not been
modified, or has been modified in accordance with the wishes
of the Copyright Holder as specified below.

"Copyright Holder" is whoever is named in the copyright or
copyrights for the package.

"You" is you, if you're thinking about copying or distributing
this Package.

"Reasonable copying fee" is whatever you can justify on the
basis of media cost, duplication charges, time of people involved,
and so on. (You will not be required to justify it to the
Copyright Holder, but only to the computing community at large
as a market that must bear the fee.)

"Freely Available" means that no fee is charged for the item
itself, though there may be fees involved in handling the item.
It also means that recipients of the item may redistribute it
under the same conditions they received it.

1. You may make and give away verbatim copies of the source form of the
Standard Version of this Package without restriction, provided that you
duplicate all of the original copyright notices and associated disclaimers.

2. You may apply bug fixes, portability fixes and other modifications
derived from the Public Domain or from the Copyright Holder. A Package
modified in such a way shall still be considered the Standard Version.

3. You may otherwise modify your copy of this Package in any way, provided
that you insert a prominent notice in each changed file stating how and
when you changed that file, and provided that you do at least ONE of the
following:

   a) place your modifications in the Public Domain or otherwise make them
   Freely Available, such as by posting said modifications to Usenet or

an equivalent medium, or placing the modifications on a major archive
site such as uunet.uu.net, or by allowing the Copyright Holder to include
your modifications in the Standard Version of the Package.

b) use the modified Package only within your corporation or organization.

c) rename any non-standard executables so the names do not conflict
with standard executables, which must also be provided, and provide
a separate manual page for each non-standard executable that clearly
documents how it differs from the Standard Version.

d) make other distribution arrangements with the Copyright Holder.

4. You may distribute the programs of this Package in object code or
executable form, provided that you do at least ONE of the following:

a) distribute a Standard Version of the executables and library files,
together with instructions (in the manual page or equivalent) on where
to get the Standard Version.

b) accompany the distribution with the machine-readable source of
the Package with your modifications.

c) give non-standard executables non-standard names, and clearly
document the differences in manual pages (or equivalent), together
with instructions on where to get the Standard Version.

d) make other distribution arrangements with the Copyright Holder.

5. You may charge a reasonable copying fee for any distribution of this
Package. You may charge any fee you choose for support of this
Package. You may not charge a fee for this Package itself. However,
you may distribute this Package in aggregate with other (possibly
commercial) programs as part of a larger (possibly commercial) software
distribution provided that you do not advertise this Package as a
product of your own. You may embed this Package's interpreter within
an executable of yours (by linking); this shall be construed as a mere
form of aggregation, provided that the complete Standard Version of the
interpreter is so embedded.

6. The scripts and library files supplied as input to or produced as
output from the programs of this Package do not automatically fall
under the copyright of this Package, but belong to whoever generated
them, and may be sold commercially, and may be aggregated with this
Package. If such scripts or library files are aggregated with this
Package via the so-called "undump" or "unexec" methods of producing a
binary executable image, then distribution of such an image shall
neither be construed as a distribution of this Package nor shall it
fall under the restrictions of Paragraphs 3 and 4, provided that you do
not represent such an executable image as a Standard Version of this
Package.

7. C subroutines (or comparably compiled subroutines in other
languages) supplied by you and linked into this Package in order to
emulate subroutines and variables of the language defined by this
Package shall not be considered part of this Package, but are the
equivalent of input as in Paragraph 6, provided these subroutines do
not change the language in any way that would cause it to fail the
regression tests for the language.

8. Aggregation of this Package with a commercial distribution is always
permitted provided that the use of this Package is embedded; that is,
when no overt attempt is made to make this Package's interfaces visible
to the end user of the commercial distribution. Such use shall not be
construed as a distribution of this Package.

9. The name of the Copyright Holder may not be used to endorse or promote
products derived from this software without specific prior written permission.

10. THIS PACKAGE IS PROVIDED "AS IS" AND WITHOUT ANY EXPRESS OR
IMPLIED WARRANTIES, INCLUDING, WITHOUT LIMITATION, THE IMPLIED
WARRANTIES OF MERCHANTIBILITY AND FITNESS FOR A PARTICULAR PURPOSE.

The End

D.9 qtchat

qtchat has been developed by Anthony Jenkins and Chad Dixon. It is distributed under
the Qt Public Source Licence, available at http://www.trolltech.com.

D.10 socket

The source code contained in the `socket` directory is copyrighted by Gnanasekaran
Swaminathan and, unless otherwise noted, is distributed under the following license.

Copyright (C) 1992-1996 Gnanasekaran Swaminathan <gs4t@virginia.edu>

Permission is granted to use at your own risk and distribute this software
in source and binary forms provided the above copyright notice and this
paragraph are preserved on all copies. This software is provided "as is"
with no express or implied warranty.

D.11 vcf

The source code contained in the `vcf` directory is copyrighted by Jim Crafton and,
unless otherwise noted, is distributed under the following license.

Copyright (c) 2000-2001, Jim Crafton
All rights reserved.

Redistribution and use in source and binary forms, with or without
modification, are permitted provided that the following conditions
are met:
   Redistributions of source code must retain the above copyright
   notice, this list of conditions and the following disclaimer.

   Redistributions in binary form must reproduce the above copyright
   notice, this list of conditions and the following disclaimer in
   the documentation and/or other materials provided with the distribution.

THIS SOFTWARE IS PROVIDED BY THE COPYRIGHT HOLDERS AND CONTRIBUTORS "AS IS"
AND ANY EXPRESS OR IMPLIED WARRANTIES, INCLUDING, BUT NOT
LIMITED TO, THE IMPLIED WARRANTIES OF MERCHANTABILITY AND FITNESS FOR
A PARTICULAR PURPOSE ARE DISCLAIMED. IN NO EVENT SHALL THE REGENTS
OR CONTRIBUTORS BE LIABLE FOR ANY DIRECT, INDIRECT, INCIDENTAL, SPECIAL,
EXEMPLARY, OR CONSEQUENTIAL DAMAGES (INCLUDING, BUT NOT LIMITED TO,
PROCUREMENT OF SUBSTITUTE GOODS OR SERVICES; LOSS OF USE, DATA, OR
PROFITS; OR BUSINESS INTERRUPTION) HOWEVER CAUSED AND ON ANY THEORY OF
LIABILITY, WHETHER IN CONTRACT, STRICT LIABILITY, OR TORT (INCLUDING
NEGLIGENCE OR OTHERWISE) ARISING IN ANY WAY OUT OF THE USE OF THIS
SOFTWARE, EVEN IF ADVISED OF THE POSSIBILITY OF SUCH DAMAGE.

NB: This software will not save the world.

D.12 X Window System

The source code contained in the XFree86-3.3 directory is copyrighted by the X
Consortium and, unless otherwise noted, is distributed under the following
license.

Permission is hereby granted, free of charge, to any person obtaining a copy
of this software and associated documentation files (the "Software"), to deal
in the Software without restriction, including without limitation the rights
to use, copy, modify, merge, publish, distribute, sublicense, and/or sell
copies of the Software, and to permit persons to whom the Software is
furnished to do so, subject to the following conditions:

The above copyright notice and this permission notice shall be included in
all copies or substantial portions of the Software.

THE SOFTWARE IS PROVIDED "AS IS", WITHOUT WARRANTY OF ANY KIND, EXPRESS OR
IMPLIED, INCLUDING BUT NOT LIMITED TO THE WARRANTIES OF MERCHANTABILITY,
FITNESS FOR A PARTICULAR PURPOSE AND NONINFRINGEMENT. IN NO EVENT SHALL THE
X CONSORTIUM BE LIABLE FOR ANY CLAIM, DAMAGES OR OTHER LIABILITY, WHETHER IN
AN ACTION OF CONTRACT, TORT OR OTHERWISE, ARISING FROM, OUT OF OR IN
CONNECTION WITH THE SOFTWARE OR THE USE OR OTHER DEALINGS IN THE SOFTWARE.

Except as contained in this notice, the name of the X Consortium shall not be
used in advertising or otherwise to promote the sale, use or other dealings
in this Software without prior written authorization from the X Consortium.

Appendix E
Maxims for Reading Code

Hell! there ain't no rules around here! We are tryin' to accomplish somepn'n!

—Thomas Edison

Chapter 1: Introduction

1. Make it a habit to spend time reading high-quality code that others have written. (*p. 3*)

2. Read code selectively and with a goal in your mind. Are you trying to learn new patterns, a coding style, a way to satisfy some requirements? (*p. 4*)

3. Notice and appreciate the code's particular nonfunctional requirements that might give rise to a specific implementation style. (*p. 4*)

4. When working on existing code, coordinate your efforts with the authors or maintainers to avoid duplication of work or bad feelings. (*p. 5*)

5. Consider the benefits you receive from open-source software to be a loan; look for ways to repay it by contributing back to the open-source community. (*p. 5*)

6. In many cases if you want to know "how'd they do that?" there's no better way than reading the code. (*p. 5*)

7. When looking for a bug, examine the code from the problem manifestation to the problem source. Avoid following unrelated paths. (*p. 6*)

8. Use the debugger, the compiler's warnings or symbolic code output, a system call tracer, your database's SQL logging facility, packet dump tools, and windows message spy programs to locate a bug's location. (*p. 6*)

9. You can successfully modify large well-structured systems with only a minimal understanding of their complete functionality. (*p. 7*)

10. When adding new functionality to a system, your first task is to find the implementation of a similar feature to use as a template for the one you will be implementing. (*p. 7*)

11. To go from a feature's functional specification to the code implementation, follow the string messages or search the code using keywords. (*p. 7*)

12. When porting code or modifying interfaces, you can save code-reading effort by directing your attention to the problem areas identified by the compiler. (*p. 8*)

13. When refactoring, you start with a working system and want to ensure that you will end up with a working one. A suite of pertinent test cases will help you satisfy this obligation. (*p. 8*)

14. When reading code to search for refactoring opportunities, you can maximize your return on investment by starting from the system's architecture and moving downward, looking at increasing levels of detail. (*p. 9*)

15. Code reusability is a tempting but elusive concept; limit your expectations and you will not be disappointed. (*p. 9*)

16. If the code you want to reuse is intractable and difficult to understand and isolate, look at larger granularity packages or different code. (*p. 9*)

17. While reviewing a software system, keep in mind that it consists of more elements than executable statements. Examine the file and directory structure, the build and configuration process, the user interface, and the system's documentation. (*p. 10*)

18. Use software reviews as a chance to learn, teach, lend a hand, and receive assistance. (*p. 10*)

Chapter 2: Basic Programming Elements

19. When examining a program for the first time, `main` can be a good starting point. (*p. 20*)

20. Read a cascading `if-else if-...-else` sequence as a selection of mutually exclusive choices. (*p. 23*)

21. Sometimes executing a program can be a more expedient way to understand an aspect of its functionality than reading its source code. (*p. 25*)

22. When examining a nontrivial program, it is useful to first identify its major constituent parts. (*p. 25*)

23. Learn local naming conventions and use them to guess what variables and functions do. (*p. 26*)

24. When modifying code based on guesswork, plan the process that will verify your initial hypotheses. This process can involve checks by the compiler, the introduction of assertions, or the execution of appropriate test cases. (*p. 28*)

25. Understanding one part of the code can help you understand the rest. (*p. 28*)

26. Disentangle difficult code by starting with the easy parts. (*p. 28*)

27. Make it a habit to read the documentation of library elements you encounter; it will enhance both your code-reading and code-writing skills. (*p. 28*)

28. Code reading involves many alternative strategies: bottom-up and top-down examination, the use of heuristics, and review of comments and external documentation should all be tried as the problem dictates. (*p. 34*)

29. Loops of the form `for (i = 0; i < n; i++)` execute n times; treat all other forms with caution. (*p. 34*)

30. Read comparison expressions involving the conjunction of two inequalities with one identical term as a range membership test. (*p. 39*)

31. You can often understand the meaning of an expression by applying it on sample data. (*p. 40*)

32. Simplify complicated logical expressions by using De Morgan's rules. (*p. 41*)

33. When reading a conjunction, you can always assume that the expressions on the left of the expression you are examining are true; when reading a disjunction, you can similarly assume that the expressions on the left of the expression you are examining are false. (*p. 42*)

34. Reorganize code you control to make it more readable. (*p. 46*)

35. Read expressions using the conditional operator `?:` like `if` code. (*p. 46*)

36. There is no need to sacrifice code readability for efficiency. (*p. 48*)

37. While it is true that efficient algorithms and certain optimizations can make the code more complicated and therefore more difficult to follow, this does not mean that making the code compact and unreadable will make it more efficient. (*p. 48*)

38. Creative code layout can be used to improve code readability. (*p. 49*)

39. You can improve the readability of expressions using whitespace, temporary variables, and parentheses. (*p. 49*)

40. When reading code under your control, make it a habit to add comments as needed. (*p. 50*)

41. You can improve the readability of poorly written code with better indentation and appropriate variable names. (*p. 50*)

42. When you are examining a program revision history that spans a global reindentation exercise using the *diff* program, you can often avoid the noise introduced by the changed indentation levels by specifying the -w option to have *diff* ignore whitespace differences. (*p. 51*)

43. The body of a do loop is executed at least once. (*p. 51*)

44. When performing arithmetic, read a & b as a % (b + 1) when $b + 1 = 2^n$. (*p. 53*)

45. Read a << n as a * k, where $k = 2^n$. (*p. 53*)

46. Read a >> n as a / k, where $k = 2^n$. (*p. 53*)

47. Examine one control structure at a time, treating its contents as a black box. (*p. 54*)

48. Treat the controlling expression of each control structure as an assertion for the code it encloses. (*p. 55*)

49. The `return`, `goto`, `break`, and `continue` statements as well as exceptions interfere with the structured flow of execution. Reason about their behavior separately since they all typically either terminate or restart the loop being processed. (*p. 55*)

50. Reason about complex loops through their *variant* and *invariant* properties. (*p. 56*)

51. Simplify code reasoning by rearranging code, using meaning-preserving transformations. (*p. 58*)

Chapter 3: Advanced C Data Types

52. By recognizing the function served by a particular language construct, you can better understand the code that uses it. (*p. 61*)

53. Recognize and classify the reason behind each use of a pointer. (*p. 61*)

54. Pointers are used in C programs to construct linked data structures, to dynamically allocate data structures, to implement call by reference, to access and iterate through data elements, when passing arrays as arguments, for referring to functions, as an alias for another value, to represent character strings, and for direct access to system memory. (*p. 62*)

55. Function arguments passed by reference are used for returning function results or for avoiding the overhead of copying the argument. (*p. 63*)

56. A pointer to an array element address can be used to access the element at the specific position index. (*p. 65*)

57. Arithmetic on array element pointers has the same semantics as arithmetic on the respective array indices. (*p. 65*)

58. Functions using global or `static` local variables are in most cases not reentrant. (*p. 66*)

59. Character pointers differ from character arrays. (*p. 72*)

60. Recognize and classify the reason behind each use of a structure or union. (*p. 75*)

61. Structures are used in C programs to group together data elements typically used as a whole, to return multiple data elements from a function, to construct linked data structures, to map the organization of data on hardware devices, network links, and storage media, to implement abstract data types, and to program in an object-oriented fashion. (*p. 75*)

62. Unions are used in C programs to optimize the use of storage, to implement polymorphism, and for accessing different internal representations of data. (*p. 80*)

63. A pointer initialized to point to storage for *N* elements can be dereferenced as if it were an array of *N* elements. (*p. 85*)

64. Dynamically allocated memory blocks are freed explicitly or when the program terminates or through use of a garbage collector; memory blocks allocated on the stack are freed when the function they were allocated in exits. (*p. 87*)

65. C programs use `typedef` declarations to promote abstraction and enhance the code's readability, to guard against portability problems, and to emulate the class declaration behavior of C++ and Java. (*p. 91*)

66. You can read `typedef` declarations as if they were variable definitions: the name of the variable being defined is the type's name; the variable's type is the type corresponding to that name. (*p. 91*)

Chapter 4: C Data Structures

67. Read explicit data structure operations in terms of the underlying abstract data class. (*p. 96*)

68. Vectors are typically realized in C by using the built-in array type without attempting to abstract the properties of the vector from the underlying implementation. (*p. 96*)

69. An array of N elements is completely processed by the sequence for (i = 0; i < N; i++); all other variations should raise your defenses. (*p. 96*)

70. The expression sizeof(x) always yields the correct number of bytes for processing an array x (not a pointer) with memset or memcpy. (*p. 97*)

71. Ranges are typically represented by using the first element of the range and the first beyond it. (*p. 100*)

72. The number of elements in an asymmetric range equals the difference between the upper and the lower bounds. (*p. 100*)

73. When the upper bound of an asymmetric range equals the lower bound, the range is empty. (*p. 100*)

74. The lower bound in an asymmetric range represents the first occupied element, the upper bound, the first free one. (*p. 100*)

75. Arrays of structures often represent tables consisting of records and fields. (*p. 101*)

76. Pointers to structures often represent a cursor for accessing the underlying records and fields. (*p. 101*)

77. Dynamically allocated matrices are stored as pointers to array columns or as pointers to element pointers; both types are accessed as two-dimensional arrays. (*p. 103*)

78. Dynamically allocated matrices stored as flat arrays address their elements using custom access functions. (*p. 104*)

79. An abstract data type provides a measure of confidence regarding the way the underlying implementation elements will be used (or abused). (*p. 106*)

80. Arrays are used for organizing lookup tables keyed by sequential integers starting from 0. (*p. 111*)

81. Arrays are often used to efficiently encode control structures, thus simplifying a program's logic. (*p. 111*)

82. Arrays are used to associate data with code by storing in each position a data element and a pointer to the element's processing function. (*p. 112*)

83. Arrays can control a program's operation by storing data or code used by abstract or virtual machines implemented within that program. (*p. 113*)

84. Read the expression `sizeof(x)/sizeof(x[0])` as the number of elements of the array *x*. (*p. 113*)

85. A structure with an element titled `next` pointing to itself typically defines a node of a singly linked list. (*p. 118*)

86. A permanent (for example, global, static, or heap allocated) pointer to a list node often represents the list head. (*p. 118*)

87. A structure containing `next` and `prev` pointers to itself is probably a node of a doubly linked list. (*p. 121*)

88. Follow complicated data structure pointer operations by drawing elements as boxes and pointers as arrows. (*p. 122*)

89. Recursive data structures are often processed by using recursive algorithms. (*p. 126*)

90. Nontrivial data structure manipulation algorithms are typically parameterized using a function or template argument. (*p. 126*)

91. Graph nodes are stored sequentially in arrays, linked in lists, or linked through the graph edges. (*p. 131*)

92. The edges of a graph are typically represented either implicitly through pointers or explicitly as separate structures. (*p. 134*)

93. Graph edges are often stored as dynamically allocated arrays or linked lists, both anchored at a graph's nodes. (*p. 137*)

94. In a nondirectional graph the data representation should treat both nodes as equal, and processing code should similarly not discriminate edges based on their direction. (*p. 139*)

95. On nonconnected graphs, traversal code should be coded so as to bridge isolated subgraphs. (*p. 139*)

96. When dealing with graphs that contain cycles, traversal code should be coded so as to avoid looping when following a graph cycle. (*p. 139*)

97. Inside complicated graph structures may hide other, separate structures. (*p. 140*)

Chapter 5: Advanced Control Flow

98. Recursively defined algorithms and data structures are often implemented by using recursive function definitions. (*p. 144*)

99. To reason about a recursive function, start from the base case test and construct an informal argument on how every recursive invocation will lead its execution closer to the nonrecursive base case code. (*p. 147*)

100. Simple languages are often parsed using a series of functions that follow the language's grammar structure. (*p. 147*)

101. Reason about mutually recursive functions by considering the recursive definition of the underlying concept. (*p. 147*)

102. Tail-recursive calls are equivalent to a loop going back to the beginning of the function. (*p. 147*)

103. You can easily locate the methods that might throw an implicitly generated exception by running the Java compiler on the class source after removing the throws clause from the method definition. (*p. 151*)

104. Code using multiprocessor machines is often structured around processes or threads. (*p. 156*)

105. The work crew parallelism model is employed to distribute work among processors or to create a pool of tasks to be used for allocating standardized chunks of incoming work. (*p. 157*)

106. The thread-based boss/worker model of parallelism is typically used to maintain responsiveness of a central task by delegating expensive or blocking operations to worker subtasks. (*p. 158*)

107. The process-based boss/worker model of parallelism is typically used for reusing existing programs or to structure and isolate coarse-grained system modules with well-defined interfaces. (*p. 159*)

108. In pipeline-based parallelism, each task receives some input, performs processing on it, and passes the resulting output to the next task for more processing. (*p. 161*)

109. Race conditions are subtle and often have the code leading to them spread over multiple functions or modules. The resultant problems are therefore difficult to isolate. (*p. 166*)

110. View with extreme suspicion data structure manipulation code and library calls that appear within a signal handler. (*p. 168*)

111. When reading code that contains macros, keep in mind that macros are neither functions nor statements. (*p. 172*)

112. Macros defined inside a do ... while (0) block are equivalent to the statements inside the block. (*p. 174*)

113. Macros can access local variables visible at the point they are used. (*p. 175*)

114. Macro calls can change the values of their arguments. (*p. 175*)

115. Macro-based token concatenation can create new identifiers. (*p. 176*)

Chapter 6: Tackling Large Projects

116. You can examine a project's organization by browsing its source code tree—the hierarchical directory structure containing the project's source code. The source code tree often reflects the project's architectural and software process structure. (*p. 181*)

117. Often the source code tree of an application mirrors the application's deployment structure. (*p. 181*)

118. Do not let huge source code collections daunt you; typically these are better organized than smaller, ad hoc efforts. (*p. 186*)

119. When you work on a large project for the first time, spend some time acquainting yourself with its directory tree structure. (*p. 186*)

120. A project's "source code" encompasses a lot more than the computer language instructions compiled to obtain an executable program; a project's source code tree typically also includes specifications, end-user and developer documentation, test scripts, multimedia resources, build tools, examples, localization files, revision history, installation procedures, and licensing information. (*p. 189*)

121. The build process of large projects is typically specified declaratively by means of dependencies. Dependencies are translated into concrete build actions by tools such as *make* and its derivatives. (*p. 191*)

122. In large projects makefiles are often dynamically generated after a configuration step; you will need to perform the project-specific configuration before examining the makefile. (*p. 192*)

123. To inspect the steps of a large build process, you can dry-run *make* by using the -n switch. (*p. 196*)

124. A revision control system provides a way to obtain an up-to-date version of the source code from its repository. (*p. 204*)

125. Use commands that display executable file revision identification keywords to match an executable with its source code. (*p. 207*)

126. Use bug-tracking code numbers that appear in revision logs to locate an issue description in the bug-tracking database. (*p. 209*)

127. Use the revision control system version repository to identify how particular changes were implemented. (*p. 209*)

128. Many different aspects of the software development process, including configuration, build process management, code generation, testing, and documentation use custom-built tools. (*p. 210*)

129. Use a program's debugging output to help you understand crucial parts of a program's control flow and data elements. (*p. 216*)

130. The places where a tracing statement is located typically mark important parts of an algorithm function. (*p. 216*)

131. Assertions are used to verify steps in the operation of an algorithm, parameters received by a function, a program's flow of control, properties of the underlying hardware, and the results of test cases. (*p. 218*)

132. Use algorithm verification assertions to confirm your understanding of an algorithm's operation or as a point to start your reasoning. (*p. 218*)

133. Often function argument and result assertions document a function's preconditions and postconditions. (*p. 219*)

134. Use assertions that test complete functions as specification statements for each given function. (*p. 220*)

135. Test cases can be a partial substitute for functional specifications. (*p. 223*)

136. Use test case input data to dry-run source code sequences. (*p. 223*)

Chapter 7: Coding Standards and Conventions

137. Knowing the file organization followed by a given code base allows you to browse efficiently through the source code. (*p. 226*)

138. Ensure that the tab setting of your editor or pretty-printer matches the style guide specifications of the code you are reading. (*p. 228*)

139. Use the indentation of a code block to quickly grasp its overall structure. (*p. 229*)

140. Inconsistently formatted code should immediately raise your defenses. (*p. 231*)

141. Pay special attention to code sequences flagged with XXX, FIXME, and TODO comments: errors may lurk in them. (*p. 233*)

142. Constants are named by using uppercase characters, with words separated by underscores. (*p. 234*)

143. In programs that follow the Java coding conventions, package names always start from a top-level domain name (for example, org., com.sun), class and interface names start with an uppercase letter, and method and variable names start with a lowercase letter. (*p. 235*)

144. The Hungarian notation prefix type tags appearing in front of the name of a user-interface control will help you determine its role. (*p. 237*)

145. Different programming standards may have incompatible notions of what constitutes a portable construct. (*p. 237*)

146. When inspecting code for portability and using a given coding standard as a guide, take care to understand the extent and limits of the standard's portability requirements. (*p. 238*)

147. When GUI functionality is implemented using an appropriate programming construct, the correct adoption of a given user-interface specification can be trivially verified by code inspection. (*p. 239*)

148. Learn how a project's build process is organized and automated to be able to swiftly read and comprehend the corresponding build rules. (*p. 240*)

149. When examining a system's release process, you can often use as a baseline the requirements of the corresponding distribution format. (*p. 240*)

Chapter 8: Documentation

150. Take advantage of any documentation you find to supplement your code-reading effort. (*p. 241*)

151. An hour of code reading can save you a minute of reading the documentation. (*p. 241*)

152. Use the system specification document to understand the environment where the code you are reading will operate. (*p. 242*)

153. Use the software requirements specification as a benchmark against which to read and evaluate the code. (*p. 242*)

154. Use a system's design specification as a road map to the code structure and as a guide to specific code elements. (*p. 242*)

155. The test specification document provides you with data you can use to dry-run the code you are reading. (*p. 242*)

156. When you are dealing with an unknown system, the functional description and the user guide can provide you with important background information to better understand the context of the code you are reading. (*p. 242*)

157. Use the user reference manual to rapidly obtain background information on presentation and application logic code components and the administrator manual to find details on interfaces, file formats, and error messages you encounter in the code. (*p. 242*)

158. Documentation provides you with a shortcut for obtaining an overview of the system or for understanding the code providing a particular feature. (*p. 243*)

159. Documentation often mirrors and therefore reveals the underlying system structure. (*p. 245*)

160. Documentation helps you understand complicated algorithms and data structures. (*p. 245*)

161. A textual description of an algorithm can make the difference between an opaque piece of code and the chance to understand it. (*p. 246*)

162. Documentation often elucidates the meaning of source code identifiers. (*p. 247*)

163. Documentation can provide the rationale behind nonfunctional requirements. (*p. 247*)

164. Documentation explains internal programming interfaces. (*p. 249*)

165. Because documentation is seldom tested and stressed in the way the actual program code is, it can often be erroneous, incomplete, or out of date. (*p. 249*)

166. Documentation provides test cases and examples of actual use. (*p. 249*)

167. Documentation often describes known implementation problems and bugs. (*p. 251*)

168. Known environment deficiencies are often documented in the source code. (*p. 252*)

169. Change documentation can indicate trouble spots. (*p. 252*)

170. Repetitive or conflicting changes to the same parts of the source code often indicate fundamental design deficiencies that maintainers try to fix by a series of patches. (*p. 252*)

171. Similar fixes applied to different parts of the source code indicate an easily made error or oversight that could conceivably exist in other places as well. (*p. 253*)

172. Documentation may often provide a misleading view of the source code. (*p. 254*)

173. Be wary of undocumented features: classify each instance as justified, careless, or malicious, and accordingly decide whether the code or the documentation should be fixed. (*p. 255*)

174. Documentation occasionally does not describe the system as implemented but as it should have been or will be implemented. (*p. 255*)

175. In source code documentation the word *grok* typically means "to understand." (*p. 256*)

176. If unknown or idiosyncratically used words hinder the code's understanding, try looking them up in the documentation's glossary (if it exists), *The New Hacker's Dictionary* [Ray96], or on a Web search engine. (*p. 256*)

177. When looking for source code documentation, consider nontraditional sources such as comments, standards, publications, test cases, mailing lists, newsgroups, revision logs, issue-tracking databases, marketing material, and the source code itself. (*p. 256*)

178. You should always view documentation with a critical mind; since documentation is never executed and rarely tested or formally reviewed to the extent code is, it can often be misleading or outright wrong. (*p. 256*)

179. You can treat flawed code as the specification of the corresponding intended implementation. (*p. 259*)

180. When reading documentation for a large system, familiarize yourself with the documentation's overall structure and conventions. (*p. 264*)

181. When confronted with voluminous documentation, you can improve your reading productivity by employing tools or by typesetting the text on a high-quality output device such as a laser printer. (*p. 264*)

Chapter 9: Architecture

182. One system can (and in nontrivial cases does) exhibit many different architectural styles simultaneously. Different styles can appear by looking at the same system

in a different way, by examining different parts of the system, or by employing different levels of decomposition. (*p. 268*)

183. Centralized repository architectures are employed in collaborative applications and when different semiautonomous processes need to cooperate to access shared information or resources. (*p. 268*)

184. A blackboard system uses a centralized repository of unstructured key/value pairs as a communications hub for a number of different code elements. (*p. 270*)

185. You will often find data-flow (or pipes-and-filters) architectures adopted when processing can be modeled, designed, and implemented as a series of data transformations. (*p. 273*)

186. Data-flow architectures are often employed in automatic data-processing batch-oriented environments, especially on platforms that efficiently support data-transformation tools. (*p. 273*)

187. A telltale sign of a data-flow architecture is the use of temporary files or pipelines for communicating between different processes. (*p. 274*)

188. Use diagrams to model the class relationships in object-oriented architectures. (*p. 278*)

189. Import source code into a modeling tool to reverse engineer a system's architecture. (*p. 279*)

190. Systems with a multitude of alternative peer subsystems are often organized following a layered architecture. (*p. 279*)

191. Layered architectures are typically implemented by stacking software components with standardized interfaces. (*p. 279*)

192. A system's layer can view lower layers as abstract entities and (as long as the layer is satisfying its requirements) does not care how upper layers will use it. (*p. 279*)

193. A layer interface can consist of either a family of complementary functions supporting a specific concept or a series of interchangeable functions supporting different underlying implementations of an abstract interface. (*p. 281*)

194. Systems implemented in C often express layer interface multiplexing operations by using arrays of function pointers. (*p. 282*)

195. Systems implemented in object-oriented languages directly express layer interface multiplexing operations by using virtual method calls. (*p. 282*)

196. A system can be organized across various axes by using different and distinct hierarchical decomposition models. (*p. 282*)

197. Use program-slicing techniques to bring together a program's data and control dependencies. (*p. 283*)

198. In concurrent systems a single system component often acts as a centralized manager, starting, stopping, and coordinating the execution of other system processes and tasks. (*p. 289*)

199. Many real-world systems adopt the best parts of multiple architectures. When dealing with such a system, do not seek in vain for the all-encompassing architectural picture; locate, recognize, and appreciate each different architectural style as a separate yet interrelated entity. (*p. 291*)

200. A state transition diagram will often help you untangle a state machine's operation. (*p. 291*)

201. When dealing with a large body of code, it is important to understand the mechanisms employed to decompose it into separate units. (*p. 292*)

202. A module's physical boundary is in most cases a single file, a directory, or a collection of files with a unique prefix. (*p. 293*)

203. Modules in C often consist of a header file providing the module's public interface and a source file providing the corresponding implementation. (*p. 295*)

204. Object constructors are often used to allocate the resources associated with an object and to initialize its state. Destructors are typically used to free the resources an object has appropriated during its lifetime. (*p. 302*)

205. Object methods often use class fields for storing data that controls the operation of all methods (such as a lookup table or a dictionary) or for maintaining state information about the class's operation (for example, a counter for assigning a unique identifier to each object). (*p. 303*)

206. In well-designed classes all fields are declared as private with access to them provided through public access methods. (*p. 304*)

207. When you encounter `friend` declarations, pause to question the actual design reason for overriding the class's encapsulation. (*p. 306*)

208. Operator overloading is used either sparingly to enhance the usability of a particular class or overreachingly to endow a class implementing a number-like entity with the full functionality associated with the built-in arithmetic types. (*p. 307*)

209. Generic implementations are realized either at compile time through macro substitution and language-supported facilities such as the C++ templates and the Ada generic packages or at runtime by using element and function pointers or object polymorphism. (*p. 313*)

210. Abstract data types are often used to encapsulate commonly used data organization schemes (such as trees, lists, or stacks) or to hide a data type's implementation details from its user. (*p. 319*)

211. Libraries are employed for a number of different purposes: to reuse source and object code, to organize module collections, to structure and optimize the build process, and to load application features on demand. (*p. 319*)

212. Large and distributed systems are often implemented as a number of cooperating processes. (*p. 323*)

213. You can decipher the structure of a text-based data repository by browsing through the data stored in it. (*p. 327*)

214. You can examine a relational database's schema by performing queries on the tables of the data dictionary or by using database-specific SQL commands such as SHOW TABLE. (*p. 327*)

215. After recognizing a reused architectural element, look up its original description to gain additional insight on the way it is used or abused. (*p. 329*)

216. When examining in-depth an application built on top of a framework, the best course of action is to begin by studying the framework itself. (*p. 330*)

217. Limit your expectations when reading wizard-generated code and you will not be disappointed. (*p. 330*)

218. Learn a few basic design patterns and you will find that the way you view code architectures will change: your vision and vocabulary will extend to recognize and describe many commonly used forms. (*p. 332*)

219. You will often encounter frequently used patterns without explicit references to their names since the reuse of architectural designs often predates their description in the form of patterns. (*p. 332*)

220. Try to understand architectures in terms of the underlying patterns, even if the patterns are not explicitly mentioned in the code. (*p. 333*)

221. Most interpreters follow a processing architecture built around a state machine whose operation depends on the interpreter's current state, the program instruction, and the program state. (*p. 336*)

222. In many cases, reference architectures prescribe a notational structure for an application domain, which is not neccessarily followed by the concrete implementations. (*p. 336*)

Chapter 10: Code-Reading Tools

223. Use lexical tools to efficiently search for patterns in a large source code file or across many files. (*p. 340*)

224. Use a program editor and regular expression search commands to browse large source code files. (*p. 340*)

225. Browse source files with your editor in read-only mode. (*p. 341*)

226. You can locate a function definition by using a regular expression search of the type ^*function name*. (*p. 341*)

227. Use regular expression character classes to look for variables with names that follow a specific pattern. (*p. 342*)

228. Use regular expression character classes with negation to avoid false-positive matches. (*p. 342*)

229. Search for symbols appearing together on the same line by using the regular expression *symbol-1.* symbol-2*. (*p. 343*)

230. Use your editor's *tags* facility to quickly locate entity definitions. (*p. 343*)

231. You can enhance the browsing functionality of your editor with specialized tag creation tools. (*p. 344*)

232. You can obtain a bird's-eye view of the source code structure by using an editor's outline view. (*p. 345*)

233. Use your editor to detect matching parentheses, brackets, and braces. (*p. 345*)

234. Search for code patterns across multiple files by using *grep*. (*p. 346*)

235. Locate symbol declarations, definitions, and uses by using *grep*. (*p. 347*)

236. When you are not sure what exactly you are looking for, search the program source code for the stems of key words. (*p. 347*)

237. Pipe the output of other tools through *grep* to isolate the items you are looking for. (*p. 347*)

238. Pipe the output of *grep* to other tools to automate sophisticated processing tasks. (*p. 347*)

239. Reuse the results of a code search by stream-editing the *grep* output. (*p. 348*)

240. Filter spurious *grep* output by selecting output lines that do not match the noise pattern (`grep -v`). (*p. 350*)

241. Match source code against lists of strings by using *fgrep*. (*p. 353*)

242. Search through all comments and through the code of languages with case-insensitive identifiers (for example, Basic) using case-insensitive pattern matching (*grep -i*). (*p. 354*)

243. Create checklists of files and line numbers that match a given regular expression by using the *grep -n* command-line switch. (*p. 354*)

244. Compare different versions of a file or program by using *diff*. (*p. 355*)

245. When running the *diff* command, you can use *diff -b* to make the file comparison algorithm ignore trailing blanks, -w to ignore all whitespace differences, and -i to make the file comparison case insensitive. (*p. 356*)

246. Do not be afraid to create your own code-reading tools. (*p. 357*)

247. When developing your own code-reading tool: exploit the capabilities of modern rapid-prototyping languages, start with a simple design and gradually improve it, use heuristics based on the lexical structure of the code, be prepared to tolerate some output noise or silence, and use other tools to preprocess your input or postprocess your output. (*p. 359*)

248. When reading code, make the compiler your friend: specify the appropriate level of compiler warnings and carefully evaluate the results. (*p. 360*)

249. Use the C preprocessor to untangle programs that abuse it. (*p. 361*)

250. To definitely understand how the compiler treats a particular piece of code, look at the generated symbolic (assembly) code. (*p. 362*)

251. You can obtain a clear picture of a source file's imports and exports by examining the corresponding object file symbols. (*p. 364*)

252. Use source code browsers to navigate through large code collections and object classes. (*p. 365*)

253. Resist the temptation to beautify foreign code to your coding standards; gratuitous formatting changes create divergent code bases and hinder organized maintenance. (*p. 367*)

254. Program pretty-printers and editor syntax coloring can make source code more readable. (*p. 368*)

255. The program *cdecl* will translate inscrutable C and C++ type declarations into plain English (and vice versa). (*p. 368*)

256. You can gain valuable insight on how the program operates by actually executing it. (*p. 370*)

257. System call, event, and packet tracing tools can improve your understanding of a program's operation. (*p. 371*)

258. Execution profilers let you target your optimization efforts, verify your input data coverage, and analyze the operation of algorithms. (*p. 372*)

259. Look for lines that are never executed to find weaknesses in your test coverage and amend your test data. (*p. 372*)

260. To explore every detail of the dynamic operation of a program you are examining, run it under a debugger. (*p. 373*)

261. Print on paper code you find hard to understand. (*p. 375*)

262. Draw diagrams to depict the code's operation. (*p. 375*)

263. You can always get a better understanding of a piece of code by explaining it to someone else. (*p. 375*)

264. To understand complicated algorithms or subtle data structures, select a peaceful and quiet environment and concentrate deeply without drawing any help from computerized or mechanical aids. (*p. 376*)

Chapter 11: A Complete Example

265. Model software additions along the lines of similar entities (classes, functions, modules). Among similar existing entities, pick one with an unusual name to simplify textual searches in the base source code. (*p. 381*)

266. Automatically generated files often start with a comment indicating the fact. (*p. 397*)

267. Any attempt to precisely analyze code will typically branch into numerous other classes, files, and modules and quickly overwhelm you; therefore, actively try to limit the extent of code you have to understand to the absolutely necessary minimum. (*p. 398*)

268. Employ a breadth-first search strategy, attacking code-reading problems from multiple sides until one of them gives way. (*p. 398*)

Bibliography

[AC75]   A. V. Aho and M. J. Corasick. Efficient string matching: An aid to bibliographic search. *Communications of the ACM*, 18(6):333–340, 1975.

[AG00]   Ken Arnold and James Gosling. *The Java Programming Language*, 3rd ed. Boston, MA: Addison-Wesley, 2000.

[AHU74]   Alfred V. Aho, John E. Hopcroft, and Jeffrey D. Ullman. *The Design and Analysis of Computer Algorithms*. Reading, MA: Addison-Wesley, 1974.

[AIS+77]   Christopher Alexander, Sara Ishikawa, Murray Silverstein, Max Jacobson, Ingrid Fiksdahl-King, and Shlomo Angel. *A Pattern Language*. Oxford: Oxford University Press, 1977.

[AKW88]   Alfred V. Aho, Brian W. Kernighan, and Peter J. Weinberger. *The AWK Programming Language*. Reading, MA: Addison-Wesley, 1988.

[Ale64]   Christopher Alexander. *Notes on the Synthesis of Form*. Cambridge, MA: Harvard University Press, 1964.

[Ale01]   Andrei Alexandrescu. *Modern C++ Design: Generic Programming and Design Patterns Applied*. Boston, MA: Addison-Wesley, 2001.

[AM86]   Even Adams and Steven S. Muchnick. Dbxtool: A window-based symbolic debugger for Sun workstations. *Software: Practice & Experience*, 16(7):653–669, 1986.

[Arm00]   Phillip G. Armour. The case for a new business model: Is software a product or a medium? *Communications of the ACM*, 43(8):19–22, 2000.

[ASU85]   Alfred V. Aho, Ravi Sethi, and Jeffrey D. Ullman. *Compilers, Principles, Techniques, and Tools*. Reading, MA: Addison-Wesley, 1985.

[Aus98]   Matthew H. Austern. *Generic Programming and the STL: Using and Extending the C++ Standard Template Library*. Reading, MA: Addison-Wesley, 1998.

[Bac86]   Maurice J. Bach. *The Design of the UNIX Operating System*. Englewood Cliffs, NJ: Prentice-Hall, 1986.

[BBL95]   Don Bolinger, Tan Bronson, and Mike Loukides. *Applying RCS and SCCS: From Source Control to Project Control*. Sebastopol, CA: O'Reilly and Associates, 1995.

[BCH+95]   Barry W. Boehm, Bradford Clark, Ellis Horowitz, Ray Madachy, Richard Shelby, and Chris Westland. Cost models for future life cycle processes: COCOMO 2. *Annals of Software Engineering*, 1:57–94, 1995.

[BCK98]   L. Bass, P. Clements, and R. Kazman. *Software Architecture in Practice*. Reading, MA: Addison-Wesley, 1998.

[BE93]   Jon Beck and David Eichmann. Program and interface slicing for reverse engineering. In *15th International Conference on Software Engineering, ICSE '93*, pp. 509–518. New York: ACM Press, 1993.

[Bec00]   Kent Beck. *Extreme Programming Explained: Embrace Change*. Boston, MA: Addison-Wesley, 2000.

[Ben86]   Jon Louis Bentley. *Programming Pearls*. Reading, MA: Addison-Wesley, 1986.

[BF01]   Moshe Bar and Karl Franz Fogel. *Open Source Development with CVS*. Scottsdale, AZ: The Coriolis Group, 2001.

[BG98]   Kent Beck and Erich Gamma. Test infected: Programmers love writing tests. *Java Report*, 3(7):37–50, 1998.

[BHH99]   L. Barroca, J. Hall, and P. Hall (eds). *Software Architectures: Advances and Applications*. Berlin: Springer Verlag, 1999.

[BK86]   Jon Louis Bentley and Donald E. Knuth. Programming pearls: A WEB program for sampling. *Communications of the ACM*, 29(5):364–369, 1986.

[BKM86]   Jon Louis Bentley, Donald E. Knuth, and Douglas McIlroy. A literate program. *Communications of the ACM*, 19(6):471–483, 1986.

[Bli95]   Bruce Blinn. *Portable Shell Programming: An Extensive Collection of Bourne Shell Examples*. Englewood Cliffs, NJ: Prentice Hall, 1995.

[BMR+96]   Frank Buschmann, Regine Meunier, Hans Rohnert, Peter Sommerlad, and Michael Stal. *Pattern-Oriented Software Architecture*, Volume 1: A System of Patterns. New York: John Wiley and Sons, 1996.

[Boe81]   Barry W. Boehm. *Software Engineering Economics*. Englewood Cliffs, NJ: Prentice-Hall, 1981.

[Boe83]   Barry W. Boehm. The economics of software maintenance. In *Software Maintenance Workshop*, pp. 9–37, Washington, DC, 1983.

[Boe88]   Hans-Juergen Boehm. Garbage collection in an uncooperative environment. *Software: Practice & Experience*, 18(9):807–820, 1988.

[Bou79]   S. R. Bourne. An introduction to the UNIX shell. In *Unix Programmer's Manual* [Uni79]. Also available online http://plan9.bell-labs.com/7thEdMan/.

[Bra86]   J. Brady. A theory of productivity in the creative process. *IEEE Computer Graphics and Applications*, 6(5):25–34, 1986.

[BRJ99]   Grady Booch, James Rumbaugh, and Ivar Jacobson. *The Unified Modeling Language User Guide*. Reading, MA: Addison-Wesley, 1999.

[Bru82]   Maurice Bruynooghe. The memory management of Prolog implementations. In Keith L. Clark and Sten-Åke Tärnlund (eds), *Logic Programming*, pp. 83–98. London: Academic Press, 1982.

[BST89]   H. E. Bal, J. G. Steiner, and A. S. Tanenbaum. Programming languages for distributed computing systems. *ACM Computing Surveys*, 21(3):261–322, 1989.

[BTS00]   Arash Baratloo, Timothy Tsai, and Navjot Singh. Transparent run-time defense against stack smashing attacks. In Christopher Small (ed), *USENIX 2000 Technical Conference Proceedings*, San Diego, CA, June 2000. Berkeley, CA: Usenix Association.

[BW98]   Alan W. Brown and Kurt C. Wallnau. The current state of CBSE. *IEEE Software*, 15(5):37–46, 1998.

[C$^+$01]   Per Cederqvist, et al. *Version Management with CVS*, 2001. Available online at http://www.cvshome.org/docs/manual/ (January 2002).

[CEK$^+$]   L. W. Cannon, R. A. Elliott, L. W. Kirchhoff, et al. Recommended C style and coding standards. Available online at http://sunland.gsfc.nasa.gov/info/cstyle.html (December 2001). Updated version of the Indian Hill C Style and Coding Standards paper.

[Chr84]   Thomas W. Christopher. Reference count garbage collection. *Software: Practice & Experience*, 14(6):503–507, 1984.

[CKV96]   J. O. Coplien, N. Kerth, and J. Vlissides. *Pattern Languages of Program Design 2*. Reading, MA: Addison-Wesley, 1996.

[Com00]   Douglas E. Comer. *Internetworking with TCP/IP*, Volume I: Principles, Protocols and Architecture, 4th ed. Englewood Cliffs, NJ: Prentice-Hall, 2000.

[Con00]   Damian Conway. *Object Oriented Perl*. Greenwich, CT: Manning Publications, 2000.

[Cre97]   Roger F. Crew. ASTLOG: A language for examining abstract syntax trees. In Ramming [Ram97], pp. 229–242.

[CS95]   James O. Coplien and Douglas C. Schmidt. *Pattern Languages of Program Design*. Reading, MA: Addison-Wesley, 1995.

[CS96]   Douglas E. Comer and David L. Stevens. *Internetworking with TCP/IP*, Volume III: Client-Server Programming and Applications (BSD Socket Version), 2nd ed. Englewood Cliffs, NJ: Prentice-Hall, 1996.

[CS98]   Douglas E. Comer and David L. Stevens. *Internetworking with TCP/IP*, Volume II: ANSI C Version: Design, Implementation, and Internals, 3rd ed. Englewood Cliffs, NJ: Prentice-Hall, 1998.

[CT90]   D. D. Clark and D. L. Tennenhouse. Architectural considerations for a new generation of protocols. In *Proceedings of the ACM Symposium on Communications Architectures and Protocols*, pp. 200–208, Philadelphia, PA, 1990. New York: ACM Press.

[CT98]   Tom Christiansen and Nathan Torkington. *The Perl Cookbook*. Sebastopol, CA: O'Reilly and Associates, 1998.

[Cun01]   Ward Cunningham. Signature survey: A method for browsing unfamiliar code, 2001. Available online at http://c2.com/doc/SignatureSurvey/ (July 2002). OOPSLA 2001 Software Archeology Workshop position statement.

[CWZ90]   D. R. Chase, W. Wegman, and F. K. Zadeck. Analysis of pointers and structures. *ACM SIGPLAN Notices*, 25(6):296–319, 1990.

[CY79]   Larry L. Constantine and Edward Yourdon. *Structured Design*. Englewood Cliffs, NJ: Prentice Hall, 1979.

[Dan02]   John Daniels. Modeling with a sense of purpose. *IEEE Software*, 19(1):8–10, 2002.

[DCS98]   Peter Duchessi and InduShobha Chengalur-Smith. Client/server benefits, problems, best practices. *Communications of the ACM*, 41(5):87–94, 1998.

[DDZ94]   David Detlefs, Al Dosser, and Benjamin Zorn. Memory allocation costs in large C and C++ programs. *Software: Practice & Experience*, 24(6):527–542, 1994.

[DE96]   Paul Dubois and Gigi Estabrook. *Software Portability with Imake*, 2nd ed. Sebastopol, CA: O'Reilly and Associates, 1996.

[Dij68]   Edsger Wybe Dijkstra. Go to statement considered harmful. *Communications of the ACM*, 11(3):147–148, 1968.

[Dij01]   Edsger W. Dijkstra. *My Recollections of Operating System Design*. Honorary Doctorate Award Lecture. Athens University of Economics and Business, Department of Informatics, 2001.

[DL99]   Tom DeMarco and Timothy R. Lister. *Peopleware: Productive Projects and Teams*, 2nd ed. New York: Dorset House, 1999.

[DLP77]   R. DeMillo, R. Lipton, and A. Perlis. Social processes and proofs of theorems and programs. In *Proc. Fourth ACM Symposium on Principles of Programming Languages*, pp. 206–214, Los Angeles, CA, January 1977. New York: ACM Press.

[Dou90]   Rohan T. Douglas. Error message management. *Dr. Dobb's Journal*, 15(1):48–51, 1990.

[DR97a]   Nachum Dershowitz and Edward M. Reingold. *Calendrical Calculations*. Cambridge: Cambridge University Press, 1997.

[DR97b]   Dale Dougherty and Arnold Robbins. *sed and awk*, 2nd ed. Sebastopol, CA: O'Reilly and Associates, 1997.

[DZ83]   J. D. Day and H. Zimmermann. The OSI reference model. *Proceedings of the IEEE*, 71:1334–1340, 1983.

[El-01]   Khaled El-Emam. Ethics and open source. *Empirical Software Engineering*, 6(4):291–292, 2001.

[ER89]   Mark W. Eichlin and Jon A. Rochlis. With microscope and tweezers: An analysis of the internet virus of November 1988. In *IEEE Symposium on Research in Security and Privacy*, pp. 326–345, Oakland, CA, May 1989.

[ES90]   Margaret A. Ellis and Bjarne Stroustrup. *The Annotated C++ Reference Manual*. Reading, MA: Addison-Wesley, 1990.

[Fel79]   Stuart I. Feldman. Make—a program for maintaining computer programs. *Software: Practice & Experience*, 9(4):255–265, 1979.

[FH82]   Christopher W. Fraser and David R. Hanson. Exploiting machine-specific pointer operations in abstract machines. *Software: Practice & Experience*, 12:367–373, 1982.

[FJ99]   M. Fayad and R. Johnson (eds). *Domain-Specific Application Frameworks: Frameworks Experience by Industry*. New York: John Wiley and Sons, 1999.

[FJS99a]   M. Fayad, R. Johnson, and D. C. Schmidt (eds). *Domain-Specific Application Frameworks: Applications and Experiences*. New York: John Wiley and Sons, 1999.

[FJS99b]   M. Fayad, R. Johnson, and D. C. Schmidt (eds). *Domain-Specific Application Frameworks: Problems and Perspectives*. New York: John Wiley and Sons, 1999.

[FNP97]   Rickard E. Faith, Lars S. Nyland, and Jan F. Prins. KHEPERA: A system for rapid implementation of domain specific languages. In Ramming [Ram97], pp. 243–255.

[FO02]   Jeffrey E. Friedl and Andy Oram (eds). *Mastering Regular Expressions: Powerful Techniques for Perl and Other Tools*, 2nd ed. Sebastopol, CA: O'Reilly and Associates, 2002.

[Fow00]   Martin Fowler. *Refactoring: Improving the Design of Existing Code*. Boston, MA: Addison-Wesley, 2000. With contributions by Kent Beck, John Brant, William Opdyke, and Don Roberts.

[Fre95]   The FreeBSD Project. *Style—Kernel Source File Style Guide*, December 1995. FreeBSD Kernel Developer's Manual: style(9). Available online at http://www.freebsd.org (March 2003).

[FS00]   Martin Fowler and Kendall Scott. *UML Distilled: Applying the Standard Object Modeling Language*, 2nd ed. Boston, MA: Addison-Wesley, 2000.

[Geh87]   Narain Gehani. *Document Formatting and Typesetting on the UNIX System*, 2nd ed. Summit, NJ: Silicon Press, 1987.

[GG00]   Richard P. Gabriel and Ron Goldman. Mob software: The erotic life of code, October 2000. Presented at the ACM Conference on Object-Oriented Programming, Systems, Languages, and Applications on October 19, 2000, in Minneapolis, MN. Available at http://www.dreamsongs.com/MobSoftware.html (May 2002).

[GHJV95]   Erich Gamma, Richard Helm, Ralph Johnson, and John Vlissides. *Design Patterns: Elements of Reusable Object-Oriented Software*. Reading, MA: Addison-Wesley, 1995.

[GKM82]   S. Graham, P. Kessler, and M. K. McKusick. gprof: A call graph execution profiler. *ACM SIGPLAN Notices*, 6(17):120–126, 1982. Proceedings of the SIGPLAN '82 Symposium on Compiler Construction.

[GKM83]   S. Graham, P. Kessler, and M. K. McKusick. An execution profiler for modular programs. *Software: Practice & Experience*, 13:671–685, 1983.

[Gla00]   Robert L. Glass. The sociology of open source: Of cults and cultures. *IEEE Software*, 17(3):104–105, 2000.

[Gol80]   Adele Goldberg. *Smalltalk 80: The Language and Its Implementation*. Reading, MA: Addison Wesley, 1980.

[Ham88]   Eric Hamilton. Literate programming—expanding generalized regular expressions. *Communications of the ACM*, 31(12):1376–1385, 1988.

[Han87]   David R. Hanson. Literate programming—printing common words. *Communications of the ACM*, 30(7):594–599, 1987.

[Hei61]   Robert A. Heinlein. *Stranger in a Strange Land*. New York: G. P. Putnam's Sons, 1961.

[HFR99]   N. Harrison, B. Foote, and H. Rohnert. *Pattern Languages of Program Design 4*. Reading, MA: Addison-Wesley, 1999.

[Hoa71]   C. A. R. Hoare. Proof of a program: Find. *Communications of the ACM*, 14(1):39–45, 1971.

[Hoa73]   C. A. R. Hoare. Recursive data structures. Technical Report AIM-223 STAN-CS-73-400, Stanford University, Computer Science Department, October 1973.

[Hoa85]   C. A. R. Hoare. *Communicating Sequential Processes*. Englewood Cliffs, NJ: Prentice-Hall, 1985.

[Hor90]   Mark R. Horton. *Portable C Software*. Englewood Cliffs, NJ: Prentice-Hall, 1990.

[HP96]   John L. Hennessy and David A. Patterson. *Computer Architecture: A Quantitative Approach*, 2nd ed. San Mateo, CA: Morgan Kaufmann, 1996.

[HT00]   Andrew Hunt and David Thomas. *The Pragmatic Programmer: From Journeyman to Master*. Boston, MA: Addison-Wesley, 2000.

[HT02]   Andy Hunt and Dave Thomas. Software archeology. *IEEE Software*, 19(2):20–22, 2002.

[Hum88]   Andrew Hume. Grep wars: The strategic search initiative. In Peter Collinson (ed), *Proceedings of the EUUG Spring 88 Conference*, pp. 237–245. Buntingford, UK: European UNIX User Group, 1988.

[Hum89]   Watts S. Humphrey. *Managing the Software Process*. Reading, MA: Addison-Wesley, 1989.

[HW01]   Daniel M. Hoffman and David M. Weiss (eds). *Software Fundamentals: Collected Papers by David L. Parnas*. Boston, MA: Addison-Wesley, 2001.

[Jac87]   Michael A. Jackson. Literate programming—processing transactions. *Communications of the ACM*, 30(12):1000–1010, 1987.

[Joh77]   Stephen C. Johnson. Lint, a C program checker. *Computer Science Technical Report 65*, Murray Hill, NJ: Bell Laboratories, December 1977.

[Joh79]   Stephen C. Johnson. Lint, a C program checker. In *Unix Programmer's Manual* [Uni79]. Also available online at http://plan9.bell-labs.com/7thEdMan/.

[Joh92]   R. Johnson. Documenting frameworks using patterns. *ACM SIGPLAN Notices*, 27(10):63–76, 1992. In John Pugh (ed) *Proceedings of the Seventh Annual Conference on Object-Oriented Programming Systems, Languages and Applications, OOPSLA '92 Conference,* October 18–22, Vancouver, BC, Canada. New York: ACM Press, 1992.

[JR94]   Daniel Jackson and Eugene J. Rollins. A new model of program dependencies for reverse engineering. In *Proceedings of the Second ACM SIGSOFT Symposium on Foundations of Software Engineering*, pp. 2–10. New York: ACM Press, 1994.

[Ker82]   Brian W. Kernighan. A typesetter-independent TROFF. *Computer Science Technical Report 97*, Murray Hill, NJ: Bell Laboratories, 1982. Available online at http://cm.bell-labs.com/cm/cs/cstr.

[Ker89]   Brian W. Kernighan. The UNIX system document preparation tools: A retrospective. *AT&T Technical Journal*, 68(4):5–20, 1989.

[KFN99]   Cem Kaner, Jack Falk, and Hung Quoc Nguyen. *Testing Computer Software*, 2nd ed. New York: Wiley, 1999.

[KGM01]   Mark F. Komarinski, Jorge Godoy, and David C. Merrill. LDP author guide, December 2001. Available online at http://www.linuxdoc.org/LDP/LDP-Author-Guide.pdf (January 2002).

[KHH$^+$01] Gregor Kiczales, Erik Hilsdale, Jim Hugunin, et al. Getting started with AspectJ. *Communications of the ACM*, 44(10):59–65, 2001.

[KL93]   Donald E. Knuth and Silvio Levy. *The CWEB System of Structured Documentation*. Reading, MA: Addison-Wesley, 1993.

[Knu86a]   Donald E. Knuth. *METAFONT: The Program*. Reading, MA: Addison-Wesley, 1986.

[Knu86b]   Donald E. Knuth. *TeX: The Program*. Reading, MA: Addison-Wesley, 1986.

[Knu89]   Donald E. Knuth. *The TeXbook*. Reading, MA: Addison-Wesley, 1989.

[Knu92]   Donald E. Knuth. *Literate Programming*, CSLI Lecture Notes Number 27. Stanford, CA: Stanford University Center for the Study of Language and Information, 1992. Distributed by the University of Chicago Press.

[Knu97]   Donald E. Knuth. *The Art of Computer Programming*, Volume 1: Fundamental Algorithms, 3rd ed. Reading, MA: Addison-Wesley, 1997.

[Knu98]   Donald E. Knuth. *The Art of Computer Programming*, Volume 3: Sorting and Searching, 2nd ed. Reading, MA: Addison-Wesley, 1998.

[Koe88]   Andrew Koenig. *C Traps and Pitfalls*. Reading, MA: Addison-Wesley, 1988.

[Kor97]   David G. Korn. Porting Unix to Windows NT. In *Proceedings of the USENIX 1997 Annual Technical Conference*, Anaheim, CA, January 1997. Berkeley, CA: Usenix Association.

[KP76]   Brian W. Kernighan and P. J. Plauger. *Software Tools*. Reading, MA: Addison-Wesley, 1976.

[KP78]   Brian W. Kernighan and P. J. Plauger. *The Elements of Programming Style*, 2nd ed. New York: McGraw-Hill, 1978.

[KP84]   Brian W. Kernighan and Rob Pike. *The UNIX Programming Environment*. Englewood Cliffs, NJ: Prentice-Hall, 1984.

[KP99]   Brian W. Kernighan and Rob Pike. *The Practice of Programming*. Reading, MA: Addison-Wesley, 1999.

[KR88]   Brian W. Kernighan and Dennis M. Ritchie. *The C Programming Language*, 2nd ed. Englewood Cliffs, NJ: Prentice-Hall, 1988.

[Kru92]   Charles W. Krueger. Software reuse. *ACM Computing Surveys*, 24(2):131–183, 1992.

[KS97]   Nils Klarlund and Michael I. Schwarzbach. A domain-specific language for regular sets of strings and trees. In Ramming [Ram97], pp. 145–156.

[Lam94]   Leslie Lamport. *LATEX: A Document Preparation System*, 2nd ed. Reading, MA: Addison-Wesley, 1994.

[LB97]   Bill Lewis and Daniel J. Berg. *Multithreaded Programming with Pthreads*. Englewood Cliffs, NJ: Prentice-Hall, 1997.

[LH86]   Kai Li and Paul Hudak. A new list compaction method. *Software: Practice & Experience*, 16(2):145–163, 1986.

[LH89]   Karl Lieberherr and Ian Holland. Assuring good style for object-oriented programs. *IEEE Software*, 6(5):38–48, 1989.

[Lib93]   Don Libes. *Obfuscated C and Other Mysteries*. New York: John Wiley and Sons, 1993.

[Lin94]   Peter Van Der Linden. *Expert C Programming*. Englewood Cliffs, NJ: Prentice-Hall, 1994.

[Lio96]   John Lions. *Lions' Commentary on Unix 6th Edition with Source Code*. Poway, CA: Annabooks, 1996.

[LMKQ88]   Samuel J. Leffler, Marshall Kirk McKusick, Michael J. Karels, and John S. Quarterman. *The Design and Implementation of the 4.3BSD Unix Operating System*. Reading, MA: Addison-Wesley, 1988.

[LS80]   B. P. Lientz and E. B. Swanson. *Software Maintenance Management*. Reading, MA: Addison-Wesley, 1980.

[Lut02]   Mark Lutz. *Programming Python*, 2nd ed. Sebastopol, CA: O'Reilly and Associates, 2002.

[LY97]   Tim Lindhorn and Frank Yellin. *The Java Virtual Machine Specification*. Reading, MA: Addison-Wesley, 1997.

[MBK96]   Marshall Kirk McKusick, Keith Bostic, and Michael J. Karels. *The Design and Implementation of the 4.4BSD Unix Operating System*. Reading, MA: Addison-Wesley, 1996.

[McM79]   L. E. McMahon. SED—a non-interactive text editor. In *Unix Programmer's Manual* [Uni79]. Also available online at http://plan9.bell-labs.com/7thEdMan/.

[Meu95]   Regine Meunier. The pipes and filters architecture. In Coplien and Schmidt [CS95], Chapter 22, pp. 427–440.

[Mey88]   Bertrand Meyer. *Object-Oriented Software Construction*. Englewood Cliffs, NJ: Prentice-Hall, 1988.

[Mey98]   Scott Meyers. *Effective C++*, 2nd ed. Reading, MA: Addison-Wesley, 1998.

[Mey00]   Bertrand Meyer. *Object-Oriented Software Construction*, 2nd ed. Englewood Cliffs, NJ: Prentice Hall, 2000.

[Mic95]   Microsoft Corporation. *The Component Object Model Specification*. Technical report, Redmond, WA: Microsoft Corporation, October 1995.

[Mic01]   Microsoft Corporation. *Microsoft C# Language Specifications*. Redmond, WA: Microsoft Press, 2001.

[MMM95] Hafedh Mili, Fatma Mili, and Ali Mili. Reusing software: Issues and research directions. *IEEE Transactions on Software Engineering*, 21(6):528–562, 1995.

[MMNS83] Richard J. Miara, Joyce A. Musselman, Juan A. Navarro, and Ben Shneiderman. Program indentation and comprehensibility. *Communications of the ACM*, 26(11):861–867, 1983.

[MRB97] R. C. Martin, D. Riehle, and F. Buschmann. *Pattern Languages of Program Design 3*. Reading, MA: Addison-Wesley, 1997.

[MW94] Udi Manber and Sun Wu. GLIMPSE: A tool to search through entire file systems. In Jeff Mogul (ed), *USENIX Conference Proceedings*, pp. 23–32, San Francisco, CA, Winter 1994. Berkeley, CA: Usenix Association.

[NBF96] Bradford Nichols, Dick Buttlar, and Jacqueline Proulx Farrell. *Pthreads Programming*. Sebastopol, CA: O'Reilly and Associates, 1996.

[Noe98] Geoffrey J. Noer. Cygwin32: A free Win32 porting layer for UNIX applications. In Susan Owicki and Thorsten von Eicken (eds), *Proceedings of the 2nd USENIX Windows NT Symposium*, Seattle, WA, August 1998. Berkeley, CA: Usenix Association.

[NR98] Cameron Newham and Bill Rosenblatt. *Learning the Bash Shell*, 2nd ed. Sebastopol, CA: O'Reilly and Associates, 1998.

[Obj02] Object Management Group. The common object request broker architecture (CORBA/IIOP), December 2002. Also available online at http://www.omg.org/technology/documents/formal/corba_iiop.htm (May 2003).

[OC90] Paul W. Oman and Curtis R. Cook. Typographic style is more than cosmetic. *Communications of the ACM*, 33(5):506–520, 1990.

[Org72] Elliot I. Organick. *The Multics System: An Examination of its Structure*. Cambridge, MA: MIT Press, 1972.

[Oss79] J. F. Ossanna. NROFF/TROFF user's manual. In *Unix Programmer's Manual* [Uni79]. Also available online at http://plan9.bell-labs.com/7thEdMan/.

[OT89] Linda M. Ott and Jeffrey J. Thuss. The relationship between slices and module cohesion. In *Proceedings of the 11th ACM Conference on Software Engineering*, pp. 198–204. New York: ACM Press, May 1989.

[OT91] Andrew Oram and Steve Talbott. *Managing Projects with make*, 2nd ed. Sebastopol, CA: O'Reilly and Associates, 1991.

[Par72] David Lorge Parnas. On the criteria to be used for decomposing systems into modules. *Communications of the ACM*, 15(12):1053–1058, 1972. Also in [HW01] pp. 145–155.

[Pet99] Charles Petzold. *Code: The Hidden Language of Computer Hardware and Software*. Redmond, WA: Microsoft Press, 1999.

[Pla93] P. J. Plauger. *Programming on Purpose: Essays on Software Design*. Englewood Cliffs, NJ: Prentice-Hall, 1993.

[PPI97] David A. Patterson, John L. Hennessy, and Nitin Indurkhya. *Computer Organization and Design: The Hardware/Software Interface*, 2nd ed. San Francisco: Morgan Kaufmann, 1997.

[Pre00]   Roger S. Pressman. *Software Engineering: A Practitioner's Approach*, 5th ed. London: McGraw-Hill, 2000. European Adaptation. Adapted by Darrel Ince.

[PT93]   Rob Pike and Ken Thompson. Hello world. In Dan Geer (ed), *USENIX Technical Conference Proceedings*, pp. 43–50, San Diego, CA, winter 1993. Berkeley, CA: Usenix Association.

[Ram97]   J. Christopher Ramming (ed). *USENIX Conference on Domain-Specific Languages*, Santa Monica, CA, October 1997. Berkeley, CA: Usenix Association.

[Ran95]   Alexander S. Ran. Patterns of events. In Coplien and Schmidt [CS95], pp. 547–553.

[Ray96]   Eric S. Raymond. *The New Hacker's Dictionary*, 3rd ed. Cambridge, MA: MIT Press, 1996.

[Ray01]   Eric S. Raymond. *The Cathedral and the Bazaar: Musings on Linux and Open Source by an Accidental Revolutionary*. Sebastopol, CA: O' Reilly and Associates, 2001.

[Ris00]   L. Rising. *The Pattern Almanac 2000*. Boston, MA: Addison-Wesley, 2000.

[Rit79]   Dennis M. Ritchie. The C programming language—reference manual. In *Unix Programmer's Manual* [Uni79]. Also available online at http://plan9.bell-labs.com/7thEdMan/.

[RJB99]   James Rumbaugh, Ivar Jacobson, and Grady Booch. *The Unified Modeling Language Reference Manual*. Reading, MA: Addison-Wesley, 1999.

[Roc75]   M. J. Rochkind. The source code control system. *IEEE Transactions on Software Engineering*, SE-1(4):255–265, 1975.

[RR96]   Kay A. Robbins and Steven Robbins. *Practical Unix Programming: A Guide to Concurrency, Communication, and Multithreading*. Englewood Cliffs, NJ: Prentice-Hall, 1996.

[RR00]   J. E. Robbins and D. F. Redmiles. Cognitive support, UML adherence, and XMI interchange in Argo/UML. *Information and Software Technology*, 42(2):79–89, 2000.

[RS90]   Henry Rabinowitz and Chaim Schaap. *Portable C*. Englewood Cliffs, NJ: Prentice Hall, 1990.

[S⁺01]   Richard Stallman et al. GNU coding standards, October 2001. Available online at http://www.gnu.org/prep/standards_toc.html (December 2001).

[Sal98]   Peter H. Salus (ed). *Handbook of Programming Languages*, Volume I: Object-Oriented Programming Languages. Indianapolis, IN: Macmillan Technical Publishing, 1998.

[SC92]   Henry Spencer and Geoff Collyer. #ifdef considered harmful or portability experience with C news. In Rick Adams (ed), *USENIX Conference Proceedings*, pp. 185–198, San Antonio, TX, Summer 1992. Berkeley, CA: USENIX Association.

[Sch90]   Douglas C. Schmidt. Gperf: A perfect hash function generator. In Jim Waldo (ed), *USENIX C++ Conference*, pp. 87–100, San Francisco, CA, USA, April 1990. Berkeley, CA: Usenix Association.

[Sch95]   Douglas C. Schmidt. Reactor: An object behavioral pattern for concurrent event demultiplexing and event handler dispatching. In Coplien and Schmidt [CS95], pp. 529–545.

[SCW01]   Randal L. Schwartz, Tom Christiansen, and Larry Wall. *Learning Perl*, 3rd ed. Sebastopol, CA: O'Reilly and Associates, 2001.

[Sed97]   Robert Sedgewick. *Algorithms in C Parts 1–4: Fundamentals, Data Structures, Sorting, Searching*, 3rd ed. Reading, MA: Addison-Wesley, 1997.

[Sed01]   Robert Sedgewick. *Algorithms in C Part 5: Graph Algorithms*, 3rd ed. Boston, MA: Addison-Wesley, 2001.

[SG95]   Mary Shaw and David Garlan. Formulations and formalisms in software architecture. In Jan van Leeuwen (ed), *Computer Science Today: Recent Trends and Developments*, pp. 307–323. Springer Verlag, 1995. Lecture Notes in Computer Science 1000.

[SG96]   Mary Shaw and David Garlan. *Software Architecture: Perspectives on an Emerging Discipline*. Englewood Cliffs, NJ: Prentice Hall, 1996.

[SG97a]   Diomidis Spinellis and V. Guruprasad. Lightweight languages as software engineering tools. In Ramming [Ram97], pp. 67–76.

[SG97b]   James M. Stichnoth and Thomas Gross. Code composition as an implementation language for compilers. In Ramming [Ram97], pp. 119–132.

[Sha95]   Mary Shaw. Patterns for software architectures. In Coplien and Schmidt [CS95], pp. 453–462.

[Sie99]   J. Siegel. A preview of CORBA 3. *IEEE Computer*, 32(5):114–116, 1999.

[Sim76]   Charles Simonyi. *Meta-programming: a Software Production Method*. PhD thesis, Stanford University, CA, December 1976. Available online at http://www.parc.xerox.com/publications/bw-ps-gz/csl76-7.ps.gz (December 2001).

[Sim99]   Charles Simonyi. Hungarian notation, November 1999. Available online at http://msdn.microsoft.com/library/default.asp?url=/library/en-us/dnvsgen/html/hunganotat.asp (December 2001). Microsoft Developer Network Library.

[Sin92]   Alok Sinha. Client-server computing. *Communications of the ACM*, 35(7):77–98, 1992.

[Spa89]   Eugene H. Spafford. The Internet worm: Crisis and aftermath. *Communications of the ACM*, 32(6):678–687, 1989.

[Spe88]   Henry Spencer. How to steal code—or—inventing the wheel only once. In *USENIX Conference Proceedings*, Dallas, TX, Winter 1988, pp. 335–345. Berkeley, CA: USENIX Association, 1988

[Spe93]   Henry Spencer. The Ten Commandments for C programmers (annotated edition). *;login:*, 18(2):29–31, 1993.

[Spi93]   Diomidis Spinellis. Implementing Haskell: Language implementation as a tool building exercise. *Structured Programming (Software Concepts and Tools)*, 14:37–48, 1993.

[Spi99a]   Diomidis Spinellis. Explore, excogitate, exploit: Component mining. *IEEE Computer*, 32(9):114–116, 1999.

[Spi99b]   Diomidis Spinellis. Reliable software implementation using domain specific languages. In G. I. Schuëller and P. Kafka (eds), *Proceedings ESREL '99—The Tenth European Conference on Safety and Reliability*, pp. 627–631, Munich-Garching, Germany, September 1999. Rotterdam: A. A. Balkema.

[Spi00]   Diomidis Spinellis. Outwit: Unix tool-based programming meets the Windows world. In Christopher Small (ed), *USENIX 2000 Technical Conference Proceedings*, San Diego, CA, June 2000, pp. 149–158. Berkeley, CA: USENIX Association.

[Spi01]   Diomidis Spinellis. Notable design patterns for domain specific languages. *Journal of Systems and Software*, 56(1):91–99, 2001.

[SR00]   Diomidis Spinellis and Konstantinos Raptis. Component mining: A process and its pattern language. *Information and Software Technology*, 42(9):609–617, 2000.

[SRC84]   J. H. Saltzer, D. P. Reed, and D. D. Clark. End-to-end arguments in system design. *ACM Transactions on Computer Systems*, 2(4):277–288, 1984.

[Sri97]   Sriram Srinivasan. *Advanced Perl Programming*. Sebastopol, CA: O'Reilly and Associates, 1997.

[SS96]   Ravi Sethi and Tom Stone. *Programming Languages: Concepts and Constructs*, 2nd ed. Reading, MA: Addison-Wesley, 1996.

[SSRB00]   Douglas C. Schmidt, Michael Stal, Hans Rohnert, and Frank Buschmann. *Pattern-Oriented Software Architecture*, Volume 2: Patterns for Concurrent and Networked Objects. New York: John Wiley and Sons, 2000.

[Str97]   Bjarne Stroustrup. *The C++ Programming Language*, 3rd ed. Reading, MA: Addison-Wesley, 1997.

[Sun88a]   Sun Microsystems, Inc. RFC 1050: RPC: Remote procedure call protocol specification, April 1988. Obsoleted by RFC1057 [Sun88b].

[Sun88b]   Sun Microsystems, Inc. RFC 1057: RPC: Remote procedure call protocol specification, Version 2, June 1988. Obsoletes RFC1050 [Sun88a].

[Sun99a]   Sun Microsystems, Inc. Java code conventions, April 1999. Available online at http://java.sun.com/docs/codeconv/ (December 2001).

[Sun99b]   Sun Microsystems, Inc. Java remote method invocation specification, December 1999. Available online at http://java.sun.com/docs/guide/rmi/spec/rmiTOC.html/ (February 2002). Revision 1.7, Java 2 SDK, Standard Edition, v1.3.0.

[Suz82]   Norihisa Suzuki. Analysis of pointer "rotation." *Communications of the ACM*, 25(5):330–335, 1982.

[Szy98]   Clemens Szyperski. *Component Software: Behind Object-Oriented Programming*. Reading, MA: Addison-Wesley, 1998.

[Tan97]   Andrew S. Tanenbaum. *Operating Systems: Design and Implementation*, 2nd ed. Englewood Cliffs, NJ: Prentice-Hall, 1997.

[Ten88]   Ted Tenny. Program readability: Procedures versus comments. *IEEE Transactions on Software Engineering*, 14(9):1271–1279, 1988.

[Tic82]   Walter F. Tichy. Design, implementation, and evaluation of a revision control system. In *Proceedings of the 6th International Conference on Software Engineering*. IEEE, September 1982.

[Tic98]   Walter F. Tichy. A catalogue of general-purpose design patterns. In *23rd Conference on the Technology of Object-Oriented Languages and Systems (TOOLS 23)*. IEEE Computer Society, 1998.

[TO90]   Edward J. Thomas and Paul W. Oman. A bibliography of programming style. *ACM SIGPLAN Notices*, 25(2):7–16, 1990.

[Tuf83]   Edward R. Tufte. *The Visual Display of Quantitative Information*. Cheshire, CT: Graphics Press, 1983.

[Uni79]   *UNIX Programmer's Manual. Volume 2—Supplementary Documents*, 7th ed. Murray Hill, NJ: Bell Telephone Laboratories, 1979. Also available online at http://plan9.bell-labs.com/7thEdMan/ (May 2003).

[VETL00]   Gary V. Vaughan, Ben Elliston, Tom Tromey, and Ian Lance Taylor. *GNU Autoconf, Automake, and Libtool*. Indianapolis, IN: New Riders Publishing, 2000.

[Vli98]   John Vlissides. *Pattern Hatching—Design Patterns Applied*. Reading, MA: Addison-Wesley, 1998.

[Wal97]   Stephen R. Walli. OPENNT: UNIX application portability to Windows NT via an alternative environment subsystem. In Ed Lazowska and Michael B. Jones (eds), *Proceedings of the USENIX Windows NT Symposium*, Seattle, WA, August 1997. Berkeley, CA: USENIX Association.

[WCSP00]   Larry Wall, Tom Christiansen, Randal L. Schwartz, and Stephen Potter. *Programming Perl*, 3rd ed. Sebastopol, CA: O'Reilly and Associates, 2000.

[Wei82]   Mark Weiser. Programmers use slices when debugging. *Communications of the ACM*, 25(7):446–452, 1982.

[WHGT99]   W. Eric Wong, Joseph R. Horgan, Swapna S. Gokhale, and Kishor S. Trivedi. Locating program features using execution slices. In *Proceedings of the 1999 IEEE Symposium on Application-Specific Systems and Software Engineering & Technology*, 1999.

[Wil99]   Alan Cameron Wills. Designing component kits and architectures. In Barroca et al. [BHH99].

[WL89]   Christopher J. Van Wyk and Donald C. Lindsay. Literate programming: A file difference program. *Communications of the ACM*, 32(6):740–755, 1989.

[WM99]   Norman Walsh and Leonard Muellner (eds). *DocBook: The Definitive Guide*. Sebastopol, CA: O'Reilly and Associates, 1999.

[WZH01]   H. E. Williams, J. Zobel, and S. Heinz. Self-adjusting trees in practice for large text collections. *Software: Practice & Experience*, 31(10):925–940, 2001.

Index

Author Index

Epigraph Credits

Preface: Graham Green. The Lost Childhood in *The Lost Childhood and Other Essays*. London: Eyre & Spottiswoode, 1951.

Chapter 1:   Donald E. Knuth. The IBM 650: An Appreciation from the Field. *Annals of the History of Computing,* 8 (1), 1986.

Chapter 2:   Werner Heisenberg. *Physics and Philosophy,* London: George Allen and Unwin, 1959, p. 58.

Chapter 3:   Douglas Adams, *Mostly Harmless,* New York: Harmony Books, 1992, p. 135.

Chapter 4:   William James. The Sentiment of Rationality. *Mind.* Series 1, Volume 4, 1879, p. 320.

Chapter 5:   P. R. Wakeling, Of Optics and Opticists, *Applied Optics,* 7 (1):19, 1968. (Quote attributed to British Admiralty Regulations.)

Chapter 6:   John Gall, *Systemantics: How Systems Work and How They Fail.* New York: Pocket Books, 1978, p. 45.

Chapter 7:   Euclid. In Stanley Gudder, *A Mathematical Journey.* New York: McGraw-Hill, 1976, p. 112.

Chapter 8:   Dick Brandon. In Robert J. Chassell and Richard M. Stallman *Texinfo: The GNU Documentation Format.* Boston: Free Software Foundation, 1999.

Chapter 9:   Frank Lloyd Wright. Frank Lloyd Wright and his Art. *New York Times Magazine,* October 4th, 1953.

Chapter 10:   Winston Churchill. Radio broadcast addressing President Roosevelt, February 9th, 1941.

Chapter 11:   Richard Phillips Feynman. Appendix to the Rogers Commission Report on the Space Shuttle Challenger Accident, June 6th, 1986.

Appendix A: From the book's CD-ROM.[1]

Appendix B: Dwight Morrow. Letter to his son, in Harold Nicholson, *Dwight Morrow.* New York: Harcourt, Brace, and Co., 1935.

Appendix C: From the book's CD-ROM.[2]

Appendix D: From the book's CD-ROM.[3]

Appendix E: Thomas Edison. In C.C. Gaither and A.E. Cavazos-Gaither. *Practically Speaking: A Dictionary of Quotations on Engineering, Technology, and Architecture.* Bristol: Institute of Physics Publishing, 1999.

Colophon: Bible, King James version.

---

[1] netbsdsrc/games/fortune/datfiles/fortunes2:29552–29553
[2] netbsdsrc/games/fortune/datfiles/fortunes2:50575–50576
[3] vcf/vcfLicense.txt:25

Colophon

Of making many books there is no end; and much study is a weariness of the flesh.

—Ecclesiastes 12:12

This book is written in 10.5 point Times-Roman, with code text set in 10.5 point Lucida Sans Typewriter. Code examples in the text appear in 8 point Lucida Sans Typewriter, and in figures in 6 point Lucida Sans Typewriter. Annotations are set in 8 point Helvetica in diagrams, and in 7 point Helvetica in the code listings.

The text was written using the *elvis*, *vim*, and *nvi* editors on several computers: a Mitac 6020 running Microsoft Windows 98 and RedHat Linux 6.1; a Toshiba Satellite 35 running Microsoft Windows 2000 and RedHat Linux 7.1; an IBM PC-340 running FreeBSD 4.1-RELEASE and later 4.6; and a Digital DNARD (Shark) running NetBSD 1.5-ALPHA.

Text was processed using LaTeX (MiKTeX 1.11 and 2.1) and converted into Postscript using *dvips* 5.86. Bibliographic references were integrated with the text by MiKTeX-BibTeX 1.7 (BibTeX 0.99c). Diagrams were specified in a declarative, textual form and converted into encapsulated Postscript by the *GraphViz* system *dot* program, version 1.8.6. Screen dumps were converted into encapsulated Postscript using programs from the *outwit* and *netpbm* systems. We also used GNU *make* to coordinate the build process and RCS to manage file revisions (480 revisions on last count).

We wrote a number of Perl scripts to automate parts of the production process. Most were processed by Perl 5.6.1. All the annotated code examples were specified textually with commented code delimited by special character sequences. A Perl script converted the annotated code into encapsulated Postscript. Similarly, the code-reading maxims, the book's index, and the source code list were generated by LaTeX macro output postprocessed by Perl scripts. Another script converted the manuscript's initial British spelling into American spelling through OLE calls to the Microsoft Word spell checker. We also wrote a Perl script (now part of the GraphViz distribution) to visualize a directory's structure as a *dot* diagram. Its output was hand-tuned to create Figures 6.1 (page 182), 6.2 (page 184), 6.3 (page 185), 6.4 (page 187), 6.5 (page 188), and 9.24 (page 321). Writing a book can be a lot more enjoyable if it involves some coding.

informIT

Register Your Book

at www.awprofessional.com/register

You may be eligible to receive:

- Advance notice of forthcoming editions of the book
- Related book recommendations
- Chapter excerpts and supplements of forthcoming titles
- Information about special contests and promotions throughout the year
- Notices and reminders about author appearances, tradeshows, and online chats with special guests

Contact us

If you are interested in writing a book or reviewing manuscripts prior to publication, please write to us at:

Editorial Department
Addison-Wesley Professional
75 Arlington Street, Suite 300
Boston, MA 02116 USA
Email: AWPro@aw.com

Addison-Wesley

Visit us on the Web: http://www.awprofessional.com

CD-ROM Warranty

Addison-Wesley warrants the enclosed disc to be free of defects in materials and faulty workmanship under normal use for a period of ninety days after purchase. If a defect is discovered in the disc during this warranty period, a replacement disc can be obtained at no charge by sending the defective disc, postage prepaid, with proof of purchase to:

Editorial Department
Addison-Wesley Professional
Pearson Technology Group
75 Arlington Street, Suite 300
Boston, MA 02116
Email: AWPro@awl.com

Addison-Wesley makes no warranty or representation, either expressed or implied, with respect to this software, its quality, performance, merchantability, or fitness for a particular purpose. In no event will Addison-Wesley, its distributors, or dealers be liable for direct, indirect, special, incidental, or consequential damages arising out of the use or inability to use the software. The exclusion of implied warranties is not permitted in some states. Therefore, the above exclusion may not apply to you. This warranty provides you with specific legal rights. There may be other rights that you may have that vary from state to state. The contents of this CD-ROM are intended for personal use only.

More information and updates are available at:
http://www.awprofessional.com/titles/0201799405